BIG COPYRIGHT VERSUS THE PEOPLE

When the idea of copyright was enshrined in the Constitution, it was intended to induce citizens to create. Today, however, copyright has morphed into a system that offers the bulk of its protection to a select number of major corporate content providers (or Big Copyright), which has turned us from a country of creators into one of consumers who spend, on average, ten hours each day on entertainment. In this alarming but illuminating book, Martin Skladany examines our culture of overconsumption and shows not only how it leads to addiction, but also how it is unraveling important threads – of family, friendship, and community – in our society. *Big Copyright Versus the People* should be read by anyone interested in understanding how Big Copyright managed to get such a lethal grip on our culture and what can be done to loosen it.

Martin Skladany is an assistant professor at Penn State Dickinson Law. Previously, as Litigation Associate at Debevoise & Plimpton, he was a member of the legal team that represented the Association of American Publishers in its copyright suit against Google over Google Books.

Big Copyright Versus the People

HOW MAJOR CONTENT PROVIDERS
ARE DESTROYING CREATIVITY AND HOW
TO STOP THEM

MARTIN SKLADANY
Penn State Dickinson Law

CAMBRIDGE
UNIVERSITY PRESS

CAMBRIDGE
UNIVERSITY PRESS

University Printing House, Cambridge CB2 8BS, United Kingdom

One Liberty Plaza, 20th Floor, New York, NY 10006, USA

477 Williamstown Road, Port Melbourne, VIC 3207, Australia

314–321, 3rd Floor, Plot 3, Splendor Forum, Jasola District Centre,
New Delhi – 110025, India

79 Anson Road, #06–04/06, Singapore 079906

Cambridge University Press is part of the University of Cambridge.

It furthers the University's mission by disseminating knowledge in the pursuit of
education, learning, and research at the highest international levels of excellence.

www.cambridge.org
Information on this title: www.cambridge.org/9781108415552
DOI: 10.1017/9781108234177

First published 2018

Printed in the United Kingdom by Clays, St Ives plc

A catalogue record for this publication is available from the British Library.

Library of Congress Cataloging-in-Publication Data
NAMES: Skladany, Martin, author.
TITLE: Big copyright versus the people : how major content providers are destroying
creativity and how to stop them / Martin Skladany.
OTHER TITLES: Big copyright vs. the people
DESCRIPTION: Cambridge [UK] ; New York, NY : Cambridge University Press, 2018.
IDENTIFIERS: LCCN 2018012452 | ISBN 9781108415552
SUBJECTS: LCSH: Copyright. | Copyright – Social aspects.
CLASSIFICATION: LCC K1420.5 .S59 2018 | DDC 346.04/82–dc23
LC record available at https://lccn.loc.gov/2018012452

ISBN 978-1-108-41555-2 Hardback
ISBN 978-1-108-40159-3 Paperback

Cambridge University Press has no responsibility for the persistence or accuracy of
URLs for external or third-party internet websites referred to in this publication
and does not guarantee that any content on such websites is, or will remain,
accurate or appropriate.

For my parents – Martin and Maria Skladany
Ďakujem Vam za všetko, čo ste pre mňa v živote urobily

Contents

Acknowledgments

I would like to thank Matt Gallaway, senior editor at Cambridge University Press, for his insightful advice, expertise, and patience working with a new author. I would also like to thank Meera Seth, Jane Bowbrick, and Emma Wilson at Cambridge University Press and Puvi Kalieperumal at Integra Software. The book was immensely improved both by the comments of the anonymous reviewers and by the skill of Mary Boniece.

I am appreciative of the support from my colleagues at Penn State Dickinson Law, especially Dean Gary Gildin.

I wish I could put in print the names of all the individuals who have taught me over the years. In particular, I am immensely thankful to a host of individuals for their contributions and inspiration, including: Akhil Reed Amar, Ian Ayres, Aubrey Abaya, Bruce Ackerman, Barton Beebe, Yochai Benkler, Spencer Bradley, Bob Brenengen, Ha-Joon Chang, J. Robert Daniell, Owen Fiss, Brenda Garland, James Grimmelmann, Henry Hansmann, Robert Harrison, Gilbert Harman, Peter Jaszi, Daniel Kahneman, Harold Hongju Koh, Michael Madison, Malcolm McDermond, Karen McGuinness, Anne Porter, Laurel Price Jones, Rhys Price Jones, Anisha Reddy, W. Michael Reisman, Paul Salerni, Tim Schnabel, Andy Scott, Peter Singer, Richard Stallman, Laurel Terry, Bruce Thomas, and James Whitman.

I would like to thank *I/S: A Journal of Law and Policy for the Information Society, Journal of the Copyright Society of the U.S.A., Journal of the Patent and Trademark Office Society, Stanford Technology Law Review,* and *University of Illinois Journal of Law, Technology, & Policy* for allowing me to reprint portions of previously published ideas.

My immigrant parents worked tirelessly to provide me with not only piano lessons but also the latest Nikes, to help me fit in at school and to ensure the experience of going to school sans shoes would end with them. More importantly, they taught me to love and not to yell at my kids if they ever accidently drive the car through the family room. Thank you.

I am appreciative of my kids for their unorthodox contributions – e.g., running inside the house loudly to keep me awake, running outside to let me doze off, providing encouragement with a smile, and motivating me to not endow them a fatally flawed world.

Finally, I would like to thank my wife for everything. She is a once-in-a-generation mind. I did not fully understand the importance of role models until I met her and witnessed the beauty of a life devoted to illuminating and passing on knowledge. I am also amazed by how much of this could be accomplished from a bathtub.

All errors are definitely either my dog's fault or mine – I leave it to you to decide.

Introduction

The law will never make men free; it is men who have got to make the law free.
— Henry David Thoreau[1]

If somebody doesn't create something, however small it may be, he gets sick. An awful lot of people feel that they're treading water – that if they vanished in smoke, it wouldn't mean anything at all in this world. And that's a despairing and destructive feeling. It'll kill you.
— Arthur Miller[2]

Hollywood paints notoriously evil portraits of corporations. Stop and think about the last film you saw where the heroic corporation battled the Nazis, cared for dying children, or defeated the sinister "environmental" nonprofits advancing the interests of big polluters. Film executives depict Wall Street bankers as wolves, oil executives as gleefully ripping up the earth, pharmaceutical executives as blithely partying on yachts within sight of the disease-stricken poor, and the military industrial complex as, well, waging war for profit. If Dante were alive today, rest assured Hollywood would have lobbied him to retrofit hell with more circles to cover multinationals' range of sins.

Film producers are adroit at demonizing other industries while deflecting attention from their own zealous efforts to increase profits at all costs. Their films function as Potemkin villages veiling the corporate power behind them. Hollywood shines the cameras on itself sporadically to poke fun at its own social norms yet never on its lobbyists and their search for the fountain of

---

[1] Henry David Thoreau, Slavery in Massachusetts (1854) (delivered at an anti-slavery rally after the conviction of Anthony Burns as a fugitive slave).
[2] Arthur Miller, What I've Learned, ESQUIRE, July 2003, at 110 (interviewed by John H. Richardson).

1

perpetual copyright. Hollywood and other major content providers (Big Copyright) lobby Congress for ever-more copyright protection, not for the good of the public or out of concern for individual artists but for the goal of holding onto their version of the Holy Grail – the Star Wars and Snow Whites in their portfolio of holdings, the beloved assets that continue to bring in vast amounts of money decades after their creation.[3]

The rewards that excessive protection provides to Big Copyright are so great that Hollywood has flooded the market with hyped consumption choices, turning the vast majority of citizens into overconsumers. Americans consume ten hours and two minutes a day of entertainment and media on average, not including social media.[4] This is more than 32.9 years of the average individual's life.[5]

Such shocking overconsumption does unsurprising harm. Excessive consumption is linked to numerous ills of the body and mind – from increased risk of heart disease to reduced ability to concentrate for extended periods of time. Studies have also shown how it negatively affects our sense of happiness and fulfillment. Overconsuming entertainment unravels the threads that hold society together – family, friends, and community. Americans spend "more time playing games than volunteering" or "going to social events."[6] I will add to this list of harms by arguing that overconsumption, precipitated by extreme copyright, makes it less likely that we will go out and create on our own. Overconsumption of entertainment crowds out life.

---

[3] For a thoughtful analysis of how copyright has lost its focus on the public good and developed into a private right instead and the need to return to its original conception, see Shubha Ghosh, *Deprivatizing Copyright*, 54 CASE W. RES. L. REV. 387 (2003). A clever alternative to the term Big Copyright is "industrial-strength copyright owners" used by Jane C. Ginsburg, *The Exclusive Right to Their Writings: Copyright and Control in the Digital Age*, 54 ME. L. REV. 195, 202 (2002). A variant of the term likely first appeared in a different context halfway around the world. See Andrew Christie, *Industrial Strength Copyright*, 51 NEW ZEALAND ENGINEERING 10 (1996). Big Copyright does not include all of corporate America. Numerous multinationals, such as consumer electronics firms, have at times come into conflict with Big Copyright in regard to copyright policy.

[4] Adding social media, which often includes corporate entertainment, brings the daily average to eleven hours and eighteen minutes. I use Nielsen's Total Audience Report data and then subtract Mediakix's statistics on social media. *The Nielsen Total Audience Report*, NIELSEN TOTAL AUDIENCE SERIES 13 (Q1 2017) (average time spent per adult eighteen and older per day) and *How Much Time Is Spent on Social Media? Infographic*, MEDIAKIX, http://mediakix .com/2016/12/how-much-time-is-spent-on-social-media-lifetime/#gs.F=eCW2M.

[5] Life expectancy in the United States is 78.8 years. CENTERS FOR DISEASE CONTROL & PREVENTION, 65 NATIONAL VITAL STATISTICS REPORTS No. 4, 1 (2016), www.cdc.gov/nchs/ data/nvsr/nvsr65/nvsr65_04.pdf.

[6] Christopher Ingraham, *It's Not Just Young Men – Everyone's Playing a Lot More Video Games*, WASH. POST: WONK BLOG (July 11, 2017), www.washingtonpost.com/news/wonk/wp/2017/07/ 11/its-not-just-young-men-everyones-playing-a-lot-more-video-games/.

Just as Thoreau states earlier, "The law will never make men free; it is men who have got to make the law free" – consuming art will never make individuals free; it is individuals who have to make themselves free through creating. We must attempt to improve copyright law, to counter the lobbying efforts of Big Copyright, so we can reduce our dependence on entertainment and become more actively engaged in civil society and culture – i.e., become more free and more creative. By discouraging the vast majority from creating, our current copyright regime, in the words of Arthur Miller, leads people to get sick. Every individual needs to create something on his or her own. The actual object or idea is secondary in importance: The process of creation is critical – it allows us to revel in new experiences and ideas. Significantly reducing copyright would loosen Big Copyright's grip on artistic production, moderate our overconsumption of corporate works, and pave the way for more of us to begin to create art for ourselves.

The history of copyright is a narrative about the heroic tension between maximizing individuals' incentives to produce copyrightable material versus maximizing the public's ability to access that very material – either for consumption purposes or to use it to create new material.[7] While this premise was a positive force 200 years ago, it is fundamentally flawed today. At the time, it would have likely been preposterous to imagine the majority of citizens overconsuming poetry, novels, and maps, while the value of supporting their creation was obvious. We should still care about creation today but in a radically different sense – to enrich the lives of everyone in society, not as passive consumers but as creators. Copyright in its current form has become an impediment to creation for most individuals, not a call to the pen or paintbrush. Instead of prompting us to generate ideas about how to structure our society, economy, and politics, or inspiring us to pursue beauty or philosophical insight, excessive copyright has, practically speaking, provided only Big Copyright and a small, talented minority, largely in Los Angeles and New York City, with realistic incentives to create art.[8] These incentives are large enough that rich societies have been flooded with commercial art, while this flood of art encourages the vast majority of individuals to consume art, not create it.[9]

---

[7] For an insightful analysis of how we might enrich copyright law through a better understanding of conflicting theoretical claims, see James Grimmelmann, *The Ethical Visions of Copyright Law*, 77 FORDHAM L. REV. 2005 (2009). For an equally thoughtful, original perspective, see Yochai Benkler, *Coase's Penguin, or, Linux and the Nature of the Firm*, 112 YALE L.J. 369 (2002).

[8] My analysis here is solely concerned with significantly weakening copyright law governing artistic works, not with other areas of intellectual property law. Furthermore, I do not address copyright on software.

[9] Extreme copyright has given multinational entertainment corporations massive incentives to capture our attention and sell it to other firms.

I agree with scholars who have argued that we should encourage more creators in order to increase the diversity of ideas in the marketplace, given that corporate entertainment, most of what we consume, will not get us new ideas – just look at how Hollywood single-mindedly churns out countless superhero sequels. Yet I also believe that we should be concerned with maximizing the number of individuals who create because creation is a key constituent of a life well lived.[10] The activity of creating is a goal in and of itself – apart from the merits or range of the artwork created or its impact on others. My theory squarely focuses on who creates, while previous scholars have stressed who creates only insofar as it factors into the diversity of ideas available to art consumers and appreciators. My position is that copyright reform should aim to encourage creativity among the general public.

Copyright maximalists might ask: Since greater copyright protection in theory means greater incentives for everyone to create, why doesn't the excessive copyright regime spur all would-be artists to go out and seek their fortune? In theory, Hollywood's relentless lobbying of Congress for ever-greater protection could benefit all current and potential creators, not just corporate entertainment companies. However, this line of thinking assumes a meaningless formal equality, as mocked by Jacques Anatole François Thibault: "The majestic equality of the law, which forbids the rich as well as the poor to sleep under bridges, to beg in streets, and to steal bread."[11] Given the nature of how we create, the excessive protection offered by our copyright regime, in practice, provides significant incentives to corporate media while discouraging lone artists.

Excessive copyright has been vigorously, and rightly, critiqued on the grounds that borrowing is essential to creativity – all new artwork builds on prior art. If I myself may borrow the most popular example used to illustrate the phenomenon, Shakespeare liberally drew on other artists' works. Igor Stravinsky proclaimed: "Lesser artists borrow; great artists steal."[12] Yet Big Copyright has lobbied Congress to so warp copyright law that such borrowing is legally perilous for individual creators. Only Hollywood can afford to pay the

---

[10]   Some argue that Hollywood largely no longer creates original art; its corporate bureaucracy simply refines a scientific process that gets us to maximally consume. Peter Bart, a former Paramount and MGM film executive, says that the greatest concern of Hollywood being "a purely corporate town resides in the creative process. It really hasn't been demonstrated, at any level, by any major corporation, that it can nurture what is euphemistically called 'creativity.'" *The Monster That Ate Hollywood*, PBS: FRONTLINE (last visited June 6, 2017), www.pbs.org/wgbh/pages/frontline/shows/hollywood/interviews/bart.html (interview with Peter Bart).

[11]   ANATOLE FRANCE (JACQUES ANATOLE FRANÇOIS THIBAULT), LE LYS ROUGE (1894) ch. 7.

[12]   LESLIE LAMPORT, LATEX: A DOCUMENT PREPARATION SYSTEM 7 n.2 (1986) (quoting Igor Stravinsky).

requisite licensing fees to make use of protected works with certainty, while the fair use doctrine is so complicated and context specific that many artists are nervous to rely on it.[13] As Lawrence Lessig once quipped, "Fair use in America simply means the right to hire a lawyer to defend your right to create ... The legal system may be tolerable for the very rich. For everyone else, it is an embarrassment to a tradition that prides itself on the rule of law."[14] Extreme copyright has, in effect, allowed Big Copyright to monopolize creativity at the expense not only of aspiring professional artists but also of any citizens who might create during their spare time. Hollywood's addiction to more legal protections has facilitated our entertainment addiction.

BEHAVIORAL ADDICTION

The nature of what Hollywood has thrust upon us is, in the eyes of many psychologists and neuroscientists, behaviorally addicting. While technology is value neutral, Marshall McLuhan's vision that the medium can be as significant as the message holds an insight into the nature of our overconsumption of entertainment. Neuroscience shows that art forms that rely on screens – TV, film, videogames, etc. – enable the use of techniques such as the orienting response that hook viewers. This is revealing, given that on average individuals consume far more screen-based art than any other kind. Furthermore, art forms that rely on screens are associated with a vast host of physical and psychological problems.

Extreme copyright leads to overconsumption because it motivates Hollywood to squeeze nonaddictive media out of the market with its all-you-can-eat buffet of entertainment that is purposefully engineered to keep us from turning away. This incentive is reinforced by the fact that excessive copyright also encourages entertainment companies to use neuroscience hook techniques in their works or risk losing market share to competitors who do not have any compunction at the prospect of exploiting consumers' neuroscience to push their products. It is a race to addiction.

---

[13] For an insightful call to level the playing field for individual artists versus corporate entertainment entities, see Sean A. Pager, *Making Copyright Work for Creative Upstarts*, 22 GEO. MASON. L. REV. 1021 (2015).

[14] LAWRENCE LESSIG, FREE CULTURE: HOW BIG MEDIA USES TECHNOLOGY AND THE LAW TO LOCK DOWN CULTURE AND CONTROL CREATIVITY 145 (2004). He continues: "And as lawyers love to forget, our system for defending rights such as fair use is astonishingly bad – in practically every context, but especially here. It costs too much, it delivers too slowly, and what it delivers often has little connection to the justice underlying the claim." *Id.* Yet also see *generally* Michael J. Madison, *Some Optimism about Fair Use and Copyright Law*, 57 J. COPYRIGHT SOC'Y U.S.A. 351 (2010).

This is not to dispute that some individuals turn to onscreen entertainment because they are depressed, lonely, stressed, or tired – i.e., the causation is likely, in part, a two-way street. Yet it is telling that those who use corporate media for relaxation or solace don't choose any of a multitude of other activities instead, such as walking along the beach, meeting a friend, consuming noncorporate art, creating, or volunteering. Consumers are enticed by profit-hungry multinationals willing to legally bribe politicians, inculcate kids, and deploy neuroscience to maximally grab our attention. Such addiction to consumption then crowds out the prospects of individuals creating on their own, reducing the competition that copyright holders might face from future creators and producers of new art.

This total reversal of the aim of copyright law as compared to its actual effects was not inevitable but happened through a combination of extreme copyright, technological advancements, and the rise of the corporatization of entertainment. The most addictive forms of onscreen entertainment are also the art forms that have been most enabled by the rise of the Internet and related technologies like advances in digital video. Other art forms have largely not been empowered to the same extent. For example, we do not need the Internet or smartphones to write poems. Further, the Internet has not spawned a poetry renaissance, nor is poetry associated with significant negative externalities. The same can be said of painting, sculpture, photography, novels, short stories, and much music. While the advent of reduced production and distribution costs ushered in by the Internet created the possibility that millions of users would be motivated to create, many more have been coaxed into simply consuming more, while some are drawn into using their creative energy in free promotion of corporate media. Through extreme copyright laws, corporate interests have largely captured the distribution revolution of the Internet. For many, the Internet is a place to read the news, mostly written by corporate actors; watch entertainment, largely produced by corporations; buy stuff, primarily corporate products on large corporate websites; and interact with our social circles, on platforms that are mediated by corporations.

COPYRIGHT AND CREATION

Reforming copyright is not necessarily the most effective way to inspire more citizens to create. However, the law of copyright exists, and the current regime has led to the overproduction of corporate art that squelches individual creativity. Thus, we have an obligation to determine how the law is causing harm and to attempt to redress the situation. Our excessively restrictive copyright regime has already been criticized on numerous fronts for having abandoned any sense of balance between providing incentives to produce and allowing others access to the creations.[15] Existing criticisms include limiting citizens' ability to shape political and cultural values and terms, restricting free speech, closing off the commons, creating countless copyright orphan works, and not leading to any real income for most artists but creating an embarrassment of riches for the most famous entertainers.

I agree with these insightful critiques, but I want to draw attention to the negative effects of overconsumption that copyright fosters in the general public. We can find a more appropriate balance between protecting corporate creators and providing individual artists and consumers access to copyrighted works by dramatically weakening copyright protection.[16] For example, we could reduce the length of copyright from the life of the author plus seventy years after her death or corporate copyright's ninety-five years of protection to as low as a year or two, such that commercial entertainment factories would substantially reduce the flow of new corporate work into the marketplace from a flood to a trickle.[17] No one can state precisely the term that is needed ex ante; we need to experiment. Yet if one thinks $200 million blockbusters would be created absent copyright, which I do not, then one must believe copyright is superfluous – if copyright has no bearing on the level of cultural production, the very point of copyright ceases to exist. Further, given most of the public's overconsumption is of entertainment that heavily relies on copyright, such as TV, it is highly unlikely that a drop-off in new blockbuster content would drive people to consume poetry or YouTube cat videos in the same excessive quantities day in and day out. More likely, they would devote their free time to other activities.

Consuming entertainment and art is vital, but too much is harmful. To be clear: I don't think the classical fine arts, such as painting and sculpture, are superior to art forms that can span the world through perfect digital reproduction. I simply demonstrate that – unlike the classical fine arts – film, TV, and video games can support techniques that keep us consuming. I am also not

---

[15] For a framework that critiques the harms of excessive copyright protection through the lens of strengthening the commons and nonmarket peer production, see YOCHAI BENKLER, THE WEALTH OF NETWORKS (2006).

[16] William W. Fisher III calls for free copying of artistic material but suggests the government should distribute tax money to artists in proportion to how often the artists' creations are consumed by the public. See WILLIAM W. FISHER III, PROMISES TO KEEP: TECHNOLOGY, LAW AND THE FUTURE OF ENTERTAINMENT (2004).

[17] Corporations can claim the shorter of ninety-five years from publication or 120 years from creation. 17 U.S.C. § 101 (2000).

arguing that certain substantive artistic content, certain messages or themes within art, should be elevated above others.[18]

Furthermore, I do not claim that creating is more important than consuming or any other important activities, from spending time with friends or family to sleeping. Yet I firmly believe we need to stress the value of creation more now because of how little of it we do and how much we overconsume. After all, copyright is a legal regime that seeks to influence creative pursuits. I argue that we should use the law to encourage certain activities (creativity) and discourage others (overconsumption), but we should not forget that we are already influencing behaviors through the existing copyright law. All I am suggesting is that we rewrite copyright so it empowers individuals instead of corporations.

THE WATER WE SWIM IN

Just as Big Pharma became villains in the eyes of much of the world – ironically thanks in part to the efforts of Hollywood, which pursues the same intellectual property strategies – so might Big Copyright suffer for refusing to dramatically reduce the excessive copyright regime to alleviate the plethora of harms it generates.[19] It took decades for the harms that Big Pharma, Big Oil, and Wall Street perpetuate to be widely recognized by the public, in substantial part because they all employed armies of public relations firms, advertised in news outlets, and silenced politicians through contributing to their campaigns.[20] The copyright fight is more challenging because Hollywood is its own Madison Avenue. Hollywood is in our homes more than half our waking hours. It inculcates our kids not for thirty seconds at a time but for their entire childhood. As if this weren't enough indoctrination, entertainment giants also hire the same public relations and lobbyist firms as the other multinationals, advertise with the same news outlets, and contribute to the same politicians.

This overconsumption problem helps to highlight another reason copyright reform is so difficult. One major potential source of resistance to it, the general public, is spending more time, on average, consuming entertainment than

---

[18] For an insightful examination of the need to consider aesthetics in copyright jurisprudence, see Alfred C. Yen, *Copyright Opinions and Aesthetic Theory*, 71 S. CAL L. REV. 247 (1998).

[19] Frank Vinluan, *Big Pharma Should Hate These Hollywood Blockbuster Movies*, MEDCITY NEWS (Dec. 26, 2011, 6:13 AM), http://medcitynews.com/2011/12/the-top-10-movies-that-big-pharma-loves-to-hate/.

[20] For an alternative take on Big Oil, see John Hofmeister, *Why We Hate the Oil Companies*, STRATEGY+BUSINESS (May 3, 2010), www.strategy-business.com/article/10207?gko=doe17.

sleeping or working. Excessive copyright protection immobilizes this possible source of resistance. Besides a group of academics and a few technology companies, there is no great source of opposition to Hollywood's influence over Congress. Others who might resist, such as the Supreme Court, benefit from the excessive protection – e.g., with million-dollar book advances – while the fourth estate, meant to be a pillar of democracy, is largely owned by corporate entertainment multinationals.

I do not view Big Copyright executives as evil. Yet we cannot deny Hollywood has an enormous vested interest in the debate, and we can justly assert that its position is diametrically opposed to that of the public.[21] While Hollywood executives and powerbrokers could, on their own, in an instant, reduce the harms they perpetuate, capitalism does not ensure enlightened corporate leadership. A few firms may make extraordinary one-off gestures acknowledging the problem of overconsumption – e.g., a British broadcaster, ITV, once purposefully blackened out its TV programs for one hour to spur consumers to take a break from TV and go exercise. In general, however, Big Copyright and multinationals will not deviate from maximizing profits unless they see a dollar in helping society or can spin the stunt to garner positive publicity.[22] Notwithstanding Kant's aspirational golden rule, history has shown that the public cannot realistically assume corporations will do anything but fixate on their bottom line. Further, they will frequently lobby to alter the laws to their own benefit, disregarding the harm doing so might cause – an observation that both liberal and conservative scholars have made.[23] Such rent-seeking activity is the nature of political systems.[24] It is our job to counter its sociopathic nature. We must fight for laws that force multinationals, and Hollywood in particular, to take into account human flourishing and health – not simply profit.

Environmental advocates were initially dismissed. Yet they persisted, and at some point it became common sense that we should demand clean air and water. The history of the environmental movement shows that the battle does not end. A 2016 investigation revealed that "excessive and harmful levels of lead" were found in more than 10 percent of tap water samples taken by the

---

[21] I would like to thank Peter Jaszi for elucidating this point.

[22] AP, *UK Broadcaster Shuts Down for Hour, Asks Viewers to Exercise*, U.S. NEWS & WORLD REPORT (Aug. 27, 2016, 6:46 AM), www.usnews.com/news/entertainment/articles/2016–08-27/uk-broadcaster-shuts-down-for-hour-asks-viewers-to-exercise.

[23] *E.g., see generally* MILTON FRIEDMAN & ROSE FRIEDMAN, FREE TO CHOOSE: A PERSONAL STATEMENT (1990).

[24] *See generally* MANCUR OLSON, THE LOGIC OF COLLECTIVE ACTION: PUBLIC GOODS AND THE THEORY OF GROUPS (rev. ed., Harvard University Press 1971) (1965).

Environmental Protection Agency from 2012 to 2015 – in almost 2,000 water systems in the United States, across all fifty states.[25] Nevertheless, the struggle is not a Sisyphean life sentence but rather an opportunity to engage in life and find collective meaning by doing good – i.e., to do more than simply consume the wares of Hollywood and suffer the negative consequences.

We need to clear away the fog that obscures the true intentions of Hollywood moguls. It serves the interests of Big Copyright to stifle the rich diversity of human interaction and divert us from pursuits that bring us meaning. Their financial motive is colonizing our motives. They will use any lever, be it political clout or the latest technology, to become our reality. They offer slick, entertaining fictions that celebrate human ingenuity while instilling mass preoccupation and dependence. Smartphones are already human prosthetics; imagine the potential profits to be made with virtual reality headsets, wearable sensors, and implanted chips.[26] While many consumers may be ecstatic about such developments and entrepreneurs such as Elon Musk find their march inevitable, the public must not assume that corporations are seriously considering the negative side effects of such a future of entertainment.

To be fair, multinationals do some good – e.g., lifesaving drugs. Yet often such benefits are inextricably mixed with significant harms – e.g., providing oil to heat our homes while sowing corruption and environmental destruction abroad. Hollywood is no exception. Its polished entertainment entertains. This is both praise and an indictment. Hollywood designs its products to be spellbinding, addictive, and ubiquitous. It doesn't just create; it pushes its creations like drug cartels do. It enlists the government's help to maximize profits, domestically and abroad, by consistently demanding that copyright laws be bent ever further in its favor.

INNOVATIVE POLICY PROPOSALS

Roughly a decade ago, Lawrence Lessig, famous for popularizing the long-held idea that excessive copyright protection inhibits creativity and innovation among existing artists, announced that he was leaving the field because copyright reform was impossible without addressing how Congress is captured by

---

[25] Alison Young & Mark Nichols, *Beyond Flint: Excessive Lead Levels Found in Almost 2,000 Water Systems across All 50 States*, USA TODAY (Mar. 11, 2016), www.usatoday.com/story/news/2016/03/11/nearly-2000-water-systems-fail-lead-tests/81220466/.

[26] *E.g., see generally* Christopher Mims, *In 10 Years, Your iPhone Won't Be a Phone Anymore*, WALL STREET J. (June 25, 2017, 9:00 AM), www.wsj.com/articles/in-10-years-your-iphone-wont-be-a-phone-anymore-1498395600.

Hollywood. We need new ideas on how to minimize corporate lobbying, reduce the power of money in elections, get politicians to internalize their decisions, compel deliberative democracy within government, demand informed governance, and ensure integrity. Yet we cannot give up on reducing the negative effects of excessive copyright through more targeted means, even if we are only striking at branches and not the root.[27]

Reform proposals that simply suggest altering part of copyright law, while important, are dead on arrival unless they squarely address the reality that Hollywood spends vast sums on lobbying while proponents of copyright reform are not even in the ring when it comes to campaign contributions. Meaningful reform of copyright without systemic reform of Congress will not come from one magic bullet. We need to try numerous novel proposals simultaneously to see what works and to build momentum so we can begin balancing out the influence that Hollywood lobbyists have with Congress. [28] At best, each new idea will modestly help, and collectively a dozen or two may only make a dent in the problems related to an extreme copyright system because we are forced to treat the symptoms instead of the disease. We cannot put all of our hopes in the systemic reform of Congress, for such a dream is as distant as copyright reform.

This book presents novel ways to alter copyright. Big Copyright must either have a compelling reason to acquiesce to copyright reform through carrots or sticks, or else reform solutions must be immune to Hollywood's influence – i.e., proposals that Big Copyright might not care for but cannot block. Hence, the chapters in the second half of this book arrange original proposals around these three strategies: effectively opposing Hollywood through pressure, bypassing or ignoring Hollywood through implementing solutions that do not require any legislative change, and actively cooperating with Big Copyright. Even if the reader is unconvinced by my theoretical justification of copyright reform as an attempt to maximize the number of

---

[27]   For an excellent examination of how copyright law's structure appears to be largely unaffected by scholars' efforts, unlike in prior cases within antitrust, privacy, and trademark law, see Timothy K. Armstrong, *Dueling Monologues on the Public Domain: What Digital Copyright Can Learn from Antitrust*, 1 UNIVERSITY OF CINCINNATI INTELLECTUAL PROPERTY & COMPUTER L. J. 1 (2016). The tree reference is to Thoreau's comment that "[t]here are a thousand hacking at the branches of evil to one who is striking at the root." HENRY DAVID THOREAU, 1 WALDEN 120 (Houghton Mifflin 1897) (1854).

[28]   The work of Bruce Ackerman has been particularly helpful in getting me to appreciate the need to design unorthodox yet practical policy proposals. For example, *see generally* BRUCE ACKERMAN & JAMES FISHKIN, DELIBERATION DAY (2004); BRUCE ACKERMAN & IAN AYRES, VOTING WITH DOLLARS (2002); and BRUCE ACKERMAN & ANNE ALSTOTT, THE STAKEHOLDER SOCIETY (1999).

artists, the reform ideas provide examples of how we might take culture back from Big Copyright, and while some reform ideas may prove more appealing and feasible than others, collectively they aim to inspire other policy suggestions.

While some of my ideas may seem radical, they are far less extreme than examples of pressure applied or incentives offered that have been used to good effect in the past. For example, if drivers are caught speeding in Finland, they are charged a percentage of their annual income. The point is to make such an infraction be felt equally across income earners. One wealthy individual was charged $103,000 for one speeding ticket – going 45 mph in a 30 mph zone.[29] Predictably, this caused outrage among some of the rich, which "might be a sign that something fair is at work" because research has shown that wealthier individuals "drive more recklessly than those who make less money."[30] Even Steve Jobs not infrequently used to park in handicapped spots, not fearing the fine.[31]

Furthermore, other countries and cities have, at times, easily eclipsed us in their willingness to experiment with novel reforms. While he was mayor of Bogotá, Dr. Antanas Mockus hired mimes to enforce traffic laws.[32] "The mimes didn't carry guns, nor could they issue tickets."[33] Rather, they "attached themselves to jaywalkers, striding behind them and mocking their every move," such that soon "the fraction of pedestrians obeying traffic signals reportedly jumped from 26 percent to 75 percent."[34] Mockus reduced traffic deaths from 1,300 to 600 a year in part by painting "stars on the spots where pedestrians (1,500 of them) had been killed in traffic accidents."[35]

Finally, some of my copyright ideas are already commonly, and largely uncontroversially, implemented in other areas. For example, unions, poison pills, and investment funds have been part of the capitalist landscape for generations.

---

[29] Joe Pinsker, *Finland, Home of the $103,000 Speeding Ticket: Most of Scandinavia Determines Fines Based on Income. Could Such a System Work in the U.S.?*, ATLANTIC (Mar. 12, 2015), www.theatlantic.com/business/archive/2015/03/finland-home-of-the-103000-speeding-ticket/3 87484/.

[30] *Id.* (citing Paul K. Piff et al., *Higher Social Class Predicts Increased Unethical Behavior*, 109 PROC. NAT'L ACAD. SCI. U.S.A. 4086 (2012), www.pnas.org/content/109/11/4086.full).

[31] *Id.*

[32] RAYMOND FISMAN & EDWARD MIGUEL, ECONOMIC GANGSTERS: CORRUPTION, VIOLENCE, AND THE POVERTY OF NATIONS 76 (2008).

[33] *Id.* at 77.   [34] *Id.*

[35] Mara Cristina Caballero, *Academic Turns City into a Social Experiment: Mayor Mockus of Bogotá and His Spectacularly Applied Theory*, HARV. GAZETTE (Mar. 11, 2004), http://news.harvard.edu/gazette/story/2004/03/academic-turns-city-into-a-social-experiment/.

Theory has been helpful to frame the harm that extreme copyright causes; now we need to practically effect change. We need to squarely address the fact that Hollywood took a modest financial incentive and turned it into a massive subsidy to itself. In formulating reform proposals, we need to acknowledge that Hollywood has vast financial resources to keep the golden egg it got Congress to lay for it. We need to (a) work against, (b) work around, and (c) work with Hollywood.

ARTISTS SHUNNING ENTERTAINMENT CONSUMPTION

If the arguments for the need to limit overconsumption and suggestions on how to do so don't convince you, ask yourself whether they have already convinced elite artists and tech entrepreneurs. Though celebrity artists endorse commercial products, they arguably define themselves less by consumption than the average American does. Perhaps they see the value in creation because of their selected career paths. There are countless examples of CEOs and stars limiting their kids' use of technology or access to entertainment despite (or maybe because of) the fact that they have made their fortunes in those fields. When asked in 2010 if his kids enjoy using the iPad, Steve Jobs famously mused, "They haven't used it. We limit how much technology our kids use at home."[36] Evan Williams, cofounder of Twitter, revealed "that in lieu of iPads, their two young boys have hundreds of books (yes, physical ones)."[37] This trend is mirrored by some in Hollywood who make hundreds of millions from TV, film, and music. William H. Macy remarked that "television itself is too powerful. That image is too overwhelming for a little kid."[38] Madonna forbids her kids from watching TV because she considers it "trash" and fears its addictive effects.[39] Helen Hunt has kept the identity of Nemo hidden from her child, while Mayim Bialik wrote a "whole blog of reasons" why she does not let her kids watch TV.[40] Other parents such as Steven Spielberg, Hugh Jackman, Megan Fox, Tom Cruise, and Gwyneth Paltrow

---

[36] Amy Fleming, *Screen Time v. Play Time: What Tech Leaders Won't Let Their Own Kids Do*, GUARDIAN (May 23, 2015, 2:30 AM), www.theguardian.com/technology/2015/may/23/screen-time-v-play-time-what-tech-leaders-wont-let-their-own-kids-do.

[37] Nick Bilton, *Steve Jobs Was a Low-Tech Parent*, N.Y. TIMES (Sept. 10, 2014), www.nytimes.com/2014/09/11/fashion/steve-jobs-apple-was-a-low-tech-parent.html?mcubz=0&_r=0.

[38] Keith, *7 Celebrities Whose Children Watch Little or No TV*, LITTLE LIGHT STUDIOS (Sept. 19, 2014), www.littlelightstudios.tv/7-celebrities-whose-children-watch-little-tv/?doing_wp_cron=1497623670.0452430248260498046875.

[39] *Id.* and *Interview: Madonna Reviews Life on Larry King Live*, CNN (Jan. 19, 1999, 6:00 PM), www.cnn.com/SHOWBIZ/Music/9901/19/madonna.lkl/.

[40] Keith, *supra* note 44.

limit access.[41] Rachel McAdams, Keira Knightley, Angelina Jolie, Susan Sarandon, Jessica Paré, Regina Spektor, Chloe Sevigny, Cynthia Nixon, Carly Rae Jepsen, Alan Cumming, and Jesse Eisenberg claim to not even own TVs.[42]

As Adam Alter perfectly observes, "It seemed as if the people producing tech products were following the cardinal rule of drug dealing: never get high on your own supply. This is unsettling. Why are the world's greatest public technocrats also its greatest technophobes?"[43] The same can be said of artists and entertainers. As he suggests, "Can you imagine the outcry if religious leaders refused to let their children practice religion?"[44]

WILL SOCIAL MEDIA KILL BIG COPYRIGHT?

Recently concern about media overconsumption has been eclipsed by anxiety about the effects of social media on society, even though currently we spend far less time on social media as compared to corporate entertainment.[45] The Internet has tended to thwart and reinforce copyright at the same time, just as social media is highly dependent on creative borrowing, such that it tends to reinforce media consumption through promotion, allusion, and mimicry. Nonetheless, if social media continues to take up more and more of our time, it might lead to the death of copyright in the long term. If we continue to fuel our behavioral addiction to social media, we have to give up something given that there is no time left in a day due to current overconsumption. While current statistics show we are increasing our consumption of both traditional entertainment and social media, at some point something has to be relinquished – be it relationships, work, or sleep. If the hook techniques of social media are more addictive than those of film and television, we might eventually renounce Hollywood

---

[41] *Id.* and Stephen M. Silverman, *Tom Cruise's Children Are TV Deficient*, PEOPLE (Sept. 26, 2002, 11:25 AM), http://people.com/celebrity/tom-cruises-children-are-tv-deficient/.

[42] Casey Chan, *A List of Celebrities Who Don't Own a TV*, GIZMODO (June 8, 2012, 7:20 PM), http://gizmodo.com/5917028/a-list-of-celebrities-who-dont-own-a-tv.

[43] ADAM ALTER, IRRESISTIBLE: THE RISE OF ADDICTIVE TECHNOLOGY AND THE BUSINESS OF KEEPING US HOOKED 2 (2017).

[44] *Id.*

[45] *See generally* James Grimmelmann, *The Law and Ethics of Experiments on Social Media Users*, 13 COLORADO TECH. L.J. 219 (2015); Amy Morin, *Science Explains How Facebook Makes You Sad and Why You Keep Using It Anyway*, PSYCHOLOGY TODAY (March 7, 2016), www.psychologytoday.com/blog/what-mentally-strong-people-dont-do/201603/science-expl ains-how-facebook-makes-you-sad, and Romeo Vitelli, *Exploring Facebook Depression*, PSYCHOLOGY TODAY (May 25, 2015), www.psychologytoday.com/blog/media-spotlight/2015 05/exploring-facebook-depression.

for Silicon Valley. If we do so, the real politik value of copyright dies, along with Hollywood, because copyright primarily benefits corporations. While excessive copyright could still be on the books, it would be a law looking for an audience.

Such a future death of Hollywood would not be an occasion to celebrate. If this world materialized, we would be no better off because we would still be overconsuming – just new stuff that profits from us in new ways. Even if we use social media to curate our personal brand or express thoughts, we would still not be creating art in the sustained and authentic fashion that makes creation so vital to human happiness. This development might even be harder to slay. Thus, conceivably, if we are unsuccessful in dramatically reducing copyright protection, social media could still kill Hollywood, by spurring an epidemic of chatter, not a creative renaissance.

PART I

THEORY

1

Capture

The point of modern propaganda isn't only to misinform or push an agenda. It is to exhaust your critical thinking, to annihilate truth.

—Garry Kasparov, Russian dissident and chess grandmaster[1]

Kasparov's point that propaganda serves three functions – misinforming, advancing an agenda, and exhausting reflection – holds true for Hollywood's assault on Congress and the public. The story its lobbyists sold initially is plausible – more protection leads to more expression – yet the counter-narrative that I espouse is as intuitive and easy to grasp. If you subsidize the soft drink industry, enabling the Pepsis and Coca-Colas of the world to substantially increase their profits, which they use not only to produce more but to push their wares on individuals through relentless advertising, then it is not surprising that you get Americans overconsuming soda. Likewise, hand the largest entertainment corporations extensive monopoly protection, and they will use the financial windfall to encourage individuals to overconsume their fare. The average American is not consuming ten hours of paintings or poetry a day on average; they are consuming highly polished entertainment coming out of Hollywood that has been enabled by excessive copyright protection.

Some argue that "corporate capture can only be part of the explanation" for the push for excessive copyright; other factors like the "honest delusion" of "maximalism," which equates more copyright with more innovation, and "authorial romance," which equates invention with absolute originality, are

---

[1] Charles J. Sykes, *Why Nobody Cares the President Is Lying*, N.Y. TIMES (Feb. 4, 2017), www.nytimes.com/2017/02/04/opinion/sunday/why-nobody-cares-the-president-is-lying.htm l?action=click&contentCollection=Opinion&module=Trending&version=Full&region= Marginalia&pgtype=article.

partially to blame.[2] While this is true, only Big Copyright hires an army of lobbyists to push for greater copyright protections. Hollywood's propaganda war on Congress is a relentless, organized offensive that has continued for decades. In such an environment, where congresspeople are being inculcated over and over about the simple alleged logic whereby more protection equals more artwork, it becomes a mantra, a quasi-religious principle or scientific fact. Further, through public relations campaigns Big Copyright deliberately perpetuates misleading justifications of the theory underlying copyright law.

That the link between greater protection and more creation is so simple to grasp makes it harder to appreciate the necessity to critically examine whether it actually holds up – whether the incentives in practice motivate industry but not individuals, whether the dramatic incentives might cause devastating negative side effects. One cannot say more is better without asking what the more is and what it does to individuals and to society. It is difficult to argue that if you give the energy industry greater financial incentives to pump more oil, it will not pump more oil, especially if it is not fined for harmful spillover effects. More surprisingly, in the case of Hollywood, negative consequences are not unintended side effects: they are the objective. Hollywood wants us to consume as much as possible, which perfectly equates to the harm of excessive copyright – overconsumption. Thus, much more successfully than Big Oil, Hollywood demanded its profits but not its waste be protected by law – that it be shielded from competition yet excused from regulation on any harm it causes. Such propaganda is so effective, one might even wonder if the significant campaign contributions Hollywood continues to make to congresspeople are overkill or simply superfluous.

Not only does Big Copyright want to exhaust our critical thinking and annihilate truth, it exploits Cicero's famous maxim: "When you have no basis for an argument, abuse the plaintiff." Big Copyright blames the public for all of the supposed ills plaguing it – e.g., copying (or piracy depending on your view) – even though copying is evidence of how effective Hollywood has been in making products addictive. It is crazy to think that Big Copyright would have the gall to cry victim when it demands so much of our attention and has Congress in its pocket, yet it does. Hollywood does this by weaving a narrative of being the struggling little guy who is barely making ends meet. If Hollywood were not in the business of masterfully spinning stories and making the illogical logical, we would balk at its attempts to paint itself as the

---

[2] *See generally* James Boyle, *Deconstructing Stupidity*, Fin. Times (Apr. 21, 2005), www.ft.com/cms/s/2/39b697dc-b25e-11d9-bcc6-00000e2511c8.html, and Eric E. Johnson, *Intellectual Property and the Incentive Fallacy* 39 Florida State University L. Rev. 623 (2012).

struggling mom-and-pop store up against consumers. Yet as Peter Bart notes, studios "live under the very handsome corporate umbrella of gigantically rich companies. I mean, they're not even companies. They're sort of nation-states. AOL Time Warner is a nation-state."[3]

Hollywood has taken over the role of the little guy – the average American – and framed the genuine little guy as the greedy evildoer – which is Hollywood. The narrative masterstroke would be worthy of an Oscar if it were not so devastatingly corrosive to society. Big Copyright portrays things as being so bad for its industries that someone reading its propaganda would not be out of line to assume Hollywood executives are on food stamps. The idea that they are collecting a subsidy is correct; simply the particular transfer – government-enforced monopoly protection – is much more valuable. Meanwhile, executive salaries have sacrificed little because of illicit downloads. For example, the head of CBS surely struggled on $69.6 million in salary in 2016, though he was probably better able to afford basic foodstuffs after his raise from a paltry $57 million in 2014.[4] While such misrepresentation by Hollywood is disappointing, you have to hand it to Hollywood that it not only had the audacity to blitz us with such a crazy reversal of roles but also in many respects pulled it off while its revenue was increasing.[5]

Hollywood's spoils of victory are nothing less than a broad, remarkable expansion of intellectual privilege in the past few decades, which some have deemed to be another "enclosure movement."[6] The length, scope, and reach of copyright protection increased dramatically – e.g., penalties for violating copyright have become more draconian, while laws have been passed limiting

---

[3] *The Monster That Ate Hollywood*, PBS: FRONTLINE, www.pbs.org/wgbh/pages/frontline/sho ws/hollywood/interviews/bart.html (last visited June 6, 2017) (interview with Peter Bart, former film executive for Paramount and MGM).

[4] Nathan McAlone, *CBS CEO Les Moonves Got a Big Pay Bump to Nearly $70 Million Last Year*, BUS. INSIDER (Apr. 7, 2017, 6:28 PM), www.businessinsider.com/cbs-ceo-les-moonves-s alary-2016–2017-4, and Meg James, *CBS CEO Leslie Moonves Received $57 Million in 2014*, L. A. TIMES (Apr. 10, 2015), www.latimes.com/entertainment/envelope/cotown/la-et-cbs-ceo-lesl ie-moonves-compensation-20150410-story.html.

[5] Not all Big Copyright fields are doing as well as others, and some are experiencing technolo- gical upheaval, yet such change is not necessarily hurting their revenue growth. *See generally* Mike Masnick, *Once Again, Piracy Is Destroying the Movie Industry . . . To Ever More Records at the Box Office*, TECH DIRT (Jan. 11, 2016), www.techdirt.com/articles/20160109/17544033291/ once-again-piracy-is-destroying-movie-industry-to-ever-more-records-box-office.shtml, and Michael Masnick and Michael Ho, *The Sky Is Rising!*, TECH DIRT (Jan. 2012), www.tech dirt.com/skyisrising/.

[6] *See generally* James Boyle, *The Second Enclosure Movement and the Construction of the Public Domain*, 66 L. & CONTEMP. PROBS. 33 (2003).

consumers' use of technology in order to further strengthen Hollywood's monopoly protections.[7]

Such big-bang expansion of copyright has caused damage to the fabric of our culture. Beyond the harms of overconsumption to be chronicled in the next chapter, excessive copyright has reduced the ability of noncorporate artists to create while failing to provide them with real income, led to an explosion of copyright orphans, restricted our free speech, and dampened our political voice.

This chapter summarizes a few examples of Big Copyright's extensive lobbying and propaganda efforts, explains how the law has been grotesquely deformed to the whims of Hollywood, and describes how such distortions have transformed the law from a helpful impetus to a harmful weapon.

MECHANICS OF CAPTURE

Hollywood employs an army of lobbyists. It pays more people to peddle its wishes to Congress than there are members of Congress.[8] To give just one example, Comcast NBC Universal "spent more on lobbying in 2013 than any other corporation in any industry except Northrop Grumman Corp.," a defense multinational.[9] Comcast employed 107 lobbyists, including former senators and members of the House, working at thirty-five different lobbying firms – thirty-seven if you count Comcast's subsidiaries.[10]

---

[7] Digital Millennium Copyright Act, 17 U.S.C. §§ 1201–1205 (2000).

[8] Bobby Calvan, *Hollywood's Impact in Washington Goes Beyond Social Issues: The Entertainment Industry's Influence in Politics Extends into International Treaties and Drones*, ALJAZEERA AM. (Dec. 28, 2013), http://america.aljazeera.com/articles/2013/12/28/hollywooda-s-impactinwashingtongoesbeyondsocialissues.html. The Center for Responsive Politics states there were 352 registered lobbyists for Hollywood in 2016, while the telecom service industry had 461 (including firms like Comcast, which owns NBC Universal). *TV/Movies/Music, Industry Profile: Summary, 2016*, OPENSECRETS.ORG: CTR. FOR RESPONSIVE POL., www.opensecrets.org/lobby/indusclient.php?id=B02&year=2016 (last visited June 23, 2017), and *Telecom Services, Industry Profile: Summary, 2017*, OPENSECRETS.ORG: CTR. FOR RESPONSIVE POL., www.opensecrets.org/lobby/indusclient.php?id=B09&year=2017 (last visited June 23, 2017). Given how the Center for Responsive Politics categorizes industries, the preceding figures do not include Internet firms dealing in entertainment such as Spotify. Plus, the Sunlight Foundation research emphasizes that the actual number of lobbyists is twice the number of lobbyists who register. Tim LaPira, *How Much Lobbying Is There in Washington? It's DOUBLE What You Think*, SUNLIGHT F. (Nov. 25, 2013), https://sunlightfoundation.com/2013/11/25/how-much-lobbying-is-there-in-washington-its-double-what-you-think/.

[9] Emily Kopp, *TV/Movies/Music: Background*, OPENSECRETS.ORG: CTR. FOR RESPONSIVE POL. (last updated April 2014), www.opensecrets.org/lobby/background.php?id=B02&year=2017 (last visited June 23, 2017).

[10] *Id.*

Hollywood does not just wine and dine congresspeople while whispering suggestions in their ears. It gives generously to their campaigns. In one election cycle, in 2012, Hollywood spent more than $69 million on campaigns, while in a recent three-year span, the total was $328 million.[11] Overall lobbying efforts in 2013 tallied $118 million.[12] Suffice to say that those who attempt to provide a counterweight to Hollywood's copyright maximalist steamroller – academics and nonprofits – cannot match even a small fraction of Hollywood's treasure chest. For all practical purposes, when it comes to doling out money, Hollywood is unopposed.

Further, Hollywood is not coy about what it expects in return. The former senator Chris Dodd, while head of the MPAA, stated: "Those who count on, quote, Hollywood for support need to understand that this industry is watching very carefully . . . Don't ask me to write a check for you when you think your job is at risk and then don't pay any attention to me when my job is at stake."[13]

Hollywood also provides generously paid jobs to the politicians, their staff, and regulators when they decide they want to cash out for their efforts representing Hollywood's interests inside government. Public Knowledge, a leading nonprofit group advocating for citizens, has written that the US Copyright Office "has a well-trodden revolving door between its leadership, its other legal and policy staff and major rightsholders and their representatives."[14] Some of these high-paying jobs are in-house while others are for lobbying firms that Hollywood funds. For example, roughly 75 percent of the outside peddlers of influence employed by Hollywood are revolvers, lobbyists who were previously employed by the federal government.[15]

These job arrangements lead to regulatory capture in two forms – material capture, where the Office's staff has a financial interest in favoring Hollywood over the public interest; and cultural capture, where the staff's "prior identities and/or relationships" sway them to select policy stances advocated by people in their "in-group," Big Copyright's army of lobbyists.[16]

---

[11] Calvan, *supra* note 8. It is unclear but unlikely that these figures include campaign funds donated by PACs and executives working at Big Copyright entities. For example, "PACs and individuals connected to Comcast and Time Warner gave away about $4.4 million and $2.3 million, respectively, during the 2012 election cycle." Kopp, *supra* note 9.

[12] *Id.* [13] Calvan, *supra* note 8.

[14] Meredith Rose, Ryan Clough, and Raza Panjwani, *Captured: Systemic Bias at the U.S. Copyright Office*, 1 PUB. KNOWLEDGE 4 (Sept. 8, 2016), www.publicknowledge.org/assets/uploads/blog/Final_Captured_Systemic_Bias_at_the_US_Copyright_Office.pdf (referencing JESSICA LITMAN, DIGITAL COPYRIGHT 74 (2001)).

[15] *TV/Movies/Music, Industry Profile: Summary*, 2016, *supra* note 8.

[16] Rose et al., *supra* note 14, at 3 (citing JAMES KWAK, PREVENTING REGULATORY CAPTURE: SPECIAL INTEREST INFLUENCE AND HOW TO LIMIT IT 75 (2014)).

Politicians' Infatuation with Celebrities and Celebrity Culture

There are some wonderful mutually beneficial relationships in the animal world, including between zebras and ostriches or clownfish and sea anemones, yet none is so multilayered as the symbiotic rapport between celebrities and politicians.[17] This unique bond reinforces politicians' urge to protect an excessive copyright regime.

First, politicians yearn for funds, and celebrities and Hollywood executives do not scoff at them either. As Ronald Brownstein describes a fundraiser with the likes of Michael D. Eisner, then chairman of Disney, attending, "Most of them come primarily for the same reason [former US Senator] Bill Bradley did on this night: money."[18]

Second, lawmakers crave fame – for its own sake but also to increase their odds of obtaining greater influence. Celebrities get something in return here also. The relationship between politicians and stars is a reciprocal one: celebrities look "to politicians to validate them as part of the company of serious men and women," while politicians look "to celebrities to validate them as part of the company of the famous."[19] Legislators desire to use the extraordinary reach of celebrities to boost their own public recognition through campaign appearances and endorsements. For example, Eva Longoria of *Desperate Housewives* fame was co-chair of President Obama's "re-election campaign in charge of outreach to the Hispanic community, while Scarlett Johansson gave a poised and eloquent speech at that year's Democratic national convention."[20] In terms of the imbalance in notoriety between celebrities and politicians, fewer than five of the top 100 followed individuals on Twitter in the world are politicians, with President Donald J. Trump accounting for two of those spots. The remaining ninety-five are predominantly celebrities. Katy Perry has more than 100 million followers, while Hillary Clinton has 16.5 million. Justin Bieber clocks 97 million followers to Bernie Sanders' 6.7 million. Taylor Swift counts 85 million to Nancy Pelosi's 1.1 million.[21]

---

[17] See ThienVinh Nguyen, *Mutually-Beneficial Animal Relationships*, HUFFINGTON POST (Mar. 18, 2010, 5:12 AM), www.huffingtonpost.com/2010/01/04/mutually-beneficial-ani ma_n_391888.html.

[18] RONALD BROWNSTEIN, THE POWER AND THE GLITTER: THE HOLLYWOOD-WASHINGTON CONNECTION 4–6 (1990).

[19] *Id.* at 10.

[20] Noah Gittell, *How Obama Blurred the Border between Hollywood and Washington*, GUARDIAN (June 2, 2015), www.theguardian.com/film/2015/jun/02/how-obama-blurred-the-border-betwe en-hollywood-and-washington.

[21] *Twitter Top 100 Most Followers*, TWITTER, https://twittercounter.com/pages/100 (last visited June 20, 2017).

At times politicians are drawn to celebrities "merely to share the intoxicating company of the famous and beautiful, the way John F. Kennedy once did. For all these reasons, and others, few roads in American politics are as well traveled as the one that leads from Washington to Hollywood, from the capital of power to the capital of glamour."[22] This cultural capture also supports the extreme copyright system, albeit less directly than through financial symbiosis. Though largely unstated or possibly subconscious, politicians' ability to indulge in their celebrity infatuation and use it to their political advantage rests on copyright. Dramatically reduce copyright and Hollywood can no longer lavishly support a multitude of celebrities to host dinner parties and galas for politicians.

Propaganda Efforts

As mentioned earlier, Hollywood plies a story of how greater incentives mean more ideas in the marketplace. Yet the storyline follows the plot of many Hollywood films – little subtlety, the omission of imperfections, and no tolerance for conflicting views. In short, Hollywood's copyright savior complex is one of absolute self-interest with no room for the devastating harmful effects on the public of overconsumption – the physical harm, the psychological harm, and the theft of most of their waking hours, of most of their waking lives.

Hollywood's inculcation machine does not spare kids. In 2013, the Motion Picture Association of America, the Recording Industry Association of America, and the largest Internet service providers, in conjunction with others, decided to pilot a series of copyright curricula in California for kindergarteners to sixth graders. Mitch Stolz, at the Electronic Frontier Foundation, called it "thinly disguised corporate propaganda" that is "inaccurate and inappropriate."[23] He pithily observed, "The overriding message of this curriculum is that students' time should be consumed not in creating but in worrying about their impact on corporate profits."[24]

The material for each grade contains talking points for teachers. The inaccuracies are numerous. First, the "educational" material fails to mention fair use. The reason given was that "K–6 graders don't have the ability to grasp it."[25] On the one hand, few can confidently apply fair use's four-factor test because Big Copyright deliberately does not want Congress to clarify it, since

[22] BROWNSTEIN, *supra* note 18.
[23] David Kravets, *Downloading Is Mean! Content Industry Drafts Anti-Piracy Curriculum for Elementary Schools*, WIRED (Sept. 23, 2013, 6:30 AM), www.wired.com/2013/09/mpaa-school-propaganda/.
[24] *Id.* [25] *Id.*

doing so would simply encourage individuals to employ it. On the other hand, if third graders can do fractions, they can understand the idea that you can borrow someone else's turn of phrase in your own poem. Second, the material inaccurately "says it's illegal to make any copies of copyright works. That's a message that essentially says it's even unlawful to rip CDs to your iPod."[26] Third, the propaganda "suggests, falsely, that ideas are property" when in fact copyright applies only to the unique expression of an idea, not to the idea itself.[27] Only after public outcry over the pilot program were the materials made less slanted.[28]

Hollywood is not satisfied with simply funding such inculcation on its own dime, especially when federal funds can be used to pay for more propaganda. In this vein, the MPAA successfully lobbied Congress to include a provision in the Every Student Succeeds Act that President Obama signed into law on December 10, 2015, to provide funds to "educate" teachers and principals about the harms of sharing and copying.[29]

Beyond in-class inculcation is the at-home variety. The Business Software Alliance created a mascot named Garret the Ferret, the Copyright Crusader, while, as Tim Armstrong notes, "Our Canadian friends took another stab at using a comic character to teach kids to think like copyright maximalists with Captain Copyright."[30] As you can imagine, both comics failed to take a fair and balanced approach. Even the Library of Congress's own fictional characters, led by Detective "Cop E. Wright," do not talk about exceptions to copyright, give no depiction of the public domain as having "any ongoing relevance today," and do not create the impression "that there are any works not protected by copyright. Whether intentional or not, that's editorial bias of a sort we shouldn't countenance from the government."[31]

To ensure that students are never without Hollywood propaganda, Big Copyright had to think of a way to reach them when they are neither at

---

[26] *Id.*   [27] *Id.*

[28] Ernesto, *MPAA and RIAA Teach Copyright in Elementary Schools, Now with Fair Use*, TF (Sept. 6, 2014), https://torrentfreak.com/mpaa-and-riaa-teach-copyright-in-elementary-school s-now-with-fair-use-140906/.

[29] Ernesto, *"Piracy Harms" Are Now Part of U.S. Education Law*, TF (Jan. 28, 2016), https://tor rentfreak.com/piracy-harms-are-now-part-of-u-s-education-law-160128/?utm_source=dlvr.it& utm_medium=twitter. The text of the Every Student Succeeds Act of 2015 (Pub. L. No. 114–95 § 114 Stat. 1177 (2015–2016)) can be found at: www.congress.gov/bill/114th-congress/senate-bill/ 1177/text.

[30] Tim Armstrong, *U.S. Government: Fair Use Is Too Complex to Explain to Kids*, INFO/LAW (Aug. 10, 2007), https://blogs.harvard.edu/infolaw/2007/08/10/us-government-fair-use-is-too-c omplex-to-explain-to-kids/.

[31] *Id.*

home nor at school. The result: insinuate copyright "lessons" into kids' groups such as Junior Achievement, which potentially provides Hollywood with access to more than one million kids.[32]

Hollywood's copyright propaganda efforts are beginning to feel as ubiquitous as its entertainment.

Co-Opting Others Besides Politicians

While using funds and propaganda, Hollywood's aim is to co-opt any potential source of resistance to its vision of extreme copyright.

The media has been largely captured by simply being bought by Big Copyright – not in the sense of favors and campaign funds but through corporate control.[33] Most TV news programs are owned by entertainment conglomerates. Online news has also largely been corporatized. The top 10 US media publications by page views are almost all corporate owned – whether entertainment multinationals (ESPN, Fox News, CNN), technology firms providing ever-greater content (MSN, Google News, Yahoo Finance, Yahoo Sports), national print newspapers (*The New York Times* and *The Washington Post* – the latter recently acquired by the largest shareholder of Amazon), or the outlier, the content-aggregator Drudge Report.[34] As Free Press, a nonprofit fighting for improving the press, states: "Massive corporations dominate the U.S. media landscape. Through a history of mergers and acquisitions, these companies have concentrated their control over what we see, hear and read. In many cases, these companies control everything from initial production to final distribution."[35] Startups suffer the same fate through acquisition. For example, in the early days of YouTube, the site was a potential source of resistance to Big Copyright – encouraging people to create videos – despite its for-profit structure. Since its takeover by Google, YouTube has been captured into producing revenue for copyright holders.

---

[32] *MPAA Expands Anti-Piracy Campaign*, Bill Board (June 21, 2004, 12:00 AM), www.bill board.com/biz/articles/news/1431307/mpaa-expands-anti-piracy-campaign.
[33] For a thoughtful analysis of a further concern regarding journalism, that for-profit online ventures will not be sufficient to supply communities the accountability journalism that is required for a vibrant democracy, see Peter M. Shane, *Introduction – "The Future of Online Journalism: News, Community, and Democracy in the Digital Age,"* 8 I/S: J. L. & Pol'y Info. Soc'y 469 (2013).
[34] Liron Hakim Bobrov, *US Media Publications Ranking May 2017*, Similar Web (June 28, 2017), www.similarweb.com/blog/us-media-publications-ranking-may-2017.
[35] *Who Owns the Media?*, Free Press, www.freepress.net/ownership/chart (last visited June 29, 2017).

Consumers are also co-opted. On average consumers are too busy over-consuming to do much of anything, let alone participate in a copyright countermovement. Even if one dislikes a habit or addiction or realizes it's harmful, that doesn't mean one has the capacity to stop, let alone advocate for change.

While not encouraging excessive copyright, possible tools of resistance potentially reinforce the concept of copyright. Just as early hopes that the Internet would be a tool for democratic liberation across the world have been dashed by Big Copyright's use of it to capture consumer attention, the Internet makes it easy for pirates to break copyright but also to be caught doing so.[36] Some have even hypothesized that open, online licenses such as those offered by Creative Commons inevitably reinforce copyright even as they stand in opposition to its most extreme forms because their existence is dependent on copyright.[37]

Co-Opting International Resistance

Big Copyright has not just appropriated domestic US copyright policy; it has held tremendous sway internationally for decades, capturing possible international sources of resistance. Hollywood commands the US government as to what its policy should be in regard to exporting excessive copyright laws abroad. Jagdish Bhagwati, a distinguished economist from Columbia University, argues that

> a "selfish hegemon" such as the United States, reflecting its own lobbies' agendas, pushed for a common, coordinated policy of excessive intellectual property protection at the WTO. In short, a socially harmful policy may be imposed, under the pretext of coordination or the provision of what economists call public goods, by powerful nations in an interdependent world.[38]

Through its proxy, the US government, Big Copyright pushed for the adoption of the World Trade Organization (WTO) Agreement on Trade-Related Aspects of Intellectual Property Rights (TRIPS), which required all WTO members to increase their domestic IP protection. Hollywood also compelled other countries to join the World Intellectual Property Organization (WIPO) Copyright Treaty (WCT), an optional agreement further strengthening

---

[36] *See, e.g., How Content ID Works*, YOUTUBE, https://support.google.com/youtube/answer/27
       9737o?hl=en (last visited July 10, 2017).
[37] Shun-ling Chen, *To Surpass or to Conform – What Are Public Licenses For?*, U. ILL. J.L.
       TECH. & POL'Y 107, 139 (2009).
[38] JAGDISH BHAGWATI, IN DEFENSE OF GLOBALIZATION 227 (2004).

copyright.[39] Developing countries only acquiesce to such damaging copyright treaties because the United States Trade Representative (USTR) threatens them with actions that would be more devastating – e.g., taking away foreign aid, revoking trade concessions in other areas like agriculture, or instigating trade sanctions. Once one treaty is swallowed, Hollywood informally sponsors another more audacious one, such as the proposed Transatlantic Trade and Investment Partnership.

More and more, the treaties are touching on topics beyond copyright in order to gain greater control, such as increasing digital restrictions (or rights, depending on your view) management (DRM) provisions and providing "legal incentives for ISPs [Internet service providers] to privately enforce copyright protection rules. This opens the door for Internet filtering, DNS blocking, repeat-infringer policies that lead to terminated accounts, and ISPs monitoring users and disclosing their identities to rightsholders."[40] Hollywood has emphasized ratifying treaties instead of domestic legislation in each foreign country not only because such an approach is more efficient but also because it bypasses "the scrutiny of transparent, democratic rule making."[41] For the first three years of negotiation of the abandoned Trans-Pacific Partnership, the USTR did not share the text of the agreement with Congress, only providing briefings to lawmakers requesting one. Once Congress complained, the USTR put "two copies of the biggest free trade deal in history" in two reading rooms for congresspeople to view but restricted them from making copies of the text or even "carry[ing] their own handwritten notes out the door."[42] Such secrecy is from politicians whom Hollywood has in its pocket.

The USTR also issues an annual name-and-shame list, the Special 301 Report, which chastises other nations for not implementing enough legal protections for Hollywood. The ridiculousness of the report is manifold. First, as the Electronic Frontier Foundation believes, the report "skirts very close to the line of transgressing international law, by strong-arming other countries into changing their laws, outside of the official channels provided for resolving trade disputes through the World Trade Organization (WTO). Whereas WTO trade disputes (although problematic in other ways) are resolved by a notionally neutral arbitrator, the Special 301 Report is unabashedly partial to the complainant – the USTR acts as its own judge, jury, and

---

[39]   H.R. REP. NO. 107–624 (2002) (Conf. Rep.), *reprinted in* 2002 U.S.C.C.A.N. 649, § 2102(b)(4).
[40]   *Trade Agreements and Digital Rights*, ELECTRONIC FRONTIER F., www.eff.org/issues/trade-agreements (last visited June 20, 2017).
[41]   *Id.*
[42]   Eric Bradner, *How Secretive Is the Trans-Pacific Partnership?*, CNN (June 12, 2015, 11:11 AM), www.cnn.com/2015/06/11/politics/trade-deal-secrecy-tpp/index.html.

executioner."[43] By ignoring international treaties, the USTR "commonly demands that countries go further than their international obligations require."[44]

Second, how the report is compiled leaves a lot to be desired: "copyright, patent and trademark maximalists send in reports to the USTR, claiming which countries don't do enough to respect US intellectual property, and the USTR – via no systematic or objective process – rewrites those complaints into a report that declares certain countries 'naughty' for their practices."[45] Mike Masnick states that he "once saw the head of the US Copyright Office openly joke about the purely arbitrary nature of the 301 report at a conference. Countries like Canada – which are regularly named to the report, despite having copyright laws that are, in many areas, more stringent than the US's – have openly declared that they do not find the Special 301 process to be legitimate."[46]

For example, the International Intellectual Property Alliance (IIPA), an IP maximalist lobby group, pushed the USTR to put Brazil and Indonesia on the report because the countries were using open source code on their government computers, which "[a]ccording to the IIPA . . . is bad for copyright as it 'fails to build respect for intellectual property rights.'"[47] This argument is a non sequitur because the governments could not infringe copyright if they use code free of copyright: "Essentially the IIPA is making the mafia-esque argument that by not dealing with copyrighted software, you are not learning to respect copyright well enough, which makes you a danger to intellectual property."[48]

In the battle for minds, copyright minimalists have words, while Hollywood has hundreds of millions of dollars to spend each year on campaigns, lobbyists, and plush jobs for former public officials; celebrity ambassadors to woo Congress; and a multibillion-dollar industry to shape public opinion.

[43] Jeremy Malcolm, *EFF Responds to USTR Bullying the World to Repeat Our Copyright Mistakes*, ELECTRONIC FRONTIER F. (Feb. 9, 2015), www.eff.org/deeplinks/2015/02/eff-respo nds-ustr-bullying-world-repeat-our-copyright-mistakes.
[44] *Id.*
[45] Mike Masnick, *US's "Naughty List" of Countries Whose Intellectual Property Rules We Don't Like Is a Joke That's No Longer Funny*, TECH DIRT (Feb. 11, 2015, 3:37 PM), www.techdirt .com/articles/20150209/17454529973/uss-naughty-list-countries-whose-intellectual-property-ru les-we-dont-like-is-joke-thats-no-longer-funny.shtml.
[46] *Id.*
[47] Michael Klurfeld, *Copyright Lobbyist Group Says Open Source Makes You an Enemy of America*, TNW (Feb. 24, 2010), https://thenextweb.com/us/2010/02/24/copyright-lobbyist-gro up-open-source-enemy-america/#.tnw_GmAXLC98.
[48] *Id.*

THE BOUNTY FROM CAPTURE: COPYRIGHT'S EXPLOSION IN PROTECTION

Copyright's length, scope, and reach are so extreme it is difficult to imagine exactly how they could be increased much further, but doubtless Big Copyright is currently working on creative ways to do so. In fact, since copyright has gotten so out of control, the law not only incentivizes the artistic elite and Hollywood to create new entertainment; it incentivizes them to create new demands for added legal protection. The excessive nature of copyright law has spawned an ecosystem aimed at constantly expanding itself.

The ballooning of copyright is best captured by Lawrence Lessig's note that copyright "was a tiny little bit of regulation of the creative process; it has since expanded dramatically."[49] The "law governing creativity has changed, transformed dramatically in the past forty years in a way that removes the opportunity for the kind of creativity that was our tradition just at the time when the technology would turn it into something extraordinary."[50]

Copyright Term

One of the most poignant examples of Hollywood's capture of Congress is the phenomenal rise in the length of the copyright term.

Big Copyright has a long history of lobbying for copyright term extensions. Thomas Babington Macaulay and others successfully fought off an attempt to extend copyright more than a century and a half ago in the United Kingdom. In an 1841 speech to the House of Commons, Macaulay vividly and skillfully described the costs of extending copyright:

> Dr. Johnson died fifty-six years ago. If the law were what my honourable and learned friend wishes to make it, somebody would now have the monopoly of Dr. Johnson's works. Who that somebody would be it is impossible to say; but we may venture to guess. I guess, then, that it would have been some bookseller, who was the assign of another bookseller, who was the grandson of a third bookseller, who had bought the copyright from Black Frank, the Doctor's servant and residuary legatee, in 1785 or 1786. Now, would the knowledge that this copyright would exist in 1841 have been a source of gratification to Johnson? Would it have stimulated his exertions? Would it have once drawn him out of his bed before noon? Would it have once cheered him under a fit of the spleen? Would it have induced him to give us one more allegory, one more life of a poet, one more imitation of Juvenal? I firmly believe not. I firmly believe that a hundred years ago, when he was

---

[49] Lawrence Lessig, *The Creative Commons*, 65 MONT. L. REV. 1, 4 (2004).   [50] *Id.*

writing our debates for the Gentlemen's Magazine, he would very much rather have had twopence to buy a plate of shin of beef at a cook's shop underground.[51]

The length of copyright protection has swelled radically, initially from fourteen years in 1790, with the possibility of another fourteen if the author was still alive at the end of the first term, to twenty-eight years with the same fourteen-year extension, to twenty-eight years with a twenty-eight-year extension.[52] Subsequently, "beginning in 1962, the copyright term has been increased for works that already exist quite regularly. Eleven times in the last 40 years Congress has extended the copyright term for existing works."[53] The most recent extension under the Copyright Term Extension Act of 1998 added twenty years of protection to existing works to stretch the length of copyright, for individuals, to the life of the author plus seventy years after her death[54] and, for corporations or within a work-for-hire context, to the earlier of ninety-five years from publication or 120 years from creation.[55]

It has been recognized that the successful campaign for an additional twenty years of copyright protection was lobbied for by the likes of Disney and recording studios to propagate their own economic welfare, not the cultural, political, and economic interests of society at large.[56] In fact, critics deride the legislation as the "Mickey Mouse Protection Act," which was possibly a strategic mistake by copyright minimalists given how widely appreciated the mouse is by the public.[57] Even pro-market publications like *The Economist* talk of "absurdly long copyright periods."[58] The publication states, "Starting from scratch today, no rational, disinterested lawmaker would agree to copyrights that extend to 70 years after an author's death, now the norm in

[51]   Thomas Babington Macaulay, Speech Delivered in the House of Commons (Feb. 5, 1841), in 8 THE LIFE AND WORKS OF LORD MACAULAY: COMPLETE IN TEN VOLUMES 200–1 (Edinburgh ed., Longmans 1897).
[52]   Copyright Act of May 31, 1790, ch. 15, § 1, 1 Stat. 124 (1790); Copyright Act of Feb. 3, 1831, ch. 16, §§ 1–2, 4 Stat. 436 (1831); and Copyright Act of Mar. 4, 1909, ch. 320, § 23, 35 Stat. 1075, 1080 (1909).
[53]   Lessig, *supra* note 49, at 5.
[54]   Sonny Bono Copyright Term Extension Act, Pub. L. No. 105–298, 112 Stat. 2827 (1998).
[55]   17 U.S.C. § 101 (2000).
[56]   Joyce Slaton, *A Mickey Mouse Copyright Law?*, WIRED (Jan. 13, 1999), www.wired.com/politics/law/news/1999/01/17327. For other reasons to possibly dislike Disney, *see generally* CARL HIAASEN, TEAM RODENT: HOW DISNEY DEVOURS THE WORLD (1998).
[57]   I would like to thank Professor Peter Jaszi for articulating this point in conversation. *Copyrights: A Radical Rethink*, ECONOMIST (Jan. 23, 2003), www.economist.com/node/1547223.
[58]   *Digital Publishing: Google's Big Book Case*, ECONOMIST (Sept. 3, 2009), www.economist.com/node/14363287.

the developed world."[59] Still, the norm usefully makes it clear that the interests being protected are those of the immortal corporation, not the mortal author.

The Copyright Term Extension Act granted copyright extensions not simply to future artwork but to existing artwork, even when the artists who created the pieces are already dead. This change demonstrates that incentives to create are often irrelevant to the drive to expand terms, since incentives will clearly neither motivate people to do something they have already done nor inspire the dead.[60]

More often than not, legislators and judges have not used historical understanding to analyze this upward surge. For example, many countries' borders or forms of government do not survive seventy years, yet copyright terms can easily last for 150 years depending on an artist's age when she created a work. In fact, when the United Nations was established roughly seventy years ago in 1945, there were only fifty-one UN member nations, compared to 193 now. The last new country, South Sudan, joined in 2011.[61]

In fact, when the Copyright Term Extension Act which was a significant expansion of copyright law, passed, its constitutionality was challenged all the way to the Supreme Court. The Constitution states that Congress shall have power "to promote the Progress of Science and useful Arts, by securing for limited Times to Authors and Inventors the exclusive Right to their respective Writings and Discoveries."[62] The question posed to the Court was whether the "for limited Times" phrase was breached with the new twenty years of added protection, given that any potential benefit from the extension was so small as to make copyright's length practically infinite.

Nobel laureates George A. Akerlof, Kenneth J. Arrow, James M. Buchanan, Ronald H. Coase, and Milton Friedman and twelve other economists submitted an Amici Curiae in Support of Petitioners in *Eldred v. Ashcroft* showing that the copyright term extensions enshrined in the Copyright Term Extension Act would only increase an author's expected income from a book, assuming the

---

[59]   ECONOMIST, *supra* note 57.

[60]   Thomas Jefferson designed the initial US copyright term to last no longer than the life of the copyright holder. While his nineteen-year term recommendation, which he calculated using actuarial tables, was never passed, the fourteen-year provision under the 1790 law, mentioned previously, with an option for a second fourteen-year renewal if the artist was still alive, essentially freed the protected works at the grave of the author. PAUL K. SAINT-AMOUR, THE COPYWRIGHTS: INTELLECTUAL PROPERTY AND THE LITERARY IMAGINATION 125 (2003).

[61]   *Growth in United Nations Membership, 1945–Present*, UNITED NATIONS, www.un.org/en/se ctions/member-states/growth-united-nations-membership-1945-present/index.html (last visited July 2, 2017).

[62]   U.S. CONST. art. I, § 8, cl. 8.

author lives for thirty years after the book's release, by no more than roughly 0.33 or one-third of 1 percent.[63] At this point in the history of US copyright, the returns from extending copyright protection had essentially vanished, yet the Court declared the giveaway to Big Copyright constitutional. In his dissent in *Eldred*, Justice Breyer states, "The present extension will produce a copyright period of protection that, even under conservative assumptions, is worth more than 99.8% of protection in perpetuity."[64]

This push to extend copyright also does not make sense given the historical data. When copyright owners were allowed to renew their holdings after 28 years, roughly only 15 percent did so in fiscal 1959.[65] Similarly, fewer than 11 percent of the "copyrights registered between 1883 and 1964 were renewed at the end of their twenty-eight-year term, even though the cost of renewal was small."[66] At least two reasons explain these low figures. First, demand for most copyrighted artwork exists primarily within the first decade or so. Second, a dollar earned seventy or eighty years from now is worth only a few pennies today; the longer the copyright term, the smaller the financial incentive to create with each additional year of protection.

Scope of Copyright

The scope of what is protected by copyright has also swollen to the point of ridicule – a toddler's scribbles on the bathroom wall potentially fall under copyright's umbrella. One has to almost conscientiously try to create something that will not have copyright protection automatically subsist in it.

The scope of what art forms are protected by copyright has dramatically increased from only books, maps, and charts to encompass not only logical areas of expanse such as musical works, photographs, and paintings but also art mediums that are a bit tangential to the threat of unauthorized copies or the goal of incentivizing artists, such as architecture.[67] The scope of copyright

---

[63] Brief of George A. Akerlof et al. as Amici Curiae in Support of Petitioners at 10–12, Eldred v. Ashcroft, 537 U.S. 186 (2003) (No. 01–618).

[64] Eldred v. Ashcroft, 537 U.S. 186, 255–56 (2003) (Breyer, J., dissenting).

[65] SUBCOMM. ON PATENTS, TRADEMARKS & COPYRIGHTS S. COMM. ON JUDICIARY, 86TH CONG., 2D SESS., COPYRIGHT LAW REVISION, STUDY NO. 31, at 187 (Comm. Print 1961) (prepared by Barbara Ringer), www.copyright.gov/history/studies/study31.pdf.

[66] WILLIAM M. LANDES and RICHARD A. POSNER, THE ECONOMIC STRUCTURE OF INTELLECTUAL PROPERTY LAW 212 (2003).

[67] Copyright Act of Feb. 3, 1831, ch. 16, § 1, 4 Stat. 436 (1831) (musical works); Copyright Act of Mar. 3, 1865, § 2, 13 Stat. 540 (1865) (photographs); Copyright Act of July 8, 1870, § 86, 16 Stat. 198, 212 (1870) (paintings); and Architectural Works Copyright Protection Act of 1990, Pub. L. No. 101–650, § 703, 104 Stat. 5089, 5133 (1990) (architecture).

protection is so broad even software is protected.[68] It includes "anything basically reduced to a tangible form."[69]

Protections that kept most new works out of the crosshairs of copyright and in the public domain have been erased. For example, the previous requirements that one had to register one's work with the US Copyright Office and affix proper copyright notice to each copy of the work in order to obtain copyright protection set scores of works free into the public domain because most individuals felt little compunction to register their works. For example, in the United States between 1790 and 1800, of the more than 21,000 works published, only 648 works were registered in order to obtain copyright protection – authors only bothered to seek copyright on 3 percent of works created.[70] Thus, copyright protection appears to be little more than an afterthought for motivating many noncorporate artists. Rather, its prime significance for many artists is a disincentive to create. Yet these registration formalities have been expunged from the law.[71]

Reach of Copyright

Finally, through the combination of anti-circumvention laws and increasing technology, the reach of copyright has substantially expanded. The Digital Millennium Copyright Act (DMCA) prohibits the circumvention of access provisions of proprietary systems like a game console or cell phone.[72] Since "the DMCA makes it illegal to circumvent software encryption, some DIY car repairs could potentially be judged illegal" if the car's software is encrypted.[73] As Glenn Harlan Reynolds argues, entertainment multinationals "shouldn't be able to leverage their intellectual property rights in software to keep you from unlocking, repairing, modifying, or reselling [your stuff] as you see fit."[74]

---

[68] Pub. L. No. 96–517, § 10, 94 Stat. 3015, 3028 (1980).   [69] Lessig, *supra* note 49, at 5.

[70] William J. Maher, *Copyright Term, Retrospective Extension, and the Copyright Law of 1790 in Historical Context*, 49 J. COPYRIGHT SOC'Y U.S.A. 1021, 1023–24 (2002).

[71] *See, e.g.*, Berne Convention Implementation Act of 1988, Pub. L. No. 100–568, § 7, 102 Stat. 2853, 2853.

[72] Digital Millennium Copyright Act, 17 U.S.C. §§ 1201(a)(1), 1201(a)(2) & 1201(b)(1) (2000). Courts have noticed that the distinction between access and copy protection measures blurs significantly. *See, e.g.*, Apple, Inc. v. Psystar Corp., 673 F. Supp. 2d 931, 941–42 (N.D. Cal. 2009). For an excellent analysis of the issue, see Alfred C. Yen, *What Federal Gun Control Can Teach Us about the DMCA's Anti-Trafficking Provisions*, 2003 WISCONSIN L. REV. 673 (2003).

[73] Glenn Harlan Reynolds, *Our Intellectual Property Laws Are Out of Control*, POPULAR MECHANICS (May 14, 2013), www.popularmechanics.com/technology/gadgets/a8937/our-int ellectual-property-laws-are-out-of-control-15467970/.

[74] *Id.*

The DMCA also forbids the sale of goods or services that help individuals circumvent technological locks – i.e., DRM technologies.[75]

Séverine Dusollier states, "The copyright industry has developed many tools to exercise the prohibitive part of copyright."[76] DRM systems in combination with the DMCA significantly restrict the legal uses of copyrighted content and works in the public domain that are accessed through proprietary systems. For example, electronic readers can limit how much of a book you can cut and paste or print, even if the book's copyright has expired.

The DMCA also has "takedown notice" provisions, which require Internet service providers to "expeditiously" remove or disable access to online material that another entity claims as its own.[77] The existence of such a law is alarming because the flagged material is taken down without any judicial determination as to whether any copyright infringement actually occurred – i.e., you can be silenced, have your speech blocked online, simply by a corporation sending an email to your ISP alleging that your speech is violating someone's copyright.[78] Worse yet, the corporation often decides to stop your speech not through having a human examine the similarities of your work to theirs but by using a computer to automate the entire process of determining infringement.[79] An ISP customer who has been censored online by Hollywood can send a counter-notice to the ISP requiring it to stop blocking the content, but the harm has already occurred.[80] Further, to protect themselves from liability, ISPs also have to create a policy to terminate repeat

[75] Digital Millennium Copyright Act, 17 U.S.C. §§ 1201–1205 (2000). Also, *see generally* Timothy K. Armstrong, *Digital Rights Management and the Process of Fair Use*, 20 HARVARD J. L. & TECH. 49 (2006).
[76] Séverine Dusollier, *The Master's Tools v. The Master's House: Creative Commons v. Copyright*, 29 COLUM. J.L. & ARTS 271, 280 (2006).
[77] The ISP does not automatically become liable for direct or contributory copyright infringement if it refuses to take down the content, though it can no longer claim safe harbor under the DMCA. 17 U.S.C. § 512(c)(A)(iii).
[78] There was an Internet monitoring program, the Copyright Alert System, developed by the Center for Copyright Information and others, including the White House, that limited free speech and handed out punishments such as slowing down a user's Internet speed without any judicial examination or decrees. The program's aim was to stop individuals from allegedly downloading corporate works from the Internet without authorization. The program was announced dead in 2017. Ted Johnson, *Internet Service Providers, Studios, and Record Labels Call It Quits on Copyright Alert System*, VARIETY (Jan. 27, 2017, 2:44 PM), http://variety.com/2017/digital/news/copyright-alerts-piracy-mpaa-comcast-att-1201971756/.
[79] This practice may change after the Ninth Circuit ruled that a copyright owner is required to perform a fair use analysis before filing a takedown notice. Lenz v. Universal Music Corp., 815 F.3d 1145, 1153 (9th Cir. 2016).
[80] 17 U.S.C. § 512(g). After a counter-notice has been filed, the original entity that requested the takedown has ten to fourteen business days to file a lawsuit; the ISP does not have to unblock access to the possibly infringing material. *Id.*

infringers, even, potentially, in instances where a court has never found the user to be a copyright infringer.[81]

While such paracopyright provisions are related to yet distinct from copyright, combined with the rise of digital technology and the explosion in copyright protection they create a copyright law thicket that deters or limits creators.

Finally, Big Copyright is not resting on its laurels. It continues to lobby and spread its propaganda in the hopes of new laws to achieve ever-greater monopoly protection. For example, Big Copyright pushed for the Stop Online Piracy Act (SOPA) in the US House of Representatives and a similar bill in the Senate, the Preventing Real Online Threats to Economic Creativity and Theft of Intellectual Property Act of 2011 (PROTECT IP Act or PIPA).[82] Big Copyright has lobbied for similar treatments internationally through the Anti-Counterfeiting Trade Agreement (ACTA) and the intellectual property provisions of the previously mentioned Trans-Pacific Partnership Agreement.[83]

While both SOPA and PIPA have lapsed, the underlying lobbying efforts of Big Copyright continue both domestically and internationally.[84] Both proposed laws were put on hold largely because technology giants like Google had the equivalent lobbying might to oppose Big Copyright's attempt to throw a net of potential liability over legitimate websites.[85] For example, SOPA would have labeled a website as dedicated to theft if it was marketed as "offering goods or services in a manner that engages in, enables, or facilitates" copyright violations.[86] The overly broad use of "enables" and "facilitates" would have meant that the proposed law would not have been limited to websites "guilty of *any* copyright infringement, direct or even contributory infringement."[87]

---

[81] 17 U.S.C. § 512(i)(1)(A).

[82] Stop Online Piracy Act, H.R. 3261 112th Cong. (1st Sess. 2011), and Preventing Real Online Threats to Economic Creativity and Theft of Intellectual Property Act of 2011, S. 968, 112th Cong. (1st Sess. 2011).

[83] Anti-Counterfeiting Trade Agreement, Oct. 1, 2011, 50 I.L.M. 239 (2011); Trans-Pacific Partnership: Intellectual Property Rights Chapter, Draft Feb. 10, 2011; and David S. Levine, *Bring In the Nerds: Secrecy, National Security, and the Creation of International Intellectual Property Law*, 30 CARDOZO ARTS & ENT. L.J. 105, 107 (2012).

[84] Andrea Peterson, *SOPA Died in 2012, but Obama Administration Wants to Revive Part of It*, WASH. POST (Aug. 5, 2013), www.washingtonpost.com/blogs/the-switch/wp/2013/08/05/sopa-died-in-2012-but-obama-administration-wants-to-revive-part-of-it/.

[85] Declan McCullagh and Greg Sandoval, *Google Will Protest SOPA Using Popular Home Page*, CNET (Jan. 17, 2012), http://news.cnet.com/8301-31001_3-57360223-261/google-will-protest-s opa-using-popular-home-page/.

[86] Stop Online Piracy Act, *supra* note 82, § 103(a)(1)(B).

[87] Marvin Ammori, *Controversial Copyright Bills Would Violate First Amendment – Letters to Congress by Laurence Tribe and Me*, AMMORI.ORG, http://ammori.org/2011/12/08/controver sial-copyright-bills-would-violate-first-amendment-letters-to-congress-by-laurence-tribe-and-me/.

Hence, the bill targeted "considerable protected speech on legitimate sites."[88]
Had SOPA been in place in the 1980s, it could have killed the Internet before
it got off the ground.

In tandem with such overbroad reach, such proposed laws would have
removed standard procedural safeguards. Mark Lemley, David Levine, and
David Post state: "Based upon nothing more than an application by a federal
prosecutor alleging that a foreign website is 'dedicated to infringing activities,' Protect IP authorizes courts to order all US Internet service providers,
domain name registries, domain name registrars, and operators of domain
name servers – a category that includes hundreds of thousands of small and
medium-sized businesses, colleges, universities, nonprofit organizations,
and the like – to take steps to prevent the offending site's domain name
from translating to the correct Internet protocol address."[89] Additionally,
SOPA would "allow rightsholders to force payment processors to cut off
payments and advertising networks to cut ties with a site simply by sending
a notice."[90] Furthermore, SOPA and PIPA remedies could have taken effect
after ex parte proceedings, where the owner of the allegedly infringing site
was not "even made aware that the action was pending against his or her
'property.'"[91]

Such weakened procedural adequacy and free speech concerns would have
harmed innovation through increased potential liability brought on by a lack
of legal clarity.[92] Presciently, Wu states: "As the pace of technological change
accelerates, copyright's role in setting the conditions for competition is quickly
becoming more important, even challenging for primacy the significance of
copyright's encouragement of authorship."[93]

THE HARMS OF CAPTURE

Scholars have powerfully articulated numerous ills resulting from our extreme
copyright laws.

The original intent of copyright was to mediate between two supposed
goods: facilitating the "free flow of ideas, information and commerce" and

---

[88] *Id.*
[89] Mark Lemley, David S. Levine, and David G. Post, *Don't Break the Internet*, 64 STAN. L. REV.
      ONLINE 34 (2011).
[90] *SOPA/PIPA: Internet Blacklist Legislation*, ELECTRONIC FRONTIER F., www.eff.org/issues/c
      oica-internet-censorship-and-copyright-bill.
[91] Lemley et al., *supra* note 89.
[92] Michael A. Carrier, *SOPA, PIPA, ACTA, TPP: An Alphabet Soup of Innovation-Stifling
      Copyright Legislation and Agreements*, 11 NW. J. TECH. & INTELL. PROP. 21, 27 (2013).
[93] Tim Wu, *Copyright's Communications Policy*, 103 MICH. L. REV. 278, 278 (2004).

motivating authors to produce by using economic incentives.[94] It worked in 1790, yet since then Hollywood decided to push for such extreme financial incentives that the other half of the bargain was significantly hampered. Excessive copyright protection reduces innovation and creativity because it does not fully acknowledge that creators need to borrow from the past.[95] No art can be wholly new, yet the slaughter of the Constitutional bargain portends that no one can freely borrow without legal risk. Decades of extending copyright's length, reach, and scope means that "no one can do to the Disney Corporation what Disney did to the Brothers Grimm."[96] Artists cannot help but borrow ideas, expression, and technique. They consciously and unconsciously reference not only art that has come before but also contemporary culture. Montaigne and Milton are but two authors who so heavily borrowed that they likely would have had permanently reserved defendants' seats in court under our current copyright laws, yet their borrowing was an essential component of their genius.[97] Copyright law is so broad and complicated that it stops individuals from creating instead of doing what it is supposed to do – motivate individuals to create.

This integral process of borrowing applies to both individual artists and corporate studios. While Hollywood may be loath to admit the need for all artists to borrow, it cleverly pushed to restructure copyright to force artists to pay for such borrowing or at least risk limbo in legal uncertainty. Given its corporate structure and deep pockets, such a pay-to-borrow-so-as-not-to-incur-legal-risk system is simply a cost of doing business for Hollywood, yet it causes havoc for the vast majority of artists.

While there are limits to the need to license – for example, the doctrine of fair use, which allows individuals to utilize a portion of a copyright work legally – such breathing space is not even a partially ajar door; it is the equivalent of the airflow under the door when it is shut.[98] Whether a use is permitted is based on four factors within the Copyright Act, yet the Supreme Court has averred that all such determinations must be made not using bright-line rules but instead on a case-by-case basis.[99] Unfortunately, the Supreme Court's refusal to set any

[94] Sony Corp. v. Universal City Studios, Inc., 464 U.S. 417, 429 (1984).
[95] *See generally* BENJAMIN KAPLAN, UNHURRIED VIEW OF COPYRIGHT (1967).
[96] Lawrence Lessig, *The Creative Commons*, 55 FLA. L. REV. 763, 764 (2003). Disney has borrowed many stories and characters from the Grimm brothers, including, for example, Pinocchio and Cinderella.
[97] MARK ROSE, AUTHORS AND OWNERS: THE INVENTION OF COPYRIGHT 2 (1993).
[98] Also, the idea/expression dichotomy holds that ideas cannot be copyrighted; only particular expressions of ideas can. See Harper & Row Publishers, Inc. v. Nation Enterprises, 471 U.S. 539, 556 (1985).
[99] Campbell v. Acuff-Rose Music, Inc., 510 U.S. 569, 577 (1994).

bright-line rules in at least some instances – e.g., you can copy 1 percent of the words in a book – has significantly reduced individuals' willingness to rely on fair use, hence substantially reducing the amount of material on which artists can draw. While adding some bright-line rules would sacrifice flexibility, they would bring a revolution of clarity. There has been recent positive movement toward improving fair use, yet artists need substantially more certainty under the doctrine and significantly more ability to borrow freely.[100]

Numerous other harms result from the current extreme copyright regime and the relentless push to extend protection. Excessive copyright impairs free speech.[101] Lessig presents the restriction from a realist perspective:

> For in a world that threatens $150,000 for a single willful infringement of a copyright, and which demands tens of thousands of dollars to even defend against a copyright infringement claim, and which would never return to the wrongfully accused defendant anything of the costs she suffered to defend her right to speak – in that world, the astonishingly broad regulations that pass under the name "copyright" silence speech and creativity. And in that world, it takes a studied blindness for people to continue to believe they live in a culture that is free.[102]

Given that such a $150,000 statutory damage threat is for one work, a defendant can easily find herself being sued for millions or more.[103] Andrew Bridges, who "has defended a handful of cases involving claims of more than $5 billion in statutory damages, called the remedy a 'nuclear weapon' in the hands of copyright claimants."[104]

---

[100] See the pathbreaking work of Patricia Aufderheide, Peter Jaszi, Michael Carroll, Barton Beebe, and others. *E.g.*, PATRICIA AUFDERHEIDE AND PETER JASZI, RECLAIMING FAIR USE: HOW TO PUT BALANCE BACK IN COPYRIGHT (2011) and Barton Beebe, *An Empirical Study of U.S. Copyright Fair Use Opinions, 1978–2005*, 156 U. PA. L. REV. 549 (2008).

[101] For powerful, broader first amendment critiques, *see generally* Jack Balkin, *Digital Speech and Democratic Culture: A Theory of Freedom of Expression for the Information Society*, 79 N. Y.U. L. REV. (2004); Neil W. Netanel, *Copyright and the First Amendment; What* Eldred *Misses – and Portends, in* COPYRIGHT AND FREE SPEECH: COMPARATIVE AND INTERNATIONAL ANALYSES (Jonathan Griffiths and Uma Suthersanen, eds., 2005); and NEIL W. NETANEL, COPYRIGHT'S PARADOX (2008). See also the insightful work of Peter M. Shane on the relationship between information policies and democracy – *e.g.*, Peter M. Shane, *Democratic Information Communities*, 6 I/S: J. L. & POL'Y INFO. SOC'Y 95 (2010).

[102] LAWRENCE LESSIG, FREE CULTURE: THE NATURE AND FUTURE OF CREATIVITY 187 (2004).

[103] *See also* No Electronic Theft Act, Pub. L. No. 105–147, 111 Stat. 2678 (1997) (enhancing criminal liability for copyright violations).

[104] Carolina Bolado, *This Song Was Made for You and Me: Copyright Challenges Seek to Protect the Public Domain* (Dec. 19, 2016), www.donaldsoncallif.com/wp-content/uploads/Law360-12.19.16.pdf.

Free speech restrictions go well beyond punishing threats of ruinous damage awards. An excessively restrictive copyright regime that allows Hollywood to cram its content into every corner of our lives and discourages individuals from creating on their own decreases the public's political voice and ability to define political discourse, party agendas, and political vocabulary.[105] It increases the ease of manipulation of the public's views on public policy.[106] In such a media-saturated environment, it is less likely for individuals to realize they have a desire to speak, let alone act on that desire through creating, which would allow them to experiment with the values and messages they want to communicate. Even if they manage to share their speech, it is harder to be heard when corporate entertainment and advertising are plastered on every surface, every screen. Defining political vocabulary becomes a marketing game that only deep-pocketed entities can play – e.g., it is no wonder that "death tax" prevailed over "silver spoon tax." The power of such rhetoric to change the political landscape and economic reality is evident in the Democratic Party's current reluctance to entertain ideas for a much more progressive income tax system despite the fact that just a few decades ago the top tax bracket was 70 percent under President Carter and 91 percent under President Kennedy.[107] Such previously successful policies that enjoyed broad support and reinforced equality and freedom are either taboo or forgotten in part because of Big Copyright's stranglehold on our political discourse.

The extreme copyright regime also restricts the digital commons and hence reduces the diversity in sources of information, which enables media to more easily selectively disclose information or skew the nature of what is communicated.[108] Moreover, exceedingly long copyright terms limit the ability of citizens to inform themselves because such terms increase the "power over the price of information... in the hands of intellectual property owners."[109]

---

[105] See generally Rosemary J. Coombe, *Objects of Property and Subjects of Politics: Intellectual Property Laws and Democratic Dialogue*, 69 TEX. L. REV. 1853 (1991) (Coombe builds off the work of Mikhail Bakhtin); Niva Elkin-Koren, *Cyberlaw and Social Change: A Democratic Approach to Copyright Law in Cyberspace*, 14 CARDOZO ARTS & ENT. L.J. 215 (1996); William W. Fisher III, *Property and Contract on the Internet*, 73 CHI.-KENT L. REV. 1203 (1998); William Fisher, *Theories of Intellectual Property*, in NEW ESSAYS IN THE LEGAL AND POLITICAL THEORY OF PROPERTY 193 (Stephen R. Munzer ed., 2001); and JOHN FISKE, TELEVISION CULTURE 95 (1987).

[106] *Id.*

[107] Compare *Jimmy Carter Administration Tax Rates*, INSIDE GOV, http://federal-tax-rates.inside gov.com/d/a/Jimmy-Carter (last visited June 27, 2017).

[108] Yochai Benkler, *Freedom in the Commons: Towards a Political Economy of Information*, 52 DUKE L.J. 1245, 1267 (2003).

[109] PETER DRAHOS and JOHN BRAITHWAITE, INFORMATION FEUDALISM: WHO OWNS THE KNOWLEDGE ECONOMY? 4 (2002).

Further, the public domain has been transformed from the natural state of our cultural world to an appendage.[110] The culprit is not copyright but extreme copyright. The dramatic and routine increase in the length of copyright over the past few decades has prevented existing art from falling into the public domain. In the twenty years following the passing of the Copyright Term Extension Act, "while one million patents will [have] pass[ed] into the public domain, zero copyrights will [have] pass[ed] into the public domain by virtue of the expiration of a copyright term."[111]

Such massive extensions in the length of copyright prevent commercially successful works and copyright orphans – artwork that is commercially unavailable and without a known copyright owner – from being freely used. The problem of orphan works is monumental. A majority of film and book holdings are estimated to be orphan works.[112] By definition, no benefit arises from the protection of these orphans because there are no known copyright holders to receive royalties. Yet hundreds of millions of orphan works are caught in the equivalent of legal purgatory, with society bearing the harm of being unable to safely use them as a basis for creation. While some works would be copyright orphans even with modest copyright laws, the longer the copyright term, the more likely it is that works will become orphans. Further, when copyright got rid of the formalities of registering work and providing notice in order to obtain and maintain copyright protection, the vast majority of works that were never motivated into existence by copyright became locked up by it.

Such lack of access is not a well-functioning market, nor is it in line with the spirit of the Constitution's Progress Clause. Whenever attempts are made to reduce the number of orphans through proposed legislation, Big Copyright lobbies against them because it views a more vibrant digital commons as a threat to its business interests. For example, the proposed Public Domain Enhancement Act,[113] now dead, was a practical attempt to lessen the harm brought on by exceedingly long copyright terms. The bill would have introduced into the public domain abandoned copyrighted works after fifty years by requiring copyright holders to pay a registration tax of $1 "due 50 years after the

[110]   For an insightful analysis of the importance of the public domain, see Shubha Ghosh, *The Fable of the Commons: Exclusivity and the Construction of Intellectual Property Markets*, 40 U.C. Davis L. Rev. 855 (2007).
[111]   Lessig, *supra* note 102, at 134–35.
[112]   James Boyle, The Public Domain: Enclosing the Commons of the Mind 9 (2008) (citing reports by the Center for the Study of the Public Domain at Duke University School of Law for film holdings).
[113]   H.R. 2408, 109th Cong. (2005).

date of first publication or on December 31, 2006, whichever occurs later, and every ten years thereafter until the end of the copyright term."[114]

The MPAA ultimately opposed this act on what Lessig calls "embarrassingly thin" grounds.[115] He goes on to argue that the underlying reason for such opposition was an

> effort to assure that nothing more passes into the public domain. It is another step to assure that the public domain will never compete, that there will be no use of content that is not commercially controlled, and that there will be no commercial use of content that doesn't require their permission first. . . Their aim is not simply to protect what is theirs. *Their aim is to assure that all there is is what is theirs*. . . [T]hey fear the competition of a public domain connected to a public that now has the means to create with it and to share its own creation.[116]

Jonathan Zittrain provides a sobering example of Big Copyright's power to even prevent meetings by international organizations from taking place on the public domain ecosystem: "When the World Intellectual Property Organization announced the prospect of a meeting devoted to studying the place of nonproprietary production models within the spectrum of intellectual property, the Business Software Alliance objected strenuously, and the meeting was cancelled."[117]

Individual creativity and our society's culture are significantly impeded not only because copyright terms on works are too long and too broad but also because the continued protection of copyright orphans prevents artists from uncovering such artwork and presenting it anew to the culture. The rediscovery of abandoned works is much more powerful now than even twenty years ago because we have a medium that makes widespread availability almost costless – the Internet.

---

[114] CONG. RES. SERV., H.R. 2408 (109TH): PUBLIC DOMAIN ENHANCEMENT ACT OFFICIAL SUMMARY, www.govtrack.us/congress/bill.xpd?bill=h109-2408&tab=summary (last visited Oct. 31, 2012). To avoid violating the Berne Convention, this requirement would have applied only to copyright holders of art created by American artists. Article 5(2) of the Berne Convention only prohibits a signatory state from imposing formalities on foreign authors. Berne Convention for the Protection of Literary and Artistic Works, Paris Act art. 5(2), July 24, 1971, 25 U.S.T. 1341, 828 U.N.T.S. 221.

[115] LESSIG, *supra* note 102, at 253.   [116] *Id.* at 255–56.

[117] Jonathan Zittrain, *Normative Principles for Evaluating Free and Proprietary Software*, 71 U. CHI. L. REV. 265, 285 (2004) (internal footnotes omitted).

2

The Overconsumption Problem

Moderation is a fatal thing. Nothing succeeds like excess.
—Oscar Wilde

Art should never try to be popular. The public should try to make itself artistic.
—Oscar Wilde

As Wilde suggests, excess may have its advantages in gaining artistic renown and its modern-day cousin – a large social media following. And while Wilde might have relished the possibility of tweeting pithy observations to millions – "There is only one thing in life worse than being talked about, and that is not being talked about" – even he would likely advocate for a dramatic reduction in copyright today if he knew of the harms it is causing, if only because to be talked about one has to interact with the world instead of simply passively consuming. Further, he recognized the value of creating: "The public should try to make itself artistic." Wilde was ahead of his time by advocating for arts programs in schools: "I would have a workshop attached to every school, and one hour a day given up to the teaching of simple decorative arts. It would be a golden hour to the children."

There is no shortage of books lambasting our society's overconsumption of all kinds of materials.[1] When we think of overconsumption, pictures of vast landfills, individuals donning masks on the streets of Beijing, and islands slowly being overtaken by the oceans often crowd our heads. While the environmental problems caused by overconsumption are undeniably serious, so are the negative effects of the overconsumption of art on individuals. Often,

---

[1] For example, *see generally* JOHN DE GRAAF, DAVID WANN & THOMAS H. NAYLOR, AFFLUENZA: THE ALL-CONSUMING EPIDEMIC (2001) (in association with Redefining Progress, a nonpartisan organization located in Oakland, California).

such stories involve children who watch too much TV or play too many video games and hence neglect their studies, become too sedentary, or do not develop the social skills we think they should develop – the absolute extremes being *hikikomori*, who lock themselves in rooms while consuming entertainment all day.[2] The image of children becoming zombies in front of screens is more vivid than that of the adult zombie, although the harms of overconsuming entertainment are equally applicable to adults.

It is not controversial to observe that overconsuming food or alcohol can be very detrimental to physical and mental health. Obviously, the more significant the overconsumption, the worse the effects on the individual. Support could also be mustered for claims that overconsuming non-agricultural consumer goods can be harmful, if not to one's physical health, then at least to one's mental health – e.g., hoarders or individuals who cannot stop buying fishing poles. So it comes as no surprise that overconsuming media can be unhealthy.[3] It is not that anything is a priori wrong with consuming art, just like there is nothing wrong with buying fishing poles or composing music. Some artwork consumption is vital to a life well lived and to maintaining a healthy sense of oneself as an ever-evolving member of society. It is the excessive, potentially addictive aspect of any consumptive activity that is worrisome.[4]

THE BENEFITS OF ART

As Goethe prescribes, "one ought, every day at least, to hear a little song, read a good poem, see a fine picture, and, if it were possible, to speak a few reasonable words."[5] While no artistic medium is devoid of merit, studies show benefits and harms vary widely between art forms and within art forms depending on the content of works.[6] For example, reading a novel increases, while watching

---

[2]   *Hikikomori* are Japanese youth who rarely if ever leave their room for months or years at a time. See Maggie Jones, *Shutting Themselves In*, N.Y. TIMES, Jan. 15, 2006, § 6 (Magazine), at 47.

[3]   *See generally* Robert Kubey & Mihaly Csikszentmihalyi, *Television Addiction Is No Mere Metaphor*, 286 SCI. AM. 74 (Feb. 23, 2002), www.sciam.com/article.cfm?articleID=0005339 B-A694-1CC5-B4A8809EC588EEDF.

[4]   I am not stating that everyone who overconsumes commercial art is addicted to such overconsumption. The important point is that people spend too much time consuming commercial art and too little time creating on their own.

[5]   JOHANN WOLFGANG VON GOETHE, 2 WILHELM MEISTER'S APPRENTICESHIP 3 (Thomas Carlyle trans., Chapman & Hall 1907) (1795–96).

[6]   Such variation is not necessarily inherent in the medium; it relates to how artists deploy technology within different artistic mediums and the fact that some art forms rely more on technology than others and are hence more prone to being used harmfully. Further, I am not attempting to dictate what popular culture ought to be. I am simply saying we cannot spend most of our waking time devoted to consuming it.

television decreases, one's theory of mind – the capacity to ascribe mental states such as beliefs and emotions to individuals and to appreciate that others living in the world can and often do have different goals and emotions than our own.[7] Furthermore, both the benefits and harms of an art form can vary, to some extent, depending on the viewer – e.g., her genetic inheritance and personal history, whether she consumes with others or alone.[8]

Brian Kisida and colleagues performed a study in which students took part in a lottery for the chance to take a tour of the Crystal Bridges Museum of American Art, funded by Alice Walton of Walmart fame. The lucky students who took part in the field trip, as opposed to those who did not have the chance to go, "demonstrated stronger critical thinking skills, displayed higher levels of social tolerance, exhibited greater historical empathy and developed a taste for art museums and cultural institutions."[9] Pamela Rutledge states that media "allows you to experience emotions, it can be cathartic and it allow[s] you to see models of different sorts of behaviors."[10] Media can help educate generally – some of the increase in rising IQs "is due to advances in media assisted learning and interactive game playing."[11] Entertainment can also convey life lessons.[12] Melissa Kearney and Phillip Levine found that regions in the United States with a higher audience for the reality TV shows *16 and Pregnant* and *Teen Mom* experienced a larger reduction in teenagers giving birth, presumably because of the portrayal of changing diapers,

---

[7] *See generally* Amy I. Nathanson et al., *The Relation between Television Exposure and Theory of Mind among Preschoolers*, 63 J. COMM. 1088 (2013).

[8] *See generally* Joseph A. Schwartz and Kevin M. Beaver, *Revisiting the Association between Television Viewing in Adolescence and Contact with the Criminal Justice System in Adulthood*, 31 J. INTERPERSONAL VIOLENCE 2387 (2015) and M. Andrejevic, *Watching Television without Pity: The Productivity of Online Fans*, 9 TELEVISION & NEW MEDIA 24 (2008). There is also a creative side to consuming art in the sense that individuals bring their own experiences to a work, providing potentially novel interpretations of the artist's work. Such interaction or dialectic is valuable and has been discussed by many European theorists, yet it is distinct from creating on one's own. Further, the lines of consumption and creation can blur. For example, there is a movement by video game makers to get video game players to help shape or create aspects of video games.

[9] Brian Kisida, Jay P. Greene, & Daniel H. Bowen, *Art Makes You Smart*, N.Y. TIMES (Nov. 23, 2013), www.nytimes.com/2013/11/24/opinion/sunday/art-makes-you-smart.html.

[10] Chris Morris, *Depression, Disease, and No Sex Are Some Dangers of Binge Watching*, CNBC (Aug. 26, 2016, 10:43 AM), www.cnbc.com/2016/08/26/depression-disease-and-no-sex-are-som e-dangers-of-binge-watching.html.

[11] Bernard J. Luskin, *Brain, Behavior, and Media*, PSYCHOL. TODAY (Mar. 29, 2012), www.psy chologytoday.com/blog/the-media-psychology-effect/201203/brain-behavior-and-media.

[12] One possible positive of overconsumption that was suggested to me is that you will at least have something to talk about with others and hence possibly forge social bonds. However, overconsumption at this level leaves little time to meet strangers or friends. Also, consuming only half the national average would likely give anyone plenty to talk about.

cleaning up vomit, and being woken in the middle of the night. Their analysis "concludes that the shows reduced teenage births by 5.7%, or 20,000 fewer teenage births each year."[13]

Some of these benefits are real, robust, and potentially long-lasting. Others are fleeting. For example, research by Daniel Kahneman and colleagues observed 909 employed women using a technique called Day Reconstruction Method to determine what people spend their time on in a particular day and how much they enjoy the activities.[14] Watching TV alone was the third most enjoyable activity behind relaxing with friends and having lunch with coworkers. Yet the study did not touch on a long-term sense of fulfillment from a life of meaningful interactions and pursuits but rather simply feelings in the moment, such as relaxation. While such emotions as relaxation are important, other activities can bring about the same sense of calm without the negative side effects associated with TV viewing. When individuals stop watching, the relaxation not only quickly dissipates but also leaves viewers drained of vitality: "The sense of relaxation ends when the set is turned off, but the feelings of passivity and lowered alertness continue. Survey participants commonly reflect that television has somehow absorbed or sucked out their energy, leaving them depleted."[15] As Blaise Pascal wrote, "Distraction is the only thing that consoles us for our miseries and yet it is, itself, the greatest of our miseries."[16]

TECHNOLOGY ENABLING ADDICTION

We go through cycles of thinking that technology is going to save us or destroy us.[17] At first, empowered by the Internet, individuals were advancing scientific research, spreading knowledge, making connections to others with unique interests, organizing politically to topple tyrants, and raising money to help

---

[13] Nicholas Kristof, *TV Lowers Birthrate (Seriously)*, N.Y. TIMES (Mar. 19, 2014), www.nytimes.com/2014/03/20/opinion/kristof-tv-lowers-birthrate-seriously.html?mcubz=3&_r=0 (citing Melissa S. Kearney & Phillip B. Levine, *Media Influences on Social Outcomes: The Impact of MTV's 16 and Pregnant on Teen Childbearing* [Jan. 2014], www.wellesley.edu/sites/default/files/assets/kearney-levine-16p-nber_submit.pdf [unpublished manuscript]).

[14] Daniel Kahneman et al., *A Survey Method for Characterizing Daily Life Experience: The Day Reconstruction Method*, 306 SCI. 1776 (Dec. 3, 2004), http://science.sciencemag.org/content/306/5702/1776/F1.

[15] Kubey & Csikszentmihalyi, *supra* note 3.

[16] THOMAS MERTON, THE ASCENT TO TRUTH 25 (Mariner Books 2002) (1951).

[17] For a prominent, nuanced understanding of this as applied to the Internet, see Alfred C. Yen, *Western Frontier or Feudal Society?: Metaphors and Perceptions of Cyberspace*, 17 BERKELEY TECH. L.J. 1207 (2002).

others. Then we could only see evil: authoritarian governments crushing free speech, dictatorships locating dissidents to torture, terrorists hatching plans, trolls blanketing comment sections with hate, corporations pushing products on the Internet regardless of their harm. These oscillations have less to do with the technology than who uses it and in what ways – i.e., the technology itself is not inherently good or bad yet can have substantial ramifications when employed by different media.[18]

Furthermore, the advent of new technology can dramatically alter long-standing incentives. A hundred and fifty years ago, the incentive of copyright appeared to work well enough to encourage the creation of books, maps, and charts while not creating significant negative externalities. Yet the same financial incentive left unaltered after the rise of a radically different techno-logical landscape led to the creation of large corporations that consolidated their position into an entrenched lobby to argue not only against the removal of such subsidies but for the strengthening of them.[19] Generally speaking, the technology advances that altered the simple elegance of copyright law devel-oped in three separate strands, each of which contributed to our present state of unprecedented overconsumption.[20] First, novel technologies created new art forms – e.g., TV, film, and video games. Second, new technology enabled the broader dissemination of content – e.g., phonorecords, Walkmans, VCRs, cable, satellite, iPads, and smartphones. Third, innovative technology empow-ered Hollywood with the ability to keep viewers' eyes glued to screens using insights from neuroscience and psychology. All three trends have continued to build over time in ways that are critical in explaining our current overconsumption.

With regard to the first technological thread, copyright protection was extended to the new art forms. With TV and film, at first, this did not lead to mass overconsumption because few owned the means to watch the new

[18]   Big Copyright has abused this reality to conclude that it should be trusted to use technology with abandon, while the public's use should be controlled and at times even prohibited. This is epitomized in Hollywood's efforts to push through the passage of the DMCA, which legally withholds technology from consumers, while demanding that Hollywood receive ever-greater copyright incentives, further encouraging it to employ technology such as neuroscience techniques against viewers.

[19]   As Mancur Olson has extensively documented, at times, all it takes is a concentrated group heavily invested in a legislative outcome facing a dispersed and diluted opposition to get what it wants. *See generally* MANCUR OLSON, THE LOGIC OF COLLECTIVE ACTION: PUBLIC GOODS AND THE THEORY OF GROUPS (rev. ed., Harvard University Press 1971) (1965).

[20]   Just as technology can alter the affects of copyright law, so can other developments or factors. Since copyright law's consequences are not eternally fixed, the shocking negative overcon-sumptive consequences of our existing laws are specific to our present day and current society.

content – TV sets – yet such extension of copyright would later prove to be important given that we currently consume more TV than almost all other art forms combined. The same trend of greater consumption of new art forms continued over decades for other art forms such as video games; at first only young kids could be seen with game consoles in their hands, but now adults consume as much as anyone, while women have caught up to men in their consumption.[21] Furthermore, it took decades to fully realize that these new art forms had features, based on the technology that allowed for their dissemination, that made them apt to be addictive.

In reaction to the second technological trend, advances in the distribution of entertainment, Big Copyright mobilized its resources to control accessibility. Historically, with each new distribution technology, the law either balanced the interests of Hollywood with the interests of those wanting to employ the new distribution technology or did not capitulate to Hollywood's demands for greater copyright protection. Within the past few decades, however, Big Copyright substantially ramped up lobbying and campaign contributions, ending any sense of balancing competing interests. Big Copyright pushed the narrative that with the rise of the Internet its treasured content could no longer be controlled because of real, yet overblown, threats of file sharing. Hollywood argued that increases in copyright and related laws were necessary to offset the harm to its interests from technological innovations that allow for works to be copied more quickly. Such calls of alarm were so successful that Congress bowed to Hollywood's demands to restrict Internet freedom, ban the use of certain technologies by consumers, and augment the strength of copyright law.

Yet this same rise in new distribution technologies has benefited Hollywood in a way that it exploits but does not publicize. Big Copyright gradually realized that such new distribution techniques could be used to its advantage, translating into greater overconsumption by the public. Regardless of where consumers are – from the bus stop to the grocery store, the office to the bedroom – they possess technology that allows them to constantly consume media. Further, even the unauthorized downloading enabled by new distribution technologies led to more harmful consumption – consumption that would not have happened if copyright laws had not motivated Hollywood to inundate the market with hyped, polished media.

---

[21] *The Nielsen Total Audience Report Q1 2017*, The Nielsen Total Audience Series 14 (2017) and Drew Harwell, *More Women Play Video Games Than Boys, and Other Surprising Facts Lost in the Mess of Gamergate*, Wash. Post (Oct. 17, 2014), www.washingtonpost.com/ news/the-switch/wp/2014/10/17/more-women-play-video-games-than-boys-and-other-surpris ing-facts-lost-in-the-mess-of-gamergate/?utm_term=.8d68b21083fd.

The third technological development was the gradual realization that Hollywood could deploy technology to hook viewers – to erect barriers preventing them from moderating their consumption of entertainment. A few of these techniques, like cliffhangers and violence, are ancient and not tied to specific art forms. Others, such as using camera angles and focus, were sporadically employed for decades by different directors experimenting with film's power to manipulate viewers. Hollywood corporations exploited this power in technologies, setting up labs to study and refine hook techniques that are specific to certain art forms, primarily entertainment displayed on screens. Within the past few years, they have chosen to use technology to design media to be as behaviorally addictive as possible. Not surprisingly, they use the same neuroscience to hawk their addictive wares.

Hollywood employs not only artists to manipulate new artistic mediums and distribution channels but also scientists who use technologies developed in other contexts, such as fMRIs to refine hook techniques that are shamelessly developed and employed by Hollywood for the express goal of getting us to perpetually consume. Big Tobacco never had the gall to publicize job openings accurately – e.g., "scientists needed to increase addictiveness of cigarettes" or "psychologists needed to hook little children" – yet Big Copyright is doing precisely this. Jacob Weisberg writes: "Today, students at Stanford and CalTech and Harvard aspire to" jobs that use "what we know about human vulnerabilities in order to engineer compulsion" within media and technology products.[22]

The economy-wide technological revolution that helped spawn these three technological developments also brought an unprecedented amount of free time to individuals starting roughly in the mid-twentieth century.[23] Previously, people toiled for inhumane hours and simply could not have survived in the world if they had consumed ten hours of entertainment a day. Nor could they have paid for it. Thus, the development of technologies like washing machines and automated manufacturing systems created household and industrial efficiencies that liberated vast amounts of time in the average person's week – opening up the possibility for untapped demand, in the eyes of Hollywood. Corresponding advances in consumer packaged goods and transportation infrastructure saved additional hours for Hollywood to capture.

[22] Jacob Weisberg, *We Are Hopelessly Hooked*, N.Y. REV. BOOKS (Feb. 25, 2016), www.nybo oks.com/articles/2016/02/25/we-are-hopelessly-hooked/.

[23] For example, Erik Barnouw states that TV viewing only became widespread after World War II in the United States. ERIK BARNOUW, TUBE OF PLENTY: THE EVOLUTION OF AMERICAN TELEVISION (1990).

These three technological strands – technology creating new art forms, novel ways of distributing content, and innovative methods to keep viewers consuming – would have done little damage and might scarcely have existed in the absence of copyright, even with the opening up of unprecedented amounts of free time in individuals' lives. Yet – adding ridicule to this absurd historical alignment of forces tipping us toward massive overconsumption – copyright exists, is extreme, and has led to our cultural pandemic. The incentives of copyright should have dramatically fallen over the past fifty years, not increased. Given the vast proliferation of technological incentives, Big Copyright no longer needs such vast legal incentives to create.

HOW SCREEN ENTERTAINMENT HOOKS VIEWERS

Neuroscience topics are the plot of numerous films and TV shows. Some such depictions are favorable and relatively accurate. Other representations are so misleading that they can harm a promising treatment tool. For example, electroconvulsive therapy (ECT), which uses electricity to induce seizures, "can be a beneficial treatment for people with severe, chronic depression," yet the "the technique has a terrible reputation among large sections of the public" because Hollywood continues to portray the procedure as barbaric, possibly because of the "dangerous application of the method in its early years."[24] Some depictions simply mislead without obviously harmful real-world consequences, such as the TV show and movie *Limitless*, which fallaciously claimed that we harness only a small portion of our brainpower.[25] Such blatant inaccuracies should not surprise lawyers who watch TV shows about the law.

Hollywood has even turned neuroscientists into stars. For example, TNT aired a TV show called *Perception* where the protagonist is a schizophrenic neuroscience professor who consults for the FBI.[26] ABC offered *Black Box*, a show about a bipolar neuroscientist.[27] PBS and the BBC hosted a show narrated by an actual neuroscientist, *The Brain with David Eagleman*.[28]

---

[24] Christian Jarrett, *10 Surprising Links between Hollywood and Neuroscience*, WIRED (Dec. 30, 2013, 6:27 AM), www.wired.com/2013/12/10-surprising-links-between-hollywood-and-neu roscience/.

[25] *Id. See also* CHRISTIAN JARRETT, GREAT MYTHS OF THE BRAIN 51 (2014).

[26] *Neuroscientist Turned Crime Solver in "Perception,"* NPR (July 20, 2012, 1:39 PM), www.npr.org/ 2012/07/20/157113794/neuroscientist-turned-crime-solver-in-perception.

[27] Matthew Gilbert, *In "Black Box," a Bipolar Doc with a Cure for What Ails Everyone Else*, BOSTON GLOBE (Apr. 23, 2014), www.bostonglobe.com/arts/television/2014/04/23/abc-black-box-bipolar-doc-with-cure-for-what-ails-everyone-else/edYtTo36PpTSUZ8ZOrokKM/story .html.

[28] *The Brain with David Eagleman*, BBC FOUR, www.bbc.co.uk/programmes/b06yjrdp.

Given such significant plot use of neuroscience, it is telling to note the topics Hollywood does not illuminate with its insights. While its fictional characters explore how to solve crime with neuroscience or how to convince a jury of a defendant's innocence, Hollywood does not cast a spotlight on how it uses neuroscience to push its products, causing overconsumption, or how it is enabled to do so because of the enormous financial incentives the law provides it. In fact, the pull to overconsume certain types of professionally made entertainment is so great that Hollywood could someday create a show about its own use of hook strategies, and consumers would sign on and tweet about the irony every week. Hulu's advertisement featuring Alec Baldwin alerting viewers that TV turns their brains to mush was an excellent example of attempting to inoculate viewers from confronting the appalling by treating the subject ironically.

While individuals consume a vast range of art in many different art mediums, most of what they consume is concentrated in certain art forms such as TV, film, video games, and content enabled by the Internet – entertainment intrinsically linked to screens. Given the importance of such hook techniques to screen entertainment, the discussion that follows will omit the fine arts and largely ignore music.[29]

The ability to control consumers' consumption habits has been dramatically enabled by developments in technology over the past hundred years. Marshall McLuhan said the medium can be as important if not more so than the specific message – that the exportation of a medium has its own effects distinct from the messages conveyed.[30] Part of his aim was to highlight that we often overlook how the message of art is delivered and how the delivery system – radio versus painting versus the Internet – can have significant ramifications for the viewer. As discussed, technology is generally neutral; it can to be used for the grandest of human aspirations, such as democratization, or for the most pedestrian of motives, such as selling bubble gum.

In an alternative world, TV and film would not have to be so prone to be overconsumed – e.g., we could have films that simply show unmoving dabs of color for hours on end. Such films would not necessarily have to be ridiculous or emotionally sterile. Individuals talk about being moved to tears in the presence of Mark Rothko's paintings, which are simple blocks of deep color, yet they do not spend hours a day, day in and day out, staring at them. TV,

[29] I realize that screens might at some point become obsolete while the underlying art forms – e.g., movies and video games – continue to enthrall viewers, yet I feel that "screen entertainment" conveniently serves as an adequate umbrella term for now.

[30] *See generally* MARSHALL MCLUHAN, UNDERSTANDING MEDIA: THE EXTENSIONS OF MAN (Massachusetts Institute of Technology Press 1994) (1964).

films, video games, and apps are addictive because of how they are deployed by profit-motivated corporations.

Uri Hasson and colleagues have demonstrated that "films can exert considerable control over brain activity and eye movements" depending on "movie content, editing, and directing style."[31] They established that if you show volunteers video clips of unscripted real life such as video of Washington Square Park in New York City, viewers' brains show little synchronous activity, across "less than 5 percent of subjects' cortex."[32] Yet using well-known audience focus techniques – careful selection of camera angles and camera focus such as fading everything into the background besides one character in a scene – directors can purposefully structure audiences' responses, dramatically increasing the control of their attention. When such structured techniques were deployed in carefully set shots from Alfred Hitchcock's *Bang! You're Dead*, "there was a significant correlation in activity across nearly 70 percent of their cortex."[33] Hasson states, "The movie takes over the brain responses of the viewers."[34]

Scarily, filmmakers have achieved such high control of consumers' brains largely through learning the craft of filmmaking along with some input from neuroscientists. Yet in the future, it is likely that artists will have even more command over the focus of viewers – e.g., Hasson suggests that filmmakers could put volunteers in fMRIs to analyze every clip of a film, using the volunteers' responses to further tweak each frame to make the work maximally controlling. Such fMRI techniques show not only entertainment's ability to hold our attention through lighting up "the primary auditory and visual cortex" but also whether our limbic system is engaged, which might suggest an emotional response to the work, and our frontal cortex, which suggests our "abstract thought and other 'higher' cognitive functions" are piqued by whatever is unfolding on the screen.[35] Thus, the possibility exists for such fMRI analyses to refine screen entertainment so that the director has even greater control – from the emotional pull of the product to how the dialogue, music, and visual components keep us glued to our many screens. Greg Miller quotes the filmmaker Darren Aronofsky of *Black Swan* and *Pi* fame saying, "It's a scary tool for the studios to have."[36]

A more established focus technique that directors and advertisers use is to literally track the movement of the audience's eyes in order to "manipulate

[31] Uri Hasson et al., *Neurocinematics: The Neuroscience of Film*, 2 PROJECTIONS: J. FOR MOVIES & MIND 1, 1 (2008).

[32] Greg Miller, *How Movies Synchronize the Brains of an Audience*, ATLANTIC (Aug. 28, 2014), www.wired.com/2014/08/cinema-science-mind-meld/.

[33] *Id.*   [34] *Id.*   [35] *Id.*   [36] *Id.*

your brain to keep you entertained."[37] For example, such knowledge can help filmmakers construct a believable reality through special effects. Jon Favreau, director of *Iron Man* and *Jungle Book*, says, "We're constantly calculating where we think the audience's eye is going to be, and how to attract it to that area and prioritize within a shot what you can fake."[38] He suggests, "The best visual effects tool is the brains of the audience" because it will "stitch things together so they make sense."[39]

Big Copyright has been experimenting with a gaggle of other biometrics beyond fMRI studies and tracking volunteers' eye movements. Viacom is in the process of deploying electroencephalograms (EEGs) to monitor volunteers' brain waves.[40] NBCUniversal is gearing up to monitor volunteers' heart rates.[41] Nielson Consumer Neuroscience uses galvanic skin response (GSR) sensors to note variation in the electrical conductance of skin – including how much someone is sweating – along with observing volunteers' breathing and facial reactions to the screen entertainment shown to them.[42] The techniques hold the promise of so much power that even some individuals working on such gadgets in an attempt to make entertainment more irresistible have qualms. Dave Poltrack, chief research officer at CBS Corporation, states: "I think we should all feel a little paranoid and a little manipulated by all of this."[43]

In addition to audience focus techniques that make entertainment more engaging through carefully controlling the viewers' attention, TV and other screen-based art forms can also readily activate individuals' "orienting response," which is the "instinctive visual (or auditory) reaction to any sudden or novel stimulus in the environment."[44] The response was hardwired into us so that we can reflexively snap to attention when there are movements around us and protect ourselves from possible dangers in the wild. When directors quickly jump from one scene to another, from one actress to another, from one

---

[37] Greg Miller, *How Movies Manipulate Your Brain to Keep You Entertained*, WIRED (Aug. 26, 2014, 6:30 AM), www.wired.com/2014/08/how-movies-manipulate-your-brain/.

[38] *Id.*   [39] *Id.*

[40] Jessica Toonkel, *TV Networks Open Labs to Read the Minds of Viewers*, REUTERS (Nov. 4, 2015, 10:14 AM), www.reuters.com/article/us-tv-neuroscience-research-insight/tv-networks-op en-labs-to-read-the-minds-of-viewers-idUSKCN0ST0IS20151104.

[41] *Id.*

[42] Aaron Souppouris, *Nielsen Wired Me with Sensors and Exposed My CES Tech Fetish*, ENGADGET (Jan. 9, 2016), www.engadget.com/2016/01/09/nielsen-consumer-neuroscience-c es-2016-video/.

[43] Toonkel, *supra* note 40.

[44] Robert Kubey, *Television, Addiction to*, in 2 ENCYCLOPEDIA OF CHILDREN, ADOLESCENTS, AND THE MEDIA, Sage Reference 799 (2007).

camera angle to another, from one musical theme to another, the orienting response is activated, instinctively altering us to engage and hence making it physiologically challenging for us to not look at the ever-changing screen. Robert Kubey and Mihaly Csikszentmihalyi state: "Typical orienting reactions include dilation of the blood vessels to the brain, slowing of the heart, and constriction of blood vessels to major muscle groups ... The brain focuses its attention on gathering more information while the rest of the body quiets."[45]

Ivan Pavlov first noted this involuntary response, while Byron Reeves and colleagues in the 1980s showed that "simple formal features of television – cuts, edits, zooms, pans, sudden noises – activate the orienting response, thereby keeping attention on the screen."[46] Annie Lang and colleagues later demonstrated that one's heart rate declines for a few seconds after an orienting response is initiated, yet such cuts, edits, zooms, pans, and other techniques associated with screen entertainment "frequently come at a rate of one per second, thus activating the orienting response continuously."[47]

In addition to such cinematographic tools, numerous content hooks can be deployed to also make it difficult for consumers to turn off a film, TV show, video game, or app. These content hooks are not unique to screen entertainment yet remain nonetheless quite effective, especially when combined with the cinematographic techniques that are unavailable to other art forms. Some important content hooks include sex, violence, cliffhangers, and serializing entertainment.

Alexandra Sifferlin suggests, "Humans are hard wired to respond to sex and violence ... Both, after all, are critical to our survival ... Sex is appealing to us on a base level – since it's our means to procreate – and we get a kick out of watching it too."[48] In terms of why violence attracts some, Anne Bartsch and Marie-Louise Mares determined: "In addition to other motivations such as suspense, some types of violent and even gory content might be sought as an opportunity for meaning-making."[49] For example, viewers may be drawn to the violence not only because of the anticipation but also because it is usually motivated by justice unmet by the law.

Cliffhangers, like the allure of sex and violence, are so common, familiar, and expected that you might assume viewers' knowledge of them would negate their effectiveness; yet this content hook continues to be used successfully in

---

[45] Kubey & Csikszentmihalyi, *supra* note 3.   [46] *Id.*   [47] *Id.*

[48] Alexandra Sifferlin, *5 Reasons Why TV's Top Shows Are So Addictive*, TIME (Jan. 17, 2014), http://healthland.time.com/2014/01/17/5-reasons-why-tvs-top-shows-are-so-addictive/.

[49] Anne Bartsch & Marie-Louise Mares, *Making Sense of Violence: Perceived Meaningfulness as a Predictor of Audience Interest in Violent Media Content*, 64 J. COMM. 956, 956 (2014).

the vast majority of corporate works. There are epic cliffhangers between TV seasons, medium cliffhangers between episodes, and mini-cliffhangers before commercials. Furthermore, by weaving numerous subplots within each episode, directors can continually have a few cliffhangers unresolved at any moment by every few minutes switching back and forth between the different storylines.

Cliffhangers are related to the trend toward serialized entertainment – e.g., TV episodes that substantially build off each other to develop a grand plot arc instead of self-contained episodes that lose little if watched out of order. The serialization of television is part of the trend toward binge-watching. Some directors argue that we have already entered the age of hyperserials, which emphasize a more pure reliance on one unified storyline. In line with this, and no doubt to encourage binge-watching, the entire first season of Netflix's *House of Cards* was released at midnight one day in 2013. Amazingly, "According to internal Netflix data, thousands of subscribers finished all 13 episodes in the first 14 hours after the show debuted online – the ultimate testament to its Hyperserial appeal."[50]

Carlton Cuse, a co-head writer for the TV show *Lost*, says, "It's like the people who make potato chips ... They know how to put the right chemicals in there to make you want to eat the next potato chip. Our goal is to make you want to watch that next episode."[51] Such admissions go to the core of the differences between corporate, onscreen entertainment and noncorporate, offscreen entertainment and why the former is overconsumed. Novelists, generally speaking, are not trying to turn their product into potato chips, even if they deploy some of the same techniques as Hollywood. Sculptors do not want to hook you; they want viewers to meaningfully connect with their work as equals. While artists would love to be able to make a living creating art, their primary motivation is not to sell you a product.

Apps and video games have their own stable of hooking tools that take advantage of their interactive nature.[52] This was not always a conscious, deliberate strategy. As Bill Davidow states:

> Until roughly 2000, compulsive behavior remained a side effect – not an intentional element of game design and other Internet applications.

[50] Andrew Romano, *Why You're Addicted to TV*, NEWSWEEK (May 15, 2013, 4:45 AM), www.newsweek.com/2013/05/15/why-youre-addicted-tv-237340.html.
[51] *Id.*
[52] These hooks can also be used to make social media more addictive. My focus is on all media except social media, given only some of the content on social media platforms is contingent on the existence of excessive copyright, unlike most of the non–social media entertainment created by Big Copyright.

Application providers were simply supplying customers with services that made their products more appealing . . . By the time Web 2.0 rolled around, the key to success was to create obsessions. Internet gaming companies now openly discuss compulsion loops that directly result in obsessions . . . In the past, society has been able to put physical barriers in place to make it more difficult to satisfy unhealthy obsessions. For example, gambling casinos were primarily segregated in Nevada. Things are very different today. In the first place, there is no physical barrier between people and the obsession in question. Smartphones and portable electronic devices travel with us in our pockets.[53]

Davidow mentions the first such tool – the compulsion loop, which is the idea of creating countless mini-goals within an app or video game, so that once one achievement is attained, consumers are presented with another in an endless loop of challenges. The loop is so engrossing because, neuroscience shows, "achieving a goal or anticipating the reward of new content for completing a task can excite the neurons in the ventral tegmental area of the midbrain, which releases the neurotransmitter dopamine into the brain's pleasure centers."[54] While "one of the defining traits of humans is that our brains possess executive functions that can override this kind of conditioning if we will it . . . often we decide to keep on going because we want the next reward."[55] Part of the reason why such goal seeking captures consumers, why we decide to keep going, is that the goals "function as placeholders that propel you forward when the daily systems that run your life are no longer fulfilling."[56] The ultimate abuse by apps and video games of our connection to goals is creating infinite format games that never end – one could play forever and never reach a conclusion.

Research on pigeons, rats, and humans has shown that if you want to maximally use feedback as a hook to encourage overconsumption, provide it in irregular intervals through multiple senses – touch, hearing, sight, and smell.[57] Furthermore, combine it with negative feedback, which can be a powerful motivator. The "bad is stronger than good" principle suggests that we not only seek out the negative (as with first reading the one-star Amazon

[53] Bill Davidow, *Exploiting the Neuroscience of Internet Addiction*, ATLANTIC (July 18, 2012), www.theatlantic.com/health/archive/2012/07/exploiting-the-neuroscience-of-internet-addiction/259820/.

[54] *Id.*

[55] JAMIE MADIGAN, GETTING GAMERS: THE PSYCHOLOGY OF VIDEO GAMES AND THEIR IMPACT ON THE PEOPLE WHO PLAY THEM 116 (2015).

[56] ADAM ALTER, IRRESISTIBLE: THE RISE OF ADDICTIVE TECHNOLOGY AND THE BUSINESS OF KEEPING US HOOKED 119 (2017).

[57] *Id.* at 127, 138, & 140.

reviews); we also remember the bad more vividly (we recollect bad childhood memories more readily than good ones, even if the bad events were infrequent and our childhood was peaceful).[58]

Tristan Harris, a former Google design ethicist, mentions a simple yet well-known way to increase consumption – the auto-play function that automatically starts the next episode of a TV show after the first ends or switches to related content on sites such as Netflix, Hulu, and YouTube.[59] A more involved process that video game designers use is termed "color coding," which entails releasing "different versions of missions . . . to different people" to see which mission elicits the most "time on device," a term borrowed from slot machine analytics.[60] Designers continue to provide different players different color-coded missions over and over again, "so what you're left with after, say, 20 generations is this weaponized evolved version of the game, or a weaponized evolved mission, that is maximally addictive."[61] Yet another hook technique is the deployment of "energy systems," where after a set period of free play, participants are locked out of the game for a few hours and must either wait to start playing again or pay to jump right back into the experience.[62]

Jacob Weisberg encapsulates the sober reality of the ubiquitous use of such hook techniques: "Aspirations for humanistic digital design have been overwhelmed so far by the imperatives of the startup economy. As long as software engineers are able to deliver free, addictive products directly to children, parents who are themselves compulsive users have little hope of asserting control."[63] We are in "'a race to the bottom of the brain stem,' in which rewards go not to those that help us spend our time wisely, but to those that keep us mindlessly pulling" the digital lever of apps that is reminiscent of "basic slot machine psychology."[64]

ADDICTION

A trope of federal democracy is that people can vote with their feet. Before the fall of Communism in East Germany, people instead used their feet to gain

[58] *Id.* at 219.
[59] *Tech Design Ethicist Works to Raise Awareness of Internet Addiction*, ALL THINGS CONSIDERED, NPR (July 10, 2017), www.npr.org/2017/07/10/536505290/tech-design-ethicist-works-to-raise-awareness-of-internet-addiction.
[60] *"Irresistible" by Design: It's No Accident You Can't Stop Looking at the Screen*, FRESH AIR, NPR (Mar. 13, 2017), www.npr.org/sections/alltechconsidered/2017/03/13/519977607/irresistible-by-design-its-no-accident-you-cant-stop-looking-at-the-screen (interview with Adam Alter).
[61] *Id.*   [62] ALTER, *supra* note 56, at 155–56.   [63] Weisberg, *supra* note 22.   [64] *Id.*

better access to television. Dresden, in the East, "experienced a crisis in labor supply when many residents moved closer to the western border to watch programs being broadcast by stations in West Germany."[65] While such movement was likely an attempt to see freedom on a screen as a substitute for the lack of freedom in their lives and gain access to free information from the uncensored West, it vivifies the idea of drawing an audience.

Dismissing a neuroscientist's concerns with the Internet and social media, *The Economist* quips: "The parallels with 20th-century concerns about radio, rock 'n' roll and television, which is presently enjoying something of a rehabilitation as a proper, serious medium, are striking."[66] I agree with *The Economist* that TV is in a renaissance period, partially because of the switch to more serialized shows, yet this does not mean that even the most aesthetically sophisticated new shows can escape inflicting harms on consumers if they continue to use hook techniques that have been enabled by screens. Again, entertainment from TV to apps can be educational, relaxing, and profound while also causing negative externalities such as swallowing up decades of one's life. The concern with much screen entertainment is that since it is engineered to maximally keep our attention, we begin to lose agency; we are unable to turn our eyes away and hence suffer the numerous harms of overconsumption.

The Economist further digs in, stating that the neuroscientist "is aware that misgivings such as hers" have a long history – at one point coffeehouses were "seen as possibly corrupting the young, making them frivolous or indolent or filling their minds with nonsense. Perhaps this time things will be different."[67] What *The Economist* fails to mention is that after we had concerns about coffeehouses, Freud trumpeted the wonders of cocaine. He became so addicted that his nose partially collapsed. While our noses are intact, our souls are in danger of crumpling under our evolutionary weaknesses as they are unabashedly exploited for profit.

The Economist and its readers might be skeptical because they are not necessarily trapped by the addiction factory that Hollywood has built. It is easy to not notice the things that do not affect us personally, as with other social ills like wage stagnation, insufficient benefits, poor job prospects, and

---

[65] Robert Kubey & Mihaly Csikszentmihalyi, Television and the Quality of Life: How Viewing Shapes Everyday Experience xi (1990) (citing M. G. Cantor & J. M. Cantor, *American Television in the International Marketplace*, 13 Comm. Research 509–20 [1986]).

[66] *Will the Internet Eat Your Brain?*, Economist (Aug. 30, 2014), www.economist.com/news/books-and-arts/21614088-neuroscientist-warns-will-internet-eat-your-brain.

[67] *Id.*

epic rising income and wealth inequality. There is a danger that we too lightly dismiss the harms of overconsumption and do nothing about it.

Experts are more and more willing to argue that overconsumption can often lead to addiction, and they are bolstering their arguments with behavioral evidence. In his book, which focuses on the effects of technology post-2000, Adam Alter argues that "addictive behaviors have existed for a long time, but in recent decades they've become more common, harder to resist, and more mainstream."[68] Whereas in the past "we swam through waters with only a few hooks: cigarettes, alcohol, and drugs that were expensive and generally inaccessible," now we are "littered with hooks" from Facebook to email, Twitter to texting.[69] For example, when a survey asked individuals between the ages of eighteen and twenty-four whether they agreed with the statement "When nothing is occupying my attention, the first thing I do is reach for my phone," 77 percent said yes.[70]

Alter avers: "These new addictions don't involve the ingestion of a substance. They don't directly introduce chemicals into your system, but they produce the same effects because they're compelling and well designed" and are getting "progressively more difficult to resist."[71] These new forms of addiction are labeled "behavior addictions" to distinguish them from traditional substance addictions. He further contends that company executives understand that "[t]here isn't a bright line between addicts and the rest of us," and thus they "run thousands of tests with millions of users to learn which tweaks work and which ones don't – which background colors, fonts, and audio tones maximize engagement and minimize frustration."[72] Alter does not believe the problem is that we lack willpower but rather, quoting Tristan Harris, that "'there are a thousand people on the other side of the screen whose job it is to break down the self-regulation you have.'"[73]

Robert Kubey largely agrees with Alter's behavioral analysis of the addictive-like tendencies of smartphones, video games, and the Internet, though he focuses on television: "Even apart from biological factors . . . television viewing can be self-perpetuating and can produce psychological dependency that is of considerable significance."[74] According to survey data, roughly 10 percent of individuals self-identify as TV addicts.[75]

---

[68] Alter, *supra* note 56, at 5.   [69] *Id.* at 4.

[70] Kevin McSpadden, *You Now Have a Shorter Attention Span Than a Goldfish*, Time (May 14, 2015), http://time.com/3858309/attention-spans-goldfish/.

[71] *Id.* at 5.   [72] *Id.* at 4–5.   [73] *Id.* at 3.

[74] Kubey, *supra* note 44, at Sage Reference 798, 799.

[75] Robert D. McIlwraith, *"I'm Addicted to Television": The Personality, Imagination, and TV Watching Patterns of Self-Identified TV Addicts*, 42 J. Broadcasting & Electronic Media 371, 371 (1998).

Kubey offers that some individuals' interactions with television fit up to five of the seven criteria used to diagnose substance dependence, while only three of these factors must be present within any twelve-month period.[76] The five potentially applicable criteria include: "(1) people ... spend a great deal of time using it; (2) people use it more often than they intend; (3) people make repeated unsuccessful efforts to reduce use; (4) people withdraw from or give up important social, family, or occupational activities; (5) people report 'withdrawal'-like symptoms of subjective discomfort when use stops."[77] As for this last criterion, numerous research projects have examined volunteers who agreed to stop watching the tube in order to glean whether withdrawal-like symptoms would be present. Charles Winick assessed these "cold-turkey studies," stating:

> The first three or four days for most persons were the worst, even in many homes where viewing was minimal and where there were other ongoing activities. In over half of all the households, during these first few days of loss, the regular routines were disrupted, family members had difficulties in dealing with the newly available time, anxiety and aggressions were expressed ... People living alone tended to be bored and irritated.[78]

HARMS OF OVERCONSUMPTION

Even if overconsumption does not lead to behavior addiction for many, it still brings a plethora of harms to viewers. Further, some of the negative effects mentioned in this section occur with even moderate consumption; thus, harm is caused without reaching a point of overconsumption. Finally, overconsumption of media has been shown to cause some of the ills mentioned in this section, while in other cases overconsumption has only been linked to or correlated with certain harms. For example, "violence in media causes desensitization to violence," yet whether violence in media is causally linked or rather correlated to actual acts of violence has been debated for decades. We have a theory as to why the relationship may be causal: "Violence may be contagious by observational learning and social agreement."[79] While correlation plus a compelling theory does not equal causation, it is nonetheless informative and at times all we can realistically expect to demonstrate.

---

[76] *Id.*   [77] *Id.*

[78] Kubey & Csikszentmihalyi, *supra* note 3 (citing Charles Winick, *The Functions of Television: Life without the Big Box, in* TELEVISION AS A SOCIAL ISSUE 221–22 [Stuart Oskamp ed., 1988]).

[79] Luskin, *supra* note 11.

Anders Grøntved and Frank Hu performed a meta-analysis of studies on TV viewing and different markers of physical illness.[80] They found that "longer duration of TV viewing time is consistently associated with higher risk of type 2 diabetes, fatal or nonfatal cardiovascular disease, and all-cause mortality."[81] Every two hours of consuming TV increased the risk of type 2 diabetes "by 20% over 8.5 years of follow-up, the risk of heart disease rose by 15% over a decade, and the odds of dying from any cause increased 13% during a seven year follow-up."[82] In an interview, Hu states: "Now we know that excessive TV watching may do more damage than other types of sedentary behaviors ... so it's a good idea to ask how much time people spend in front of the TV and for doctors to give advice not only about exercise but about how to reduce TV watching."[83] Every added two hours of watching a day was also shown to increase the risk of fatal pulmonary embolisms by 40 percent.[84] Lilian Cheung, director of health promotion and communication at Harvard School of Public Health, states: "There's convincing evidence in adults that the more television they watch, the more likely they are to gain weight or become overweight or obese."[85] Television has a range of ills beyond those associated with a lack of exercise and bad diet. In the United States, 80 percent of individuals state "that they watch TV in the hour before going to sleep," which leads to sleep loss.[86] One starts watching and "the next thing you know, it's 2 o'clock in the morning."[87] Researchers at Copenhagen University even discovered that watching more than five hours of TV per day is associated with reducing men's sperm count by a third.[88]

[80] Anders Grøntved & Frank B. Hu, *Television Viewing and Risk of Type 2 Diabetes, Cardiovascular Disease, and All-Cause Mortality: A Meta-Analysis*, 305 J. AMER. MED. ASSOC. 2448 (June 15, 2011).
[81] *Id.* at 2454.
[82] Alice Park, *Too Much TV Linked with Disease and Early Death*, TIME (June 15, 2011), http://healthland.time.com/2011/06/15/too-much-tv-watching-linked-with-disease-and-early-death/. Hu goes on to state that TV consumption and exercise are mutually exclusive. *Id.*
[83] *Id.*
[84] Pat Hagan, *Why Too Much TV Makes Men Less Fertile: Watching More Than Five Hours a Day Can Cut a Man's Sperm Count by a Third*, DAILY MAIL (Aug. 12, 2016), www.dailymail.co.uk/health/article-3738308/Why-TV-makes-men-fertile-Watching-five-hours-day-cut-man-s-sperm-count-THIRD.html.
[85] Susmita Baral, *Netflix and Chew: How Binge Watching Affects Our Eating Habits*, NPR (Dec. 31, 2015, 4:57 PM), www.npr.org/sections/thesalt/2015/12/31/461594989/netflix-and-chew-how-binge-watching-affects-our-eating-habits.
[86] *Science Friday: TV and Smart Phones May Hamper a Good Night's Sleep*, NPR (Mar. 11, 2011), www.npr.org/2011/03/11/134459354/TV-And-Smart-Phones-May-Hamper-A-Good-Nights-Sleep.
[87] *Id.* [88] Hagan, *supra* note 84.

In addition to being associated with many detrimental physical effects, TV is linked to reducing the quality and quantity of our interactions and increasing psychological struggles. Heather Kirkorian and colleagues found that both the value and amount "of parent-child interaction decreased in the presence of background television. These findings suggest one way in which early, chronic exposure to television may have a negative impact on development."[89]

A study of heavy-media-using kids aged eight to eighteen consuming more than three hours of entertainment a day found that 47 percent reported getting "fair or poor grades (mostly C's or lower), compared to 23% of light media users" consuming under three hours a day of entertainment.[90] The heavy media users were also "more likely to say they get into trouble a lot, are often sad or unhappy, and are often bored."[91] The study found that "the relationships between media exposure and grades, and between media exposure and personal contentment, withstood controls for other possibly relevant factors such as age, gender, race, parent education, and single vs. two-parent households."[92]

Bernard J. Luskin states: "Attention spans are decreasing because of exposure to excessively stimulating and fast-paced media. A direct link between exposure to media stimulation and Attention Deficit Disorder (ADD) has surfaced."[93] Further, television watching has also been correlated to reduced cognitive development in infants and toddlers.[94]

A Cambridge University statistician, David Spiegelhalter, says that binge-watching, smartphones, and other digital devices are to blame for a 40 percent decrease in the amount of sex couples have from, on average, five times a month in the 1990s to three times a month now.[95] Other harms of overconsuming TV include "creating political or social biases," "increased fear of being victimized," "predicting later cigarette smoking," "avoidance of relationship maintenance," and "poorer body image among women."[96]

---

[89] Heather L. Kirkorian et al., *The Impact of Background Television on Parent-Child Interaction*, 80 CHILD DEV., 1350, 1350 (2009). Additional work by Kirkorian also suggests a decrease in the quantity of interaction between child and parent if the TV show in the background is a kids' program, not a show directed at adults. *Id.* at 1357.

[90] VICTORIA J. RIDEOUT et al., GENERATION M2: MEDIA IN THE LIVES OF 8- TO 18-YEAR-OLDS, KAISER FAMILY FOUNDATION STUDY 15 (2010), https://kaiserfamilyfoundation.fil es.wordpress.com/2013/04/8010.pdf.

[91] *Id.*   [92] *Id.*   [93] Luskin, *supra* note 11.

[94] *See generally* Heather L. Kirkorian, Ellen A. Wartella, & Daniel R. Anderson, *Media and Young Children's Learning*, 18 FUTURE OF CHILDREN 39–61 (2008).

[95] Morris, *supra* note 10.

[96] Steve Sussman & Meghan B. Moran, *Hidden Addiction: Television*, 2 J. BEHAV. ADDICTION 125, 126 (2013) (citing various studies).

Finally, a Gallup poll demonstrates that many of us recognize that we are overconsuming entertainment. Individuals aged eighteen to twenty-nine years old voluntarily admitted that they "spend too much time" using their smartphones (58 percent), using the Internet (59 percent), and watching television (26 percent).[97]

Similar negative results have been found for other forms of screen entertainment such as video games and Internet use. Excessive Internet use and smartphone use are correlated to sleep loss, lower empathy, and mental and physical problems.[98] In the United Kingdom, "More women filing for divorce are complaining that their husbands spend too long playing video games, according to research. Of those wives who cite unreasonable behaviour for ending their marriage, 15 per cent believe their partners put gaming before them."[99] There are Internet and video game addiction camps in China, South Korea, and the United States; adults are dying from uninterrupted questing; and crushingly, a South Korean couple let their three-month-old daughter die of malnutrition "while they were raising a virtual child in an online game."[100]

While overconsumption of screen entertainment has been linked to many physical and psychological ills, negative effects can go beyond the individual to harm society. While everyone needs downtime and while moderate

---

[97] Frank Newport, *U.S. Young Adults Admit Too Much Time on Cell Phones, Web*, GALLUP (Apr. 12, 2012), www.gallup.com/poll/153863/young-adults-admit-time-cell-phon es-web.aspx. The percentage of all adults admitting too much cell phone use was 27 percent; too much Internet use, 26 percent; and watching too much TV, 33 percent. *Id.*

[98] Aviv Weinstein & Michel Lejoyeux, *Internet Addiction or Excessive Internet Use*, 36 AM. J. DRUG & ALCOHOL ABUSE 277, 281 (2010); Yolanda Reid Chassiakos et al., *Children and Adolescents and Digital Media*, 138 PEDIATRICS e1, e8 (2016); Eunusk Cho, *Therapeutic Interventions for Treatment of Adolescent Internet Addiction – Experiences from South Korea*, *in* INTERNET ADDICTION: NEUROSCIENTIFIC APPROACHES AND THERAPEUTICAL IMPLICATIONS INCLUDING SMARTPHONE ADDICTION 168 (Christian Montag & Martin Reuter eds., 2015); Éilish Duke & Christian Montag, *Smartphone Addiction and Beyond: Initial Insights on an Emerging Research Topic and Its Relationship to Internet Addiction*, *in* INTERNET ADDICTION: NEUROSCIENTIFIC APPROACHES AND THERAPEUTICAL IMPLICATIONS INCLUDING SMARTPHONE ADDICTION, *supra*, at 367; Chien Chou et al., *A Review of the Research on Internet Addiction*, 17 EDUC. PSYCHOL. REV. 363 (2005).

[99] Lydia Warren, *Video Games Being Blamed for Divorce as Men "Prefer World of Warcraft to Their Wives,"* DAILY MAIL (May 31, 2011, 3:32 AM), www.dailymail.co.uk/news/article-1392 561/World-Warcraft-video-games-blamed-divorce-men-prefer-wives.html.

[100] Simon Parkin, *The Sometimes Fatal Attraction of Video Games*, GUARDIAN (Aug. 9, 2015, 3:30 P.M.), www.theguardian.com/technology/2015/aug/09/who-killed-the-video-gamers-sim on-parkin-taiwan; Mez Breeze, *A Quiet Killer: Why Video Games Are So Addictive*, NEXT WEB (Jan. 12, 2013), https://thenextweb.com/insider/2013/01/12/what-makes-games-so-addic tive/#.tnw_MlosDBLR; Andrew Salmon, *Couple: Internet Gaming Addiction Led to Baby's Death*, CNN (Apr. 2, 2010, 10:07 AM), www.cnn.com/2010/WORLD/asiapcf/04/01/korea.pa rents.starved.baby/index.html.

consumption of art provides some benefits, if able-bodied adults are forgoing work altogether to overconsume, then our economy suffers.[101] Think this is only a theoretical possibility? *The New York Times* recently ran an article with the following title: "Why Some Men Don't Work: Video Games Have Gotten Really Good."[102] It is not just our economy that might be adversely affected; if Americans continue to spend more time playing video games than volunteering, as they currently are doing, then we are casting aside those in need of help.

The exposition of Hollywood's various hook techniques, brazen research to make its products harder to turn off, and relentless pushing of harmful addictive content leads us to the question: Should we care that by spending countless hours a day overconsuming entertainment, citizens are missing out on a host of activities commonly considered essential to life? If consumers were not being manipulated to overconsume by corporations that care only about maximizing profit, their lived experience would be dramatically different.

Such a concern could be couched in terms of utilitarian theory – the opportunity cost of overconsuming plus the mental and physical harms of overconsumption are greater than any benefit from overconsuming. It can also be situated within a Kantian or deontological framework – Hollywood is dictating to individuals how they should spend their time and doing so through hook techniques that can effectively strip away individuals' agency instead of leaving them to freely make their own decisions, treating consumers as means instead of ends. The worry can be expressed within virtue ethics – individuals are being blocked from practicing virtuous behavior and hence are unable to serve as role models and help others through Hollywood's non-Aristotelian actions. There are other situations in which many of us could agree that a variety of normative theories support the same ideal. For example, we can all deeply believe in women's equality yet can debate which normative ethical framework is the best grounding for it.

Furthermore, my theory could arguably fit under modern political liberalism as conceived by John Rawls, Charles Larmore, and Martha C. Nussbaum, especially if I stress how creation, like education, is critical to the public sphere in providing the space for and cultivating the ability of citizens to engage in rational dialogue about public matters as equals.[103] Yet my theory can as likely be viewed as a form of perfectionist liberalism, under which Mill's classical

---

[101] I would like to thank Glynn Lunney for this important observation.

[102] Quoctrung Bui, *Why Some Men Don't Work: Video Games Have Gotten Really Good*, N.Y. TIMES (July 3, 2017), www.nytimes.com/2017/07/03/upshot/why-some-men-dont-work-video-games-have-gotten-really-good.html?mcubz=3.

[103] Martha A. Nussbaum, *Perfectionist Liberalism and Political Liberalism*, 39 PHIL. & PUB. AFF. 3, 37–42 (2011).

liberalism fits, if I emphasize the private sphere value of creation – how creation is a good in and of itself to a life well lived. As will be shown in Chapter 3, I argue for the value of creation in both ways – as a way to demonstrate the "equality of citizens" and the "importance of equal respect" and as a way to touch our soul, to give everyone personal meaning.[104] Again, as with the phenomena that we can agree to a particular value yet differ as to its best normative underpinnings, we can concur that women's equality is sacrosanct yet disagree on whether it should fall under political liberalism as Nussbaum argues or under perfectionist liberalism as Susan Moller Okin believes.[105]

Regardless of how this concern is framed, it is not terribly controversial to argue that certain things like human interaction, helping others, and peace and quiet are valuable.[106] In fact, scientific studies back up our theoretical understanding as to why they are critical.[107] While talking about how to address the bargain presented to us by ad men, Tim Wu's elegant words are equally applicable to addressing Hollywood's desire to steal large portions of our lives: "Ultimately, it is not our nation or culture but the very nature of our lives that is at stake. For how we spend the brutally limited resource of our attention will determine those lives to a degree most of us may prefer not to think about. As William James observed, we must reflect that, when we reach the end of our days, our life experience will equal what we have paid attention to, whether by choice or default. We are at risk, without quite fully realizing it, of living lives that are less our own than we imagine."[108] Even the Epicureans

[104] *Id.*, at 37–38. Either way, my theory squarely fits within a modern liberal conception.

[105] *Id.*, at 40–41. Okin believes in "the endorsement of a comprehensive perfectionist doctrine including, prominently, women's equality in every sphere of life, not simply in the public culture." *Id.* Furthermore, one can accept both my arguments for reducing overconsumption and my vision of the value of creation or simply one or the other.

[106] Pico Iyer, *The Joy of Quiet*, N.Y. TIMES (Dec. 29, 2011), www.nytimes.com/2012/01/01/opinion/sunday/the-joy-of-quiet.html?pagewanted=all. While I outline a few general propositions of a good life, I am not suggesting that such endeavors be mandated by law nor prohibited by law. Furthermore, I agree with Mill's harm principle and do not desire to ban the consumption of commercial art, no matter how possibly excessive the overconsumption. I also do not want to make it illegal for anyone to produce art. Instead, by notably reducing copyright, I desire to remove a considerable subsidy to the production of commercial art, prompting both moderate consumers and overconsumers of art to cut back on their consumption and begin to create on their own.

[107] *See generally* Rodlescia S. Sneed & Sheldon Cohen, *A Prospective Study of Volunteerism and Hypertension Risk in Older Adults*, 28 PSYCHOL. & AGING 578 (2013), and Jane E. Brody, *Social Interaction Is Critical for Mental and Physical Health*, N.Y. TIMES (June 12, 2017), www.nytimes.com/2017/06/12/well/live/having-friends-is-good-for-you.html?mcubz=3.

[108] TIM WU, THE ATTENTION MERCHANTS: THE EPIC SCRAMBLE TO GET INSIDE OUR HEADS 7 (2016).

believed in balance and valued friendship despite their mistaken reputation for sensual hedonism.[109]

DATA ON OVERCONSUMPTION

It goes without saying that the ubiquity of technology enables us to consume media at almost any moment. In the United Kingdom, individuals check their phones 221 times a day on average, a feat that is difficult to accomplish without omnipresent access.[110] Also, the time individuals spend consuming can vary tremendously from individual to individual, generation to generation – e.g., a study of Baylor University female students found that they used their smartphones on average ten hours a day, four times the national average.[111] For some individuals, ten hours of consumption a day might be appropriate. For example, if much of it is for their profession – a writer reading other novelists, a composer listening to others' music. Yet for the vast majority of individuals, such daily consumption is extraordinary.

According to Nielsen's *Total Audience Report*, the average adult in the United States spent four hours and twenty minutes per day watching live TV in the first quarter of 2017.[112] On top of this, the average individual also watched thirty-four minutes of DVR/time-shifted TV, seven minutes on a DVD or Blu-ray device, and nineteen minutes of entertainment on a multimedia device (Apple TV, Roku, Google Chromecast, smartphone, computer/laptop connected to a TV, etc.).[113] Further, the average adult spent two hours and nineteen minutes per day using apps or the web on a smartphone, thirty-three minutes using apps or the web on a tablet, and one hour using the Internet on a PC.[114] Finally, the average individual listened to AM/FM radio for one hour and fifty-one minutes a day and played on a game console for fourteen minutes.[115] This adds up to eleven hours and eighteen minutes of use per day on average.

Most, though not all, of this is straight up consumption of entertainment.[116] The remainder, one hour and sixteen minutes a day, is social media

---

[109] *See generally* LES EPICURIENS (Daniel Deattre & Jackie Pigeaud eds., 2010).
[110] Weisberg, *supra* note 22.   [111] *Id.*
[112] *The Nielsen Total Audience Report Q1 2017, supra* note 21, at 13.   [113] *Id.*   [114] *Id.*
[115] *Id.* The amount played is likely higher given that the Nielsen figures do not apparently include video games played on tablets and cellphones. Also, video game playing is quite concentrated – "[i]f you exclude people who played no games at all, the typical gamer spent over two hours per day playing games in 2016." Christopher Ingraham, *It's Not Just Young Men – Everyone's Playing a Lot More Video Games*, WASHINGTON POST, July 11, 2017.
[116] The statistics do not appear to differentiate between entertainment and news, but it is unlikely that individuals spend most of the time absorbing news. Furthermore, the statistics do not distinguish between commercial versus non-commercial entertainment consumption, yet it

consumption, which is a mix of consuming material contingent on copyright –
e.g., music videos or TV clips – and material that does not practically speaking
rely on copyright, such as reading tweets that may at times support or reference
corporate media.[117] Further, some of the activity on social media is posting
photos or updating the world about your activities, not consuming. While we
know how much time individuals spend on different social media platforms, it
is difficult to get Facebook and the rest to tell us how much of this time is spent
doing what – on copyright-contingent versus non-copyright-contingent media,
consuming versus posting. The average individual in the United States is on
Facebook for thirty-five minutes, Snapchat for twenty-five minutes, Instagram
for fifteen minutes, and Twitter for one minute.[118] Collectively this adds up to
one hour and sixteen minutes a day on average across America. Thus, while
some of this time is consuming media that is contingent on copyright, since I
have not found a way to know how much, I discard the one hour and sixteen
minutes of social media consumption and rely on the remaining ten hours and
two minutes per day of consumption that we consume.

The US Bureau of Labor Statistics states that the "average hours per day
spent" on leisure and sports is 5.13 hours."[119] There are numerous reasons for
this vast discrepancy, reasons that support Nielsen's higher figures.

First, Nielsen tracks people's actual consumption using technology, while
the Bureau asks individuals for estimates.[120] For example, Nielsen's
"Electronic Mobile Measurement (EMM) is an observational, user-centric
approach that uses passive metering technology on smartphones and tablets to
track device and application usage."[121] Conversely, the Bureau's reliance on
self-reporting can lead to incongruous figures. For example, the Bureau

appears that the vast majority of art consumption is commercial art consumption given the
nature of the artistic forms consumed. Finally, as Adorno and other theorists have noted, the
distinction between corporate and non-corporate or commercial and non-commercial artwork will never be absolute, yet often, practically speaking, is clear in practice.

[117] *YouTube Top 100 Most Subscribed Channels List – Top by Subscribers*, VidStatsX, https://vidstatsx.com/, and *YouTube Top 100 Most Viewed Video Producers*, VidStatsX, https://vidstatsx.com/youtube-top-100-most-viewed.

[118] *How Much Time Is Spent on Social Media? Infographic*, Mediakix, http://mediakix.com/2016/12/how-much-time-is-spent-on-social-media-lifetime/#gs.F=eCW2M (last visited July 30, 2017). Again, while some disagree, I do not treat YouTube as mainly social media, so I include the forty minutes a day on average that individuals spend on YouTube in the entertainment figures, not the social media figures.

[119] *Average Hours per Day Spent in Selected Activities by Sex and Day, 2016 Annual Averages*, American Time Use Survey, U.S. Bureau Lab. Stat., www.bls.gov/charts/american-time-use/activity-by-sex.htm (last visited July 30, 2017).

[120] *Frequently Asked Questions, American Time Use Survey*, U.S. Bureau Lab. Stat., www.bls.gov/tus/atusfaqs.htm#8 (last visited July 30, 2017).

[121] *The Nielsen Total Audience Report Q1 2017*, supra note 21, at 32.

numbers suggest that only 20.9 percent of the population engage in telephone calls, mail, and email on average per day.[122] Another example may illustrate the flaws in self-assessed data. Relying on volunteers' answers also creates the possible conundrum that only 94.7 percent of Americans eat or drink each day by the Bureau's analysis – that more than 10 million adults a day don't drink anything.[123] On the other hand, Nielsen's EMM monitoring is so refined that it automatically excludes "other types of activity such as making/receiving phone calls, sending SMS/MMS messages etc." from its statistics on app usage and browsing the web on a phone.[124]

Besides the apparent reality that few can remember, let alone precisely calculate, how much entertainment they consume, some individuals might assume they accomplish more in an average day than they actually do and hence do not want to admit to themselves the extent of their overconsumption, just as a large majority of individuals consider themselves to be above-average drivers. Put in starker terms, many alcoholics do not consider themselves to overconsume alcohol. Further, admitting to some consumption is socially acceptable, but some might be reticent to admit too much consumption. This parallels the phenomenon of individuals curating their Facebook profiles so that they look like they lead the most exciting and successful lives imaginable.

Second, the Bureau admits that it does not do a good job tracking Internet or computer usage: The American Time Use Survey "is not a good source of information about how people use the Internet"[125] and "does not have good data on computer use."[126]

Third, the Bureau does not track overlapping activities, with one exception – secondary childcare – while Nielsen takes such multitasking into account.[127] For example, with the American Time Use Survey, "if a respondent reports listening to music while reading the news for pleasure, the interviewer will ask her if she can separate the two activities into two different time intervals. If she cannot separate these activities, the interviewer will only collect the activity she reports as the main activity."[128] Furthermore, "Travel activities are an exception to this rule; if a respondent reports traveling along with another activity (e.g., 'I was listening to the

---

[122] *Percent of the Population Engaging in Selected Activities, Average per Day by Sex and Day, 2016 Annual Averages*, U.S. Bureau Lab. Stat., www.bls.gov/charts/american-time-use/civ-pop-by-sex-and-day.htm (last visited July 30, 2017).

[123] *Id.*   [124] *The Nielsen Total Audience Report Q1 2017, supra* note 21, at 32.

[125] *Frequently Asked Questions, American Time Use Survey, supra* note 120.   [126] *Id.*

[127] *Id.* "The only simultaneous activity ATUS collects is secondary childcare. Secondary childcare is care for children under age 13 that is done while doing something else as a primary activity." *Id.*

[128] *Id.*

radio while driving to work'), the interviewer always records traveling."[129] It is likely that relatively few individuals listen to the radio without simultaneously doing something else, such as driving. Nielsen takes into account the fact that individuals can simultaneously watch TV and cook – it would record all the time spent watching TV, even if it was while cooking, as consuming entertainment, while the Bureau might completely ignore all of such consumption.

Thus, while extraordinary in amount, the Nielsen figures demonstrate the vast scope of the problem.

OVERCONSUMPTION BASELINE

Given that overconsumption is harmful, when do we cross the line into the abyss? Determining a universal baseline of what constitutes overconsumption is challenging, yet given the vast amounts we consume, we are well beyond every measure set in scientific studies. Thus, one can ask this without, I believe, questioning whether ten hours a day on average of media consumption is too much. There is a strong and weak version of this critique. A strong version of this critique would demand that I discover a precise baseline "normal" level of consumption that holds for all individuals and for all the different harms from media overconsumption. It is a critique that appears absolutely reasonable at first glance – until one realizes not only that it is an impossible task, given how much individuals and art forms vary, but that even if it were possible, it would only be dangerous or at a minimum banal.

The same applies to social norms – e.g., to survive as a society we must have working understandings of what justice and fairness and harmful overconsumption are, yet we must also acknowledge that we cannot rationally proclaim that consuming exactly four hours and eleven minutes of entertainment a day is the boundary line of overconsumption without looking ridiculous and dangerously committing our society to an overly determinate definition. People vary. The amount of entertainment any one individual can healthily consume in a day will depend on many variables – e.g., her age, abilities, and interests. While we cannot and should not try to set overprecise baselines of "normal" consumption, this is not to say we cannot clearly agree on what is well beyond the bounds. In fact, when we significantly deviate from any imaginary norm is when we can make helpful assertions. Besides rare exceptions, who among us would not be concerned if their significant other or friend was consuming ten hours of entertainment and news on average every day?

[129] *Id.*

Furthermore, this is an average, so you likely consume much less, meaning someone else in society has to consume even more in order for us to get to an average level of consumption that is substantially more than half of our waking hours.

The weak version of this critique is appropriate and simply asks for a presentation of the relevant data and scientific studies without suggesting that an all-encompassing general "baseline" can exist. Different studies suggest various different "baselines" for when harm occurs, yet all point to a few hours of Internet surfing or TV viewing, not ten hours. We saw above that more than two hours of television a day on average is associated with greater risk of type 2 diabetes, cardiovascular disease, pulmonary embolisms, and death in general. Such relatively modest consumption routinely serves as the baseline for dangerous side effects. For example, Kristine Yaffe and colleagues conducted a twenty-five-year study that demonstrated "[h]igh television viewing and low physical activity in early adulthood were associated with worse midlife executive function and processing speed." In the study, high TV viewing was defined as three hours or more a day on average, which is well below the national average.[130]

Steve Sussman and Meghan Moran state, "Trying to establish a consistent normative threshold of addictive viewing time may be impossible. For example, among U.S. university students back in 1998, self-identified TV addicts were found to watch TV an average of about 21 hours a week, whereas those who did not so identify watched an average of approximately 13 hours per week."[131]

EXCESSIVE COPYRIGHT CAUSING OVERCONSUMPTION

Extreme copyright provides a massive financial incentive to Big Copyright to create vast amounts of profitable entertainment. Hollywood has capitalized on new technologies as well as copyright in order to control our consumption of its products. It overwhelms us with consumption choices that are available to us anywhere, at any time, and are embedded with neuroscientific and psychological hooks to keep us consuming. A dramatic reduction in copyright would cause a vast diminution in financial incentives for Hollywood to create, for if

---

[130] Kristine Yaffe et al., *Effect of Early Adult Patterns of Physical Activity and Television Viewing on Midlife Cognitive Function*, 73 JAMA PSYCHIATRY 73, 73 (2016). "This is one of the first studies to demonstrate that these risk behaviors may be critical targets for prevention of cognitive aging even before middle age." *Id.*

[131] Steve Sussman & Meghan B. Moran, *Hidden Addiction: Television*, 2 J. BEHAVIORAL ADDICTION 125, 130 (2013).

copyright did not exist, Hollywood would not exist, at least not in any recognizable manner. Hollywood could not afford to invest millions in works without the monopoly protection of excessive copyright. If Hollywood were not pumping out engineered entertainment that is purposefully aimed to addict consumers, then there would be dramatically less polished media to view, stemming the tide of overconsumption. If this entertainment were not enabled by the artificially excessive copyright regime, Hollywood would not fight tooth and nail to maintain the legal spoils and demand more.

It is worth inquiring as to what else could possibly be causing individuals to consume so much. People who are tired after a long day, depressed, isolated, or hoping to escape tension in the home may look to entertainment for relaxation, comfort, or distraction and wind up stuck in front of the screen. Yet, as Wei-Na Lee at the University of Texas reminds us, "'for now researchers don't know if one factor causes the other, simply that they're correlated.'"[132] It is likely that the causal street runs in both directions, yet it is telling that so many of us turn to television rather than reading novels or poetry, volunteering, walking the dog, or creating on our own. That we turn to screen entertainment, at a minimum, intimates that our choice is predetermined by Hollywood's conscious designs to surround us with attractive, addictive products. Otherwise, we would be as likely to turn to a thousand other activities as to consume corporate works.

Alvin Swonger and colleagues have argued that the component of a drug that most characterizes its "abuse liability is not its ability to produce tolerance . . . but rather its ability to reinforce the drug-taking behaviors."[133] Thus, "both the speed of a drug's effect and how quickly it leaves the body are often critical factors in whether or not dependence develops" because the faster the effects, the easier it is for the user to notice them.[134] Just like individuals could initially be drawn to try heroin for many reasons, from loneliness to simply wanting to relax, many quickly get hooked because of the drug's effects and suffer negative consequences as a result. The harms they experience and their inability to stop taking more drugs are not caused by the loneliness or desire to relax; they are caused by the drug.

Similarly, many who are depressed or lonely, or simply want to escape or relax, turn to screen entertainment and then get quickly hooked because

---

[132]   Anna Daugherty, *UT Study Links Binge-Watching, Depression*, ALCALDE (Feb. 16, 2015, 11:17 AM), https://alcalde.texasexes.org/2015/02/ut-study-links-binge-watching-depression/ (quoting Wei-Na Lee).

[133]   Kubey, *supra* note 44, at Sage Reference 800 (quoting ALVIN SWONGER & LARRY CONSTANTINE, DRUGS AND THERAPY: A PSYCHOTHERAPIST'S HANDBOOK OF PSYCHOTROPIC DRUGS [1976]).

[134]   *Id.*

"relative to other means available to bring about relaxation (and distraction), television is among the quickest [in its effects] and certainly among the cheapest."[135] The reason they continue to view even though it is causing them harm is because they get hooked – "viewers' vague learned sense that they will feel less relaxed if they stop viewing may be a significant factor in not turning the set off. Viewing begets more viewing."[136] They are "conditioned to associate watching TV with rest" and to associate not watching with "stress and dysphoric rumination."[137] Thus, individuals' loneliness or desire to relax may have led them to experiment with drugs or screen entertainment, but then the drug or screen entertainment takes over and compels more and more consumption. The more free time we have, the more is taken away by Hollywood entertainment. For example, retirees not only have more free time; they consume significantly more than working-aged individuals do.

While not necessarily another cause of overconsumption, our unique economic circumstances have provided the free time and disposable income to be enticed by Hollywood's products. Before our society industrialized, individuals needed to routinely create in order to survive. If you wanted shelter, food, clothing, or even soap, there was a good chance you would have to make it yourself or barter for it in exchange for something you created. Either way, you were an artist. Just as Amish communities continue to come together for barn raisings, villagers were routinely building, cooking, knitting, and gardening individually or collectively. Furthermore, if communities wanted entertainment, no one outside their circle of relations was going to provide it for them. During long winter nights, family members would play a musical instrument, tell stories, or sing, possibly not only performing existing songs but improvising new tunes on the spot.[138] Individuals and local communities were responsible for the creative destiny of their lives by necessity. It was not simply that supply of media was scarce in the marketplace; there was essentially no marketplace besides the occasional traveling dramatic troupe of actors.

This is not to romanticize all aspects of a life long gone. Individuals lacked some basic necessities that we take for granted, such as antibiotics; and foundational values, such as gender equality, were brushed aside. Yet, with the advent of the industrial age, little remained the same in terms of economic production. Few have improved on Adam Smith's understanding of the changes unleashed through the division of labor. His pin factory example

---

[135] *Id.*   [136] *See generally* Kubey & Csikszentmihalyi, *supra* note 3.   [137] *Id.*
[138] Emilie Carles & Robert Destanque, A Life of Her Own: The Transformation of a Countrywoman in Twentieth-Century France (1992).

publicized this modest-in-stature yet transformative force. In combination with increasingly powerful machines and the concentration of labor in cities, the reorganization of labor began an economic revolution that practically wiped out the ability of many individuals to create on their own. While in the past individuals killed their own animals and baked their own bread, trades like butchers, bakers, and candlestick makers thrived. Thus, some individuals were able to specialize without losing the opportunity to create on the job, but most were not so lucky. Scores were pushed into factories, never to return the same. As Marx observed, not only were they losing their economic independence; they were losing their creative spirit.

It got worse before it got better. In the struggle against gilded capitalists, the idea of carving out time to create was lost. In their brief moment of respite, some workers turned to music and art to keep their souls from collapsing under the darkness. Many an illiterate Welsh miner could recite a poem with an ale in his hand and black dust on his face. Songs were sung, tales were told, yet few created besides giving such private performances. The world we had created killed creation.

Through this long struggle with capital emerged a material golden age for blue-collar workers in the middle of the twentieth century. Many workers could afford to buy their own homes and take to the road in their own cars, yet they forgot to demand the ability to create on their own. Winning safer working conditions and a livable wage are two of the greatest battles ever fought. Yet workers celebrated by acquiring their own machines – washers and dryers – in order to save time, which they promptly spent using other machines – televisions. The *Mad Men* malaise of living without creating quickly set in.

Thus, historically we are at a distinct juncture where we have time and money, which has set up the possibility of vast demand for entertainment. Hollywood not only happily provides the supply; it manipulates demand by encapsulating numerous hook techniques into the product, making us dependent on it. While causality in some instances invariably runs to a certain extent both ways, Hollywood preys on the young, the old, and the struggling. Big Copyright openly engineers media to be addictive and continues to spend resources to make it more addictive.

Each film and TV studio and each game developer uses hook techniques because they feel that if they don't, other firms will, driving them out of business. The tools they have developed are so effective, they can quickly capture our attention and market share. For example, Cuse suggests that competition between content providers to maximize profit significantly contributes to making creative decisions that are more apt to hook consumers because "as a storyteller you can't hold back. You have to spend your bullets quicker and sooner. The event that used to be the series finale better happen by episode six now."[139] Davidow makes the same point for other forms of screen entertainment, saying app developers and Internet startups "face an interesting, if also morally questionable imperative: either they hijack neuroscience to gain market share and make large profits, or they let competitors do that and run away with the market."[140]

For the foreseeable future, the best we can do is theorize about such connections based on the facts – e.g., consumption statistics, the tactics Big Copyright openly employs against us, the fact that Hollywood spends a fortune on lobbying. We cannot, and may never be able to, demonstrate causality through regression analysis, but such mathematical tools can be in practice quite limiting and shed little clarity on significant portions of life. Further, theory informed by available data is quite revealing and is exactly what Hollywood relies on as well.

First, the data does not exist to run such regression analysis, but there is ample data demonstrating the extent of the average American's overconsumption. It was possible to study a twenty-year increase in the copyright term from an already practically infinite term of the life of the author plus fifty years after his death, as Hui and Png did, because the data exists. It is effectively impossible to do the same for a dramatic decrease in the copyright term to say two or ten years because to prove empirically what would happen in regard to Big Copyright's production and the public's consumption, we would need to get Congress to pass legislation that profoundly reduces the length of the copyright term. We could attempt to look back to 1790, a time when the copyright term was reasonable (fourteen years, with the possibility of a second fourteen-year term), yet the historical gap makes finding usable data a monumental task, plus the main forms of overconsumption today – TV, video, apps, and Internet surfing – did not exist.

Second, even when the data exists and is relatively reliable, it does not mean that a clear answer can emerge given the number of different factors that can influence an outcome, even given our efforts to control for other factors. For example, Charles Kenny, a development economist, observed that between 2001 and 2007 alone there were 14,600 papers written "referring to the analysis of cross-country [economic] growth," yet there was no consistent pattern linking "any particular policy" to growth, which "appears to be a more complex process than can be captured by universal models."[141] This is not to say

[139] Romano, *supra* note 50. [140] Davidow, *supra* note 53.
[141] Charles Kenny, Getting Better: Why Global Development Is Succeeding – and How We Can Improve the World Even More 36 (2011).

that no empirical analysis can be done within the field of copyright. Rather, such studies may not definitively show anything to be statistically significant over the long run. For example, seemingly each new empirical economic growth study appears to contradict past findings, even though we know something has to cause economic growth – it doesn't just happen on its own.

Third, there is little to no empirical evidence showing the counterfactual can be empirically proven. Why should we not criticize the fact that we have a law that regulates something that affects ten hours of the average American's day, though we have no empirical validation that the flood of Big Copyright's creations do not cause overconsumption? If the burden of proof is to fall anywhere, then it should likely fall on corporations that are provided with substantial monopoly protection in the form of excessive copyright law. Without regression analysis, we are left to examine competing theories. There is no compelling argument why extreme copyright does not cause overconsumption. On the other hand, I use Big Copyright's theory, that increasing copyright protection increases production, to strengthen, theoretically, my analysis of the contrary – that excessive copyright has turned us into overconsumers.

If something else were causing our epic overconsumption, Hollywood would put vast resources into it and abandon the protection of extreme copyright and its endless quest to expand it. If eating onions or carrots were singularly responsible for keeping us glued to our screens consuming entertainment, then rest assured Hollywood would rather spend the tens of millions a year it currently does on copyright lobbying efforts not just to increase the production of onions or carrots but to create a legal regime that effectively gives it the exclusive right to farm onions and carrots.

With many if not most complex social policies and dynamics, regression analysis breaks down because there are too many variables to attempt to take account of, because there is a lack of data, and because it is often impossible to accurately gauge causation. Thus, lawyers must acknowledge the limits of empirical analysis. This is not a fault of the law; it is simply the recognition that lawyers must find nonempirical ways to articulate conceptions of justice, equality, freedom, and the good life using reason and common sense – in essence, to practice law.

3

The Value of Creativity

Since boredom advances and boredom is the root of all evil, no wonder then, that the world goes backwards, that evil spreads. This can be traced back to the very beginning of the world. The gods were bored; therefore they created human beings ... [T]he population of the world increased and the nations were bored *en masse*. To amuse themselves, they hit upon the notion of building a tower so high that it would reach the sky. This notion is just as boring as the tower was high and is a terrible demonstration of how boredom had gained the upper hand.

—Søren Kierkegaard[1]

We have constructed a digital Tower of Babel occupied by virtual Greek sirens who lure individuals to overconsume. Extreme copyright prevents genuine communication not by force but by distraction. We are politically disengaged not by guns but by phones. We try to fill the emptiness inside with more entertainment, yet the isolation in part stems from the proposed cure. We need to defenestrate the sirens.

You are likely familiar with numerous reasons why experiencing artwork can be beneficial – e.g., how it can provide insight and introduce us to beauty – yet less emphasis has been placed on articulating why the act of creation is critical to the individual well-being of each of us.[2] Charles Horton Cooley said: "An artist cannot fail; it is a success just to be one." Cooley's idea that we win simply by doing art sounds too good or even banal. It evokes the ridiculous side of participation trophies. Yet creation can be this straightforward a good. As Kurt Vonnegut has stated, "To practice any art, no matter how well or badly, is a way to make your soul grow. So do it." Creating on one's own

---

[1] HOWARD V. HONG & EDNA H. HONG, THE ESSENTIAL KIERKEGAARD 51 (2000).
[2] *See generally* Martin Skladany, *Alienation by Copyright: Abolishing Copyright to Spur Individual Creativity*, 55 J. COPYRIGHT SOC'Y U.S.A. 361, 362 (2008).

provides a host of benefits – it enables individuals to communicate through different channels, to achieve a greater sense of autonomy, and to experience the freedom of mastering an art form or area of knowledge through extended practice.

We simply have to take up creation once more, for as Pablo Picasso remarked, "Every child is an artist. The problem is how to remain an artist once we grow up." In the process of being bent toward the needs of economic forces and cultural norms, we lose the part of our childhood that came naturally, the time we would sit down every day and scribble on the walls, bang on pots, or build spaceships or castles with used cardboard boxes. Life is challenging and full of time-consuming responsibilities. That does not mean we cannot once more take up creation. In fact, many reading this may have consciously selected their career by forgoing a higher-paid job in order to have more autonomy to read, reflect, and create.

A brief aside about how I define art is necessary.[3] I use a very broad definition of art, a definition that is more expansive than the definition contained or implied by copyright statutes. Creating art can mean building a shack, painting, sculpting, or writing comic books or novels, screenplays or short stories, poems or philosophical treaties. Art, for the purposes of this book, also includes all forms of music, from smacking a spoon against one's cheek to

---

[3] My broad definition of art is meant to demonstrate that the benefits of creating can come from a vast number of activities. Such an approach to defining art is different from a legal attempt to delineate what constitutes copyrightable material. Under copyright law, certain traditional artistic mediums like cooking and fashion are largely excluded, while other objects that involve creativity but are not traditionally thought of as art, such as spreadsheet software, are protected. Since nonartistic, copyrighted commercial goods like tax software do not consume a significant portion of individuals' free time that could be spent creating, especially in comparison to the average number of hours Americans spend consuming commercial art, this book does not argue for or against significantly weakening copyright protection for nonartistic goods. Of course, like much of life, there is a fine line between commercially useful, nonexpressive copyrighted material and purely artistic copyrighted material. Perhaps a rigorously logical line could be drawn through this spectrum, by which we could maintain traditional copyright protections for certain nonexpressive, nonartistic material and not for others. If we could not draw a perfectly principled line, the integrity of remaining copyright law could be damaged somewhat, but it would not be the first such bruise to the logical integrity of law. Also, the beneficial effects of considerably reducing the scope of copyright on art would not be threatened. On the margins people might tend to stretch the definition of what constitutes non-artistic, copyrighted material in an attempt to provide greater copyright protection to entertainment. For example, video games or movies could be incorporated into word processing software in the hopes of having the video game or movie protected under the more robust copyright protection granted to the software application. Such pushing of the borders could be limited through legislation, and any marginal examples of exploiting the boundary between artistic and nonartistic goods would have an insignificant impact on the value of extensively weakening copyright law for art.

composing symphonies. Creative or experimental hobbies such as gardening or cooking can also be a form of art. The key to my view of art is that the individual has significant discretion while engaged in the process of creation. Thus, a builder who has a large amount of discretion in laying tiles on a kitchen floor and a lawyer writing an amicus brief both have the potential to create art.

A purposeful, aesthetic component is also necessary.[4] I have the discretion to throw soap bubbles up against the shower wall either to dislodge a piece of dirt or in a conscious attempt to create artistic, yet ephemeral, soap bubble patterns. Putting aside whether beauty is in the eye of the beholder, the ultimate judge of whether a physical manifestation is an act of creation is solely in the hands of the one performing the act. This is because, as long as one believes oneself to be creating, one is deriving fulfillment from this belief. If one believes oneself not to be creating, one might enjoy some value from the act but not the fulfillment that comes from the conscious reordering of the world.

Even given this broad definition of art, most jobs do not provide the necessary freedom to allow workers to create. Yet those who do not have the opportunity to create on the job can hopefully find inspiration and a few spare moments away from the pressing demands of life to create. Finally, there is no tension in using such a broad definition of art because I believe the creation of copyright-protected commercial art, which is more restrictively defined, should be reduced to make way for more individuals within society to create art, more broadly defined.

THE VALUE OF CREATING

The act of creating cannot directly solve nuclear standoffs or get a stray kitten out of a tree, but it can do more good than is commonly assumed. Regardless of how imaginative or banal, beautiful or pedestrian the outcome is, as Kurt Vonnegut suggests, the artist benefits. Romantic aid to the soul or pragmatic gains to one's cholesterol are available to all.

Historically, some have considered having the opportunity to create a privilege that generations would struggle to provide to their distant offspring. As John Adams mentioned in 1780: "I must study Politicks and War that my sons may have liberty to study Mathematicks and Philosophy. My sons ought to study Mathematicks and Philosophy, Geography, natural History, Naval Architecture, navigation, Commerce and Agriculture, in order to give their

---

[4] For an alternative vision, *see generally* NICK ZANGWILL, AESTHETIC CREATION (2007).

Children a right to study Painting, Poetry, Musick, Architecture, Statuary, Tapestry, and Porcelaine."[5]

Creating helps us actively engage with our humanity, with the world, with life. Alienation is often considered one of the fundamental aspects of modernity.[6] While there are many possible roots of alienation, I will argue that one of the aspects of a life of non-alienation involves an individual creating art, broadly defined, on his or her own.[7] Our personalities will succumb to ossification if we do not experiment and revel in new experiences. This is the metaphysical position of Roberto Mangabeira Unger,[8] who states:

> As we pass through childhood each of us, a storehouse of alternative ways of becoming a person, imagines many different courses of action and of life he may later take. However, we cannot be everything in the world. We must choose a path, and reject other paths. This rejection, indispensable to our self-development, is also a mutilation. In choosing, as we must, we cast aside many aspects of our humanity. If, however, we cast them aside completely, we become less than fully human. We must continue somehow to feel the movements of the limbs we cut off. To learn how to feel them is the first major work of the imagination.[9]

In the preceding passage, Unger is partially pleading that we not specialize completely. Regardless of whether we are nurses or composers, Unger wants us to be open to new experiences, which speaks primarily not to consuming new types of movies but to doing new things, creating, and interacting meaning-fully with others. He articulates a metaphysical vision in which we are infinite spirits bound by finite physical and social realities. We are born into specific classes, countries, and families. While we cannot rebel against the physical limits of our bodies, he beseeches us to fight for our own sake against the "alliance between chance and society."[10] Experiencing art contributes to this

---

[5] John Adams, Letter to Abigail Adams, May 12, 1780, *in* Fred R. Shapiro, The Yale Book of Quotations (2006).

[6] I use the terms "alienation" and "ossification" interchangeably throughout this chapter. Also, my use of the term "alienation" does not transform my thesis that individuals need to stop overconsuming commercial art and to create art on their own into a piece of Marxist theory.

[7] I claim that this active use of our capacity to create is a necessary condition to being fulfilled. I do not claim that it is or is not a sufficient condition. Further, I leave open the possibility that there are many paths and activities that can bring about fulfillment.

[8] For a good review of some of the ideas mentioned in this section and their philosophical underpinnings, see James Boyle, *Modernist Social Theory: Roberto Unger's Passion*, 98 Harv. L. Rev. 1066 (1985) (book review).

[9] Letter from Roberto Mangabeira Unger, Law Professor, Harvard Law School, to a class of school children passing from sixth to seventh grade (May 6, 2002), www.law.harvard.edu/fac ulty/unger/english/docs/passion2.doc.

[10] *Id.*

struggle only insofar as it helps individuals become aware of the need to struggle or helps them develop the necessary tools for such a fight.

Unger recognizes that "[a]s society and culture must take a certain hardened form, so must the personality lean on habit."[11] He goes on to state, "This habitual form of the person – of his dispositions toward others as well as toward the prospects of his own existence – is his character. We have been taught that his character becomes his fate, which is simply this hardened self."[12] All of us face a constant struggle to prevent the ossification of our selves. Unger maintains that "[t]he point is not to make war against habit or to make war against one self."[13] The only way to resist ossification is "to fashion a style of existence, a mode of the self, in which we lower our defenses enough to strengthen our readiness for the new, our attachment to life, and our love of the world."[14] One aspect of accomplishing this is striving for "work that both expresses us and changes us and does both by mastering and transforming some aspect of the structure of arrangements and beliefs within which we move. By changing the world, we relieve it of some of its dumb facticity and its burdensome alienness; we set our imprint upon it."[15] Unger believes through such work we "make ourselves more fully into the originals that we all know ourselves to be and develop the conditions on which we can give ourselves, as individuals, more fully to one another."[16] Thus, Unger ties the importance of experiencing the new, one central component of which is creating, to our "obligations" to those we love.

Within Unger's conception of work, "the goals of self-fulfillment and service to society combine with the notion that such service requires you to press against things and conceptions as they are."[17] In his view, this is only accomplished when individuals pursue artistic, philosophical, or scientific endeavors or when they help those in need.[18] For example, Karim Lakhani and Robert Wolf state: "Academic theorizing on individual motivations for participating in F/OSS [Free/Open Source software] projects has posited that external

---

[11] *Id.*

[12] Roberto Mangabeira Unger, The Self Awakened: Pragmatism Unbound 130 (2007).

[13] *Id.*   [14] *Id.*

[15] Roberto Mangabeira Unger, The Present of Architecture and the Future of Democracy 7 (letter to William Saunders) (Apr. 3, 1995), www.law.harvard.edu/faculty/unger/english/pdfs/architecture2.pdf.

[16] *Id.*

[17] Roberto Mangabeira Unger, Politics: The Central Texts, Theory against Fate 415 (1997).

[18] *Id.* at 416.

motivational factors in the form of extrinsic benefits (e.g., better jobs, career advancement) are the main drivers of effort."[19] They find, "in contrast, that enjoyment-based intrinsic motivation, namely how creative a person feels when working on the project, is the strongest and most pervasive driver."[20] Creation meets all of the requirements for the state of flow as elaborated by Mihaly Csikszentmihalyi.[21]

Ideally, all of us could have such vocations. But for those of us who cannot, all is not lost; we can resist ennui through creating on our own, after work. While time constraints make it difficult for many to spend significant amounts of time creating, what is critical is that we recognize the importance of creating and strive to do it whenever we get a break from the practical struggles of surviving.

Unger wants us to be gripped by transformative work. At the same time, he wants us to not be overly devoted to such work because he believes in experimenting with new experiences outside work. Creating art is central to such experimentation because, unless one writes the same novel over and over, the process of creation is experimentation.

As cited at the beginning of the chapter, Kierkegaard argues that boredom is the root of evil and intimates that it might be relieved through creating. Friedrich Nietzsche struggles with a similar concern: "We must get beyond this skepticism, we must *forget* it! How much must we forget in this world! . . . Not in *knowledge*, in *creating* lies our salvation."[22] Leslie Paul Thiele argues that for Nietzsche art is needed to counteract skepticism: "Socrates' denial of art, of its merit and necessity, was interpreted by Nietzsche as an attempt to flee the terrible truths of existence. Anyone who was brave enough to confront these truths knew the need of art for recuperation. He who denied the worth of art was denying himself the therapy required by all true 'warriors of

[19]   Karim R. Lakhani & Robert G. Wolf, *Why Hackers Do What They Do: Understanding Motivation and Effort, in* PERSPECTIVES ON FREE AND OPEN SOURCE SOFTWARE, Abstract (J. Feller, B. Fitzgerald, S. Hissam, & K. R. Lakhani eds., 2005), http://freesoftware .mit.edu/papers/lakhaniwolf.pdf.

[20]   *Id.*

[21]   MIHALY CSIKSZENTMIHALYI, FLOW: THE PSYCHOLOGY OF OPTIMAL EXPERIENCE (1990).

[22]   LESLIE PAUL THIELE, FRIEDRICH NIETZSCHE AND THE POLITICS OF THE SOUL: A STUDY OF HEROIC INDIVIDUALISM 122 (1990) (citing Friedrich Nietzsche, Gesammelte Werke 6:35). Nietzsche also argues: "Good and evil and pleasure and pain and I and thou – coloured smoke they seemed to me before creative eyes. To look away from himself was what the creator wanted – so he created the world." FRIEDRICH NIETZSCHE, THUS SPOKE ZARATHUSTRA: A BOOK FOR EVERYONE AND NOBODY 27 (Graham Parkes trans., Oxford 2008) (1885). One interpretation of this passage is that creation is valuable in going beyond constant self-examination, doubt, or boredom.

knowledge'.... In such times art has an indispensable role to play in making life bearable."[23]

John-Paul Sartre echoes this sentiment: "One of the chief motives of artistic creation is certainly the need of feeling that we are essential in relationship to the world. If I fix on canvas or in writing a certain aspect of the fields or the sea or a look on someone's face which I have disclosed, I am conscious of having produced them by condensing relationship, by introducing order where there was none, by imposing the unity of mind on the diversity of things. That is, I feel myself essential in relation to my creation."[24] Albert Camus further suggests that creation is "staggering evidence of man's sole dignity: the dogged revolt against his condition, perseverance in an effort considered sterile."[25]

Reflecting on the artistic process, Monroe C. Beardsley states: "I do not forget that man is the maker – of nearly all the great works we have, or are likely to have, but the finest qualities of a work of art cannot be imposed on it directly and by fiat; the artist can, after all, only manipulate the elements of the medium so that they will make the quality emerge."[26] In his view, for example, a musician creates a joyful melody by discovering in nature a "sequence of notes that will have that quality."[27] While such a conception is debatable, Beardsley's argument from this assumption is hopeful. He suggests that the miracle an artist "makes is a miracle that celebrates the creative potentialities inherent in nature itself."[28] If an artist continues to reveal "the marvelous richness of nature's potentialities, he also presents us with a model of man's hope for control over nature, and over himself."[29]

Beardsley believes: "It is in our intelligent use of what we are given to work with, both in the laws of the universe and in the psychological propensities of human beings, that we show our mastery and our worthiness to inhabit the earth. In this broad sense, we are all elected, or perhaps condemned, to be artists."[30] Finally, in his view, "what keeps us going in the roughest times is the reminder that not all the forms and qualities and meanings that are to emerge in the fullness of time have already appeared under the sun – that we do not know the limits of what the universe can provide or of what can be accomplished with its materials."[31]

---

[23] THIELE, *supra* note 22.
[24] JOHN-PAUL SARTRE, WHAT IS LITERATURE? 39 (Bernard Frechtman trans. 1949). *See also* ALBERT CAMUS, THE REBEL, AN ESSAY ON MAN IN REVOLT (trans. Anthony Bowen, 1992).
[25] ALBERT CAMUS, THE MYTH OF SISYPHUS: AND OTHER ESSAYS 115 (2012).
[26] MONROE C. BEARDSLEY, THE AESTHETIC POINT OF VIEW: SELECTED ESSAYS 261 (Michael J. Wreen & Donald M. Callen eds., 1982).
[27] *Id.* [28] *Id.* [29] *Id.* at 261–62. [30] *Id.* at 262. [31] *Id.*

Hannah Arendt's theory of freedom in the political realm has much to offer to my criticism of copyright law in regard to the harm of overconsumption inhibiting freedom and creation. She does not desire life to be solely about labor (necessity) and consumption (conformity). Such a life is not a life of freedom, which can only be brought about through equality of interaction with others in the political realm. Her vision of such equality is one not of superficiality but of political equality akin to that of male citizens in ancient Greece. Arendt refers to the freedom found in equality of interaction in the political sphere as allowing for creative action, an aspect critical to the human condition.[32] Thus, just as a conversation dominated by one person is likely unsatisfying and may reveal imbalances in power, having an individual only consume others' creations, while never reciprocating, can be similarly unsettling and potentially instructive about power dynamics.[33]

Another advantage to stressing the value of maximizing the number of individuals creating is that this is an antidote to an Internet filling with trash, hate, gossip, pettiness, and material that can most generously be described as a mere distraction – empty calories for the soul. There are few other strategies for saving the idea of the Internet, which is at heart about sharing information and communicating. The information on the Internet has turned into clickbait; the communication has turned into rant porn. Both are generated by a relatively small subset of the population, from celebrity-chasing tabloids to fly-by-night content factories, from angry, lonely outcasts in basements to scared, lonely adolescents wanting to be part of a group to escape the alternative of being ridiculed by it.

Potential solutions, from getting rid of anonymity to building monitored walled gardens, leave unplugged holes the size of the Internet. Current solutions are bound to be unsatisfying in whole or in part because they take the default norm to be consumption by all with some creating rather than creation by all. If we want to sideline vacuous content with meaningful interaction, we need to flip the cultural norm so that the expectation is creation – heartfelt, playfully humorous, or profound communication. Encourage everyone to imagine and there is a greater chance they will take ownership of their lives, realizing how consumption on its own is stunting but becomes more valuable mixed with creation. Motivate others to memorialize their thoughts, and the Internet will be less of a hollow swamp of trolls and

---

[32]   *See generally* HANNAH ARENDT, THE HUMAN CONDITION (1958).

[33]   For a more contemporary, related exposition of Arendt on this point, see Kerry Freedman, *Rethinking Creativity: A Definition to Support Contemporary Practice*, 63 ART EDUC. 8 (2010). "I would argue that creativity is an aim of democratic curriculum, as is, for example, the concept of freedom." *Id.* at 10.

bots. Dramatically reducing copyright will open up people's schedules to imagine their own dreams instead of living in others' nightmares, but it is not enough. We need to create and implement numerous strategies to get people to take the leap into their own heads and hearts and share what they discover.

Physical health and mental health flow from creating. For example, creating visual works of art is positively related to "psychological resilience" at a neural level.[34] Arts and crafts activities "in midlife and late-life" have been correlated with reduced rates of mild cognitive impairment.[35] Speaking about playing a musical instrument, Nina Kraus states: "There really is now so much evidence showing that musical experience has a pervasive [positive] effect on how the nervous system gets molded and shaped throughout our lifetimes."[36] For example, Rachel Ehrenberg mentions that "[i]n the long run, musical training appears to improve a suite of verbal and nonverbal skills."[37] Creating art is also tied to helping the sick cope.[38]

POSSIBLE CONCERNS

I would like to address a few potential concerns before moving on to how dramatically reducing copyright would transform our current abyss.

Someone could argue that even if copyright reform helps more individuals gain substantially more free time, the best way to fill it would be not creating but rather taking a vacation, spending more time with friends or family, etc. This position is a tough sell; I'm glad I don't have to argue it. There are few activities that I would claim are not worthy endeavors in the classical liberal view. That said, I am willing to admit that kicking puppies, making children cry, and consuming ten hours of media a day are not part of a life well lived. I would never argue that creation is more important than other important aspects of life. However, there are a few things that I believe need to be

---

[34] Anne Bolwerk et al., *How Art Changes Your Brain: Differential Effects of Visual Art Production and Cognitive Art Evaluation on Functional Brain Connectivity*, 9 PLOS ONE (2014), https://doi.org/10.1371/journal.pone.0101035. *See also* Girija Kaimal, Kendra Ray, & Juan Muniz, *Reduction of Cortisol Levels and Participants' Responses Following Art Making*, 33 ART THERAPY 74 (2016).

[35] *See generally* Rosebud O. Roberts et al., *Risk and Protective Factors for Cognitive Impairment in Persons Aged 85 Years and Older*, 84 NEUROLOGY 1854 (2015).

[36] Rachel Ehrenberg, *Music of the Hemispheres: Playing Instruments Gives Brains a Boost*, 178 SCI. NEWS 30, 30 (2010).

[37] *Id.*

[38] Cathy Malchiodi, *Creativity as a Wellness Practice*, PSYCHOL. TODAY (Dec. 31, 2015), www.psychologytoday.com/blog/arts-and-health/201512/creativity-wellness-practice.

emphasized as part of a life well lived – in this context, creation – because I am writing about a body of law that regulates artistic endeavors.

One could argue that there is no way of knowing whether spending time creating is any better than consuming. I am not arguing that both are not important nor am I arguing that a minute of creation is better than a minute of consumption. I am simply arguing that ten hours of consumption and no creation on a daily basis for the average individual is less valuable than fewer hours of consumption daily and a little creation.

A skeptic could agree that creating is a valuable act yet still be concerned over allegedly formulating copyright law to take into account that the public would benefit from creating more because such a position could be deemed paternalistic. In fact, the law is already doing what the skeptic doesn't want it to do – copyright incentivizes creation. I am simply arguing that we need to reform it to benefit individuals more and corporations less.

An additional critique could suggest Americans are creating enough already. Sadly, the data does not point in this direction. Tens of millions of individuals create sporadically, yet government data clearly shows that there are many more millions of individuals who don't. Further, our national consumption statistics are reported on the daily level, while our creation statistics are stated on an annual basis – the switch from daily to yearly units of analysis is quite telling.

Moreover, I make a philosophical argument that creating is a central component of the good life for everyone. Those who upload original content to YouTube or sell their creations on Etsy have already discovered this, but it is a non sequitur to suggest that the existence of some amateur creators proves that there is no need to encourage creation by those who simply consume. I do not claim that dramatically reducing copyright will make everyone creators or that it would even be the most powerful policy change to get more individuals to create. I simply suggest that if we regulate artistic creativity, which we do through copyright, we must not ignore how the regulation is currently causing massive overconsumption and that reducing copyright protection will cause some individuals, possibly only 5 percent of the public, to create with some of the free time it opens up in their lives. Such a modest percentage should be cheered given that it would translate into more meaning for millions of individuals.

Another possible critique is that even in places with little copyright enforcement, such as Nigeria, allegedly there are still copious amounts of creation. While it is true that Nollywood creates ten times as many films as Hollywood every year, there is a reason very few individuals in America watch Nollywood creations. Respectfully, their production value is not at the level of the polished professionalism of Hollywood. While Americans might experiment by watching a few Nollywood films, it is difficult to believe that Americans would watch hours a day, every day of Nollywood creations. In essence, the reach of Nollywood is small: The average production cost is roughly $125,000 relative to the tens of millions spent on one Hollywood film or TV episode. Further, it takes at least 500 Nollywood films to generate the same revenue as one Hollywood film, which speaks volumes about the actual consumption of Nollywood films despite the fact that they fill a cultural niche in West Africa.[39]

Others might suggest that fan communities are proof that abundant creation occurs where copyright cannot be ruthlessly enforced. In terms of fan communities and questioning whether "we don't create as much or enough," I do not dispute that some individuals use Big Copyright content to create on their own through fan communities, which I celebrate. Yet this is a niche phenomenon occupied by a small fraction of the American public. Hollywood has calculated that it is better for their profit margin to allow the noncommercial derivative works because they generate massive sales of merchandise – e.g., *Star Wars* light sabers, costumes, figurines, and lunchboxes. Once fan communities step over into commercial adaptations, they are almost always swiftly and ruthlessly put down.

A skeptic could retort: How do we know that consumers creating on their own would not simply create fan fiction based on Hollywood's wares, which we already have too much of? First, if this result occurs, it would be an unequivocal improvement because more individuals would be creating. Stemming the flood of corporate art is a means to an end – more free time and more creating – not an end in itself. Second, I do not want to dictate what others should create or how they should create it. Finally, one only has to look at Renaissance paintings to realize that all creation is derivative to different degrees. This is something to be celebrated and appreciated – as it is by many other minimalist copyright scholars who use this as the basis of their critique of copyright.[40]

THE EFFECTS OF DECREASING COPYRIGHT ON ARTISTIC PRODUCTION

Samuel Johnson famously averred, "No man but a blockhead ever wrote, except for money."[41] Yet he did not always take his own advice. While there

---

[39] Of course, this result is partially because Nigerians have a lower per capita income also. For a thoughtful, novel approach to applying IP to regulating traditional culture that flips the previous conception, see Sean A. Pager, *Folklore 2.0: Preservation through Innovation*, 2012 UTAH L. REV. 1835 (2012).

[40] I do not address whether creating, as opposed to consuming, in different art forms has different effects.

[41] JAMES BOSWELL, THE LIFE OF SAMUEL JOHNSON (1791).

are numerous factors that may go into an individual's decision to create, corporations generally care about the money. Consequently, corporations' singular focus is convenient for an analysis of whether a dramatic decrease in copyright protection would lead to a significant drop in production of new works by Big Copyright because we do not have to consider the host of reasons why individuals might create, which are largely irrelevant to multinationals. For the purpose of the argument, it is also fortuitous that most of the art individuals overconsume is corporate, not the work of amateurs or sole professionals. This is largely a result of the fact that the forms of art we overconsume are the ones dominated by Hollywood – TV, film, video games – art forms that allow Hollywood to employ a plethora of hook techniques. Thus, I will focus on Big Copyright's focus on the money.

Robert Merges states, "I have become convinced that with our current tools we will never identify the 'optimal number' of patented, copyrighted, and trademarked works ... I simply cannot justify our current IP system on the basis of verifiable data."[42] William Patry, senior copyright counsel at Google, expresses a similar sentiment: "[I]n my 27 years of practicing copyright law, I have never seen a study presented to Congress that even makes a stab at demonstrating that if the proposed legislation is passed, X number of works that would not have been created will be."[43]

Merges and Patry are not claiming that copyright does not provide a financial incentive to create. They are articulating that the relationship between a set amount of copyright protection and the number of works it will inspire to be created is imprecise at best. Merges asks simply whether our current copyright protection is correct given the tension at the heart of copyright law between attempting to provide incentives to artists to create and wanting to disseminate their artwork as widely as possible. These two goals are diametrically opposed in that the monopoly protection copyright grants would in the abstract reduce the circulation of artwork given that monopolists tend to capture some of the social utility of a good by charging higher prices. Merges is not contemplating that other equally important considerations should count. I am attempting to advance this uncertain state of affairs by suggesting we look to how much entertainment the average person in America consumes. If we do, it proffers a new response to the debate. By expanding the universe of relevant considerations, I am attempting to move the ball forward – not precisely, of course, because empirical analysis is out of our reach. I am attempting to create a new theoretical architecture that informs the question –

---

[42]   ROBERT P. MERGES, JUSTIFYING INTELLECTUAL PROPERTY 3 (2011).
[43]   WILLIAM PATRY, MORAL PANICS AND THE COPYRIGHT WARS 62 (2009).

my argument on overconsumption sheds relevant light on how copyright laws are extreme, using existing data and theory to advance our understanding. It is a theoretical counter-narrative to an assumption, without any data supporting it, we have had for centuries – that it is always beneficial to encourage more creation, and more dissemination, regardless of who is creating, what actually gets widely disseminated, and how much overconsumption it causes.

Reducing the strength of copyright could go a long way toward alleviating the numerous concerns already elucidated – e.g., strengthening and clarifying fair use doctrine could substantially expand the scope of creative and political freedom by opening up artists' access to the language and symbols of our culture. But reductions in copyright protection, unless robust, would be less effective in reducing the amount of commercial art produced and hence would not provide enough breathing space to enable some individuals to begin creating on their own. For example, reducing copyright terms for corporate authors to forty years from ninety-five years might not appreciably decrease the number of Hollywood movies produced.[44] Thus, copyright terms must be dramatically reduced to well below the twenty years of protection provided by patents, well below the fourteen-year first term offered by the first Copyright Act of 1790, possibly to the point of a few months or a handful of years.

Given space constraints and the fact that the reform with the most potential impact on reducing Hollywood's output is addressing copyright's length, I will limit the discussion that follows to the effects of reducing copyright terms on the production and consumption of artworks. I will not discuss how scaling back copyright in other ways could affect production and consumption, though doubtless employing a range of tactics – besides reductions in copyright length – would reduce the amount of corporate or commercial art being produced, which would reduce the number of hours individuals spend consuming commercial art.[45] For example, we could simply restrict which art forms are eligible for copyright protection. Under the 1790 Act, only books, charts, and maps received such

[44] Copyright terms for works of hire are ninety-five years from publication or 120 years from creation. Sonny Bono Copyright Term Extension Act, 17 U.S.C. § 302(c) (2000).
[45] Ultimately, significant reductions across all aspects of copyright protection might not be as effective as contemplating the complete elimination of copyright for artistic creations, which would most dramatically reduce commercial art consumption and increase the public's creation of art. By desiring to potentially abolish all of copyright law, I include laws like the Digital Millennium Copyright Act. Digital Millennium Copyright Act of 1998, 17 U.S.C. §§ 1201–1205 (2000). See Pamela Samuelson, *Intellectual Property and the Digital Economy: Why the Anti-Circumvention Regulations Need to Be Revised*, 14 BERKELEY TECH. L.J. 519 (1999).

a privilege. While not having to scale back all the way to the 1790 Act's restrictiveness, we could conceivably deny copyright protection to the art forms that lead to the most overconsumption – the art forms that are corporate dominated and squeeze out individual creators. Yet such exclusion of entire fields from copyright protection is less realistic than dramatically reducing copyright terms for all works, which itself is a monumental task.

Supply Side Effects: Would Less Corporate Art Be Created?

It is hypothetically possible that if we weaken copyright to eliminate a dramatic portion of the economic incentive to create art commercially, all entertainment companies would go on creating art in the same amounts just out of love. In this scenario, for-profit firms would simply continue accumulating multibillion-dollar expenses with drastically less money coming in the door. This may sound like pie in the sky, and it is for the most part, yet there is a possibility that one of the richest persons on the globe would simply subsidize an entertainment company's losses because she thinks the art produced is so compelling that it needs to be seen by the world.

However, it is clear that at least some of the multinationals that comprise Big Copyright, if not all, are keenly motivated by the prospect of profits. Thus, the altered financial landscape of a world with dramatically less copyright protection would most likely cause much of for-profit Hollywood that produces most of what we overconsume – television shows, movies, video games, music – to significantly scale down its operations. Given that the heart of copyright is to incentivize the creation of works, if a sizable decrease in the production of new commercial art did not follow an extensive reduction in copyright, there would be little utility in retaining copyright law in the first place.

One cannot argue that a significant decrease in copyright protection would not decrease Hollywood's production without simultaneously negating the entire point of copyright. If significant decreases in copyright protection do not matter, then why would any protection matter? While copyright minimalists and maximalists do not agree on much, we widely concur with the view that copyright does matter and does increase the amount that Big Copyright creates. This is not to say that if copyright were abolished, no corporate works would be created or that no other economic or noneconomic considerations touch on how much Hollywood makes; it is simply to make explicit that unless one believes copyright is completely irrelevant and should be eliminated, the argument that a dramatic decrease in copyright would not bring about significant reductions in corporate works is mistaken.[46]

For a few moments, let's assume copyright is abolished. The fall in the amount of corporate art created would vary markedly among different artistic mediums, with art forms dominated by corporations hit much harder than art fields that Big Copyright has less of a grip over.[47] The variation would hinge on the structure of the industries, which vary in how they fund, distribute, and seek to generate revenues from works.

The Hollywood film industry would be ravaged. Even with the possibility of alternative revenue sources such as product placement, using contractual licenses instead of relying on copyright, and attempting to invent new revenue models, film studios would likely no longer be able to afford much at all, let alone multimillion-dollar pay packages and lavish accoutrements.[48] This is because there would be no effective legal restriction on simply copying Hollywood's creations. Plus, we have the technology to quickly and cheaply do so. This threat is nothing new; in fact, Hollywood has sounded alarm bells on a version of this premise for decades, alleging that without more

---

[46] A half century ago, Justice Breyer argued that some inducements, e.g., lead time to market, to create corporate art do not rely on copyright. Yet, given our digital era, lead time, in particular, would likely no longer be such a non-copyright inducement to create given the speed, ease, and little cost of copying in a copyrightless world. See Stephen Breyer, *The Uneasy Case for Copyright: A Study of Copyright in Books, Photocopies, and Computer Programs*, 84 HARV. L. REV. 281 (1970). But see Barry W. Tyerman, *The Economic Rationale for Copyright Protection for Published Books: A Reply to Professor Breyer*, 18 UCLA L. REV. 1100 (1971).

[47] The radical reduction in corporate works would, of course, affect how many artists Hollywood employs. Thus, after copyright is greatly weakened, some of the hundreds of individuals who are needed to make one Hollywood blockbuster might stop creating art altogether, while others would switch to creating independent films or art in another medium – e.g., trying their hand at poetry. A few newly unemployed corporate artists could attempt to continue making corporate entertainment on their own, not out of financial motivation but because of a love of creating in a specific field or hopes of fame, yet they could not employ an army of artists with a seemingly unlimited budget to help realize their artistic vision, which makes the product less likely to be overconsumed. There are two important implications that follow. First, most if not all of the hundreds of individuals who previously worked on creating one Hollywood film would no longer be creating corporate art because corporate art is expensive to create. Second, reducing copyright would rob them of their jobs but not the opportunity to gain fulfillment through creating in another artistic medium.

[48] Attempting to rely solely on contracts instead of copyright would likely be ineffectual because, in the absence of copyright protection, it would be too difficult to prove which consumer broke such an agreement out of the multitude of consumers. Without copyright, it would not be illicit to post material as long as one did not sign a contract with Big Copyright not to do so; thus, Big Copyright could not necessarily go after the person who released the content freely on the Internet.

protection – never mind standing pat or eliminating all of copyright –
Hollywood could not survive given the risk of illicit copying.

Besides film, TV would also suffer significantly. Revenue to TV producers
from DVD sales and iTunes sales would evaporate. Subscriptions to network
TV websites providing access to shows and licensing revenue from streaming
services such as Netflix might disappear. Syndication revenues generated from
one TV channel selling rebroadcast rights to another TV channel would likely
vanish. Furthermore, copycat TV stations or apps could cannibalize the
advertising revenue of the largest stations by immediately replaying another
station's original broadcast. Of course, as with film, product placement within
TV shows could increase, but it is unclear how much room there is for more
product placement or how valuable such advertising would be if a whole slew
of brands are competing for visibility in a scene.

In a world without copyright, other art forms would also be devastated by the
proliferation of cheap or readily obtainable free copies. For example, many
commercially produced video games would also take a substantial hit from the
proliferation of copying.[49] Of course, the extent of the financial slump would
depend on the revenue model of different games, with free online games that
rely on "energy system" hooks and add-ons potentially doing better than games
that sell copies to consumers; yet even such initially free games could have
their economic model wiped out if others copy the games, eliminate the need
to pay to continue playing or to buy added lives or weapons, and then
redistribute the games. In commercial publishing, million-dollar book
advances and possibly royalties would be a thing of the past. Music consumers
might be willing to pay for streaming services such as Spotify for the conve-
nience, but without copyright similar free services could emerge to cannibalize the business.

While most art forms that have been dominated by Hollywood would suffer,
fine artists' or visual artists' economic incentives and artistic production would
be largely unaffected.[50] Thus, the art forms that are not responsible for our
present overconsumption, which are presently niche fields that do not generally rely on copyright for their success, would continue essentially
unscathed. Only a small percentage of painters, sculptors, and classical

---

[49]   Even relying on revenue from the growing practice of inserting advertisements into video
games, video game makers would still see their revenues devastated because an overwhelming
percentage of their revenue comes from selling copies of their video games. Advertisers spent
"$76 million on in-game advertising last year." *Got Game*, ECONOMIST (June 7, 2007), www
.economist.com/node/9304254.

[50]   See Daniel J. Gifford, *Innovation and Creativity in the Fine Arts: The Relevance and
Irrelevance of Copyright*, 18 CARDOZO ARTS & ENT. L.J. 569 (2000).

composers would lose significant royalty payments because most fine artists have very little to lose to begin with in this regard. Amy Adler forcefully states that "there is no resale value for most works of art, let alone for copies of it."[51] Further, those at the absolute pinnacle of the visual art market might lose thousands or millions, yet such losses are spare change to them. For example, Andy Warhol is a rare artist whose works have a market for copies.[52] In fact, since sales of his original pieces have made him the highest selling artist in the world recently, it is not surprising that Warhol also "has the most active market for copies of any contemporary artist."[53] His foundation licenses his works for roughly $4 million a year, yet his original works sell for $80 to $105 million a piece.[54] Partially because most fine artists do not make anything from copyright, Adler has argued that "copyright law does not and cannot incentivize the creation of visual art.'"[55] Those who hold the copyright to recordings of classical music compositions would probably be the most affected of fine artists, yet, again, the revenue from such recordings is modest, given that sales of classical music amount to less than 3 percent of all music sales.[56]

In a new creative landscape with no copyright, symphonies would still commission composers to write new pieces; art foundations would continue to distribute grants to artists; universities would continue to employ visual art, drama, music, and writing professors and to support academic publishing across all disciplines; and museums would continue to buy new artwork.[57] Patrons would continue to cultivate young and distinguished artists by providing them with financial support. Regional libraries would improve significantly.

In a world of dramatically reduced copyright as opposed to no copyright at all, the preceding effects would be mitigated to varying degrees – the creation of new works would be reduced and would vary between art forms, primarily between corporate works and noncorporate works. While ex ante we cannot

---

[51] Amy Adler, Why Art Does Not Need Copyright 16, (Oct. 4, 2017) (draft paper on file with author).

[52] *Id.* at 18. [53] *Id.* [54] *Id.* at 19. [55] *Id.* at 48.

[56] Mark Vanhoenacker, *Requiem: Classical Music in America Is Dead*, SLATE (Jan. 21, 2014, 11:52 PM), www.slate.com/articles/arts/culturebox/2014/01/classical_music_sales_decline_is_classi cal_on_death_s_door.html.

[57] Academic authors' incentives to write academic research books and articles would not be diminished given that academics, for the most part, produce such work to advance their academic careers, not to line their pocketbooks, and because they enjoy the scholarly enterprise. Even though academic authors' incentives to publish would not decrease or would decrease only slightly, academic publishers might take a large financial hit, potentially forcing academia to rely more heavily on new publishing models such as open access works distributed online.

definitely know how large a reduction in the copyright term is necessary to
significantly scale back the production of new Hollywood entertainment, we
need to take a knife to copyright and see what happens. If the anticipated level
of reduction does not materialize, we should take the knife out again. If we
continued to reduce the copyright term, at some point before we hit zero,
Hollywood would stop producing new works. Again, if Hollywood continued
to create as many works after the elimination of copyright as before, the entire
premise in the United States for the law – to provide a financial incentive to
stimulate the creation of new works – would be negated.

The shorter the copyright term, the more consumers would be willing to
wait to see a film or play a video game – negatively affecting Hollywood's
revenue. For example, just because *Wonder Woman* can rake in $103 million
in its opening weekend does not mean that if the copyright term were only two
days, the same bounty would be had.[58] An appreciable number of people
would simply wait out the two-day copyright term in order to see it for free
later. This wait-to-pay-less tactic would be nothing new; it already exists as
a sizable additional revenue stream – today people forgo seeing a film in
theaters and instead wait for the movie to be released on DVD or on demand
or hold off even further until it appears on a streaming service.[59]

If copyright's term is only a year or two, some forms of revenue that are
contingent on copyright would continue to operate to some degree, yet some
might collapse. For example, even though 1.32 billion movie tickets were sold
in the United States and Canada in 2016, film theaters are not currently
thriving even with extreme copyright because consumption of corporate
entertainment has shifted to different distribution formats.[60] Thus, with
a radically reduced copyright term, theater sales might disappear. Two revenue streams likely to remain robust with falling copyright terms are merchandising and foreign sales. For example, kids would still probably want figurines

[58]   Camila Domonoske, *"Wonder Woman" Smashes Domestic Box Office Record for Female
       Directors*, NPR (June 5, 2017, 3:05 PM), www.npr.org/sections/thetwo-way/2017/06/05/531588
       482/wonder-woman-smashes-domestic-box-office-record-for-female-directors.
[59]   There are numerous considerations that might be affected by or impact the effects of copyright
       term reductions. For example, Brian Lee has suggested in conversation that the extensive
       franchising of Hollywood (*Star Wars, Spiderman, Batman*, etc.) would potentially lead to
       a greater decrease in creation with any given amount of copyright term reduction than a world
       without such emphasis on rolling out sequels over decades. Also, it would adversely affect
       Hollywood's calculus in deciding whether to create new franchises.
[60]   Julie Miller, *2016 Is on Track to Be Hollywood's Worst Year for Ticket Sales in a Century*,
       VANITY FAIR (June 13, 2016, 4:20 PM), www.vanityfair.com/hollywood/2016/06/hollywood-
       movie-ticket-sales, and Ryan Faughnder, *Global Box Office Barely Grew in 2016. Blame It on
       China*, L.A. TIMES (Mar. 22, 2017, 4:15 PM), www.latimes.com/business/hollywood/la-fi-ct-
       mpaa-box-office-20170322-story.html.

of their favorite characters, and adults might still want to buy movie-themed T-shirts.[61] Dina Zipin suggests that merchandising as a significant revenue "strategy obviously doesn't work for every film (action figures for a comedy like Amy Schumer's 'Trainwreck' probably wouldn't bring in billions), but for big-budget films that appeal to kids and Comic-Con junkies alike, merchandising is a cash cow. See Disney's 'Toy Story' franchise, which has brought in about $2.4 billion in retail sales."[62] Again, we would have to wait and see what happens to such merchandising sales after a dramatic reduction in copyright, especially since the more expensive films to make – action and animated films – are usually the ones that most effectively exploit retail sales as a revenue source.

Especially for film, foreign sales have become more important. Zipin states: "When a producer cobbles together the budget for an independent film modestly budgeted at, say, $25 million, selling the distribution rights in foreign territories is crucial to cover the film's budget and, hopefully, bring in revenue."[63] Foreign film sales have steadily risen to be larger than US domestic sales.[64] Thus, one could argue that a short copyright term in the United States would not inhibit Hollywood from creating for foreign markets. Yet, given the United States has lobbied for excessive copyright across the globe, if we take the lead in decided to limit copyright first, other nations might follow suit. Given the size of the US market, other countries were pressured into accepting excessive copyright in return for access for their goods. Thus, because of fear of significant trade retaliation, no other country in the world would take the initiative to dramatically reduce copyright on its own. Furthermore, if the United States decided to limit copyright first, other nations would be loath to continue to subsidize Hollywood through maintaining extreme copyright regimes in their own countries – continuing to doing so could be viewed as allowing American consumers and corporations to ride the coattails of foreigners, just as some currently believe Americans heavily subsidize the rest of the world's consumption of pharmaceuticals, given that prices for the same drugs are significantly lower across the world relative to within the United States.

It has been argued by Kal Raustiala and Chris Sprigman that the fashion industry, which is currently unprotected by copyright, thrives because it "rests on attributes specific to fashion, in particular the status-conferring, or

---

[61] This revenue stream would also be partially contingent on trademark law.

[62] Dina Zipin, *How Exactly Do Movies Make Money?*, INVESTOPEDIA, May 22, 2017, 1:36 PM), www.investopedia.com/articles/investing/093015/how-exactly-do-movies-make-money.asp.

[63] *Id.* [64] Faughnder, *supra* note 60.

positional, nature of clothing."[65] The same argument is extended to creative cuisine, furniture design, hairstyles, and tattoos.[66] I mention their argument not simply to point out that art forms not already protected by copyright would be unaffected by the abolition of copyright[67] but to address their question "whether the positional nature of fashion is present in other creative industries, and if so, whether similar, if perhaps more muted, effects exist."[68] If film and television have positionality, then Hollywood production might not substantially fall with a dramatic decrease in copyright. Raustiala and Sprigman suggest music displays some positionality – in that becoming mainstream causes certain musicians to lose their original fans – but admit that "music choices are more private than fashion choices and hence it is easier to maintain 'guilty pleasures' in music than in clothing."[69] In addition to such private "guilty pleasures," another major difference between the two artistic mediums is that a copied song costs essentially nothing, but even a knockoff handbag will set you back roughly $20. Positionality seems as remote if not more remote in film, TV, video games, etc. – media that share the almost costless copying nature of music. Thus, the fact that a few artistic fields are commercially successful without copyright protection does not change the reality that if copyright laws are significantly weakened, a substantial decrease in corporate art would occur in the industries that command ten hours of the average American's day.

Substantial reductions in the creation of commercial art would, in the short term, lead to reduced gross domestic product (GDP) growth attributable to the entertainment industry and likely even declines in overall GDP.[70] Yet in no way is it a foregone conclusion that long-run economic growth would be hurt.

---

[65] Kal Raustiala & Chris Sprigman, The Piracy Paradox: Innovation and Intellectual Property in Fashion Design, UCLA School of Law Research Paper No. 06–04 (Aug. 2006 draft), http://ssrn.com/abstract=878401. *See also* Kal Raustiala & Chris Sprigman, *The Piracy Paradox Revisited*, 61 STAN. L. REV. 1201 (2009).

[66] *Id.*

[67] It appears unlikely that after the fall of copyright a flood of copyright refugees would pour into artistic fields that have operated without copyright protection for some time – either for artistic reasons or for financial reasons.

[68] Raustiala & Sprigman, *supra* note 65 (2006).   [69] *Id.*

[70] The operating revenue of the motion picture and video industries was $71.77 billion in 2004 or 0.61 percent of 2004 US GDP. The operating revenue of the sound recording industry was $16.5 billion during the same period or 0.14 percent of US GDP. U.S. Census Statistical Abstract 2007, tab. 1122 (Motion Picture and Sound Recording Industries – Estimated Revenue and Inventories 1998 to 2004). Book revenue was $51.92 billion in 2005 or 0.44 percent of 2004 US GDP. U.S. Census Statistical Abstract 2007, tab. 1119 (Books Sold: Value of U.S. Domestic Consumer Expenditures 2004 to 2009). The 2004 US GDP figure of $11.7125 trillion comes from the Bureau of Economic Analysis, National Economic Accounts, http://bea.gov/national/txt/dpga.txt.

It is eminently possible that the extensive reduction of copyright protection would actually lead to an increase in long-term economic growth. First of all, if the average American considerably reduces her consumption of entertainment, not only would such reduction open up time for her to create, but it would also open up time for other pursuits that are directly or indirectly beneficial to the US economy.[71] Second, the public's reduced consumption could lead to a modest increase in national savings, which could be channeled into increased investment.[72]

Even if profoundly weakening copyright protection for artistic creations does not lead to an increase in long-term economic growth, as a society we cannot be afraid to lose a small fraction of our income if the loss would help a broader group of society find fulfillment through creating. In 2010, two Nobel Prize–winning economists, Joseph Stiglitz and Amartya Sen, urged us to end our fixation on economic growth to the exclusion of all else.[73] This is in part because it has been shown repeatedly that after having enough money to meet basic needs (food, shelter, etc.), individuals do not become happier or more fulfilled with increases in their wealth or income.[74]

A skeptic might mistakenly, yet understandably, attempt to think through what a limited decrease in copyright protection would mean for production starting from our current extreme regime instead of a more reasonable level of

[71] Numerous individuals could contribute beneficially to scientific, engineering, or technological advancements or discoveries on a part-time, nonpaid basis. More individuals pursuing such hobbies could potentially accelerate the rate of progress in such fields. For example, Jay McNeil, a TV satellite dish installer, recently discovered a new nebula. Clive Thompson, *Professional Amateurs*, N.Y. TIMES MAG. (Dec. 12, 2004), www.nytimes.com/2004/12/12/magazine/12PROFESSIONAL.html.

[72] Third, individuals who lost their jobs creating commercial art after the elimination of copyright would in the medium to long term be redeployed in the economy – potentially in jobs with higher productivity.

[73] *See generally* JOSEPH STIGLITZ, AMARTYA SEN, & JEAN-PAUL FITOUSSI, MISMEASURING OUR LIVES: WHY GDP DOESN'T ADD UP (2010).

[74] "Money doesn't buy happiness – or even upgrade despair, as the playwright Richard Greenberg once wrote – once our basic needs are met. In one well-known survey, Ed Diener of the University of Illinois determined that those on the Forbes 100 list in 1995 were only slightly happier than the American public as a whole; in an even more famous study, in 1978, a group of researchers determined that twenty-two lottery winners were no happier than a control group (leading one of the authors, Philip Brickman, to coin the scarily precise phrase 'hedonic treadmill,' the unending hunger for the next acquisition)." Jennifer Senior, *Some Dark Thoughts on Happiness*, N.Y. MAG. (July 17, 2006), http://nymag.com/news/features/17573. This conclusion has been refined to suggest that incremental amounts of added happiness can come from added consumption if such spending, for example, is used to obtain added experiences. Elizabeth Dunn, Daniel Gilbert, & Timothy Wilson, *If Money Doesn't Make You Happy Then You Probably Aren't Spending It Right*, 21(2) J. CONSUMER PSYCHOL. 115–25 (2011).

protection. In essence, modest copyright decreases would not reduce Big Copyright's production because copyright protection is presently at such an extreme level, yet this does not negate the fact that the financial incentives of copyright are critical to Hollywood's ability to produce, outside the absolute tail end of excessive protection.

As mentioned in Chapter 1, five Nobel Prize–winning economists argued that the 1998 Copyright Term Extension Act, which extended the copyright term from the life of the author plus fifty years after her death to the life of the author plus seventy years, would not incentivize Hollywood to create new works but instead simply protect existing works that were about to expire – hence the law's "Mickey Mouse Protection Act" nickname. The economists reasoned that the copyright term of life plus fifty years was already so long that it was for practical purposes infinite, and at infinity incentives break down. Adding or subtracting twenty years of protection when we are near infinity means little, yet the same does not hold on the opposite end of the spectrum – adding or subtracting a decade of protection if the copyright term were only ten years would have enormous effects on the amount Hollywood chose to produce. This was later partially confirmed empirically by Kai-Lung Hui and I. P. L. Png, who in 2002 demonstrated that the twenty-year extension did not increase the number of movies Hollywood created.[75] On this point, I agree with the Nobel Prize–winning economists and Hui and Png. In fact, we can all agree on this and also believe that much shorter copyright terms – six months or two years in total – would decrease Big Copyright's production. As Hui and Png's study suggests, a minor decrease in a virtually infinite copyright term would make little impact, which is why I argue for a dramatic reduction. We need to get the copyright length to approach zero, not infinity.

Numerous respected scholars have shown that almost all of the economic benefits from copyrights accrue early on in most cases – not decades later.[76] James Boyle observes, "For most works, the owners expect to make all the money they are going to recoup from the work with five or ten years of exclusive rights. The rest of the copyright term is of little use to them except as a kind of lottery ticket in case the work proves to be a one-in-a-million perennial favorite."[77]

[75] *See generally* Kai-Lung Hui & I. P. L. Png, *On the Supply of Creative Work: Evidence from the Movies*, 92 AM. ECON. REV. PAPERS & PROC. 217 (2002)
[76] HM TREASURY, GOWERS REVIEW OF INTELLECTUAL PROPERTY 52 (2006) (U.K.) www .official-documents.gov.uk/document/other/0118404830/0118404 830.pdf.
[77] JAMES BOYLE, THE PUBLIC DOMAIN: ENCLOSING THE COMMONS OF THE MIND 11 (2008).

At a dramatically lower copyright term, Big Copyright would still continue to produce new material (which I do not object to) but would produce significantly less of it, which is what is needed given the extent of overconsumption. Thus, while the order of magnitude of the decrease is understood, we have to wait and see whether the copyright term would significantly reduce Hollywood's output at two years or six months or some length in between because it is safe to assume that no $200 million Hollywood films would be created without any copyright.

Demand Side Effects: Would the Public Consume Less?

Granting that dramatic reductions in copyright protection will significantly reduce the amount of new content Big Copyright creates, one might question whether this reduction would lead to less overconsumption – i.e., if no new blockbusters are released, individuals could simply overconsume different stuff, such as movies or shows from Hollywood's vast library that they have already watched or have yet to try; new art forms; or new content that they previously would not have considered. Such substitution would likely be modest and not nearly enough to offset the significant decrease in consumption due to Hollywood producing fewer works. There are numerous reasons for this.

One big reason is that, thanks to Hollywood, consumers are accustomed to carefully targeted and increasingly sophisticated products. After having watched what they consider to be the best or highest-quality entertainment, they will only be willing to lower their standards so much to watch shows that they previously scoffed at or associate with an earlier time in their lives. For example, if someone is a fan of the BBC series *Sherlock*, she might be willing to watch the CBS series *Elementary*, or vice versa, but that doesn't mean she would settle for *Psych* or rewatch *Scooby-Doo*, regardless of how much enjoyment the dog detective brought during childhood. This hesitancy applies to older works, foreign works, and amateur content.

A significant amount of commercial art has already been produced, but its shelf life for consumers is relatively short. More than a decade ago, Brewster Kahle, the founder of the Internet Archive, stated: "'It looks like there's about two to three million recordings of music. Ever. There are about a hundred thousand theatrical releases of movies . . . and about one to two million movies [distributed] during the twentieth century. There are about twenty-six million different titles of books.'"[78] Yet comparatively little current consumption is of

---

[78] Lessig quotes Brewster Kahle making the preceding statement. LAWRENCE LESSIG, FREE CULTURE: THE NATURE AND FUTURE OF CREATIVITY 114 (2004).

old works, let alone works made only a few years ago. For example, all of the thirty most-rented films on DVD in 2015 were released in the preceding two years.[79] The same for DVD sales in 2016 – all of the thirty top-selling movies on DVD in 2016 were released in the preceding two years.[80] On August 14, 2017, twenty-seven of the top thirty music singles sold on iTunes were from 2017, while the remaining three were from 2016.[81]

The consumption of older commercial art would cushion but not prevent a significant drop in commercial art consumption by the public. Very few movies or television shows age well because they are strongly marked by the fashions, pop trends, and production values of their time. If there were a sudden, significant decrease in Hollywood output tomorrow, the visual quality of today's material would still set a very high bar for future productions, diminishing audience willingness to watch anything beneath its level – and yet today's content would still lose its luster as it aged. Furthermore, advertisers would continue to produce high-quality, polished ads and "rich media" experiences, which might deter individuals from watching older or amateur video because of the stark contrast in aesthetic quality, not to mention the wow factor. Brands would continue to pay advertisers to create high-quality marketing content because their raison d'être is to sell stuff – stuff that will continue to be as valuable after a dramatic drop in copyright protection.

Another factor that could dampen the reduction of commercial art consumption if copyright is markedly reduced is the flow of commercial art created under copyright in foreign countries. A minor difficulty of sizably weakening copyright only in the United States and not globally is that copyright-protected commercial art from abroad could be freely copied and distributed in the United States much sooner than in other countries. If US citizens do not have a great longing to consume foreign commercial art, then this factor should not change the general assumption that the significant weakening of copyright would significantly lessen overconsumption.[82] While no perfect indicator of US interest in foreign commercial art exists, an example or two quickly hint at the limited nature of such demand.

---

[79] *Top Rentals – 2015*, FOR MOVIES, https://formovies.com/awards/top_rentals.html?year=2015 (last visited August 14, 2017).

[80] *Top-Selling DVDs in the United States 2016*, NUMBERS, www.the-numbers.com/home-market/dvd-sales/2016 (last visited August 14, 2017).

[81] *iTunes Charts*, APPLE, www.apple.com/itunes/charts/songs/ (last visited August 14, 2017).

[82] US demand for foreign commercial art might increase if, instead of folding, some US corporations that produce commercial art are able to survive by copyrighting and selling US-style commercial art abroad. If this were the case, then more US-style commercial art could make its way back to the copyrightless United States. This is further discussed in Chapter 5.

Only 5.8 percent of film rentals through Netflix are of foreign films.[83] Furthermore, Netflix's audience most likely does not precisely reflect a cross section of the US population – it is probably biased toward a segment that seeks hard-to-obtain rentals. While this statistic is in no way conclusive proof that the availability of foreign films is not a factor, it is certainly suggestive. A better indicator of feasible US demand for foreign commercial art may be that "[i]n 2005, just 10 foreign-language films had ticket sales of more than $1 million in the United States . . . The top grosser, Stephen Chow's *Kung Fu Hustle*, ranked No. 116 at the domestic box office, with $17.1 million in receipts."[84] Not much has changed since then. The top-grossing foreign film in the United States from 2007 to 2010 was *Ponyo* at only $15 million.[85] Such lack of commercial success for foreign titles is only getting more pronounced. For example, "In 2013 the top five foreign-language releases earned collectively just $15 million at the U.S. box office."[86] Further, "U.S. box office for the top five foreign-language films has declined by 61% in the last seven years."[87] These statistics are probably indicative of US demand for foreign commercial art in other artistic media. US demand for foreign video games may be higher than US demand for foreign films, but US demand for foreign TV shows may be even weaker than US demand for foreign films.

The same limits of changing one's consumption patterns apply to amateur content, which lacks professional video production, from cinematography to wardrobe, lighting, and makeup (forget special effects). Watching a handful of videos filmed with iPhones on YouTube can be good fun, as I previously mentioned, but few of us have the fortitude to watch five hours of such amateur entertainment on a daily basis. This idea that there are limits to what individuals will consume is indirectly supported by the fact that current statistics show that Americans consume miniscule amounts of amateur

[83] Anthony Kaufman, *Is Foreign Film the New Endangered Species?*, N.Y. Times (Jan. 22, 2006), www.nytimes.com/2006/01/22/movies/is-foreign-film-the-new-endangered-species.html?mcubz=3.
[84] *Id.*
[85] David Cook, *Top Grossing Foreign Films in the US*, Amazon.com, www.amazon.com/Top-Grossing-Foreign-Films-US/lm/RE0CCL2BJTS2F.
[86] Anthony Kaufman, *The Lonely Subtitle: Here's Why U.S. Audiences Are Abandoning Foreign-Language Films*, IndieWire (May 6, 2014, 9:18 AM), www.indiewire.com/2014/05/the-lonely-subtitle-heres-why-u-s-audiences-are-abandoning-foreign-language-films-27051 /. "This doesn't count films catering specifically to immigrant or diaspora populations, whether Spanish-language films for Hispanic Americans or Bollywood films for Indian-Americans." *Id.*
[87] *Id.*

content relative to professionally made content.[88] There is nothing to suggest that this non-habit would explode into hours a day if less corporate art is created.

Just like, invariably, there are some individuals who prefer time-honored classics, there may be those who are steadfastly devoted to amateur or foreign content. Exceptions exist but do not invalidate the fact that most Americans do not consume significant amounts of old, foreign, or amateur content. Also, while we all love rewatching our favorite films and series, adults are unlikely to do so on a frequent basis, especially since we are accustomed to Hollywood's nonstop delivery of suspenseful, fast-paced serialized fare. When the available viewing options are less compelling, there will come a point when it is preferable to choose another activity, such as catching up on sleep, calling a friend, or even creating a little ourselves.

I have stressed that Americans' overconsumption rests on too much TV, video, and online entertainment because scientific research shows such mediums allow Hollywood to deploy a vast array of hook techniques that are addictive-like in nature in addition to being harmful if overconsumed. There is little danger that the average American would overconsume amateur or even professional poetry or sculpture for ten hours a day because the artists do not deploy such hook techniques nor do they spend liberally to advertise their work each year. This is not to dispute that a counter-shift toward consuming more offscreen works could facilitate the shift away from onscreen entertainment. In fact, such a switch would be beneficial because it would entail fewer harms of consumption. More individuals might pick up a novel or go to a concert, but there is little likelihood that they will do so in excess on a daily basis. To the extent they continue to look to their screens to while away the hours, the stark contrast between Hollywood fare and amateur productions – the combined mastery of hundreds of professional artists versus the developing artistry of one or a few novices – would place a limit on how much amateur onscreen entertainment they find appealing.

Finally, it is possible that reducing copyright protection will actually lead to an increase in new amateur artwork to consume. This is exactly the point: more noncorporate creators. Such a development would be healthy; it would signify equality of communication among individual creators instead of a one-way flow of content from corporate creator to consumer. Moreover, having

---

[88] *The Nielsen Total Audience Report Q1 2017*, THE NIELSEN TOTAL AUDIENCE SERIES 13 (2017) and *How Much Time Is Spent on Social Media? Infographic*, MEDIAKIX, http://media kix.com/2016/12/how-much-time-is-spent-on-social-media-lifetime/#gs.F=eCW2M.

more content options is very different from actually consuming more, especially given that the type of new content – amateur rather than slick – is not what we have been groomed to overconsume.

At least in part, increases in consumption of amateur content are likely to come from increased creation and sharing of creations among family and friends. The enjoyment of this new noncommercial art would have beneficial spillover effects – loved ones and social circles interacting, communicating, and possibly creating together.

Thus, if copyright is dramatically scaled back, it is likely that Americans will consume more fine art, foreign works, and new amateur content as well as preexisting professional entertainment. However, these substitutes for new blockbusters are not just substitutes; they signal a movement away from dependence on Hollywood toward freer interaction with a variety of creators through a variety of aesthetic experiences, some even offscreen. Moreover, the amount of time we spend consuming would pale in comparison to the ten hours a day we currently spend glued to our screens – enthralled, sedentary, and cut off from life.

Supply Side Effects: Would the Public Create More?

Not everyone will instantaneously begin to create if copyright is significantly reduced. A significant reduction in the consumption of entertainment might cause only a modest increase in the number of individuals beginning to create art. It is impossible to know, ex ante, the extent of the increase, yet the transformation for those who start would be meaningful, potentially revelatory. I do not claim that reforming copyright is the most effective way to inspire more citizens to create. Some individuals might spend more time with their loved ones while others take up soccer, fix their motorcycle's carburetor, nap, or create. Yet this is wonderful. If only some of these events occur, I would hope we would think that reforming copyright was worth it.

If all citizens find themselves with a few extra hours a day to do other things and only 5 percent of them take a few minutes of their new time to occasionally create, I would call the reform a great success. To put such an increase into perspective, the 2012 US Census Statistical Abstract (the last produced before the series was discontinued) states that in 2008, 9 percent of the adult population painted, drew, sculpted, or engaged in printmaking at least once in the prior twelve months; 5.2 percent sang in a choir or chorale; 14.7 percent engaged in photography; 3.1 percent played classical music on an instrument; 6 percent made pottery; 13.1 percent partook in sewing, weaving, crocheting, quilting, or needlepoint; and 6.9 percent wrote creatively.[89] Comparably more adults took part, at least once in the prior twelve months, in the following leisure activities: charity work (32 percent) and exercise (52.9 percent).[90]

A little dancing, improvising jazz, writing code for an open source or free software project, or gardening – this is all that it takes to break free from the prison of overconsumption if the supply of addictive entertainment dries up. Dana Gioia, a poet and the former chairman of the National Endowment for the Arts, gave a commencement speech at Stanford, the title of which speaks volumes – "Trade Easy Pleasures for More Complex and Challenging Ones." In it he states that those who "read for pleasure and participate in the arts" remarkably "exercise, play sports, volunteer and do charity work at about three times the level" of individuals who do not "read for pleasure and participate in the arts."[91]

Since copyright law exists, we have an obligation to determine how the law is causing harm and to attempt to redress the situation. Copyright allows corporate creators to ensnare our lives to satisfy their unrestrained and insatiable quest for increased profits. My proposal aims to reform the law so it helps us restore our lives and create room for a wealth of other important things. I realize that potentially only a modest fraction of these activities will include more creation. Ultimately, the goal is to maximize the number of people who create.

Combining a significant reduction in copyright protection with other public policies or programs aimed at strengthening the commons and directly encouraging people to create would increase the number of individuals who pick up a trumpet, chisel, or pen in their newly opened-up free time. While such policies on their own would likely increase the number of creators, collectively with dramatic copyright reform they could be transformative – i.e., freeing up to almost half of people's waking days as well as filling part of the void with a communal atmosphere conducive to arts education, interactivity, and collaboration.

---

[89]   U.S. Census Statistical Abstract 2012, tab. 1237 (Personal Participation in Various Arts or Creative Activities: 2008).

[90]   U.S. Census Statistical Abstract 2012, tab. 1239 (Attendance/Participation in Various Leisure Activities: 2008). In no way do I mean to imply that creating art is more important than assisting those in need.

[91]   While we cannot know for sure if the art participation causes the exercise and volunteer work or is simply correlated with the additional activity, either scenario is encouraging. Dana Gioia, *Gioia to Graduates: "Trade Easy Pleasures for More Complex and Challenging Ones,"* STAN. REP. (June 17, 2007), http://news-service.stanford.edu/news/2007/june20/gradtrans-062007 .html (speech delivered at Stanford University's commencement).

Such existing policies include renewed emphasis on the arts and music in schools and in community education programs.[92] Public schools should reestablish and reinvigorate art curricula. The public educational system has the potential to expose millions of children and teens to the satisfaction of engaging in the process of creation. Art, music, and drama programs were once staples in the American public educational system.[93] Sadly, "[t]his once visionary and democratic system has been almost entirely dismantled by well-meaning but myopic school boards, county commissioners, and state officials, with the federal government largely indifferent to the issues. Art became an expendable luxury, and 50 million students have paid the price."[94] Given how critically important creating art is to battling ossification, a student's access to arts education should not be "largely a function of his or her parents' income," as is currently the case.[95]

Creative new approaches to art education for children and adults should also be explored. Let's pursue the complex and challenging pleasures of developing innovative ways to stimulate creativity and maximize the number of citizens who make art.

Would More Great Art Be Created?

While some might assume that less great art would be produced if copyright is considerably reduced, I caution against such a conclusion. Even if weakening copyright reduces the number of masterpieces created, the reduction would be marginal in certain artistic media. Precise forecasts are difficult for numerous reasons. To begin with, there is significant divergence over what art is – e.g., whether video games count as art as opposed to "mere" entertainment. Also, many individuals disagree over what constitutes greatness – e.g., whether an individual work of art merits such a distinction, whether the structural contours of an entire artistic medium prohibit the birth of masterpieces in that medium, or whether any commercial artwork can be a masterpiece, regardless of the artistic medium.

First, some believe that geniuses are oblivious to the outside world in regard to what motivates them, which may be part of their genius. As Ludwig von

---

[92] Ideally, many different types of community art education programs aimed at encouraging the general population to create should be tried to determine the optimal approaches. Many different factors would have to be tested, from the size of the art program to the method of instruction to the form of advertising used to promote the art program. Most likely, different groups of individuals would respond best to different types of programs. Also, art education programs should be offered in many subject matters to include creative activities consistent with a very broad view of art.

[93] Gioia, *supra* note 91. [94] *Id.* [95] *Id.*

Mises has argued, creative geniuses "do not produce and work in the sense in which these terms are employed in dealing with the affairs of other people. They do not let themselves be influenced by the response their work meets on the part of their contemporaries. They do not wait for encouragement."[96] Oscar Wilde's take is even pithier though likely too deterministic: "Genius is born, not paid."[97]

Second, the commercial pressures blamed for possibly corrupting art by some today would be significantly diminished. In essence, instead of having artists create "art for art's sake" as Pierre Bourdieu argues, extreme copyright has enabled the corporatization and commodification of art – bourgeois art – that risks compromising artists' aesthetics, vision, and values in pursuit of profit.[98] Any such erosion of the artist's autonomy could lead to works that are more readily consumed by the public but at the expense of losing some potentially great art. As Albert Camus instructed, "The freedom of art is not worth much when the only purpose is to assure the artist's comfort."[99]

Further, as mentioned earlier, the fall of copyright would have virtually no negative effect on the production of fine art and by extension great fine art. The predominant economic incentives for fine art come not from copyright but instead from a web of institutions that support the fine arts. Universities, foundations, symphonies, ballet companies, opera houses, and private patrons would all continue to search for talent and financially support those individuals once they were found.

If many commercial artists, after the extensive weakening of copyright, started creating noncommercial art – either in the same artistic medium or in a new artistic medium – and we can assume that their rate of creating masterpieces would be the same, which appears to be a reasonable assumption, then any fall in new commercial masterpieces would be offset by an increase in new noncommercial masterpieces created.

Not only would no sizable decrease in the creation of great art come about with a vast reduction in the scope of copyright, but also the amount of masterpieces produced might increase overall. With the pronounced weakening of copyright, if a substantial segment of the public, widely distributed

[96] Ludwig von Mises, Human Action 657 (Scholar's Ed.) (1949).
[97] Bruno Fey, *State Support and Creativity in the Arts: Some New Considerations*, 23 J. Cultural Econ. 71, 78 (1999) (Wilde was inverting the expression "genius is born, not made").
[98] Martin Senftleben, *Copyright, Creators and Society's Need for Autonomous Art – the Blessing and Curse of Monetary Incentives*, in What If We Could Reimagine Copyright? 28–31 (Rebecca Giblin & Kimberlee Weatherall eds., 2017)
[99] Albert Camus, Create Dangerously (Dec. 14, 1957) (lecture delivered at the University of Uppsala).

among different groups within society, begins to create, society might discover future Mozarts whose talents would otherwise have gone undetected.[100]

Even if slightly less great art would be created, would it really matter significantly? Historians like Ann Blair have found information overload back in sixteenth-century Europe.[101] Some cultural commentators of today would claim that so much art is produced that the institutions set up to identify great art can no longer operate effectively. Given that an extensive amount of great art already exists, it seems worth the trade-off to have more of the public creating on their own than to have possibly a few extra Paul Klees or Gustav Klimts. Finally, some great artists might not have been as great as they were if they had been privileged enough to make a living as full-time artists. Would Franz Kafka have been Kafka if he did not work in an insurance company?[102]

On this last point, permit me a brief aside. By arguing for dramatically less restrictive copyright law, I am not looking to punish artists. The current regime does not meaningfully help most artists outside of a relative handful of elite, mostly commercial artists. In fact, this book proposes alternative ideas to generate new revenue for artists, ideas that do not encourage vast overconsumption. If some artists are adversely affected by dramatic reduction in copyright, such pain will be worth the benefit of getting many others to create on their own and/or not overconsume.

We cannot hold onto a vision of copyright enabling artists to concentrate full time on their craft when this story largely only applies to the commercial elite artists and the harm is so devastating to the public. First, many artists can sustain themselves through their art yet in a way that has little to do with copyright – e.g., working for or in partnership with universities, symphonies, opera houses, galleries, museums. Further, while not necessarily ideal, there is no reason some artists cannot hold a day job and create in the evening and on weekends. Artists themselves have at times cultivated such struggle as part of the mystique of the artist. More important, such sacrifice can provide untold

[100]   Anupam Chander and Madhavi Sunder's observation about the public domain – that different individuals will have unequal access to make use of the commons given differences in income, wealth, education, etc. – is relevant to my argument, insofar as the commons can motivate or assist individuals to create because as a society we should take steps to equalize individuals' opportunities to use the commons to create and communicate. The same can be said about stemming overconsumption. *See generally* Anupam Chander & Madhavi Sunder, *The Romance of the Public Domain*, 92 CAL. L. REV. 1331 (2004).

[101]   *See generally* ANN BLAIR, TOO MUCH TO KNOW: MANAGING SCHOLARLY INFORMATION BEFORE THE MODERN AGE (2010).

[102]   There would be famous artists even if copyright did not exist. The interesting question is whether society would place such a great premium on the ethos of professionalism versus being an amateur if copyright did not exist.

insight, as suggested previously with Kafka but applying equally to Anton Chekhov, Henri Rousseau, Williams Carlos Williams, Charles Ives, David Hume, Pablo Neruda, Octavio Paz, Adam Smith, Wallace Stevens, Morton Feldman, Joseph Conrad, and many other artists.

Furthermore, especially given my desire to see everyone take up creation, I am also sympathetic to artists' need to maintain a deep personal connection to their works. In the United States, the justification behind copyright is not about a right to own the creations of one's mind but rather a monopoly privilege granted to artists to further a societal good of incentivizing the creation and distribution of ideas and expression. Yet many American artists' vision of copyright seems to more closely align with the European view of moral rights and their justifications for the existence of copyright – that to allow others to openly take one's work is akin to taking the artist's arm or soul. At a minimum, this misunderstanding of US copyright points to the importance of attribution. However, even greater legal privileges could be in harmony with not getting the public hopelessly addicted to entertainment through the corporate use of hook techniques if such privileges are tailored to individual artists, not corporations spanning the globe. Such a challenge would be intimately related to our current struggle and would be a monumental undertaking. Yet it is possible to structure copyright to protect individual artists and consumers and ideally make them one and the same.

THE MECHANICS OF HOW COPYRIGHT COULD BE REDUCED

Big Copyright captured Congress in order to make the copyright laws excessive because this was the easiest and least risk-averse way to increase its profits without having to care about the public interest or think seriously about new, alternative revenue streams. Thus, one can view our present state of overconsumption as having two problems. First, we have excessive copyright protection, which leads to overconsumption. Second, Congress has been captured by Hollywood. Solving the second problem (capture by Big Copyright) will potentially enable legislators to see that copyright is extreme (the first problem). As Upton Sinclair once quipped, "It is difficult to get a man to understand something when his salary depends upon his not understanding it."[103]

Assuming for a moment that we could divorce legislators' job security from Hollywood's campaign contributions, how would we go about making

---

[103] Upton Sinclair, quoted in EVAN ESAR, THE DICTIONARY OF HUMOROUS QUOTATIONS (1949).

copyright law reasonable again? Copyright law without Congress wearing Hollywood's lobbying blinders could be radically limited in all aspects. In fact, the reforms would be conceptually quite simple, such as reversing much of copyright's expansion over the past few decades.

First, the copyright term could be reduced to its origins under the 1790 Act – fourteen years – or as low as a few months or a handful of years if fourteen years does not stop the avalanche of corporate entertainment. Such a significant reduction would likely have the most noticeable effect on stemming the flood of hyped corporate entertainment.

Second, we could reduce the scope of copyright protection – the different types of works eligible for copyright protection. We could conceivably limit copyright's scope by excluding from its protections all forms of onscreen entertainment given they are the forms most prone to be abused by corporations to hook consumers. Doing so would stop the flow of corporate entertainment even more effectively than dramatically reducing the length of copyright.

Third, we could revise copyright law so that once a work generates revenues over a set amount, $10,000 or $100,000, it would automatically lose its copyright protection. Jon Pareles has stated: "Sometimes I'm tempted to suggest that any song that has sold more than a million (or maybe two million or five million) copies ought to go directly into the public domain, as if its fans have ransomed it from the copyright holders."[104] I find Pareles's suggestion not only innovative but also appealing – its ransom imagery touches on copyright as a monopoly that was supposedly bargained for with society and hence should be theoretically subject to renegotiation, especially since all the recent escalation in protection has in practice been Hollywood negotiating with itself, given how it has paid off the side at the other end of the table through campaign contributions. Further, if we are skeptical that copyright protection for large corporate entities generates meaningful new ideas for the marketplace – either because vast bureaucracies are not known for their originality or because for-profit entities are interested in getting consumers addicted to their products, not in doing good for society – then capping copyright's monopoly protection would disable Hollywood's addiction factories while enabling individual artists to still generate revenue from their ideas.[105]

---

[104] Jon Pareles, *Parody, Not Smut, Has Rappers in Court*, N.Y. Times (Nov. 13, 1993), www .nytimes.com/1993/11/13/arts/critic-s-notebook-parody-not-smut-has-rappers-in-court.html.

[105] We might consider crafting a copyright policy that allows copyrights to be held only by individuals, not by corporations, yet such a policy could run up against constitutional concerns, which capping revenue from each copyright would not face. A more workable, related exposition of this is Tim Wu's vision of authorial copyright, as opposed to a copyright system that vests rights in commercial intermediaries, because it may "act as a check on the

If appropriately implemented, the preceding reforms could transform countless lives, bringing the possibility of layers of added richness to existences that are currently too preoccupied by what Hollywood pushes on us. While each of the preceding policies on its own could potentially halt much of our overconsumption, combined they would likely be more effective.

There is also a set of reforms that would not lead to appreciably less overconsumption but would help solve other harms that excessive copyright protection has created, such as the copyright orphan works epidemic and the uncertain legal landscape of employing copyright's fair use doctrine. For example, we could resurrect historical limitations of copyright such as the former requirements that works be registered with the US Copyright Office and have a notice provision attached to them – e.g., a © mark to notify the public – in order to receive copyright protection.[106]

As for other reforms, we could enhance the scope of copyright's fair use doctrine, such as possibly creating some bright-line rules for fair use.[107] We could scrap most if not all of the laws that go beyond strictly regulating creative expression – paracopyright laws – such as aspects of the Digital Millennium Copyright Act.[108] We could support the Access to Knowledge (A2K) movement's numerous goals such as free

---

market power of dominant distributors." Tim Wu, *On Copyright's Authorship Policy*, U. CHI. LEGAL F. 335, 341 (2008). Wu contends that the "principal means for achieving" a neutral copyright system is "to maximize the decentralization of copyright ownership and enforcement." *Id.* at 349.

[106] Christopher Sprigman has argued that the reformalization of copyright by creating new-style formalities would allow for substantial reform to "take place without damaging the interests of copyright owners who would otherwise have strong incentives to oppose the creation of a less restrictive copyright regime." See Christopher Sprigman, *Reform(alizing) Copyright*, 57 STAN. L. REV. 485, 568 (2004). Sprigman argues that such a reform would "ease[] access to commercially valueless works for which protection (or the continuation of protection) serves no purpose and [would] focus[] the system on those works for which protection is needed to ensure that the rightsholder is able to appropriate the commercial value of the expression." *Id.* Sprigman's new-style formalities reform is a reasoned policy option that should be seriously considered, yet simply bringing back the mandatory registration and notice provisions would effect more change more quickly.

[107] *See generally* William W. Fisher III, *Reconstructing the Fair Use Doctrine*, 101 HARV. L. REV. 1661 (1988); Haochen Sun, *Fair Use as a Collective User Right*, 90 N.C. L. REV. 125, 131 (2011); and Martin Skladany, *Copyright Corvée: Inverting the Ancien Régime*, 34 EUR. INTELL. PROP. REV. 741 (2012).

[108] *See generally* Joshua Schwartz, *Thinking outside the Pandora's Box: Why the DMCA Is Unconstitutional under Article I, § 8 of the U.S. Constitution*, 10 J. TECH. L. & POL'Y 93, 97 (2005).

and broad dissemination of information to those in developing countries.[109]

Thus, the mechanics of how we reform copyright law are not a mystery; the challenge is breaking Big Copyright's capture of Congress. It is likely that we cannot mitigate most of the harms of our current extreme copyright regime without reform. Niva Elkin-Koren makes a prescient point about how even efforts to create alternative systems to stem the harms of copyright might inevitably depend on copyright reform: "Conceptualizing an alternative to the current regime may require an option of opting out of the proprietary system, and at the same time safeguard against capture and abuse. In the long run, creating an alternative to copyright will require copyright reform."[110]

STEPS FORWARD

While academics and policy advocates do not have the lobbying power to roll back legislation, they have largely prevented it from getting worse. One example of a successful effort to halt the added insanity was when a collection of Internet companies, academics, and nonprofits prevented the Stop Online Piracy Act (SOPA) from becoming law. SOPA was a terrible attempt to hand over the Internet to Hollywood to censor with abandon. Resisting Big Copyright is no small feat, and new dangers can emerge swiftly. The present fragile stalemate, which rests at an extreme level of copyright protection, cannot be the best we can do.

In this age of ever-expanding copyright protections, there is a widespread countermovement to aid the commons, that is, to nurture and protect art, knowledge, and expression that are given freely to all.[111] The free culture

---

[109] *See generally* Lea Shaver & Caterina Sganga, *The Right to Take Part in Cultural Life*, 27 WISCONSIN INT'L L. J. 637 (2009); Molly Beutz Land, *Protecting Rights Online*, 34 YALE J. INT'L L. 1, 3 (2009); Amy Kapczynski, *The Access to Knowledge Mobilization and the New Politics of Intellectual Property*, 117 YALE L.J. 804 (2008); and Martin Skladany, *The Revolutionary Influence of Low Enlightenment: Weakening Copyright in Developing Countries to Improve Respect for Human Rights and the Rule of Law*, 95 J. PAT. & TRADEMARK OFF. SOC'Y 285 (2013).

[110] Niva Elkin-Koren, *What Contracts Cannot Do: The Limits of Private Ordering in Facilitating a Creative Commons*, 74 FORDHAM L. REV. 375, 422 (2005).

[111] "Rousseau said that the first person who wanted a piece of nature as his or her own exclusive possession and transformed it into private property was the person who invented evil." David Berry, *The Commons*, FREE SOFTWARE MAG. (Feb. 21, 2005), www .freesoftwaremagazine.com/articles/commons_as_ideas. While I take an expansive yet flex-ible view of the commons in this book, for example, by including works technically deemed to be in the semicommons, my view is not as expansive as Rousseau's. Further, even if a website is not under a Creative Commons license, individuals can still potentially benefit from the

tradition "is as important as any tradition of freedom in our history . . . Not the tradition that celebrated the power to steal Britney Spears' music, but the ability of people to build on the past without apology."[112] The free software movement[113] and Creative Commons "see the expansion of copyright as a threat to the stated goal of copyright law itself: the promotion of science and useful arts."[114]

While continuing to advocate for the public domain, we need to expose the dirty underbelly of excessive copyright – overconsumption – and broadcast its harms. We also need to champion the act of creation and its value to each of us.

Creating is an essential component of the good life. It is an invigorating and exhilarating activity that leads to a range of other goods. Through creating, we can turn inward – to reflect and imagine, to look for meaning, to find our humanity, to challenge ourselves. Creating provides mental and physical health benefits. It can help us counteract ennui, find solace, confront reality, and become an active participant in life. Through creating, we can engage with the world – communicate through new means, develop and express our thoughts, and collaborate with other creators. Through creating, we can experience mastery and control, attain a fuller sense of autonomy – and discover new ways to surmount the practical limits we routinely run up against in politics, in the economy, and in culture. Creating empowers us to contribute to society and shape the world.

cultural creation. Additionally, I assume any increase in the commons is a positive development because it provides more cultural creation for people to discover and to learn and create from.

[112] Lawrence Lessig, *The Creative Commons*, 55 FLA. L. REV. 763, 777 (2003).

[113] The free software movement is distinct from open source software. For a discussion of open source software, *see generally* ERIC RAYMOND, THE CATHEDRAL AND THE BAZAAR: MUSINGS ON LINUX AND OPEN SOURCE BY AN ACCIDENTAL REVOLUTIONARY (2001).

[114] Shun-ling Chen, *To Surpass or to Conform – What Are Public Licenses for?*, U. ILL. J.L. TECH. & POL'Y 107, 107 (2009). Feist Publ'ns, Inc. v. Rural Tel. Servs. Co., 499 U.S. 340, 349 (1991) (averring that the main objective of copyright is not to compensate authors for their effort).

PART II

PRACTICAL PROPOSALS FOR CHANGE

4

Pressuring Big Copyright

God forbid we should ever be 20 years without such a rebellion . . . What country can preserve its liberties, if their rulers are not warned from time to time that their people preserve the spirit of resistance? Let them take arms . . . What signify a few lives lost in a century or two?

—Thomas Jefferson, Letter to William Stephens Smith, Nov. 13, 1787

Putting aside the rash call for blood, Congress needs to better understand Jefferson's warning. Our elected officials should represent us, not the faceless corporations that pour money into their campaign coffers. However, the implausible dream of a legislative fix to Big Copyright should not stop us from seeking policy remedies that attack the problem from new, less direct angles. This second part of the book investigates different kinds of proposals that might help.

How to accomplish a citizen-centered copyright regime is uncertain. For example, Creative Commons' founding was based on the premise that a staggered, two-stage copyright reform movement is necessary: first remake how people think about the social norm of copyright, including through advocating for the widest adoption of Creative Commons licenses, and then push for political reform to limit the excesses of copyright.[1] This approach

---

[1] Lawrence Lessig, Free Culture: How Big Media Uses Technology and the Law to Lock Down Culture and Control Creativity 275 & 282 (2004). Creative Commons is a nonprofit that freely provides copyright licenses that allow artists to share their works with others in a more liberal manner than copyright allows. Creative Commons supports numerous different types of licenses so artists can choose how they want to share their works with others. For example, an artist can decide to allow others to create adaptations of her work or disallow others to use her work in a commercial manner. Creative Commons also works with other online platforms such as YouTube, Wikipedia, and PLOS. More than 1.1 billion works have been shared through these partnerships. Finally, Google and others allow users to search for artwork under a Creative Commons license, so, for example, if you do a search for cat

makes sense – few realize that the average individual consumes ten hours of entertainment a day, let alone copyright's role in stoking such overconsumption. Yet the two initiatives do not have to be sequential, and efforts in both areas can reinforce each other. For example, a grassroots effort to pressure Congress to reform copyright can simultaneously inform more of the public through traditional and social media coverage of the effort. To achieve these two aims, citizens will need to create institutions or partner with existing nonprofits and academic centers.

The first half of this book argued that copyright law should be concerned with maximizing the number of artists, rather than the number of works created, by encouraging citizens to consume less and create more. The second half presents a tripartite schema for copyright reform – proposing tactics that range across a spectrum from openly confronting Big Copyright to implementing ideas that ignore Hollywood to working with it on reform efforts. Some ideas across the next three chapters aim to directly increase creation by individuals, while others aim to do so indirectly through decreasing overconsumption. A few ideas seek to partially alleviate other ills brought about by excessive copyright – such as copyright orphans and low pay for artists. Furthermore, the proposals are suitable for implementation by many different organizations, from legislators to unions, businesses, and nonprofits.

I am not expecting readers to like all of the ideas. In fact, I'll be happy if I can make you smile at the thought that just one or two of them could be fun, cool, or devious as well as helpful. As Oscar Wilde once quipped, "An idea that is not dangerous is unworthy of being called an idea at all." Chances are readers will widely disagree as to which ideas, if any, are worth attempting. Also, I can't predict which might work until they are tested and refined by others. Few people thought Wikipedia was necessary before it came into existence, and it now has 470 million unique users a month and provides incredible coverage of topics.[2] Even if my roughly twenty proposals work, I am not suggesting that any of them will be game-changing. They cannot be complete solutions because the direct and most impactful route – legislative reform – is blocked by

---

photos, every result will have a Creative Commons license attached. Such options have proven helpful in lessening the severity of our excessive copyright regime, yet online open source licenses, like almost any improvement to the status quo, cannot be reasonably expected to solve even one of the numerous existing problems with copyright – e.g., excessive consumption, orphan works, poor pay for all but the most famous artists, and overly restrictive borrowing provisions. Creative Commons has done an admirable job alleviating restrictive borrowing law and encouraging creation over consumption, but more tools need to be implemented to attack these problems.

[2]   *Wikipedia: About*, WIKIPEDIA, http://en.wikipedia.org/wiki/Wikipedia:About#cite_note-1 (last visited June 9, 2013) (citing Wikimedia Report Card).

Hollywood, and research has shown that by arguing against a concept one reinforces and legitimizes it. I am simply optimistic that a few of them would be implemented and collectively they could make a dent. We need new practical ideas for addressing the many ills of excessive copyright laws because calling for legislative reform has gotten us little.

I admit that some of my proposals are more feasible than others – that many could be introduced without legislation while others would require legislation and hence would need to get through Big Copyright's lobby. The point is to bombard Hollywood with creative proposals it would have to fight against, depleting its resources. Moreover, in this unequal battle against big money, a good offense would be a welcome change in strategy. The copyright minimalist movement has been on the relative defensive in terms of proposing new ideas and proposals, possibly helping to legitimize Big Copyright's ideas more than having them reinforce and legitimize ours.[3]

The traditional paths to compel compliance by corporations or Congress include lobbying for legislative change, advocating for administrative inquiries, and consumer boycotts. Yet none of these strategies will be as effective as we would like given Big Copyright's capture of Washington, DC, and stranglehold over consumers. Big Copyright well understands how it has co-opted most threats and so has little fear. Thus, creative new efforts must be attempted. This chapter presents practical ideas that aim to decrease consumption by pressuring Congress and Hollywood in various novels ways to reform copyright.[4]

TECHNOLOGY UNIONS

Google, Apple, Facebook, and other big technology companies have largely rebuffed pressure from government regulators and civil society to reform questionable practices, leaving many to wonder whether the profitability, ubiquity, and influence of such giants render them effectively immune from

---

[3] If you like any of the ideas, please run with them (ideas may be borrowed freely; only their expression is protected by copyright).

[4] For numerous ideas listed in the next three chapters, I will briefly discuss possible concerns or criticisms. There are two general concerns that I will not address: (1) that an individual idea will have little impact and (2) that it will be difficult to find funding for a particular program. To do so again and again would be tedious, given the number of ideas. Change is often incremental, and while some of the ideas might have little impact if implemented, they are probably better than nothing and collectively could create significant momentum. As for finding funding, this is a reality faced by nonprofits and for-profits. The concern is real, but it is universal and is overcome on a daily basis by organizations across the globe.

outside pressure.[5] Investigations, proposed legislation, class action lawsuits, and public shaming efforts by nonprofits, think tanks, authors, agencies, and legislatures have created little lasting change.[6] The situation is not hopeless, however, because technology giants have an unanticipated internal vulnerability. Their greatest strength – their highly skilled and talented labor force – may be the only group capable of exerting enough pressure to convince them to improve their most egregious policies. External efforts have failed; it is time to attempt reform from within.

The war for human capital means that skilled employees at large technology companies do not need to lobby for added pay or perks but in fact have substantial potential power to encourage social change from within their companies. The only thing stopping them from doing so (other than their own level of political engagement) is the lack of an organization or structure to help represent their ideals. This is where unions should step into a unique role – to advocate for the betterment of society, not just their own members, and from a position of historical strength, not weakness.[7] This would be an inverted union, focused on the upper echelon of talent at technology corporations, not on contract workers, consumer technology support personnel, or unskilled employees. This structural twist to the vision of unions would be reinforced by the likelihood that their intentions would be embraced and celebrated by society, not viewed skeptically. Such public approbation would give technology unions further leverage in their quest to advocate for more socially responsible policies by their employers on issues such as copyright, Internet freedom, and the

---

[5] For more information on technology unions, see Martin Skladany, *Technology Unions: How Technology Employees Can Advocate for Internet Freedom, Privacy, Intellectual Property Reform, and the Greater Good*, 97 J. PAT. & TRADEMARK OFF. SOC'Y (2016) and, relatedly, M. J. Coren, *Silicon Valley Tech Workers Are Talking about Starting Their First Union in 2017 to Resist Trump*, QUARTZ, (March 24, 2017), https://qz.com/916534. For an example of how governments have unsuccessfully regulated technology firms, see Robert Peston, *Is Government Too Scared of Google, Amazon and Starbucks?*, BBC NEWS (Dec. 3, 2012), www.bbc.com/news/business-20579264.

[6] Juliette Garside, *Google Did Not Lobby Us into Submission, US Trade Watchdog Says*, GUARDIAN (Mar. 26, 2015, 2:49 PM), www.theguardian.com/technology/2015/mar/26/us-fed eral-trade-commission-google-lobbying-accusations; Vanessa Barford & Gerry Holt, *Google, Amazon, Starbucks: The Rise of "Tax Shaming,"* BBC NEWS (May 21, 2013), www.bbc.com/ news/magazine-20560359.

[7] Unlike highly skilled and talented workers with considerable power in technology firms, unskilled workers have seen their bargaining power significantly diminish because of the increased use of robotics in factories, "globalisation, which makes it harder for unions to regulate work, the rise of a more flexible service sector, and government policies" – all of which has coincided with a substantial lull in union membership. *Why Trade Unions Are Declining*, ECONOMIST (Sept. 28, 2015, 8:54 PM), www.economist.com/blogs/economist-exp lains/2015/09/economist-explains-19.

commons and to urge their employers to challenge other entities – from domestic and foreign governments to competitors – that violate such policies.[8]

Another way of conceptualizing the need for technology unions is to situate them within the structural evolution of organizations. When one policy fails to address problems or unmet needs within society, organizations – firms, nonprofits, and unions – typically search for a more effective tool. Given that the problems in need of a new policy are problems that touch on the organizations' missions, the new proposed solutions are consistent with the organizations' goals.[9] Thus, companies lobby for policies that benefit them, unions struggle to advance the position of their workers, and nonprofits advocate not for their own workers or for their own fiscal benefit but for what, in their view, is best for society.[10]

Yet simply changing policies within existing organizations might not be enough to tackle social ills or unaddressed needs. Rather, what might be needed in certain situations is a new form of organization. This is either because the goals of the existing organizations are inconsistent with addressing the societal need or because a new form of organization would more effectively tackle the problem. This switch in thinking from policy experimentation to structural experimentation acknowledges that how an organization is structured – its membership, size, legal designation, access to resources, ability to engage with other entities, and goals – can impede or increase its effectiveness. Thus, for example, a mélange of the corporate and union forms can be seen in

---

[8] *See generally* James P. Nehf, *Recognizing the Societal Value in Information Privacy*, 78 WASH. L. REV. 1 (2003); SANJA KELLY, MADELINE EARP, LAURA REED, ADRIAN SHAHBAZ, & MAI TRUONG, FREEDOM HOUSE, FREEDOM ON THE NET 2014: SUMMARY OF FINDINGS (2014); and SIVA VAIDHYANATHAN, COPYRIGHTS AND COPYWRONGS: THE RISE OF INTELLECTUAL PROPERTY AND HOW IT THREATENS CREATIVITY (2001).

[9] Of course, organizations can have multiple goals or advocate for goals that are beyond their core mission. For example, it is possible for companies or unions to benefit society tremendously, but their raison d'être is to benefit shareholders and union members, not to advocate for policies that benefit society first and foremost. Thus, sometimes what companies lobby for aligns with the campaigns of nonprofits. *See, e.g.*, Kyle Peterson & Marc Pfitzer, *Lobbying for Good*, STAN. SOC. INNOVATION REV., Winter 2009, at 44, 44–49. Also, unions often fight for policies that not only benefit their members but also might help society at large. *See, e.g.*, Donna Brazile, *What Have Unions Done for Us?*, CNN (Sept. 4, 2012, 8:03 AM), www.cnn .com/2012/09/04/opinion/brazile-unions/.

[10] *See, e.g.*, John Hasnas, *Lobbying & Self-Defense*, 12 GEO. J.L. & PUB. POL'Y 391 (2014); Vincent R. Johnson, *Regulating Lobbyists: Law, Ethics, and Public Policy*, 16 CORNELL J.L. & PUB. POL'Y 1, 37 (2006); Ellen J. Dannin, *Cooperation, Conflict, or Coercion: Using Empirical Evidence to Assess Labor Management Cooperation*, 19 MICH. J. INT'L L. 873, 926 (1998); and John Morgan & Veronica Sandoval, *Pacific Northwest Perspective: The Impact of the America Invents Act on Nonprofit Global Health Organizations*, 9 WASH. J.L. TECH. & ARTS 177, 185–86 (2014).

age-old collectives and cooperatives, and the corporate and nonprofit forms have combined to create social entrepreneurship.[11] These organizational hybrids not only mix structural forms but can also alter the goal or purpose commonly associated with traditional forms such as nonprofits, firms, and unions.

Technology unions are an addition to these innovations in organizational structure – they would create a new hybrid between unions and nonprofits. Their sole function would be to advance policies to benefit society, though, unlike nonprofits, technology unions would take a union form and be associated with a corporation in the sense that its members would be employees.

Technology unions could make a substantial difference because the companies they would be negotiating with are formidable by many measures – e.g., Facebook has more than 1.4 billion users around the world, Apple sits on more than $170 billion in cash, and Google runs more than 3.5 billion searches a day.[12] Further, these companies provide important services to users around the world – numerous ways to connect with individuals and communities, search for and share information and news, learn, buy, and create. Finally, these companies have considerable political leverage in Washington, DC.[13]

Attempts have been made to unionize unskilled workers at technology giants and to prevent technology firms from using subcontracted low-wage workers, and at least one association has been created to help unionize contract workers at technology companies. However, all of these efforts have employed the standard approach to unionization.[14] For example, at least two different unions have attempted to unionize Amazon workers. The Washington Alliance of Technology Workers targeted "customer service workers at Amazon's corporate headquarters in Seattle," and the United Food and Commercial Workers International Union distributed "union authorization cards in an attempt to organize Amazon workers at distribution centers" across

[11] *See generally* Jennifer Dasari, Frank Vargas, & Michael Vargas, *Recognizing Social Entrepreneurship: Minnesota Embraces the Public Benefit Corporation*, 71 BENCH & B. MINN. 18 (2014).

[12] *Company Info*, FACEBOOK, http://newsroom.fb.com/company-info/ (last visited July 23, 2015); Paul R. La Monica, *Apple Has Mind-Boggling $178 Billion in Cash to Spend*, CNN MONEY (Jan. 29, 2015, 5:52 AM), http://money.cnn.com/2015/01/28/investing/apple-cash-178-billion/; and *Google Search Statistics*, INTERNET LIVE STATS, www.internetlivestats.com/google-search-statistics/ (last visited July 23, 2015).

[13] Tony Romm, *Tech Giants Get Deeper into D.C. Influence Game*, POLITICO (Jan. 21, 2015, 6:49 PM), www.politico.com/story/2015/01/tech-lobby-apple-amazon-facebook-google-114468.

[14] Llewellyn Hinkes-Jones, *Why IT Workers Should Unionize*, ATLANTIC (June 21, 2011), www.theatlantic.com/technology/archive/2011/06/why-it-workers-should-unionize/240810/ (arguing that information technology workers should unionize for improvements in their own working conditions and job security).

the country.[15] These unions alleged that Amazon workers were "concerned about job security, wages, mandatory over-time, and 'worthless' stock options."[16] The focus of technology unions would differ significantly from such traditional union efforts in two fundamental ways. First, technology unions would aim to foment collective action among highly skilled and talented technology workers such as programmers, scientists, and engineers, not individuals working in unskilled jobs such as at call centers and warehouses. Second, technology unions would fight to change the policies of their employers that negatively affect society, not to improve wages, benefits, or working conditions.

In theory, the only issues that might limit the ability of a company's employees to effectively establish a technology union are whether the employees have substantial bargaining power and adequate employment benefits and whether the company's products or services touch on important societal concerns. Thus, highly skilled employees at pharmaceutical firms, robotics firms, hospitals, universities, and possibly even military firms could form such unions.

As with traditional unions, technology unions could use numerous tools, including negotiating in private with their company or using the prospect of going public as an incentive for their firm to alter its course. Moreover, the interactions between technology unions and their respective companies do not always have to be confrontational – e.g., technology unions could hold internal debates on policy issues with company executives in front of employees and could come together with their companies to lobby more effectively for responsible social practices.

Benefits

The creation of technology unions could have numerous benefits for society and for technology firms.

The potential societal benefits could range across a vast spectrum of policies, depending on the research and development priorities of and products or services offered by technology firms. The list of benefits could be further expanded to include technology or intellectual property issues that do not directly touch on one particular firm's focus but that nonetheless could be potentially improved by lobbying efforts on behalf of society by the firm vis-à-

---

[15] Hinkes-Jones also suggests that "[o]ut of the approximate 3,000,000 tech workers in the United States, maybe 5,000 in total are union members." *Id.* This estimate includes members of the Washington Alliance of Technology Workers. *Id.* Many of these 5,000 are contract or temporary workers. *Union Activity Across the Country*, 5 No. 8 PAC. EMP. L. LETTER 6, 6 (2001).

[16] *Id.*

vis government or competitors. Thus, benefits could arise with regard to the Internet, communications regulation, privacy, intellectual property, pharmaceuticals, robotics, and artificial intelligence. Simply taking one field as an example to demonstrate the number of topics where technology unions could possibly make a difference, a sampling of robotic concerns include creating proper government and industry oversight regulations, stemming potential significant job losses in the future, attempting to ensure the efficacy of autonomous military killing machines, and more existential apprehensions.[17] Plus there are a host of other non-technology-related public policy issues in need of improvement, including the control of human capital, government transparency and accountability, improper supervision of foreign subcontractors regarding labor practices, insufficient wages for unskilled employees or employees of subcontractors, and non-technological issues such as tax minimization.[18]

Given that technology firms touch on many of the most important aspects of our lives from how we access information or lifesaving drugs to how we communicate, learn, and work, it is understandable that there is a vast policy space within which technology unions could operate.

Technology unions could also significantly benefit corporations. First, if the advent of technology unions causes firms to listen to their employees more, even if out of necessity, firms could reap the benefits of higher productivity from more engaged employees – e.g., employees who want to contribute to teams have been shown to be more creative and to catch more

---

[17] See generally Ryan Calo, *Robotics and the Lessons of Cyberlaw*, 103 CALIF. L. REV. 513 (2015); Aviva Hope Rutkin, *Report Suggests Nearly Half of U.S. Jobs Are Vulnerable to Computerization*, MIT TECH. REV. (Sept. 12, 2013), www.technologyreview.com/s/519241/re port-suggests-nearly-half-of-us-jobs-are-vulnerable-to-computerization/; Jens David Ohlin, *The Combatant's Stance: Autonomous Weapons on the Battlefield*, 92 INT'L L. STUD. 1 (2016); and Samuel Gibbs, *Apple Co-Founder Steve Wozniak Says Humans Will Be Robots' Pets*, GUARDIAN (June 25, 2015, 8:42 AM), www.theguardian.com/technology/2015/jun/25/ap ple-co-founder-steve-wozniak-says-humans-will-be-robots-pets.

[18] See generally Orly Lobel, *The New Cognitive Property: Human Capital Law and the Reach of Intellectual Property*, 93 TEX. L. REV. 789 (2015); Jennifer Shkabatur, *Transparency with(out) Accountability: Open Government in the United States*, 31 YALE L. & POL'Y REV. 79 (2012); Mary LaFrance, *Steam Shovels and Lipstick: Trademarks, Greed, and the Public Domain*, 6 NEV. L.J. 447 (2005–06); Michael Kan, *Low Wages, Long Hours Persist at iPhone Factory, Says Labor Group*, CNET (Oct. 22, 2015, 1:14 AM), www.cnet.com/news/low-wages-and-long-hours-still-persist-at-iphone-factory-claims-labor-group/; Josh Harkinson, *Google's Low-Wage Contract Workers Are Poised to Unionize*, MOTHER JONES (July 27, 2015, 5:08 PM), www.m otherjones.com/politics/2015/07/google-low-wage-contract-workers-union; and Jesse Drucker, *Google 2.4% Rate Shows How $60 Billion Is Lost to Tax Loopholes*, BLOOMBERG (Oct. 21, 2010, 6:00 AM), www.bloomberg.com/news/2010–10-21/google-2-4-rate-shows-how-60-billion-u-s-re venue-lost-to-tax-loopholes.html/.

mistakes.[19] Further, employees who feel as if their employer hears what they say could demonstrate not only greater motivation but also more job satisfaction and loyalty, making the company more likely to attract and retain top talent.

Second, technology giants could raise consumer perceptions of their brands not only by adopting the recommendations of technology unions but also by negotiating with the unions in good faith.[20] Moreover, they could enhance their profitability as well as their reputation because the unions would fight for societal causes that are widely popular, and consumers are more likely to trust a company and purchase its product or service after being assured that their privacy is protected and that the company is fighting for the greater good.[21]

Technology unions and technology giants could reach numerous mutually beneficial accommodations if firms realize that it is in their best interest to not overly antagonize their valued and possibly irreplaceable employees. Confrontation will be unavoidable, yet it can be spirited and reasonable. Further, both sides will need to compromise. Finally, the forms and types of concessions and collaboration in such negotiations are almost infinite and allow for creative, mutually beneficial progress.

The Structure of Technology Unions

Governed by the National Labor Relations Act (NLRA) and enforced by the National Labor Relations Board (NLRB), federal labor law is one of the most highly centralized legal regimes.[22] Yet this centralized labor law regime is

---

[19]   *See generally* Susan Sorenson, *How Employee Engagement Drives Growth*, GALLUP: BUS. J. (June 20, 2013), www.gallup.com/businessjournal/163130/employee-engagement-drives-growt h.aspx.

[20]   *See generally* Ilana Tyler-Rubinstein, *How to Improve Trust in Business? Look beyond Profits*, IPSOS MORI (Jan. 22, 2015), www.ipsos-mori.com/newsevents/blogs/makingsenseofsociety/162 8/How-to-improve-trust-in-business-Look-beyond-profits.aspx ("Only a third [34 percent] of the general public would trust business leaders to tell the truth, while more than half [57 percent] would not."); Jacquelyn Smith, *The World's Most Reputable Companies*, FORBES (June 7, 2012, 12:02 AM), www.forbes.com/sites/jacquelynsmith/2012/06/07/the-worlds-most-reputable-compa nies/ ("'People's willingness to buy, recommend, work for, and invest in a company is driven 60 percent by their perceptions of the company and only 40 percent by their perceptions of their products.'") (quoting Kasper Ulf Nielsen, executive partner of Reputation Institute).

[21]   *See generally* Rafael Laguna, *Comcast, Time Warner, and Verizon Should Fight the NSA to Engender Trust among Their Users*, PANDO (Nov. 22, 2013), https://pando.com/2013/11/22/com cast-time-warner-verizon-should-fight-the-nsa-to-engender-trust-among-their-users/.

[22]   National Labor Relations Act, 29 U.S.C. §§ 151–169 (2006). I will use "NLRA" to designate the 1935 Act as amended on two separate occasions, in 1947 and 1959. Also, I will use the term "labor law" to refer to the federal law governing the topic, not state law, which generally relates to public sector unions at the state or local level. Further, I will generally exclude public sector unions from the discussion.

widely viewed today as ineffective in fulfilling its mission – assisting employees in their efforts to collectivize.[23]

Beyond the NLRA's inability to effectively prevent companies from taking illicit action in more than a dozen different forms against any organizing efforts before a union election, such as dismissing employees for their attempts to unionize, federal labor law and the NLRB are also ineffectual in assisting employees after a majority have successfully voted to establish a union. For example, roughly 50 percent of newly recognized unions are unable to "persuade the employer to agree to a collective bargaining agreement" because employers have significant incentives to stall negotiations or refuse to bargain in good faith.[24] Unfortunately, the NLRB does not have the "power to remedy even the most egregious cases of refusal to bargain in good faith, except to order the recalcitrant party to bargain more."[25]

Furthermore, the NLRA's broad jurisdiction and preemptive powers over state and local labor laws have aggravated the law's difficulty in keeping up with societal transformations because the one source of legislative improvements – Congress – has failed to take into account how the evolution from an industrial age to an information age has affected the nature of jobs.[26] In essence, numerous employers find the costs of illegally infringing employees' rights to attempt to unionize to be inconsequential relative to the advantages of squashing union attempts, even if accomplished through illicit means.[27] Further, "private rights of action under the NLRA simply do not exist."[28] Numerous scholars have articulated reform proposals to alleviate the significant limitations to the NLRA, yet there has been no substantial improvement.[29] Fortunately, the NLRA's ineffectualness has not

---

[23]   See generally Cynthia L. Estlund, *The Ossification of American Labor Law*, 102 COLUM. L. REV. 1527 (2002).

[24]   Catherine L. Fisk & Adam R. Pulver, *First Contract Arbitration and the Employee Free Choice Act*, 70 LA. L. REV. 47, 47 (2009).

[25]   *Id.*

[26]   See generally KATHERINE V. W. STONE, FROM WIDGETS TO DIGITS: EMPLOYMENT REGULATION FOR THE CHANGING WORKPLACE (2004).

[27]   See generally Paul C. Weiler, *Hard Times for Unions: Challenging Times for Scholars*, 58 U. CHI. L. REV. 1015 (1991) (responding to Robert J. LaLonde & Bernard D. Meltzer, *Hard Times for Unions: Another Look at the Significance of Employer Illegalities*, 58 U. CHI. L. REV. 953 [1991], which itself is a response to Paul C. Weiler, *Promises to Keep: Securing Workers' Rights to Self-Organization Under the NLRA*, 96 HARV. L. REV. 1769 [1983]).

[28]   James J. Brudney, *The National Labor Relations Board in Comparative Context: Isolated and Politicized: The NLRB's Uncertain Future*, 26 COMP. LAB. L. & POL'Y J. 221, 233 (2005).

[29]   Zev J. Eigen & Sandro Garofalo, *Less Is More: A Case for Structural Reform of the National Labor Relations Board*, 98 MINN. L. REV. 1879 (2014).

prevented the growth of novel efforts at unionization that circumvent the act's reach.[30]

One such innovation involves completely disregarding federal labor law and seeking voluntary, private labor agreements with companies regarding union organizing campaigns and subsequent recognition of any union that successfully emerges from such a campaign with the support of a majority of employees.[31] Specifically this entails employees and their employers setting up their own mutually agreed-upon rules for how a union campaign should proceed through contract law – i.e., it is a private re-creation of the super-structure or legal framework of the NLRA and NLRB.[32] When employees agree to such an arrangement, they consciously give up the statutory protections provided to them by the NLRA because they believe such protections are inconsequential at best and harmful at worst. Unlike the one-size-fits-all NLRA regime, private labor agreements can take almost any form because they are voluntary contracts between two parties.[33]

Technology unions should adopt the voluntary, private labor agreement model instead of the traditional NLRA union form not only because it is more appropriate for the circumstances but also because the traditional union form is unavailable to them. First, from the employees' perspective, the major purpose of technology unions is to better align the policies of their employer with their own individual views of social justice and freedom. This is significant to the programmers, scientists, and engineers employed by technology giants because they create the projects integral to the company. Thus, the employees are seeking a greater partnership with their employer to ensure their creations are appropriately deployed by senior management.[34]

[30] Benjamin I. Sachs, *Labor Law Renewal*, 1 Harv. L. & Pol'y Rev. 375, 376 (2007).
[31] Such contracts are legally enforceable as the NLRA positively affirms such voluntary arrangements. *See* 29 U.S.C. § 185 (2006).
[32] Employees and their employer do not necessarily have to disregard all of the NLRA but can still agree to privately modify its rules. Most prominently this involves consenting to a "neutrality agreement" while pursuing an NLRA union election campaign. *See generally* George N. Davies, *Neutrality Agreements: Basic Principles of Enforcement and Available Remedies*, 16 Lab. Law. 215 (2000).
[33] For example, instead of employees and employers agreeing to a card check regime, they can sign a pact to hold a privately conducted election to determine if a majority of employees desire to form a union. *See generally* Charles I. Cohen, *Neutrality Agreements: Will the NLRB Sanction Its Own Obsolescence?*, 16 Lab. Law. 201 (2000).
[34] Each technology giant could have its own technology union – e.g., Google Union, Facebook Union, Twitter Union, Microsoft Union. Over time it would be beneficial to create an umbrella association of different technology unions so that coordination among them could be improved. Such an umbrella association would also encourage friendly competition among technology unions. Such competition could even be formalized into league tables that compare how enlightened technology companies are.

Voluntary, privately negotiated labor agreements are more suitable because they would likely lead to a less hostile relationship between the parties. Not having to be concerned with federal labor law restrictions on a host of issues such as the form of the union or how voting and negotiation to establish the union should take place would create more room for amicable compromise.[35]

Second, some though not all programmers, engineers, scientists, and other skilled workers at technology giants will be unable to qualify for the protections to collectively organize under the NLRA.[36] The reasoning for such exclusion is that the NLRB has defined "supervisors" with a wide scope and all supervisors are explicitly left out of the NLRA's grasp.[37] The NLRA defines a supervisor as someone who has "authority, in the interest of the employer, to hire, transfer, suspend, lay off, recall, promote, discharge, assign, reward, or discipline other employees, or responsibly to direct them, or to adjust their grievances, or effectively to recommend such action, if in connection with the foregoing the exercise of such authority is not of a merely routine or clerical nature, but requires the use of independent judgment."[38] Workers who use "independent judgment" to "responsibly direct" others for a small fraction of their time at work (as little as 10 percent) may be deemed supervisors.[39] Given the nature of skilled work at technology giants – significant collaboration among peers with team members sharing supervisory roles – skilled workers at technology giants should strategically opt for privately contracted voluntary labor agreements with their employers.[40]

---

[35]   Another possible advantage of having technology unions rely on voluntary, privately negotiated labor agreements instead of the NLRA is that a technology union might not qualify as a "labor organization" under federal law, which defines the term to mean "any organization of any kind, or any agency or employee representation committee or plan, in which employees participate and which exists for the purpose, in whole or in part, of dealing with employers concerning grievances, labor disputes, wages, rates of pay, hours of employment, or conditions of work." 29 U.S.C. § 152(5) (2006).

[36]   *See generally* Bashar H. Malkawi, *Labor and Management Relationships in the Twenty-First Century: The Employee/Supervisor Dichotomy*, 12 N.Y. City L. Rev. 1 (2008).

[37]   29 U.S.C. § 152(11).   [38]   *Id.*

[39]   Oakwood Healthcare, Inc., 348 N.L.R.B. 37 (2006). *Oakwood Healthcare* and two other decisions – *Croft Metals* and *Golden Crest Healthcare* – are known as the "Kentucky River Trilogy," given they were all issued in 2006 after the Supreme Court case NLRB v. Ky. River Cmty. Care, Inc., 532 U.S. 706 (2001). Croft Metals, 348 N.L.R.B. 38 (2006); Golden Crest Healthcare, 348 N.L.R.B. 39 (2006).

[40]   Under the NLRA, if a majority of workers in a bargaining unit vote to establish a union, the new union will represent all of the employees within the bargaining unit, regardless of the fact that some of the employees did not vote affirmatively. Since technology unions would not operate under the NLRA, this rule need not apply, and its omission is in line with the spirit of technology unions. Given that technology unions will engage in collective bargaining not to improve wages and benefits but rather to revise company policies that touch on social or

A potential alternative to technology unions would be a less formal association of skilled workers within a technology firm. Such an alliance would still seek to improve the social ramifications of the company's policies but through more informal and less public channels. An alliance of skilled workers at an Uber or a Snapchat would have less clout on issues such as collection of dues, use of certain advocacy tools, and whether to negotiate a voluntary, private understanding with the employer.

A technology alliance would have some potential benefits over a technology union, including being simpler to form without opposition from the firm and possibly having an easier time gaining members, yet without the formal negotiation framework vis-à-vis the company, such an alliance would not give the appearance of an equal partner.[41]

One potential concern with the creation of a technology alliance instead of a technology union is that the less official structure would not give members enough clout to achieve significant change. A technology union would command a stronger voice in internal negotiations but also externally if it makes a case for policy change to the public. Furthermore, a technology union would likely provide more legal and career protection to members than a technology alliance in case the relationship between the workers and the employer became adversarial. Plus, a technology union would be on stronger footing and less easily pressured by a technology giant into acquiescing on any particular organizational policy or disagreement.

Finally, a technology alliance could not legally include unskilled workers, but a technology union could potentially decide to open its doors to all workers at a particular technology giant. This is because the technology union would have an official structure, and the NLRA does not allow a firm to "dominate or interfere with the formation or administration of any labor organization."[42] Since the NLRA applies to unskilled workers but not to programmers, scientists, and engineers if they are deemed to be supervisors, the NLRB would not oppose the formation of a technology alliance; however, the alliance's

---

political issues, forcing all skilled workers at a technology giant to join the union, even if some are opposed to the union's policy stances, would be counterproductive to all parties. Thus, voluntary membership should be an intuitively appealing approach not only to employees but also to employers. 29 U.S.C. § 159 (2006).

[41] A poll of workers found that 45 percent stated they desired a union (a "strongly independent workplace organization"), while 43 percent desired a more informal association (an "organization with more limited independence from management"). RICHARD B. FREEMAN & JOEL ROGERS, WHAT WORKERS WANT 35 (1999).

[42] James Sherk, *How to Give Workers a Voice without Making Them Join a Union*, ATLANTIC (Mar. 11, 2014), www.theatlantic.com/politics/archive/2014/03/how-to-give-workers-a-voice-wit hout-making-them-join-a-union/284328/.

inclusion of unskilled workers would potentially prompt the NLRB to shutter its doors.

Potential Limitations

Conceivably, a technology firm could view any effort by its employees to unionize in order to advocate for better company policies on a range of societal issues as an expression of ingratitude, a threat to the company's bottom line, or a provocation akin to war. Even if a company's corporate leadership has any or all of these views, it does not necessarily follow that the firm would retaliate. Yet, given the history of how corporations have responded to traditional unionization efforts in the past, it would not be surprising if technology firms took aggressive measures. Even recent events suggest this could likely transpire at some technology firms – e.g., Apple, Adobe, Google, and Intel settled a lawsuit for allegedly illicitly refusing to hire workers from each other's companies in order to prevent a talent bidding war.[43]

Companies could possibly respond with a host of legal or illegal retaliatory measures, including threatening to close a division or group, firing employees, discharging supervisors, surveillance, violence, interrogation, reducing wages and benefits, outsourcing jobs, holding captive audience meetings, calling the police, hiring anti-union consultants, and assisting anti-union committees.[44] A company can also reply with numerous different types of lawsuits using antitrust law or defamation law.[45] A particularly aggressive form of retaliation is to bring a lawsuit "alleging a pattern of unlawfully extortionate activities under the Racketeer Influenced and Corrupt Organizations Act ('RICO')."[46]

Even if technology giants have a mountain of available methods to disincentivize employees from creating technology unions, they may determine that it is not in their best interest to deploy any of them. For example, employers have acknowledged that they have numerous economic incentives to not oppose a neutrality agreement and/or card check procedures and to allow employees to attempt to unionize without anti-union corporate

---

[43] Jeff John Roberts, *Tech Workers Will Get Average of $5,770 under Final Anti-Poaching Settlement*, FORTUNE (Sept. 3, 2015), http://fortune.com/2015/09/03/koh-anti-poach-order/.

[44] Kate L. Bronfenbrenner, *Employer Behavior in Certification Elections and First-Contract Campaigns: Implications for Labor Law Reform*, in RESTORING THE PROMISE OF AMERICAN LABOR LAW 80–82 (Sheldon Friedman et al. eds., 1994).

[45] *See generally* Daralyn J. Durie & Mark A. Lemley, Comment, *The Antitrust Liability of Labor Unions for Anticompetitive Litigation*, 80 CALIF. L. REV. 757 (1992).

[46] James J. Brudney, *Collateral Conflict: Employer Claims of RICO Extortion against Union Comprehensive Campaigns*, 83 S. CAL. L. REV. 731, 733 (2010).

pressure.[47] Some surveyed firms admitted that they did not want to have to deal with the possibility of diminished profits or loss of goodwill if employees attempted numerous strategies associated with comprehensive union campaigns.[48] Even Google was recently successfully pressured into increasing the wages of security guards through a public shaming campaign.[49]

Further, technology firms are much less likely to retaliate than a nontechnology firm because they cannot afford to drive away a significant number of highly skilled and talented employees who are in such short supply. Even if employees at technology companies are not once-in-a-generation geniuses, they are still incredibly valuable contributors, especially when the contributions of all the union members are aggregated. Technology firms would be quite shortsighted if they retaliated against the reasonable demands of hundreds or thousands of such talented employees. Even the recent scheming of Apple, Adobe, Google, and Intel to prevent a talent bidding war is a significant acknowledgment that technology giants realize how incredibly valuable their skilled employees are. It is an affirmation that employee contributions are so integral to the success of technology companies that retaliation instead of constructive negotiation would be foolish.

A second concern is corporate preemption or co-option. At the first sign of possible unionization, a technology company might quickly alter a few of its policies to bring them more in line with what its employees would be advocating for, in order to preempt the creation of a technology union. Other possible forms of preemption include offering better benefits, creating an in-house group to explore how corporate policies affect society but designing it to move slowly and go nowhere, or establishing internal or external publicity efforts to mask the firm's unenlightened policies by highlighting its enlightened policies.

It is not beyond the pale that at least some technology firms would attempt to employ one or more of these preemption or co-option strategies. It is difficult to gauge how successful such strategies would be in averting the creation of a technology union at any particular technology firm. While some employees might view such preemption attempts suspiciously or even

---

47   *See generally* ADRIENNE E. EATON & JILL KRIESKY, *Dancing with the Smoke Monster: Employer Motivations for Negotiating Neutrality and Card Check Agreements, in* JUSTICE ON THE JOB: PERSPECTIVES ON THE EROSION OF COLLECTIVE BARGAINING IN THE UNITED STATES 139 (Richard N. Block et al. eds., 2006).
48   *Id.*
49   Kevin Montgomery, *Google Shamed into Paying Their Security Guards a Living Wage,* VALLEYWAG (Oct. 3, 2014, 12:20 PM), http://valleywag.gawker.com/google-shamed-into-pay ing-their-security-guards-a-livin-1642110689.

be offended by them, depending on how obvious or superficial they are, the company's tactics could make other employees less inclined to push for a technology union. Thus, such preemption efforts may do harm in terms of reducing the long-term positive impact technology unions can have, but it is impossible to determine how much harm with any certainty before efforts to create technology unions begin in earnest. That said, even if some attempts to establish technology unions fail because of such strategies, all such attempts will not be deterred.

A potential third concern is that employees have a lack of political awareness. For various reasons, employees might either not be politically informed or not have the time or interest to pursue policies aimed at improving social justice and freedom. One possible scenario is that employees are overly consumed with work, which is, at times, either genuinely believed to be a badge of honor or, at least, publicized as such.[50] Another possibility is that they prefer to spend time with family or friends. Alternatively, technology employees might simply want to pursue outside interests or side projects within their field of expertise, such as open source or collaborative programming or scientific projects – e.g., Linux or Wikipedia.[51]

A skeptic might ask why handsomely paid employees would risk confronting their employers. The only possible answer is that fighting for justice and helping others are integral components of most conceptions of the good life, bringing not only a sense of purpose but also a sense of humility and fulfillment to individuals. Furthermore, employees' lobbying could begin to dispel the belief that "collaboration" is merely corporate jargon and that all employees except for top executives have little say in the decisions of firms.[52] Ultimately, the political activism of technology employees could empower other workers to voice their concerns and ideas and to organize – especially knowledge workers, who "see themselves as equal to those who retain their services, as 'professionals' rather than as 'employees.'"[53]

Finally, some employees of technology companies might share their employer's views on policies that harm society. Ultimately, given the sheer

---

[50] *See generally* Drake Baer, *The Many Reasons Long Hours Are Awful for You, Your Work, and Your Clients*, FAST COMPANY (Nov. 11, 2013, 5:30 AM), www.fastcompany.com/3021408/lea dership-now/the-many-reasons-long-hours-are-awful-for-you-your-work-and-your-clients.

[51] *See generally* James Grimmelmann, *The Virtues of Moderation*, 17 YALE J.L. & TECH. 42 (2015).

[52] See Ned Smith, *If You Listen Up, Your Employees Will Step Up*, BUS. NEWS DAILY (Jan. 19, 2012, 2:18 PM), www.businessnewsdaily.com/1934-leadership-listening-employee-input-initia tive.html.

[53] Peter Drucker, *The New Workforce*, ECONOMIST (Nov. 1, 2001), www.economist.com/node/770847.

number of employees at technology giants, it is likely that any large firm would employ a mixture of individuals with a range of opinions and that the greater number of employees would lean significantly toward the policies discussed here. This is because it is commonly understood that programmers, scientists, and engineers at technology giants widely share certain basic assumptions, foremost of which is that information wants to be free.[54] From this basic axiom, many of the policies earlier discussed – such as a more robust commons, net neutrality, less restrictive intellectual property policies, and greater access to lifesaving drugs in developing countries – can be derived.

Furthermore, it is irrelevant whether some employees share the same stance on the rightness or wrongness of each policy a company pursues. Technology unions are meant to allow employees to advocate for policies benefiting society, irrespective of whether some employees at the same firm disagree and side with weakening privacy protections, restricting the public domain, and hampering Internet freedom.

Cynthia Estlund suggests that collective bargaining is capable of being more effective than legislation in terms of governing labor law because collective bargaining is decentralized and "potentially flexible, responsive to local conditions and to changing needs, cooperative, and democratic."[55] Given technology giants' apparent immunity to legislative and regulatory attempts to hem in their more suspect policies, it is time to see if Estlund's vision of the superiority of collective bargaining over legislation in the labor law context can hold in the realm of nonlabor law policies – i.e., if technology unions, unlike regulatory and legislative efforts, can succeed in reforming technology giants.

Gregory Ferenstein recently averred:

> Unions may be quite valuable in other parts of the country, but they haven't been needed much in the Valley. Despite having no union, Facebook, Google and other tech companies are consistently voted the "best" companies to work for in America. Cushy salaries, luxurious dining amenities, and decentralized management structures provide an elite class of high-tech workers all the benefits and influence that unions have long hoped for.[56]

---

[54] See generally Hinkes-Jones, supra note 14, and R. Polk Wagner, Information Wants to Be Free: Intellectual Property and the Mythologies of Control, 103 COLUM. L. REV. 995 (2003).

[55] CYNTHIA ESTLUND, REGOVERNING THE WORKPLACE: FROM SELF-REGULATION TO CO-REGULATION 136 (2010).

[56] Gregory Ferenstein, Why Labor Unions and Silicon Valley Aren't Friends, in Two Charts, TECH CRUNCH (July 29, 2013), http://techcrunch.com/2013/07/29/why-labor-unions-and-silicon-valley-arent-friends-in-2-charts/.

While technology giants provide stimulating work and generous benefits to their most talented and skilled employees, this does not negate a role for unions to do well within technology firms. By modifying the traditional union form, technology unions can focus their efforts on improving social justice and freedom through advocating for improved policies at their firms.

COPYRIGHT TROLLING CONGRESS

Patent trolling justifiably has a bad name. In essence, it is when shell companies, who are not commercially exploiting discoveries that they hold a patent on, are set up for the sole purpose of suing other companies actually producing stuff consumers want. In 2013, President Obama suggested patent trolls, or more euphemistically "patent assertion entities," are "just trying to essentially leverage and hijack somebody else's idea and see if they can extort some money out of them."[57] The practice verges on extortion because when a productive business is threatened with a patent infringement suit, its calculus often suggests quickly settling rather than fighting the baseless or close-to-baseless threat. The legitimate company will often conclude that the legal costs of a full trial will be much more expensive than a settlement, and a loss at trial, however remote the risk, could be financially devastating.

The practice of patent trolling is far from obscure. In 2012, the government estimated that patent trolls mailed in excess of 100,000 demand letters, "threatening everyone from Fortune 500 companies to corner coffee shops and even regular consumers to pay a settlement or face a day in court."[58] In 2015, more than 5,700 patent infringement cases were brought of which 67 percent were deemed to be from patent trolls.[59] Patent trolls "cost defendant firms $29 billion per year in direct out-of-pocket costs; in aggregate, patent litigation destroys over $60 billion in firm wealth each year."[60] Furthermore, the damages awarded at present are at all-time highs. The average damage amount in a patent lawsuit was roughly "$50,000 (in today's dollars) at the time [of] the telegraph," while today the average damage award runs "about $21 million."[61]

---

[57] Gene Sperling, *Taking on Patent Trolls to Protect American Innovation*, WHITE HOUSE (June 4, 2013), www.whitehouse.gov/blog/2013/06/04/taking-patent-trolls-protect-american-innovation.

[58] *Id.*

[59] *2015 Patent Dispute Report*, UNIFIED PATENTS (Dec. 31, 2015), www.unifiedpatents.com/news/2016/5/30/2015-patent-dispute-report.

[60] James Bessen, *The Evidence Is In: Patent Trolls Do Hurt Innovation*, HARV. BUS. REV. (Nov. 2014), https://hbr.org/2014/07/the-evidence-is-in-patent-trolls-do-hurt-innovation.

[61] *Id.*

In May 2017, the Supreme Court effectively put an end to patent troll plaintiffs making a habit of strategically suing others in the Eastern District of Texas, where 44 percent of all US patent litigation was filed in 2015 because of the favorable trial conditions.[62] While forum shopping was expected to be significantly curtailed as a result, companies had already become so frustrated by such tactics that they had donated substantial funds to cities in the Eastern District of Texas to shape potential future jurors' opinions. For example, Samsung famously gave the city of Marshall an outdoor ice skating rink.[63] Samsung even put its name on a Marshall tradition – the "Samsung Holiday Celebration Show" that opened the annual "Wonderland of Lights Festival," featuring 250,000 lights draped over the historic courthouse.[64]

The practice of trolling has also relatively recently spread to the world of copyright, where it mirrors the activity in the patent world. A lawyer, law firm, or company aims to acquire an exclusive copyright license or have a copyright assigned to it not in order to commercially exploit the work itself but rather with the express purpose of suing others who may or may not have potentially infringed the work.[65] One example of such "mass copyright litigation" was when the US Copyright Group filed "predatory lawsuits implicating thousands of unnamed John Does, subpoena[ed] their identities from the ISP's, and then sue[d] the individuals themselves" for having supposedly illegally downloaded certain films from BitTorrent.[66] The same approach to copyright trolling can be applied to stocks of photographs or any work of authorship, including software and pornography, where the copyright owner is also hoping to threaten potential defendants with the possible embarrassment of having their identities disclosed.

---

[62]   TC Heartland LLC v. Kraft Foods Group Brands LLC, No. 16–341, slip op. (May 22, 2017), www.supremecourt.gov/opinions/16pdf/16–341_8n59.pdf. The statistics come from *2015 Patent Dispute Report*, UNIFIED PATENTS (Dec. 31, 2015), www.unifiedpatents.com/news/2 016/5/30/2015-patent-dispute-report.

[63]   Bruce Berman, *For Samsung Charity Begins at "Home,"* Marshall, Texas, IP CLOSEUP (Feb. 25, 2015), https://ipcloseup.com/2015/02/25/for-samsung-charity-begins-at-home-mar shall-texas/.

[64]   *27th Annual Wonderland of Lights Festival Begins with Samsung Holiday Celebration Show*, MY EAST TEXAS (Nov. 21, 2013), http://myetx.com/27th-annual-wonderland-of-lights-festival-begins-with-samsung-holiday-celebration-show/.

[65]   *Copyright Trolls*, ELECTRONIC FRONTIER FOUND., www.eff.org/issues/copyright-trolls (last visited Mar. 26, 2017). The entity can also approach copyright owners offering to collect damages on their behalf from consumers who allegedly illicitly downloaded their works. *Id.* *See also* Shyamkrishna Balganesh, *The Uneasy Case against Copyright Trolls*, 86 S. CAL. L. REV. 723 (2013), and James DeBriyn, *Shedding Light on Copyright Trolls: An Analysis of Mass Copyright Litigation in the Age of the Statutory Damages*, 19 UCLA ENT. L. REV. 79 (2012).

[66]   The US Copyright Group's efforts did not go far. *Copyright Trolls, supra* note 65.

It is time to take this practice of ill repute and turn it on its head. We should be copyright trolling Congress so our lawmakers can experience firsthand how copyright protection has gotten out of hand. The purpose of such an endeavor would be to make them rethink their stance on excessive copyright – to understand how difficult it is to not violate copyrighted works given the extreme legal overprotection they have enabled.[67]

Advocates for a more robust public domain and a reasonable copyright regime need to create a nonprofit organization that would research potential copyright violations by members of Congress and also field suggestions from individuals as to instances of possible copyright infringement by congresspeople. The nonprofit would be looking for any use of digital images, video, music, or written text in a congressperson's communications with the public that might have infringed the works of others instead of simply being a fair use. The nonprofit would then attempt to obtain the copyright or an exclusive license in the work in order to sue the congressperson. Even if the nonprofit does not acquire the copyright or license, it could publicize the potential infringement to alert the congressperson that the actual copyright owner could sue her.

Unlike most copyright trolls who brush aside fair use considerations in their haste to sue others, the nonprofit should attempt to determine, to the best of its judgment, whether the congressperson's use of another's artwork was in fact an instance of fair use. Furthermore, the nonprofit should see if any copyright exemptions apply. For example, did the congressperson read another's poem in a religious setting or within a classroom, where such performance is allowed, as opposed to during a fundraising speech?[68]

Also, any nonprofit that copyright trolls congresspeople would have to be cognizant of the limits to copyright infringement presented by the Speech or Debate Clause of the Constitution.[69] This clause immunizes congresspeople from liability for any words spoken, reports or proposed legislation presented, or votes cast within the walls of Congress and for speech that is essential to the deliberations of Congress.[70] Such limitation is meant to promote free speech by preventing the intimidation of members of Congress through threats of litigation for defamation or libel. Its conception dates back to the struggle between monarch and parliament in pre–Glorious

---

[67] Though the federal government can be held liable for copyright violations, targeting individual congresspeople would make more sense than going after the government itself because congresspeople would feel the sting of a copyright infringement suit more acutely than a federal bureaucracy funded by taxpayer money would. 28 U.S.C. § 1498(b).

[68] 17 U.S.C. § 110.   [69] U.S. CONST. art. I, § 6, cl. 1.

[70] Kilbourn v. Thompson, 103 U.S. 168 (1881).

Revolution Britain. While such protection is fundamental to our separation of powers, a wide range of speech lies unprotected from potential copyright infringement suits or other claims. For example, a congressperson who distributed a "Golden Fleece of the Month Award" press release highlighting wasteful spending by a government employee would not be shielded against a defamation suit.[71]

The copyright trolling nonprofit could even broaden its victim base to possibly include the policy staffers of senators and representatives as well as other high-ranking government officials in the legislative, executive, and judicial branches. The nonprofit might consider whether it is appropriate to copyright troll family members and friends of congresspeople. This might be wildly out of bounds, but Congress bears sole responsibility for having created the legal system that has enabled copyright (and patent) trolls to operate on such questionable ethical grounds. Additionally, even mainstream content holders, such as the recording industry, have done worse, attacking the parents and grandparents of little kids who arguably ran afoul of copyright laws. In one instance, the Motion Picture Association of America sued a grandfather for $600,000 because his visiting twelve-year-old grandchild downloaded four movies from a file-sharing site, even though his family already legally owned copies of three of the movies.[72] It did not matter that it was clear to everyone what had happened – that the potential infringement was that of the child, not the grandfather. The recording industry did not flinch because its strategy, at the time, was to instill fear into the general consuming public. Admittedly, the recording industry ultimately recognized that its actions were so beyond the pale that it ended this sue-everyone-regardless-of-the-clear-circumstances strategy. Yet other members of Big Copyright, such as large photo agencies, continue similar practices to this day. In 2016, Carol Highsmith, a photographer, was sent a threatening letter by an affiliate of Getty Images that claimed she violated the copyright in her own photo. She decided to fight back, suing Getty Images for more than $1 billion in damages, "accusing the agency of illicitly claiming rights to 18,755 of her photographs."[73]

---

[71] Hutchinson v. Proxmire, 443 U.S. 111 (1979).

[72] *Grandpa Is Sued over Grandson's Downloads*, USA TODAY (Nov. 2, 2005), http://usatoday30 .usatoday.com/tech/news/techpolicy/business/2005-11-02-grandpa-movie-download_x.htm? csp=34.

[73] Michael Hiltzik, *Photographer Sues Getty Images for $1 Billion after She's Billed for Her Own Photo*, L.A. TIMES (July 29, 2016, 1:15 PM), www.latimes.com/business/hiltzik/la-fi-hiltzik-g etty-copyright-20160729-snap-story.html.

There is a story that President Lyndon Johnson, well before ascending to the presidency, instructed his campaign manager in a Texas race to start a false rumor that his political opponent was sleeping with barnyard animals. When his aide said that no one would believe it, Johnson replied, "But let's make the son-of-a-bitch deny it."[74] Given the mud-slinging nature of politics, a potential concern of this proposal is that warning congresspeople that they could be sued is not enough; only actual lawsuits will bring home the point. This understandable concern could be overcome by actually suing the members of Congress for copyright infringement. Since Congress has created such a punishing remedial regime for copyright infringement – where one willful, illicit copy of a poem or photo could bring up to $150,000 in statutory damages even if the illicit use caused actual economic damages of only $10 – hardened congresspeople would likely take any such suit seriously. The statutory damages provisions they enacted could threaten to financially ruin them, just as they have savagely punished individual citizens. For example, if one could prove that a congressperson copied a ten-song musical album in an illicit manner, she could be liable for $1.5 million in statutory damages if each song counts as a separate $150,000 instance of copyright infringement.

A second potential concern is that antagonizing congresspeople might upset them more than convince them. In essence, the idea could backfire. Yet there are good reasons to believe that it would not. An advocacy nonprofit is effectively immune from counterpressure tactics – i.e., is not a fellow congressperson who can be frozen out of information or punished internally. More important, the copyright lawsuits would be quite public and embarrassing, and retaliation would be ill-advised from a public relations standpoint. A counterattack would not impress voters any more than Governor Christie's bridge closure scandal did. Rather, it is more likely that some congresspeople will finally understand that the current copyright law needs to be pared back significantly because of the difficulties that artists face trying to create without borrowing. Finally, even if some congresspeople attempted to get even, it is not clear how they could by skewing copyright law even further, given how unbalanced it already is. None of this guarantees that a congressperson would not respond irrationally and simply strike back out of anger, yet it does significantly dampen the concern that congresspeople would be quick to retaliate.

---

[74] Jack Shepherd, *This Hunter S. Thompson Passage Is Particularly Poignant in Light of That David Cameron and the Pig Story*, INDEPENDENT (Sept. 21, 2015, 10:40 BST), www.indepen dent.co.uk/arts-entertainment/books/news/this-hunter-s-thompson-passage-is-particularly-poi gnant-in-light-of-that-david-cameron-and-the-pig-10510787.html.

RECUSEMENT BY ROYALTIES

When Supreme Court justices can make millions – ten to twenty times their annual salary – through royalties on one book, they need to be encouraged to either (1) recuse themselves from copyright cases if they have authored any copyrighted works that generate significant royalties or (2) donate all of their royalties to charity on any work they have authored or may author in the future that generates such extraordinary returns.

If federal judicial recusal rules require judges to recuse themselves from a case involving a company that they directly hold stock in, then recusement, for example, from a case disputing the length of copyright by a justice who has earned anything substantial from her work, let alone more than $3 million as an advance on one autobiography, seems equally appropriate.[75] I am not claiming that the Code of Conduct for United States Judges, the American Bar Association's Model Code of Judicial Conduct, Title 28 of the US Code on Judiciary and Judicial Procedure, the Constitution's Due Process Clause, or any other existing rule necessarily compels this perspective.

These two things might seem completely distinct – a justice having a personal stake in a particular case through a connection to the parties versus a justice with no ties to the parties possibly benefiting from a garden-variety dispute of a general legal principle. Yes, in almost all conceivable scenarios they are, and should remain, distinct. Yet we all know that any boundary's border can become porous – from the well-trodden law school example of a prohibition on vehicles in parks (and asking if bikes or baby strollers qualify as vehicles) to deconstructivist literary and legal work that aims to destabilize boundaries to show how they could be manipulated to advantage the powerful against the powerless.[76] We take an arguably infinitely complex world and attempt to organize it into laws versus social norms, different substantive areas of the law, different forms of regulation – often reasonable endeavors, yet many of the most interesting legal disputes straddle such constructed walls.

The distinction between having a financial stake in one party to a dispute and simply being affected by a change in general legal principle in a case can become so blurred as to lose meaning. The way recusal rules are currently constructed, a judge could conceivably have to recuse herself for holding $100 in a public stock yet be allowed to rule on the constitutionality of a copyright

[75] Royalties can also add significantly to a book advance. Justice Sotomayor's annual government salary is slightly over $200,000. Greg Stohr, *Sotomayor's Book Advances from Knopf Surpass $3 Million*, BLOOMBERG (June 7, 2013), www.bloomberg.com/news/articles/2013–06-07/sotomayor-s-book-advances-from-knopf-surpass-3-million.
[76] See works by Jacques Derrida or Duncan Kennedy, among many others.

reform that could cause her to lose millions in future royalties. While it is unlikely that one change to the copyright laws could cause a justice to lose most of her expected future royalties, the higher the expected advances and royalties, the smaller the change in copyright law that would produce a significant loss of income. We can imagine a copyright payday so extraordinary that it would at the very least create the appearance that the judge's impartiality might be less than bulletproof. Would that sum be the $65 million book advance that Barack and Michelle Obama received for a memoir from each of them?[77] I realize that the argument is more difficult than maintaining our current separation regarding recusal policies for justices, especially since my first instinct is often to maintain legal boundaries, yet copyright law, likely more than any other law for many justices, is responsible for the lion's share of their income.

Furthermore, the existing recusal standards could pass the laughter test in being construed to suggest justices reconsider stepping aside for a copyright case, depending on its substantive content, or donating their royalties if they are substantial. For example, the section of Title 28 of the US Code on Judiciary and Judicial Procedure dealing with disqualification of judges states: "Any justice, judge, or magistrate judge of the United States shall disqualify himself in any proceeding in which his impartiality might reasonably be questioned."[78] It also maintains that a judge should recuse himself not simply when he has a "financial interest in the subject matter in controversy or in a party to the proceeding" but also if he has "any other interest that could be substantially affected by the outcome of the proceeding."[79] These two standards speak to how the line can meaningfully vanish between a justice having a direct financial interest in a party to a dispute and a justice being affected by a change in a general legal principle as the result of the outcome of a case. For the average citizen, potentially losing any part of a future book deal worth $2 to $4 million if a court ruling reduced the excessive copyright laws could be viewed as a "substantially affected" interest, whether specific or general. Plus, it is not ludicrous to think that possibly losing a portion of a multimillion-dollar future book deal could call into question a justice's impartiality.

To avoid bothering with justices' academic articles and their other copyrighted works that generate little or no income, Justice Kennedy's analysis on a recent case could serve as a useful yardstick. In *Caperton v. A.T. Massey Coal*

---

[77] Laura Miller, *Just How Outrageous Is the Obamas' Alleged $65 Million Book Deal?*, SLATE (Mar. 2, 2017, 7:31 AM), www.slate.com/blogs/browbeat/2017/03/02/just_how_outrageous_is_the_obamas_alleged_65_million_book_deal.html. In fact, high-ranking members of the executive and legislative branch along with lower court judges could also be encouraged to donate their royalties.

[78] 28 U.S.C. § 455(a).   [79] 28 U.S.C. § 455(b)(4).

Co., which dealt with a judge who refused to recuse himself from a case even though the litigant had made $3 million in contributions to the judge's election campaign, Justice Kennedy stated that "[t]he inquiry centers on the contribution's relative size in comparison to the total amount of money contributed to the campaign, the total amount spent on the election, and the apparent effect such contribution had on the outcome of the election."[80] Thus, certain copyright cases will only trivially affect justices, if at all, while others could conceivably be viewed differently.

One could argue that pressuring justices who have received significant funds from copyrighted works to recuse themselves from copyright cases will create a slippery slope allowing different advocacy groups to push for recusal on a host of other issues. However, Supreme Court justices have lifetime appointments and hence can simply rebuke any pressure – i.e., they should listen to the arguments for recusal but decide on their own course of action. Further, I am not arguing that justices must recuse themselves but rather that they should do so or donate their royalties to charity.

There is a possibility that justices will attend to this concern, especially since scholars have called for transparency in recusal given the personalized and unreviewable nature of such decisions. In 2011, more than a hundred law professors sent a signed letter to the House and Senate Judiciary Committees "outlining the need for new recusal legislation to protect the integrity of the Supreme Court."[81] The letter urged justices to publicly issue explanations for their recusal decisions and to have the Code of Conduct for United States Judges applied to Supreme Court justices.[82] Virelli argues:

> Critics of the Court's recusal practices argue that the Justices' failure to submit their decision to more traditional legal processes has damaged the integrity and reputation of the Court. The Justices' increasingly publicized involvement in political causes and organizations has highlighted concerns about the fairness and impartiality of the Justices' decisions and has resulted in calls for more stringent ethics and recusal standards.[83]

In recent years, Justices Alito, Breyer, Ginsburg, Sotomayor, and Thomas have all been critiqued for their contacts with politically interested entities that either have been or may come before the Court.[84] If enough

---

[80] Caperton v. A.T. Massey Coal Co., 129 S. Ct. 2252, 2264 (2009).
[81] Louis J. Virelli III, *Congress, the Constitution, and Supreme Court Recusal*, 69 WASH. & LEE L. REV. 1535, 1546 (2012).
[82] *Id.*   [83] *Id.* at 1551.
[84] Louis J. Virelli III, *The (Un)Constitutionality of Supreme Court Recusal Standards*, 2011 WIS. L. REV. 1181, 1182–83 (2011).

light is shed on the matter, the resulting public pressure could reach a tipping point. Chief Justice William H. Rehnquist admitted: "Judges, so long as they are relatively normal human beings, can no more escape being influenced by public opinion in the long run than can people working at other jobs."[85]

I appreciate Judge Kozinski's position that "the more rules you have, the more hoops judges have to jump through to avoid the appearance of impropriety, the more likely they are to feel that the hoop-jumping is the alpha and omega of their ethical responsibilities, and the less likely they are to give careful thought to the job's real ethical pitfalls," such as "[g]iving short shrift to small cases, signing on to the work of staff and calling it my own, bending the law to reach a result I like."[86] I also see Lessig's point that "[w]henever the Court acts to impose a new constraint or new requirement, it must ask both whether the legal materials justify this constraint (fidelity to meaning), and whether the judicial institution can effectively impose it (fidelity to role)."[87] I am not advocating for new legislation, simply urging advocates to attempt to get justices to reconsider their current stance or, more likely, to get them to stop and think about an issue they may not have considered.

We wouldn't expect a judge to recuse herself from cases regarding murder in the abstract simply because of the substantive content of a case – for example, if taking justice into one's own hands is a mitigating factor when the justice system fails victims. However, if yesterday a justice secretly offed a brutal murderer who was acquitted on a technicality, the calculus of recusal changes because now a court case addressing a substantial change in the criminal law could significantly affect the judge's life trajectory, and letting her decide the new appeal is undesirable. This is similar to how we don't allow a judge to hear a case on appeal if she was previously involved as a lawyer or judge on the matter in a lower court. To put it in starker terms: the likelihood of a justice ending up on death row – highly unlikely; the chance that a justice will earn millions on a book deal simply because of her position – more likely than not, if she chooses to write a book. It's time to encourage justices to reconsider their multimillion-dollar payouts that are contingent on going along with Hollywood's capture of Congress.

---

[85] William H. Rehnquist, *Constitutional Law and Public Opinion*, 20 SUFFOLK U. L. REV. 751, 768 (1986) (found in Eric E. Johnson, Law, Science, and Unknown Unknowns 31 [Mar. 14, 2017] [draft paper on file with author]).

[86] Alex Kozinski, *The Real Issues of Judicial Ethics*, 32 HOFSTRA L. REV. 1095, 1105 (2004).

[87] Lawrence Lessig, *What Everybody Knows and What Too Few Accept*, 123 HARV. L. REV. 104, 118 (2009).

COPYRIGHT POISON PILLS

Martin Lipton, a mergers and acquisition partner at the renowned law firm Wachtell, Lipton, Rosen & Katz, wrote a 1979 article on his philosophical and legal approach to hostile takeovers that in the words of Lipton was "ridiculed in academia."[88] Noting that in the 1970s "[w]e had reached a whole new plateau of hostile takeovers, and there was really very little in the way of defense to them," Lipton invented a novel solution to block unwelcomed takeovers: the idea of a shareholder rights plan or corporate "poison pill."[89] While he devised the anti-takeover defense in 1982, it took an additional three years for it to gain popularity, after a 1985 Delaware Supreme Court decision first upheld the innovation.[90]

The poison pill, which is passed by a corporate board, is triggered when a potential acquirer of a firm buys enough shares to breach a predefined threshold, e.g., 10 percent of all outstanding shares. At this point, the poison pill bestows a benefit to all other shareholders, which in practice substantially harms the would-be acquirer.[91] The most common benefit granted to shareholders, besides the potential acquirer, is the opportunity to purchase additional shares equal to their existing holdings at a steep discount. Thus, if all non-bidding shareholders can purchase new stock at 40 percent of the market value, the bidding shareholder's existing stock is substantially diluted. Further, after the poison pill is triggered, the would-be acquirer would have to buy even more shares to obtain enough to force through a buyout. Thus, the poison pill, by diluting the value of the bidder's shares, makes a potential acquisition not worth it financially to hostile bidders.[92]

The essence of the shareholder poison pill – a protective measure to ensure a greedy power play does not materialize – can be transplanted into the world of copyright. In corporate America, poison pills make sense only for companies that are valuable – otherwise there would be little desire to take them over. Thus, to transfer the idea of a poison pill into the artistic world, we have to lure Big Copyright with something shiny. What Hollywood covets is the output of

---

[88] Shira Ovide, *Marty Lipton: Why I Invented the Poison Pill*, WALL ST. J.: DEAL J. (Dec. 29, 2010, 1:33 PM), https://blogs.wsj.com/deals/2010/12/29/marty-lipton-why-i-invented-the-poison-pill/.

[89] *Id.* [90] Unocal Corp. v. Mesa Petroleum Co., 493 A.2d 946 (Del. 1985).

[91] There are numerous variations of a defensive poison pill, some, such as the Dutch Poison Pill, even receiving their own moniker. Leonard Chazen & Peter Werdmuller, *The Dutch Poison Pill: How Is It Different from an American Rights Plan?*, HARV. L. SCH. F. ON CORP. GOVERNANCE & FIN. REG. (Dec. 1, 2015), https://corpgov.law.harvard.edu/2015/12/01/the-dutch-poison-pill-how-is-it-different-from-an-american-rights-plan/.

[92] Christine Hurt, *The Hostile Poison Pill*, 50 U.C. DAVIS L. REV. 137, 147 (2016).

famous artists. Because celebrity artwork is sought after, this minority of well-known artists has economic leverage – unlike their many peers who are not commercially successful but may be every inch as good artistically.

Famous artists should leverage their desirability to demand that a copyright poison pill be inserted into their contracts and licensing agreements. This poison pill would commit Big Copyright to not attempt to influence Congress on copyright issues. If Hollywood, the recording industry, or the publishing world is found to be making campaign contributions or lobbying Congress, the poison pill clause would require the corporate party to forfeit or dilute its copyright interests in the artist's work.

Just as a corporate poison pill would create a substantial financial disincentive to pursue a hostile takeover, a copyright poison pill would create a significant pecuniary impediment dissuading Big Copyright from demanding more favors from Congress. It should go without saying that the copyright poison pill would have to be carefully crafted to prevent Hollywood from finding loopholes. While our immediate impulse might be that such precise drafting is impossible given the innumerable tax-dodging techniques in existence, we should remind ourselves that the corporate poison pill has largely held up to questions about its legitimacy and efforts to undermine it for decades.[93] Thus, the copyright poison pill would have to be carefully designed to prohibit both direct and indirect attempts by Big Copyright to influence Congress on copyright matters. Not only would lobbying efforts on the part of Hollywood employees be circumscribed but also such efforts by hired third parties. This could be challenging since law firm lobbying efforts on behalf of clients would have to be separated, and prohibited, from the legal advice law firms provide their Hollywood clientele, which could continue. Other thorny issues to be addressed include how to handle individual political donations by executives of entertainment companies and how to address personal, private contact between Hollywood executives and members of Congress.

As mentioned earlier, only famous artists who are committed to reducing the harms of excessive copyright protection would be encouraged to insist on copyright poison pills. Some skeptics might argue that this could pose a danger to the artists. For example, either one entertainment company or all of Big Copyright could conceivably retaliate by refusing to work with them. However, the reputation and fame of the artists would enable them to simply find another Big Copyright firm that is willing to accept millions or hundreds

[93] For example, *see generally* Lucian A. Bebchuk & Robert J. Jackson, Jr., *Toward a Constitutional Review of the Poison Pill*, 114 COLUM. L. REV. 1549 (2014).

of millions in additional profits in exchange for walking away from the unreflective assumption that lobbying for added copyright perks should be a central pillar. Putting aside antitrust concerns, if the entire entertainment establishment banded together to blacklist any celebrated artists demanding a copyright poison pill clause, such artists could simply turn to new media companies that desire to break the stranglehold of Big Copyright. Such alternative media companies could include startup book publishers or movie studios. Famous artists could even create their own entertainment companies, as numerous stars, such as Oprah Winfrey and JAY-Z, have successfully done already. In addition to her existing record label, Beyoncé recently announced her intention to establish a TV network in the next decade.[94]

Thus, if famous artists are recruited to insist on copyright poison pills, progress will be made in bringing back reasonableness to the copyright regime, regardless of Big Copyright's response. If some firms acquiesce to the artists' demands, less lobbying would result, which would open up more space for copyright reform that serves citizens, not corporations. Even if all of Big Copyright blacklists such famous artists, the copyright minimalist movement would still win because Big Copyright would take a substantial financial hit – in the form of no longer profiting from the artists – for its reluctance to stop lobbying. To put such a strategy on the part of Big Copyright into perspective, think of the windfall that Taylor Swift alone has made for her recording label or Tom Hanks for Hollywood. Publishers that failed to sign J. K. Rowling did not collapse, yet the mistake of passing on a jackpot was surely deeply felt.

The remaining issue is simply whether any well-known artists would push for copyright poison pills. Some might support stronger copyright even if they are willing to admit that they didn't understand copyright when they became an artist or that they would continue to create without it. There will never be political uniformity on most issues, but there are plenty of artists who understand that the current form of copyright is harmful. Whether these copyright minimalists would fight for change by demanding a copyright poison pill in their own licenses and contracts is difficult to know in the abstract. It is possible that no celebrity artist has ever thought of such a tool for influencing the actions of Big Copyright, so we have to introduce the idea and wait and see.

---

[94] Dan Wootton's Bizarre Column, *Bey-BC Beyonce to Follow in Footsteps of Oprah Winfrey by Creating Own TV Network*, SUN (July 29, 2016, 6:02 PM), www.thesun.co.uk/tvandshow biz/1524139/beyonce-to-follow-in-footsteps-of-oprah-winfrey-by-creating-own-tv-network/ (last updated July 30, 2016, 10:02 AM).

PUBLICIZING THE FOREIGN POLICY COSTS OF COPYRIGHT

A country constantly interacts with other nations. Such contact is on multiple fronts – antiterrorism cooperation, trade negotiations, environmental partnerships, contagious disease prevention monitoring, and so forth. Further, each of these areas of support or conflict has numerous subcomponents. One such area, environmental dealings, reveals interaction in regard to air pollution, climate change, nuclear power, deforestation, etc. Finally, each of these subareas can be further broken down and can overlap with other fronts. For example, nuclear energy issues of international concern include waste disposal, plant safety from potential terrorist attacks, the spread of nuclear weapons knowledge, and so on. I belabor the point to stress the enormous possibilities of weighing these foreign policy considerations against each other in negotiations.

Each country must decide which international interactions are most critical to it and then engage other states to back its vision. To convince other nations to collaborate instead of either retaliating or ignoring its policy priorities, a country must use carrots and sticks. There are a few other policy options such as soft power, yet these are more amorphous, less immediate, or weaker. For example, wining and dining delegates in the present moment might help only on the margins. Since a country cannot expect to constantly wield threats in a credible manner and only has so many positive incentives to hand out before breaking the bank, careful stewardship of both levers of influence is needed.

Excessive copyright protection brings riches to Big Copyright and a group of elite artists at the expense of the rest of the globe. If developing countries truly desired extreme copyright protection, they would have implemented it on their own without the need for other countries to threaten them. Instead, for decades Hollywood has dictated the US government's stance on copyright both domestically and internationally.[95] Hollywood has strong-armed developing countries into acquiescence by lobbying the US government to use trade negotiations to pressure developing countries to adopt ever-more-stringent copyright regimes.[96] In this vein, trade sanctions have been instigated against and trade concessions withheld from developing countries that have not lived up to Hollywood's stringent expectations.[97]

---

[95] Jessica D. Litman, *Copyright, Compromise, and Legislative History*, 72 CORNELL L. REV. 857 (1987).

[96] PETER DRAHOS & JOHN BRAITHWAITE, INFORMATION FEUDALISM: WHO OWNS THE KNOWLEDGE ECONOMY? (2002).

[97] Peter Drahos, *Developing Countries and International Intellectual Property Standard-Setting* (Comm'n on Intell. Prop. Rts., Study Paper No. 8, 2001), www.iprcommission.org/papers/p dfs/study_papers/sp8_drahos_study.pdf.

The pressure the US government places on developing countries to submit to extreme copyright laws not only hurts individuals abroad but also comes at the expense of myriad other foreign policy considerations that would have benefited the entire US public, not simply an elite group of artists and entertainment executives. Foreign policy scholars and practitioners must forcefully and repeatedly articulate to politicians and the general public how ridiculous this approach is.

Up until the 1960s, the Department of State led US trade and investment diplomacy.[98] American corporations were dismayed at the idea that the federal government was granting trade concessions to other nations in exchange for foreign policy objectives it believed were more important to US national security than economic handouts to massive industrial conglomerates. To end this folly of putting the public interest first and corporate pocketbooks second, companies lobbied Congress to change the situation by establishing a Special Representative for Trade Negotiations, later to become the Office of the US Trade Representative. In the words of the USTR, the 1962 Trade Expansion Act (TEA) "reflected Congressional interest in achieving a better balance between competing domestic and international interests in formulating and implementing US trade policy."[99] This is as close as any government bureaucracy will get to admitting that the TEA was meant to end the use of trade concessions as a foreign policy tool and instead make US firms' financial interests paramount in trade negotiations. This was accomplished by putting the responsibility of promoting US trade interests in a stand-alone institution concerned solely with trade, not with the totality of foreign policy interests. This strategy on the part of corporations has been wildly successful, insulating their singular focus on profit maximization from having to be sacrificed for the common good.

To alter our currently perverse stance of extreme copyright promotion across the globe would not necessarily require significant structural changes to our current trade promotion apparatus. Reforms could take numerous forms but would in essence either require the USTR to take into account other issues of national interest or institutionally abolish the office and put trade negotiation matters back into the hands of the State Department.

Our nation needs to stop putting Hollywood and Big Business first. We need to publicize the foreign policy costs of exporting our unwanted extreme copyright laws. We must get Congress to end the insanity of wasting our

---

[98] *History of the United States Trade Representative*, OFF. U.S. TRADE REPRESENTATIVE, https://ustr.gov/about-us/history (last visited Feb. 1, 2017).

[99] *Id.*

limited policy levers coercing developing countries into enacting ever-greater copyright protection. Instead, our nation should be using trade concessions to advance important public policy issues.

NATIONAL SECURITY COPYRIGHT TASK FORCE

In planning for the long-term security of our nation, US military leaders attempt not only to isolate every potential external threat but also to identify any internal weaknesses in preparedness. Yet foreign concerns get the lion's share of media attention. We are apprised of multiple aspects of terrorism on a seemingly daily basis – from which countries are funding or hosting terrorists to their methods of recruitment to their social media presence to their methods of weaponizing different vehicles like drones or trucks. We hear about dictators to such an extent that we know details of their personal lives and some of their proclivities and obsessions. For example, we know that former North Korean leader Kim Jong-il "amassed arguably the world's largest personal film collection" of "over 20,000 bootlegged 35mm screening copies," which, due to the country's "stringent information-control policies, he was the only person in the country authorized to watch."[100] His son and the current leader, Kim Jong-un, was even the subject of a Hollywood movie, titled *The Interview*, which sparked accusations that a foreign entity, possibly the North Korean government, was behind the hacking of Sony Pictures' computer systems in retaliation for the unflattering depiction.[101]

Despite the vivid portrayal of foreign threats in news media, movies, and political rhetoric, the size of the national security apparatus is difficult to comprehend. *The Washington Post* reports: "Some 1,271 government organizations and 1,931 private companies work on programs related to counterterrorism, homeland security and intelligence in about 10,000 locations across the United States."[102] Further, an estimated 854,000 government employees and private contractors hold top-secret security clearances.[103] While not all of these people work directly in the national security space, many of them do.

---

[100] Paul Fischer, *Kim Jong-il and the Great Movie-Star Kidnap*, GUARDIAN (Feb. 21, 2015, 3:00 EST), www.theguardian.com/books/2015/feb/21/kim-jong-il-movie-star-kidnap-plot-north-so uth-korea-godzilla.

[101] *North Korea Berates Obama over* The Interview *Release*, BBC NEWS (Dec. 27, 2014), www.bbc.com/news/world-asia-30608179.

[102] Dana Priest & William M. Arkin, *A Hidden World, Growing beyond Control*, WASH. POST: TOP SECRET AM. (July 19, 2010, 4:50 PM), http://projects.washingtonpost.com/top-secret-a merica/articles/a-hidden-world-growing-beyond-control/.

[103] *Id.*

To put this whopping number of individuals with top-secret security clearances in perspective: Google employs 57,000 workers, while Facebook pays a mere 13,000.[104] In fact, the world's largest private employer is Walmart with 2.1 million employees globally, though it comes in third place if one includes public bureaucracies.[105] The US Department of Defense tops the worldwide list at 3.2 million employees, followed by the People's Liberation Army in China at 2.3 million.[106] The United States has so many individuals working in national security that if all those with top-secret clearances worked for the same employer, it would be one of the largest employers in the world. There are more people working in the US national security space than people living in all of Boston (636,000), Seattle (634,000), or Washington, DC (632,000).[107] The vast size of the national security framework should enable it to explore an impressive number of issues in depth, including how copyright laws affect national security.

Governments should establish copyright task forces as part of their national security apparatus to address how an excessive copyright regime adversely affects issues of national security. As mentioned previously, we should no longer be willing to pander to Big Copyright by offering concessions on national security and other issues in exchange for other countries agreeing to accept greater copyright protections.[108]

In the United States, the sedentary lifestyle abetted by our addiction to Hollywood entertainment has affected military recruitment. Tellingly, retired US military officers issued a public call to arms against providing unhealthy food to students in public schools because of their concern that obesity in young adults makes it more challenging for different branches of the military to recruit highly qualified soldiers. Our military leaders should also be concerned that excessive screen time is tied to higher obesity

[104] Julie Bort, *Google's Hiring May Have Slowed, but It's Still Adding Thousands of New Employees*, Bus. INSIDER (July 17, 2015, 12:28 PM), www.businessinsider.com/google-has-5 7000-employees-2015-7, and *Number of Facebook Employees from 2004 to 2015 (Full-Time)*, STATISTA, www.statista.com/statistics/273563/number-of-facebook-employees/ (last visited Nov. 17, 2016).

[105] Niall McCarthy, *The World's Biggest Employers*, FORBES (June 23, 2015, 8:20 AM), www.fo rbes.com/sites/niallmccarthy/2015/06/23/the-worlds-biggest-employers-infographic/ #16839c6851do.

[106] *Id.*

[107] *The Largest US Cities: Cities Ranked 1 to 100*, CITY MAYORS STAT., www.citymayors.com/ gratis/uscities_100.html (last visited Nov. 16, 2016).

[108] For the opposite perspective, see Maureen K. Ohlhausen & Dan Schneider, *Intellectual Property and the National Security Issue*, WASH. TIMES (Dec. 1, 2015), www.washingtontimes.com/news/2015/dec/1/maureen-ohlhausen-dan-schneider-intellec tual-prope/.

rates.[109] Overconsumption of corporate entertainment limits physical activity and, more often than not, does little to increase intellectual acuity,
knowledge, or skills. While some video games such as flight simulators
can prove educational, we must curtail excessive screen time to increase
the pool of potential recruits. Thus, the military establishment should
consider innovative ways to counter Hollywood's enthrallment of children
and young adults through excessive copyright.

In addition to supporting our military's ability to recruit qualified
soldiers, a national security copyright task force could initiate research
into the ways in which imposing excessive copyright protections on
other countries harms global stability and peace. Doing so would reveal
other national security reasons for reforming copyright to reasonable
standards.

In the field of intellectual property, most publicity on the harmful effects
of stringent IP protection of US exports to developing countries has focused
on patents for agricultural products and lifesaving drugs.[110] While the Access
to Knowledge movement has fought back against Big Copyright by attempting to open up access to informational material such as textbooks, it has not
recognized the value of greater access to entertainment for citizens in
developing countries or how developed countries might also benefit in the
long term if citizens in developing countries consumed more artwork.[111]
While Hollywood artwork is quite variable and at times far from ideal, it
often implicitly or explicitly communicates valuable messages of human
rights, equality, and freedom that studies have shown to be quite powerful.
For example, Robert Jensen and Emily Oster examined the consequences of
introducing cable television in villages in rural India on the status of women.
In the span of months, they observed not only significant improvements
in women's perceptions of themselves but also substantial behavioral

---

[109]   *Television Watching and "Sit Time,"* OBESITY PREVENTION SOURCE (Harvard University T.
        H. Chan School of Public Health), www.hsph.harvard.edu/obesity-prevention-source/obe
        sity-causes/television-and-sedentary-behavior-and-obesity/ (last visited Aug. 16, 2017).
[110]   Dan Hunter, *Culture War,* 83 TEX. L. REV. 1105, 1116–17 (2005).
[111]   My argument is that we need dramatically less copyright in both rich and poor countries yet
        for different reasons. In developed countries, we need less to stop the flood of polished new
        entertainment from taking over consumers' lives, while in developing countries, less copyright
        is desirable to help increase the flow of ideas such as human rights and gender equality. There
        is little risk of overconsumption in developing countries on the scale found in developed ones.
        Further, if history is precedent, in developing countries the entertainment does not have to be
        new, since parts of these countries are still media dark. For information on A2K, *see generally*
        ACCESS TO KNOWLEDGE IN THE AGE OF INTELLECTUAL PROPERTY (Gaëlle Krikorian &
        Amy Kapczynski eds., 2010).

progress – e.g., women being more assertive in advocating to educate their daughters, not just their sons.[112]

By restricting access to art among the poor in developing countries, excessive copyright protection also harms US security. If the introduction of developed or developing artwork to Indian villages can have such a rapid and robust impact on conceptions of women, imagine the promise for having human rights further internalized across the globe simply through greater access to entertainment and other media. Given the secret nature of our national security apparatus, it is difficult to know if this lesson has been forgotten. Yet this approach must have been on policy planners' minds when they created Radio Free America and Radio Liberty, a CIA-financed group specifically targeting the former Soviet empire.[113] For example, a branch of Radio Liberty secretly gave away copies of banned books such as Vladimir Nabokov's *Pnin* and George Orwell's *Animal Farm* for decades, to the likes of Svetlana Stalina, the daughter of the late Soviet tyrant, and Alexander Solzhenitsyn, the dissident Russian novelist. In at least one scholar's views, such a "Marshall plan for the mind" performed a "decisive role, by contributing . . . to the West's ideological victory. They did so at a relatively low financial cost and without loss of lives."[114] This example comes from a point in time when Hollywood did not yet equate with multinationals and copyright was largely an afterthought.

Today, China fully understands the potential liberating power of ideas and words – just look at their massive anti-free speech big brother censorship machine. Plus, China's state broadcaster, Central China TV, recently announced plans to rebrand its international networks and online content to gain a greater international audience.[115] President Xi congratulated the effort to "tell China's story well, spread China's voice well, let the world know a three-dimensional, colorful China, and showcase China's role as a builder of world peace."[116]

---

[112] Robert Jensen & Emily Oster, *The Power of TV: Cable Television and Women's Status in India*, 124 Q. J. ECON. 1057, 1059 (2009).

[113] It is hard to know what the national security apparatus is doing in this space given the practice of classifying government records for decades. As for Radio Liberty's efforts, see Adam Bernstein, *Isaac Patch, Who Led CIA-Financed Program to Distribute Books in the Soviet Union, Dies*, WASH. POST (June 9, 2014), www.washingtonpost.com/entertainment/books/is aac-patch-who-led-cia-financed-program-to-distribute-books-in-the-soviet-union-dies/2014/06 /09/3aea5fe2-efdc-11e3-9ebc-2ee6f81ed217_story.html?utm_term=.0db5bb9ec95b.

[114] *Id.* (citing ALFRED A. REISCH, HOT BOOKS IN THE COLD WAR [2013]; the Marshall plan quip is from John P. C. Matthews).

[115] AP, *China State Broadcaster Rebrands in International Push*, CNBC (Dec. 31, 2016, 5:41 AM), www.cnbc.com/2016/12/31/china-state-broadcaster-rebrands-in-international-push.html.

[116] *Id.*

The security benefits to the United States would be clear – democracies that aspire to human rights do not go to war with each other.[117] Whether or not such a long-term goal could be realized globally, it would be a significant gain to get more individuals in developing countries to support ideas such as equality and freedom rather than disdain them as Western poison meant to weaken their country. Greater access to entertainment will not guarantee this switch, but less access will not help facilitate it. Further, while excessive copyright protection may be secondary in importance to the need for tools such as Internet service in developing countries, both are barriers that should be addressed.[118]

Thus, there are at least two fronts in the fight to increase access to art in developing countries: first, in poor countries where conceptions such as gender equality are not widely held but the wider spread of artwork is not a political issue, and second, in dictatorships where the free flow of art is deemed an overt offense against the state. The first would immediately improve through relaxing copyright laws, while the second would require a more complex approach beyond copyright reform in order to get the art in the hands of citizens.[119]

The military could even consider paying Hollywood to make custom artwork with subtle targeted messages about gender equality to be freely distributed to individuals in "media dark" swathes in developing countries – compensation that would be in exchange for weakened copyright protection domestically or internationally. We have done this to undermine political dictators and communism. Dictators have retaliated in kind. For example, Kim Jong-il kidnapped "two of South Korea's biggest film names and forced them to shoot pro-North versions of foreign hits, including a communist Godzilla."[120] This may have been a lesson he learned when he began his

---

[117] For a discussion of democratic peace, *see generally* Michael W. Doyle, *Liberalism and World Politics*, 80 AM. POL. SCI. REV. 1151 (1986).

[118] Also, access to different forms of content is limited by access to such tools. For example, Global Voices Online (GVO) is an Internet-based "citizen media community dedicated to amplifying independent online voices from outside North America and Western Europe." The editorial team helps "curate and translate the best blogs and other online citizen media in their countries and regions." GVO aims to help "more communities who are generally underrepresented in media coverage to get their voices heard through blogging, podcasting, and online sharing of videos and images." *Global Voices*, BERKMAN KLEIN CTR. FOR INTERNET & SOC. HARV. U., https://cyber.harvard.edu/research/globalvoicesonline# (last visited Feb. 5, 2017).

[119] *See generally* Martin Skladany, *The Revolutionary Influence of Low Enlightenment: Weakening Copyright in Developing Countries to Improve Respect for Human Rights and the Rule of Law*, 95 J. PAT. & TRADEMARK OFF. SOC'Y 285 (2013).

[120] Fischer, *supra* note 100.

political career in 1968 as the "head of the state's propaganda and agitation department, the main organ of which was the film studios."[121]

There is precedent for such a national security copyright task force. In 1982, the President's National Security Telecommunications Advisory Committee under the auspices of the Department of Homeland Security was established. Its mission is to provide guidance on the availability, reliability, and security of communication networks. Specific issues it has addressed include commercial satellite survivability, intrusion detection, emergency communications, and cybersecurity. The committee comprises executives from the telecommunications and military industries, including Apple, AT&T, Intel, Lockheed Martin, Raytheon, and Verizon.[122] Unlike this advisory panel of private sector individuals with vested interests in the field of telecommunications, a copyright task force would comprise government officials who can look objectively at the harms to national security that our excessive copyright regime poses.

One could reasonably be concerned that military personnel maintain the historic neutrality of the military and avoid publicly expressing their beliefs on domestic matters.[123] It is telling that retired, not active duty, military officers authored the press release voicing concerns about obesity in children and young adults. Yet creating a national security copyright task force does not have to breach the policy of neutrality. Rather than publicizing their opinions, military personnel could advise Congress, the president, and others within government on how they believe a particular domestic or nonmilitary international policy harms their ability to protect the country.

Currently, we are not only sacrificing foreign policy interests by bartering them away for greater copyright protection abroad; we are actively harming our national security through the negative effects of excessive copyright both domestically and abroad. The national security and military establishment should examine these issues and use its considerable weight to counterbalance the lobbying efforts of Big Copyright.

A copyright task force would not have to be composed solely of government employees – i.e., an internal unit within a federal agency. An agency task force could work in tandem with an outside advisory group comprising academics,

121 *Id.*
122 *Fact Sheet*, President's Nat'l Security Telecomm. Advisory Committee (Dec. 2016), www.dhs.gov/sites/default/files/publications/NSTAC%20Fact%20Sheet%20%2812-14-16%29-%20508%20Compliant.pdf. There is also a Homeland Security Information Network Advisory Committee, which was established in 2006.
123 *See generally* Bruce Ackerman, The Decline and Fall of the American Republic (2010).

nonprofit analysts, and others. Finally, similar task forces studying the effects of excessive copyright could be set up for other federal institutions such as the Department of State, the US Agency for International Development, and the US Copyright Office, which amazingly appears to have no advisory panel of outside experts.[124] Similar advisory boards of copyright scholars and public advocacy nonprofit directors could be constructively set up for international institutions such as the Organisation for Economic Co-operation and Development, the United Nations Development Programme, and the World Bank.

There are a plethora of advisory groups to governmental institutions. The Department of State has close to two dozen such groups of external experts to counsel on a wide spectrum of international law issues.[125] The US Federal Advisory Committee Act database allows individuals to search for existing advisory groups to government entities. Users can search by more than 150 different interest areas to see how many different advisory committees exist on a particular topic. A search for "Railroads" results in twenty-one committees, "Mining and Minerals" yields twenty-four, and "Grazing Areas" generates twenty-seven. Copyright law does not even get its own interest area, let alone register dozens of advisory committees.

The national security apparatus needs to follow suit. An advisory group of academics advising the military could act as a modest counterweight to Hollywood's army of lobbyists.

BOLSTERING INSTITUTIONAL SUPPORT FOR THE PUBLIC DOMAIN

The public domain is a critical component of our culture. It is the intangible equivalent of public parks, the highway system, and water systems. The public domain provides us the intellectual space and infrastructure to help us imagine and create. It contains our language, thoughts, discoveries, ideas, and art – our cultural heritage to the extent that it has escaped or been freed from the clutches of copyright. The public domain enables us to freely learn and borrow from the past – from authors and artists who themselves relied on previous authors and artists. It is Newton's formulation of Bernard of Chartres's expression, which was possibly borrowed from another earlier source: "If I have seen further it is by standing on the shoulders of

---

[124] Chairman Bob Goodlatte, H.R. Judiciary Committee, *Reform of the U.S. Copyright Office*, https://judiciary.house.gov/wp-content/uploads/2016/12/Copyright-Reform.pdf.
[125] *Advisory Groups*, U.S. DEP'T ST., www.state.gov/r/pa/ei/rls/dos/160060.htm (last visited Feb. 6, 2017).

Giants."[126] Of course, many have borrowed this expression since – most recently Google Scholar and Stephen Hawking along with dozens of others.

The physical commons – e.g., shared grazing lands, fisheries, and water – have been subject to intense study in order to avoid the tragedy of the commons.[127] This is the view that without law, resources that are collectively managed but not privately owned will be overused until they are depleted. While some peasants and citizens have overused such resources, many communities have not. As David Bollier, a respected advocate of the commons, states, "Two billion people around the world manage" shared physical resources "to meet their everyday needs."[128] In fact, the most dramatic devastation of such treasures may have occurred at the hands of powerful interest groups – e.g., multinational companies across the globe polluting our air, land, and water with abandon.

Our intellectual commons is presently experiencing a similar crisis, yet despite the billions that have been spent attempting to protect our physical commons from overuse and the scholarly recognition that the issue has received from award-granting institutions such as the Nobel Prize committees, the public domain has largely been an afterthought. Given the nature of the intellectual commons, overgrazing is impossible. The existential threat to the public domain is enclosure – restricting access to our cultural heritage by granting ever-greater copyright protection to the powerful. History provides precedent. As James Boyle illuminates, the gentry of England took the public grazing lands of the commoners for themselves by capturing Parliament. The aristocracy's justification was that they were protecting the land from the commoners' inevitable proclivity to abuse community custom. As an anonymous poem from this first enclosure movement states:

> The law locks up the man or woman,
> Who steals the goose from off the common,
> But leaves the greater villain loose,
> Who steals the common from off the goose.[129]

---

[126] Lotus Dev. Corp. v. Paperback Software Int'l, 740 F. Supp. 37, 77 n.3 (D. Mass. 1990) (quoting Isaac Newton).

[127] Garrett Hardin, *The Tragedy of the Commons*, Sci., Dec. 13, 1968, at 1243, www.scien cemag.org/site/feature/misc/webfeat/sotp/pdfs/162–3859-1243.pdf.

[128] David Bollier, Think Like a Commoner: A Short Introduction to the Life of the Commons 2 (2014).

[129] James Boyle, *The Second Enclosure Movement and the Construction of the Public Domain*, 66 Law & Contemp. Probs. 33, 33 (2003), and James Boyle, The Public Domain: Enclosing the Commons of the Mind (2008) (while not arguing for a government institution devoted to protecting the public domain, Boyle explains that a portion of the environmental movement's success was attributed to the creation of institutions such as Greenpeace).

Big Copyright has successfully enclosed our common culture – it has bought and brainwashed politicians to enact and extend legislation that prevents existing creations from falling into the public domain and makes almost any new creation subject to private ownership.

In one of the earliest formulations of the need for a groundswell of support to protect the public domain, the intellectual commons was compared to the environment.[130] Both provide invaluable, free benefits to everyone – the public domain enables our culture, while the environment enables our existence. Environmental activists realized that they needed to not only continue their own efforts but also agitate for the creation of a governmental watchdog to help oversee the environment. Their efforts came to fruition in 1970, with the establishment of the US Environmental Protection Agency (EPA).

Today, at the micro level, the idea of protecting the environment is so ingrained in many individuals that it is a reflexive, natural response. When we finish our bottle of soda or beer, we turn our heads in hopes of locating a recycling bin. At the macro level, the national tenor regarding environmental protection has also fundamentally shifted. Our government is no longer satisfied that it properly disposed of dangerous pathogens such as anthrax by simply putting them in glass jars and burying them in a field next to Fort Detrick. We have banned some toxic insecticides, and through regulation we encourage power plants to put air pollution scrubbers on top of exhaust stacks. While we fiercely debate how we should create energy for 7 billion individuals, few of us think it a good idea to legally allow nuclear facilities to sprinkle waste across any part of the earth, not even their own privately owned patches. No politician would say that there should be absolutely no rules against throwing whatever you want into a river or lake. Many individuals and organizations prefer renewable energy such as wind and solar to natural gas, while most of us recognize that using natural gas produces significantly less pollution than burning coal.

Without trivializing the vast differences of opinion on certain environmental policies, collectively we humans appreciate the value of the environment more than we did in the 1960s. We accept that without protection, we all suffer. The elite within developing countries and middle-income countries recognize this with their feet and wallets. For example, some of the wealthy in China do not trust that their domestic food sources are not polluted, so they import not just bottled water but milk from Australia. They send their kids to

---

[130]   See generally James Boyle, A Politics of Intellectual Property: Environmentalism for the Net?, 47 DUKE L.J. 87 (1997).

universities in the United States, Canada, and Europe not only because of the quality of the education and reputation of the schools but because they want their kids to breathe clean air. The coverage of the Beijing Olympics made this palpable to everyone.

As we have seen, Big Copyright has cultivated Congress for decades through expensive lobbying, political contributions, and sophisticated propaganda. Hollywood has given congresspeople every incentive to believe that they are doing the work of America, ensuring maximal creativity, and expanding the economy to its fullest without ever giving the public domain a moment's thought. Since civil society is not nearly as well funded as Hollywood and is much more diffuse, countervailing forces need to be cultivated. Big Copyright has Congress; the public domain needs at least a modest office within a small federal agency. Someone within government needs to explicitly protect the public domain on a full-time basis. Someone within government has to fight to expand it. Someone needs to counter the narrative Big Copyright has spun for years about copyright.[131] We need a federal government institution – a Department of the Public Domain (DPD).[132]

At some point before the creation of the EPA, the idea of Congress establishing a bureaucracy to protect the environment might have sounded at best incredibly naive. To many doing the same for the public domain might sound ridiculous. Politically, it may be at this point. Yet this shouldn't stop us from mobilizing broad and robust action to coalesce into a powerful movement that demands copyright reform and aims to create another bureaucratic acronym. If the EPA attempts to prevent multinational corporations from swamping our environment with toxic pollution, the DPD needs to be established to prevent Big Copyright from flooding our culture with polished, addictive, entertaining stuff.

If we cannot initially successfully advocate for an entire agency devoted to the protection of the public domain, we should demand a public domain

---

[131] There is an academic Center for the Study of the Public Domain at Duke Law School. It was the first such university-based organization in the world centering on the protection of the public domain. *About*, Ctr. for Study Pub. Domain, https://law.duke.edu/cspd/about/.

[132] Thomas Folsom calls for a public domain protection agency in an entirely different context. The purpose of his new agency is to provide reduced, patent-like protection to obvious but valuable inventions. *See generally* Thomas C. Folsom, *Designing Food, Owning the Cornucopia: What the Patented Peanut Butter & Jelly Sandwich Might Teach about GMOs, Modified Foods, the Replicator and Non-Scarcity Economics*, 8 Akron Intell. Prop. J. 53 (2015). Similarly within the realm of patents is the Public Patent Foundation, an organization dedicated to protecting "the public domain from being recaptured in new patents through both litigation and the filing of requests for re-examination with the PTO." *Protecting the Public Domain*, Pub. Patent Found., www.pubpat.org/Protecting.htm (last visited Aug. 16, 2017).

defender's office (PDDO) that would fight for distributive justice within our culture, just as we increase the chances that criminal justice is done by having a public defender's office.[133] A PDDO might not even require formal authorization. The Copyright Office or possibly the Justice Department or the National Science Foundation could reassign a handful of attorneys to a newly established internal PDDO to defend and advocate for the digital commons.

The DPD or PDDO could help raise awareness of not just the existence of the public domain but also how important it is to our culture. Further, it could highlight steps individuals can take that are the equivalent of recycling and not driving a Hummer, such as affixing the Creative Commons' CC0 license (no rights reserved) on works they create.

The DPD could also help federal agencies more clearly publicize how their work is in the public domain; convince companies and nonprofits to not overreach in their copyright claims; perform research on issues relevant to the public domain; litigate copyright issues – e.g., when entities deceitfully assert ownership over works in the public domain; prevent any attempts by individuals to obtain exclusive control over works in the public domain through non-copyright regulations; advance solutions to the copyright orphan works problem; and attempt to harmonize the public domains in different countries so that when a work falls into the public domain in its country of origin, it is also in the public domain in every other country in the world.[134]

In addition to a domestic agency looking after the public domain, we need an international organization to do the same, just as the establishment of the United Nations Environmental Programme in 1972 followed the creation of the US EPA.[135] While no institution is perfect, the public domain needs all the advocates it can get, including on the international level. Given that Big Copyright already has its own sympathetic international agency, the World Intellectual Property Organization (WIPO), having an international presence for the public domain is even more important to counterbalance WIPO's working assumptions, such as their belief that locking up creations until seventy years after the death of the artist is socially beneficial instead of destructive to individuals' ability to create.

---

[133] I would like to thank Tim Schnabel for the idea of formulating a PDDO within the Copyright Office.

[134] See general recommendations 4, 5, 6, and 3, respectively, in the Public Domain Manifesto, www.publicdomainmanifesto.org/manifesto.html (last visited Mar. 17, 2017).

[135] *Background*, UNEP FIN. INITIATIVE, www.unepfi.org/about/background/ (last visited Aug. 16, 2017).

Of course, the public servants at WIPO most likely possess a range of opinions as to whether copyright law is excessive both domestically and internationally and, if so, how excessive. Yet the WIPO leadership, just like Congress, has been cultivated by Hollywood into believing simple assumptions about protecting artwork. The more-stuff-is-always-better assumption is compelling as long as one doesn't think about consequences. If WIPO officials have doubts about the efficacy of excessive copyright, they probably do not want to rock the boat. Or, more likely, such freethinking individuals are screened out beforehand as leaders select who ascends the heights of the WIPO hierarchy.

A newly minted United Nations Public Domain Programme (UNPDP) could support the commons in ways similar to a domestic agency or a division within the US Copyright Office with the same mission.[136] Furthermore, an international organization tasked with advocating for the public domain could continue a United Nations tradition of convincing celebrities to promote the mission of the organization as honorary goodwill ambassadors. Such open-minded luminaries would introduce the public domain to those who never conceived of it as a separate entity and would remind the rest of us why it matters.

We can realistically expect that if a UNPDP is established, Hollywood would not fall on its sword. Thus, the UNPDP's initiatives would be fought tooth and nail behind the scenes in prime minister residences and legislative corridors across the West. Successes may not be frequent or revolutionary. Yet the existence of the international organization will serve, like the Statute of Liberty, as a reminder of what is worth protecting.

One possible concern is that creating a PDDO would harmfully pit different parts of government against each other on both the domestic and international level. Yet this could easily be viewed as a positive safeguard in the spirit of how our balance of powers provides checks and balances. Also, such a competing dynamic exists throughout government. The Department of Energy fights behind-the-scenes turf wars with the EPA, among other agencies, while the Department of State,

[136] While there is no intergovernmental agency devoted to the public domain, there is a nongovernmental group of international "activists, researchers and practitioners from universities, NGOs and SME" called COMMUNIA. *About,* COMMUNIA, www.communia-association.org/about/ (last visited June 19, 2017). Also, WIPO is slowly becoming more open to the idea of taking into account views held by non-Hollywood actors. For example, they are working on a "Development Agenda." *Development Agenda for WIPO,* WIPO, www.wipo.int/ip-development/en/agenda/ (last visited Aug. 28, 2017).

the Department of Defense, the National Security Agency, the Department of Homeland Security, the CIA, and the Department of Justice battle over international diplomacy, intelligence gathering, and national security.

COPYRIGHT-FREE ZONES

A free-trade zone (FTZ) is a plot of land, often next to a large body of water or an international airport, where activities related to goods in transit are not taxed by the host government. FTZs are a modern formulation of freeports, which were first enacted more than a century ago to reduce the transaction costs associated with importing and then exporting goods such as food staples, by exempting such activities from ordinary customs laws.[137] Yet FTZs, also referred to as "foreign-trade zones," exploited the exemption first associated with freeports by allowing the imported materials to be transformed before export – turning warehouses into factories.[138] In essence, raw materials or components of particular manufactured goods could be brought into the FTZ from abroad and then assembled into finished products such as cell phones without incurring any tariffs.[139] Further, the import and export requirements were relaxed at times to allow domestic and foreign inputs and to enable the finished products to end up in domestic markets, not just foreign ones.[140] Governments were not completely unaware of such expanded activity and would at times explicitly encourage it in the hopes that it would create jobs for citizens.[141] FTZs were thus used by one state in competition with another to entice domestic and foreign companies to relocate their manufacturing facilities.

The idea of exempting a plot of land from legal regulation can be applied to copyright law. Congress should be encouraged to create a physical zone – an entire state, county, city, or neighborhood or simply a building – where copyright law would not apply. Thus, any copyrighted material could be brought into the copyright-free zone without penalty. Visitors could create

---

[137] Freeports will be discussed in Chapter 6 in a different context – how the modern freeport is often effectively used as a secure, tax-free, and long-term storage facility for fine art.

[138] Donald E. deKieffer & George W. Thompson, *Political and Policy Dimensions of Foreign Trade Zones: Expansion or the Beginning of the End?*, 18 VAND. J. TRANSNAT'L L. 481, 485 (1985).

[139] *Id.*

[140] FOREIGN-TRADE ZONES BOARD, 52ND ANNUAL REPORT TO THE CONGRESS 1–2 (1990).

[141] *See generally* BANGLADESH ECON. ZONES AUTHORITY, EXPLORE YOUR INVESTMENT IN ECONOMIC ZONES OF BANGLADESH 8 (2015), www.beza.gov.bd/wp-content/uploads/2015/10/BEZA-Brochure-2015.pdf.

anything and borrow as liberally as they like as long as they are physically within the copyright-free zone. Further, as with the original formulation of FTZs, copyright law would apply only if artwork created in the copyright-free zone is taken beyond the zone's bounds.[142]

The question then becomes why Congress would ever consider implementing such a copyright-free zone. The answer is twofold – a historical argument and a call for rigorously analyzed experimentation.

History has shown that FTZs are successful, to a greater or lesser degree, in creating intense industrial hubs that provide positive spillover effects such as offering economies of scale to enable specialization and greater idea generation because many manufacturers are in close proximity to each other. There is no reason to believe that the same might not occur if a free zone is established for artistic creations. Yes, a manufacturing hub and a creativity hub produce different types of products, but that does not conclusively suggest the result would be different. In fact, it could be convincingly argued that artwork would have significantly greater spillover effects on education and idea generation than toys, textiles, or even tablets would.

Plausible attempts at experimentation are worth trying. Congress itself needs to rethink its assumptions about copyright and get creative. Putting aside the good of the nation for a moment, one can imagine the intangible benefits to lawmakers who innovate – a boost of excitement, the thrill of taking a gamble, the anticipation of potential success, and the opportunity to conceive of themselves as creative thinkers willing to take a calculated chance with little risk.

The idea of a copyright-free zone is in harmony with the goals of decreasing overconsumption, reducing copyright orphans, and enabling greater sharing of noncorporate artwork. The zone would facilitate sharing of works because there would be no legal restrictions preventing it. It would eliminate the problem of copyright orphans within the zone for the same reason. Finally, it could reduce consumption by inspiring individuals to visit the zone in order to create uninhibited by copyright law. This might sound like a stretch, and it's impossible to predict behavior without a test launch. Some art lovers would inevitably visit a copyright-free zone strictly to consume, while others will visit to experience unrestrained creation, and still others will choose to do both. Furthermore, a copyright-free zone might attract artists looking to relocate. Such artists would still consume others' work but as inspiration or material to

---

[142] For a related concept, *see generally* Brian D. Wassom, *Unforced Rhythms of Grace: Freeing Houses of Worship from the Specter of Copyright Infringement Liability*, 16 FORDHAM INTELL. PROP. MEDIA & ENT. L.J. 61 (2005).

learn or borrow from rather than as pure, passively consumed entertainment. This outcome would also help reduce overconsumption and increase creativity.

Even if an artist borrows others' works to create within the copyright-free zone and cannot subsequently export her new creations, the zone would allow for needed experimentation. Many famous artists have preferred not to publicly distribute their studies and pilots, instead destroying them because their ideas were not yet fully developed. Further, if an artist determines that her work created in the zone has merit and is ready to be made public, she could attempt to gain licenses to any borrowed works in order to export her new piece outside the zone. If this tactic works, such a twist to our existing copyright regime might be reasonable to implement across the country – e.g., artists could substantially borrow from existing copyrighted works but would only infringe the copyright of the borrowed works if their own work becomes a commercial success.

A potential concern is that a copyright-free zone would simply legalize copying – not just within the zone but also outside of it. As a friend pointed out, "It would stimulate people buying things through front companies established there," even if laws disallowed such exportation. This skepticism is unwarranted given that the Internet has technologically enabled such skirting of the law; in fact, unauthorized copying on the Internet is significantly less common than is widely assumed. Such unauthorized copying, or justified rebellion against the enclosure of all material, is a small fraction of Internet traffic – possibly less than 10 percent of what happens online is file sharing.[143] This is important precedent. Just because something is easy to do (unauthorized copying online or exporting material out of the copyright-free zone) doesn't mean most individuals will not respect the reasonable norms of a particular ecosystem.

A second possible apprehension is that while a creatively robust copyright-free zone would put pressure on Big Copyright to justify its desire for excessive copyright protection, it would be difficult to establish a copyright-free zone in the first place given Hollywood's lobbying prowess in

---

[143] Paul Resnikoff, *File-Sharing Now Accounts for Less Than 10% of US Internet Traffic . . .*, Digital Music News (Nov. 12, 2013), www.digitalmusicnews.com/2013/11/12/illegalfile sharing/. Predictably, reports from Big Copyright state a higher figure. For example, *The Daily Dot* cites a study performed by NetNames "at the behest of über content creator NBCUniversal, [which] estimated that nearly one-quarter of the Internet's total bandwidth is taken up by the illegal distribution of copyrighted content." Aaron Sankin, *24 Percent of Internet Traffic Is Devoted to Piracy, Study Says*, Daily Dot (Sept. 23, 2013, 12:48 PM), www.dailydot.com/business/nbcuniversal-comcast-piracy-study/ (last updated Dec. 10, 2015, 9:54 PM).

Washington, DC.[144] This is true. Yet resisting the implementation of a modestly sized copyright-free zone might be a strategic misstep on Hollywood's part, making greedy multinationals appear exactly how they are when it comes to copyright – unwilling to compromise and only concerned with profit.

[144] If it is impossible to convince Congress to enact such a copyright-free zone, one could theoretically be established without legislative decree. A nonprofit could lease or buy a disused offshore platform in the high seas. This is an idea out of the libertarian playbook. Peter Thiel, a PayPal founder, has donated money to the Seasteading Institute, which has the realization of such "floating cities" as its goal. Granted, it could be tough to attract a significant number of artists to live on an old oil rig in order to be unfettered by excessive copyright laws. One could even explore the hypothetical of making part of the Internet a copyright-free zone. For more on ocean platforms, see Alexis Madrigal, *Peter Thiel Makes Down Payment on Libertarian Ocean Colonies*, WIRED (May 18, 2008, 9:00 PM), www.wired.com/2008/05/peter-thiel-makes-down-payment-on-libertarian-ocean-colonies/.

5

Ignoring Big Copyright

Every nation, and if need be, every human being, has authority on behalf of humanity and of justice.

— William Ewart Gladstone[1]

If Congress is unwilling to help, we need to take action on our own, as Gladstone suggests. Very promising developments have resulted from non-profit efforts and informal collaboration among individuals either to alleviate some of the problems caused by copyright or to encourage citizens to create. Yet the scope for additional improvement through ideas that are immune to Big Copyright's influence can be increased. Some examples of such tactics follow.

COMMONS EXCHANGE

A man Caesar is born, and for ages after, we have a Roman Empire . . . An institution is the lengthened shadow of one man.

— Ralph Waldo Emerson[2]

Contrary to Emerson's suggestive remark, few institutions actually last for ages.[3] For instance, most democracies in the world are less than 100 years

---

[1] The quote is from a speech by Gladstone on the atrocities in Armenia. THE ANNUAL REGISTER: A REVIEW OF PUBLIC EVENTS AT HOME AND ABROAD FOR THE YEAR 1894 196 (1895).

[2] RALPH WALDO EMERSON, THE ESSAYS OF RALPH WALDO EMERSON 35 (Alfred Ferguson et al. eds., Belknap Press 1987) (1841).

[3] For more information on a commons exchange, see Martin Skladany, *A Commons Exchange: Aiding the Commons through Facilitating Website and Digital Art Adoption*, 10 I/S: J. L. & POL'Y INFO. SOC'Y 43 (2014).

old. The majority of countries in much of Latin America, Asia, Africa, and Eastern Europe and parts of Western Europe – Spain under Franco, Portugal under Salazar, Germany under Hitler, Italy under Mussolini – have been relatively recently liberated from domestic or foreign (colonial) dictatorships. As previously noted, United Nations membership has grown from only 51 in 1945 to 193 today.[4] A third wave of democratization swept the globe two decades ago with the fall of communism, yet "[t]here are at least 40 dictators around the world today."[5] Both democracies and dictatorships are fragile.[6]

While igniting and passing on the torch of democracy have been immensely complex, successful transfers of less complicated endeavors have also been challenging. For example, family-run businesses often are sold, underperform, or do not survive if one generation does not have a passion or aptitude for the trade.[7] The tradition of scholarship as a family enterprise – i.e., multiple generations producing scholarly works in the same field and even working on the same grand research projects – was, even in its prime in Europe during the early modern period, fiendishly difficult to maintain.[8] Handing off any cultural, social, academic, or business enterprise to friends rather than family members is no easier. If we have trouble finding a friend to temporarily watch our dog or cat while we are away, we cannot rest assured that our friends will be the best qualified and most inclined to permanently adopt our website or digital artwork.[9]

The challenges of transition extend beyond the difficulty of finding a good fit. When attempting to continue a tradition of democracy, societies are routinely confronted by forces with personal or financial motives to weaken the rule of law, transparency, accountability, and the voice of the people.

---

4   *Growth in United Nations Membership,* 1945–Present, UNITED NATIONS, www.un.org/en/se
    ctions/member-states/growth-united-nations-membership-1945-present/index.html (last visited
    Aug. 26, 2017).
5   SAMUEL P. HUNTINGTON, THE THIRD WAVE: DEMOCRATIZATION IN THE LATE
    TWENTIETH CENTURY (1991) and George B. N. Ayittey, *The Worst of the Worst: Bad Dude
    Dictators and General Coconut Heads,* FOREIGN POL'Y (July/Aug. 2010), www.foreignpolicy
    .com/articles/2010/06/21/the_worst_of_the_worst.
6   Collier mentions that "[g]lobally since 1945 there have been some 357 successful military
    coups," many of which have been against dictators. PAUL COLLIER, WARS, GUNS, AND
    VOTES: DEMOCRACY IN DANGEROUS PLACES 8 (2009).
7   *See generally* DAVID S. LANDES, DYNASTIES: FORTUNES AND MISFORTUNES OF THE
    WORLD'S GREAT FAMILY BUSINESSES (2006).
8   *See generally* Caroline R. Sherman, The Genealogy of Knowledge: The Godefroy Family,
    Erudition, and Legal-Historical Service to the State (Jan. 2008) (unpublished Ph.D. thesis,
    Princeton University) (on file with Mudd Library, Princeton University).
9   Also, studies have shown that community ties are fraying. See ROBERT D. PUTNAM,
    BOWLING ALONE: THE COLLAPSE AND REVIVAL OF AMERICAN COMMUNITY (2000).

Similarly, cultural creation – artwork and knowledge-based material created by diverse groups such as academia, nonprofits, and individuals – is also confronted by a focused yet powerful lobby of entertainment and content producers, Big Copyright, set against expanding the commons and reducing competitive pressures in the production of artwork. In societies and other institutions, longevity is often achieved through social and cultural rigidity, as was the case for many ruling dynasties and cultural institutions through time.[10] We need to find a compromise for the Internet that would achieve both longevity and flexibility.

The open cultural creation movement can be restricted by at least three avenues. First, material that is privately owned may never reach the commons. Second, information in the public domain may be lost – because the creator no longer has the time or does not keep up with code updates or due to external reasons like software no longer being supported, such as Microsoft's discontinuation of the content management system FrontPage.[11] Third, the commons' development can be limited by insufficient legal, technological, or institutional support mechanisms.

Existing nonprofit organizations have greatly aided the commons by addressing aspects of all three constraints. Creative Commons pushes back against the first restriction by providing more options to creators for sharing their work. The Internet Archive tackles the second restraint: It prevents the loss of information by saving pages to document the historical progression of the Internet over time. Wikipedia confronts the third constraint by providing an obvious outlet for the creation of free, easily accessible knowledge.

Yet the commons needs other novel legal and technological tools to further support it. Creative Commons cannot envelop all possibilities for enhancing sharing. The Internet Archive likewise cannot practically save all data, nor can it support the continued growth and development of the dead websites it memorializes.[12] Wikipedia cannot cover all information, nor again does the

---

[10] *See generally* CHARLES DE MONTESQUIEU, THE SPIRIT OF THE LAWS (Anne M. Cohler et al. eds., Cambridge University Press 1989) (1748).

[11] ComputerGeekMatt, *Microsoft FrontPage Discontinued in Late 2006*, DIGITAL J. (Dec. 8, 2006), http://digitaljournal.com/article/70028.

[12] The ideal solution to get all the information from a webpage is to go to the source – the person who owns the rights to the information on the website – not to a third party like Google or the Internet Archive. For example, the Internet Archive is at times blocked by robots.txt from collecting information from a website. Plus, it cannot get to password-protected information, etc. Finally, copyright concerns restrict what it can put online – as Brewster Kahle, the Internet Archive's founder, mentioned, "We can't put all our music on the Internet." Jill Lepore, *Can the Internet Be Archived?*, NEW YORKER (Jan. 26, 2015), www.newyorker.com/magazine/2015/01/26/cobweb.

commons want only one source of information, regardless of how benevolent it might be. These are not criticisms but rather acknowledgments that no idea or institution, regardless of how helpful or transformative, can solve all problems. The commons needs additional complementary institutions to strengthen its vitality.

What happens when someone running a website wants to move on to another project or retire? What happens when she dies? All too often, the website, no matter how useful, either goes dark or stagnates. And yet there is always fresh talent willing to make a mark on the Internet. Every possible area of human interest has aficionados who would gladly work for free on relevant websites. But there is no way to match up those who want to pass on the torch for a cultural creation with those who would like to pick it up. The Internet has no adoption agency.

Websites that are not handed over to a new generation usually suffer their fate because of a lack of contacts, even in this interconnected age. Moreover, taking over another person's site requires navigation of uncertain legal waters that a nonlawyer might hesitate to grapple with. A parallel problem exists for digital artwork. It can be difficult for artists to find an executor they are comfortable with. Creative Commons licenses do not practically resolve the issue of owners transferring all their rights to others when they can no longer maintain them.

Jagdish Bhagwati states: "Cultures will certainly change over time, as invention, organizational innovation, political change such as democratization, and globalization on many dimensions occur."[13] He believes that "[t]his process of decay of the old and evolution of the new always evokes nostalgia among more sensitive observers."[14] Thus, "[a]s cultures evolve and elements of them vanish, we must decide what we need to remember and retain in our midst. All of the past cannot be frozen endlessly in time."[15] While some websites and artwork might deserve to fade away quietly, countless others are not only worth preserving but also capable of evolving.

The Proposal

Copyright did not create the problem of lost or stagnant cultural creation, yet it has significantly exacerbated the problem. Even without copyright, knowledge and art would be lost en masse, not updated, or rendered useless by being contained within obsolete code. I propose a new legal idea to bolster the

---

[13] Jagdish Bhagwati, In Defense of Globalization 112 (2004).   [14] *Id.*
[15] *Id.* at 113.

commons and lessen the harmful effects of excessive copyright: a commons exchange that facilitates contacts between those who are looking to hand off a project and those who are willing to take one up. A commons exchange would connect individuals who have existing cultural creations – digital photos, online poetry, blogs, and websites – but can no longer maintain them to individuals who would like to adopt established works.[16] For example, if someone created a website on a particular galaxy but no longer has the time to run it, she could post information about her site on a commons exchange and ask others to take it over for free.

A commons exchange would also provide this same free adoption or matching service for artists looking to hand over digital artwork. Even artists who have material under a Creative Commons license and archive their works might still desire to set in place plans to transfer ownership of their artwork in the future.[17] While a license and archive policy would entail slightly lower transaction costs than a commons exchange, such a plan is realistically a death knell for art. How often do you use material from a blog that stopped updating a decade ago? How likely are you to search the Internet Archive for a large collection of bird photos instead of simply going to Google? The blog and photos still technically exist, but they are buried deeply. Idle websites are hard to find because search engine ranking algorithms measure the quantity and quality of external and internal page links to ensure that the most interactive websites dominate search results. This isn't to claim that having someone adopt your life's collection of 600,000 bird photos will instantaneously make it a top search result for anyone looking for bird pictures, yet we cannot discount the fact that certain art mediums are built on the premise of continued evolution and that the visibility of many other works could benefit from a curator.

A policy of licensing and archiving is at best the equivalent of consigning a painting to the Museum of Modern Art (MoMA)'s storage facilities, while having someone adopt your work is akin to having it hung in a bathroom at PS1, MoMA's exhibition space in Queens – unlike the artwork gracing the walls of Midtown Manhattan, your painting will probably never be seen by millions, but it isn't in a dungeon and could still affect the lives of others, however modestly.

Further, even in a world of online sharing, artists who put their works under Creative Commons licenses remain emotionally attached to them, just as

---

[16] There are a few creations that would likely be unsuitable for adoption on a commons exchange such as online platforms that support other works and open collaborative projects.

[17] Even works under a CC0 (no rights reserved) or CC BY (attribution rights reserved) license could benefit from some of the arguments for adoption mentioned in this section.

a homeowner who rents to a stranger still maintains a bond to the premises. Remove that intimate sense of ownership, and the house will gradually fall apart from disrepair – i.e., at times, ownership of a creation, however open, nurtures stewardship. Also, few simply take all of another's Creative Commons–licensed works. We borrow one or a few pictures out of homage to the artist because we acknowledge a norm of not assuming another's entire creative identity without an explicit agreement with the artist. There is a legal and cultural difference between free licensing and assigning, between sampling and taking ownership, even if they overlap.

Even the word "archiving" suggests putting something away that is not commonly used – storing out of sight rather than actively promoting, sharing, and nurturing. We don't archive pets; we adopt them. This is not to say that using a policy of Creative Commons licenses and archiving is bad or the best we can do in many instances, nor is this to trumpet a commons exchange as a revolution. It is simply to argue for the possibility that a commons exchange can play a part in the online ecosystem, along with other innovative policies and other not-yet-dreamt-of developments to encourage a robust commons. A commons exchange would facilitate transition planning through free legal and technological assistance. It would clarify the necessary legal steps – such as the transfer of artwork and URLs – to aid such transitions, just as Creative Commons has done for sharing. It would be a modified peer-to-peer network for "preserving the vision of artists" while allowing the works to evolve under new artist vision, just as each new generation interprets a George Balanchine classic in its own unique way.[18]

In Jean-Paul Sartre's note read in Stockholm explaining why he was declining the Nobel Prize for literature, he stated: "A writer must refuse to allow himself to be transformed into an institution."[19] A commons exchange would not institutionalize cultural creation in the sense of having it become an instrument of propaganda or profit for the powerful – the very thing that Big Copyright does with the material it owns. The purpose behind a commons exchange is not to help large, well-known institutions – i.e., the Googles and Facebooks of the world. Furthermore, owners of sites visited by millions of individuals a day do not doubt their ability to find a suitable suitor to carry on the legacy. Often this is because the most popular sites are run by established institutions, with substantial internal history, support mechanisms, and stable

---

[18] I'd like to thank James Grimmelmann for the nice turn of phrase and insightful analysis.

[19] *Sartre Explains Stand*, NY TIMES (Oct. 23, 1964), www.nytimes.com/1964/10/23/sartre-explains-stand.html (quoting Jean-Paul Sartre, declaration read in Stockholm, Sweden [Oct. 22, 1964]).

finances. Finally, online collaborative projects where a robust group of dedicated volunteers collectively work together have little need for an external transfer mechanism because future transitions will organically take place between group members. Rather, a commons exchange is meant to thicken the supportive netting underneath cultural creations that have limited audiences but that make up a vast portion of the web. While it is estimated that there are roughly 180 million websites globally, the top million are "responsible for the great majority of web traffic."[20] A commons exchange is meant to help many of the creators of the remaining 179 million websites – 99.4 percent of all websites – when they can no longer support their site or determine that it is time to take a new direction artistically. Just as in the collaborative development of software "given enough eyeballs, all bugs are shallow," so through a commons exchange that brings together enough suitors all cultural creation can find a new home.[21] Unless we find a more stable way to transition the ownership of cultural creation, the demand for a commons exchange will remain robust – while most cultural creation will not need to be adopted at any given moment, over time all cultural creation not owned by institutions and a good amount of material from institutions will need to find new suitors.[22]

Tim Wu maintains that the "production of expressive works can be broken down into three standard stages" – creation, dissemination, and improvement.[23] In his analysis, "At each stage, production can be fully open, fully closed, or somewhere in between."[24] Depending on the nature of the cultural creation, a commons exchange would aim to support it in one or more of these stages. For example, certain websites providing information on new economic events, novel theories of philosophy or literature, or efforts to catalogue new archeological or evolutionary findings can be supported by a commons exchange at all three stages. On the other hand, if a commons exchange helps facilitate the adoption of digital photographs, its assistance would primarily be through having maintained

---

[20] *July 2013 Web Server Survey*, Netcraft, ttp://news.netcraft.com/arhives/category/web-server-survey/ (last visited Sept. 5, 2017), and *Hosting Locations of the Million Busiest Websites*, Netcraft, www.netcraft.com/internet-data-mining/million-busiest-websites/ (last visited Sept. 5, 2017).

[21] Eric Raymond, The Cathedral and the Bazaar: Musings on Linux and Open Source by an Accidental Revolutionary 30 (2001).

[22] The problem a commons exchange aims to solve is partially related to the problem of temporal interoperability – ensuring that existing cultural creations can be opened and understood in the future, given, for example, the rapid changes in code. *See generally* Robert E. Kahn, Perspectives on Interoperability of Systems (May 23, 2011) (presentation at Institute of Medicine Roundtable on Value & Science-Driven Health Care).

[23] Tim Wu, *On Copyright's Authorship Policy*, U. Chi. Legal F. 335, 343 (2008).   [24] *Id.*

public access to the work. Yet someone adopting a digital photo could always display the original online next to a revised version that has been updated by the new steward.

A commons exchange would allow anyone to post a cultural creation for adoption and would give anyone the ability to search the entire database of available material. It would allow the owner of the artwork to summarize the creation and tailor the application requirements for those interested in adopting the work. Once an adoption is agreed to, the commons exchange would provide the parties with a free legal document that would enable the assignment or transfer of the copyrighted material. Following in the path-breaking steps of Creative Commons, a commons exchange could slightly modify Creative Commons' famous three-layer design of licenses to create three levels of assignments – the legal, human-readable, and machine-readable layers.[25] A commons exchange could also provide a manual on how to update code, create a forum for individuals to discuss related issues, and possibly even foster a group of volunteers to assist website owners in updating their sites. Numerous other ideas could be incorporated into a commons exchange, such as advocating for vendor relationship management (VRM) software, formulating prelaunch publicity, requiring foundation grantees to use a commons exchange, and presetting automatic adoption code.[26] In certain jurisdictions such as the European Union, legal issues including database regulations, privacy laws, and moral rights issues would need to be addressed.[27] Finally, a commons exchange could explain the vision and benefits behind Creative Commons licenses and ask those looking to hand off their work to consider using such licenses before assigning the work.[28]

---

[25] The machine-readable layer could consist of websites up for adoption posting a commons exchange "adopt me" logo that could be identified by search engines. This would create a second way for individuals to discover what works are up for adoption in addition to browsing the commons exchange website listings.

[26] DOC SEARLS, THE INTENTION ECONOMY: WHEN CUSTOMERS TAKE CHARGE xii (2012). A commons exchange could theoretically provide ready-to-use code for individuals to insert into their websites that would automatically put the site up for adoption if a particular condition is met, such as the site not being updated for two years or the site getting fewer than, for example, 1,000 hits in a year.

[27] See J. H. Reichman & Pamela Samuelson, *Intellectual Property Rights in Data?*, 50 VAND. L. REV. 51 (1997); Michael D. Birnhack, *The EU Data Protection Directive: An Engine of a Global Regime*, 24 COMPUTER L. & SECURITY REP. 508 (2008); and Cyrill P. Rigamonti, *The Conceptual Transformation of Moral Rights*, 55 AMER. J. COMP. L. 67 (2007).

[28] Those giving away their cultural creations could attempt to stipulate that the adopter not change the openness of the license to make it more restrictive to discourage any potential adopter from adopting a work primarily for commercial reasons.

The Benefits of a Commons Exchange

It is easiest to see the loss of cultural creation by recalling high-profile losses. For example, the number of different websites and services sponsored by technology giants that died in only one year, 2009, strongly suggests that countless smaller websites routinely die off. In the course of that year, Google killed Dodgeball and Notebook, Yahoo let Briefcase die off, Microsoft called it quits with Encarta, Hewlett-Packard ended Upline, and Wikia pulled the plug on Wikia Search.[29] The fact that even technology giants are getting rid of websites shows how much more difficult survival must be for websites without institutional support. The lack of institutional support and the overly restrictive copyright regime have led to a staggering number of works that are either orphans – works under copyright where the owner is either unknown or unreachable – or in danger of becoming orphans. For example, 90 percent of photos held by museums in the United Kingdom are orphan works.[30] This equates to 17 million works in just one artistic medium in a country with five times fewer individuals than the United States.[31] While other artistic mediums have a smaller percentage of orphan works, the figures still add up to possibly billions of neglected, unusable works.[32]

Some family members might adopt a relative's website or a friend might step in, but such serendipity is not a strategy. Further, no formal institutional structure exists to facilitate digital adoption. An institutional adoption mechanism for cultural creation, a commons exchange, would substantially lower the current high transaction costs of passing on one's work to another and also of creation in general. Lowering such costs – primarily temporal, financial, and legal – would bring numerous substantial benefits.

First, a dedicated institution would significantly alleviate the orphan works problem in the future by providing a method of publicizing that a work is up for adoption, by creating a process for easily soliciting interest and selecting the right person to take over, and by offering free legal tools to formally complete the adoption. Creators have put sweat and blood into what they have brought to life and do not want to see their creations disappear. Regardless of whether such individuals put their digital content up for adoption because they no longer have the time or money to continue creating, cannot fix technical

---

[29] Josh Lowensohn, 15 *Sites That Died in 2009*, CNET (Dec. 23, 2009), http://news.cnet.com/2300-27076_3-10002066-1.html.

[30] Anna Vuopala, Assessment of the Orphan Works Issue and Costs of Rights Clearance 5 (May 2010) (report prepared for the European Commission, DG Information Society and Media, Unit E4 Access to Information), http://ec.europa.eu/information_society/activities/digital_libraries/doc/reports_orphan/anna_report.pdf.

[31] *Id.*   [32] *Id.*

problems, or simply want to move on to new projects, a commons exchange would prevent their creations from being discarded. Part of the value of preserving artwork is that no one knows when great art will be recognized as such – e.g., Vincent van Gogh sold only one painting during his lifetime.[33] Furthermore, preservation matters because the disappearance of artwork or excessive restriction of its availability not only is needless but discourages creation. Peter Drahos and John Braithwaite recognize that a restricted commons reduces creativity and dampens innovation.[34]

By reducing the amount of lost material and the number of copyright orphans, a commons exchange would lessen the harmful effects of our overly restrictive copyright regime. It would support the continued life of artistic endeavors by providing free legal forms to resolve the uncertainty around taking over another's work. Even if one is simply passing on work to a friend, there is legal uncertainty in the transfer that makes some people feel uncomfortable or reluctant to spend the time and money to have a lawyer draft a copyright assignment. For example, friends not steeped in copyright law might not realize that in order to reduce possible confusion in the future, they could be explicit about what a website adoption would entail – i.e., the transfer of all or only part of a website's many copyrighted components including text, images, video, stylesheets, and code.[35] A commons exchange would facilitate the transfer for free and without hassle.

Second, having more cultural creations available for much longer periods instead of disappearing is beneficial in and of itself, yet a commons exchange would go beyond the simple static preservation of artwork because it would enable newly adopted works to evolve dynamically under the direction of the new owners. Of course some adopted pieces will not be dramatically reworked, but this is not a limitation. Depending on the form and content of the cultural creation and the vision of the new creator, adopted works will evolve to different degrees. This is a key limitation to existing attempts such as the Archive Team that take a static snapshot of sites in danger of disappearing.

Information, knowledge, and artwork need to live and breathe, not stagnate in the attic. A map of the world from 2010 is already outdated on the country level, let alone on the state or local level. A 2011 history of the Nazi persecution during World War II is incomplete because it excludes the recently released

---

[33] VALERIE BODDEN, VAN GOGH 39 (2008).
[34] PETER DRAHOS with JOHN BRAITHWAITE, INFORMATION FEUDALISM: WHO OWNS THE KNOWLEDGE ECONOMY? 2 (2002).
[35] Such considerations need to also be made for licensing. *See Considerations for Licensors and Licensees*, CREATIVE COMMONS, http://wiki.creativecommons.org/wiki/Considerations_fo r_licensors_and_licensees (last visited Aug. 26, 2017).

first comprehensive study on the total number of concentration camps, forced labor camps, prisoner-of-war camps, brothels, ghettos, and other detention centers.[36] We have a new understanding of the link between eating red meat and heart disease – "a little-studied chemical that is burped out by bacteria in the intestines after people eat red meat."[37]

As discussed earlier, such dynamism often makes cultural creation more valuable to us because it provides up-to-date information or allows for a dialogue. Shun-ling Chen reminds us that "[a]ll works, embodiments of ideas, and expressions are intermediaries that channel the ideas of one to others."[38] Yet "no one will be able to know how well one is understood until one actually hears other people's responses" in the form of comments, borrowing portions of the artistic expression under the fair use doctrine, or creating derivative works.[39] Such "ability to communicate between members is key for any community to remain vital."[40] Michel Foucault argues that through their work creators begin a "discursive practice."[41] Their work "gives other creators the opportunity to pursue the creative process."[42]

Third, the existence of a commons exchange would not only help ensure the dissemination and improvement of existing artwork but also motivate more individuals to create and innovate. This would occur for numerous reasons. A more robust commons would provide creators with more material – the previously unavailable work – to use as building blocks for their artwork. More individuals would be inspired to create because they would have more assurance that their creations would have the time and means to evolve and find an audience. More individuals looking to test the creative waters would be encouraged by the possibility of adopting another's site, which could be less daunting than striking out on their own. Furthermore, both individual and collaborative production would be fostered by a growing sense of community where members help each other through adopting established works.[43] For

---

[36]   Eric Lichtblau, *The Holocaust Just Got More Shocking*, N.Y. Times, Mar. 3, 2013, at SR3.

[37]   Gina Kolata, *Culprit in Heart Disease Goes beyond Meat's Fat*, N.Y. Times, Apr. 8, 2013, at A14.

[38]   Shun-ling Chen, *To Surpass or to Conform – What Are Public Licenses for?*, U. Ill. J.L. Tech. & Pol'y 107, 137 (2009).

[39]   *Id.*   [40]   *Id.* at 138.

[41]   Séverine Dusollier, *The Master's Tools v. The Master's House: Creative Commons v. Copyright*, 29 Colum. J.L. & Arts 271, 286 (2006) (citing Michel Foucault, *What Is an Author?*, in Textual Strategies: Perspectives in Post-Structuralist Criticism 141, 154 [Josué Harari ed., 1979]).

[42]   *Id.*

[43]   Michael Carroll, a pioneer and leading light in helping us understand the importance of the commons, discusses the example of the project Connexions at Rice University. He believes this example shows how "Creative Commons facilitates not only dissemination, but also

example, a group of peers could decide to adopt and update a website together. Or one individual who adopts a website could encourage others to add content or comment about the newly adopted site. Conversely, a group could adopt a website and incorporate its content into its existing site. Alternatively, groups of individuals interested in certain topics could band together and adopt numerous sites on related topics, with the aim of creating something greater than the sum of its parts. Such efforts would not only create better sites but encourage deeper commitment to collaborative, peer-based production.

The Limits of Creative Commons in Preventing the Stagnation of Works

The properties of software and the milieu of the programming community suggest that free software in general may not need a commons exchange to the same extent that other cultural creation does. If an active community exists that collectively creates and continually updates a project under a free software or open Creative Commons license, the existence of a commons exchange will not add any present value to the project because such collaborative production is in essence a quasi-institutional structure – a community that sustains itself through passing on the project from one generation to the next.[44]

However, Creative Commons and the free software movement cannot fulfill the role of a commons exchange for all cultural creation. Even though many prominent examples of successful cooperation exist outside of software, such an intensely rich collaborative milieu is unlikely to materialize for the majority of artistic, academic, or personal creative pursuits.[45] There are numerous reasons for this distinction.[46]

First, only cultural creation, such as software, that can be divided into small pieces, "each of which can be performed by an individual in a short amount of time," will likely allow collaborative, peer-based production to

---

collaboration and community-building." Michael W. Carroll, *Creative Commons and the New Intermediaries*, 2006 MICH. ST. L. REV. 45, 58 (2006).

[44] Theoretically, even if all cultural creation is initially created in Wikipedia-like collaborative environments, one could argue that a commons exchange could still play a valuable role by acting as free insurance for projects in case their communities collapse. Wu reminds us that although "a project like Wikipedia seems undeniably popular now, its volunteer-based mode of production may simply lose favor one day." Wu, *supra* note 23, at 348.

[45] For example, while DeviantArt, the "largest online social network for artists," has more than 38 million registered members, it is more a blend of Facebook and Amazon than a peer-based artistic collaboration. *About DeviantArt*, DEVIANTART, http://about.deviantart.com (last visited Aug. 25, 2017).

[46] The strokes that follow are general and not meant as absolute truth. Further, counterexamples will likely exist for each distinction discussed.

flourish.[47] These individual modules should be able to be created independently of the other modules. Yochai Benkler states: "This enables production to be incremental and asynchronous, pooling the efforts of different people, with different capabilities, who are available at different times."[48] The effort to complete most components should be minimal in order to increase the number of potential contributors. Benkler concludes that "[n]ovels, for example, at least those that look like our current conception of a novel, are likely to prove resistant to peer production."[49] Furthermore, Benkler maintains that he is not suggesting that peer collaboration "is always the more efficient model of production for information and culture."[50]

Second, collaborative production taking the place of an Internet adoption agency works more successfully for software because inferior software has a lack of utility while art's value is more in the eye of the beholder. Software often has a practical, targeted purpose – e.g., to be the best operating system or the most user-friendly e-calendar – that sets the standard for one version being judged superior to another. While peer production in one light can be viewed as sharing, it can also be thought of as an unyielding, fiercely competitive challenge where numerous programmers modify an existing program and generally only the best modifications get reproduced in future versions of the software. This form of competition does not apply to artwork whose value is more subjective. I adore Henryk Górecki's Third Symphony, but my family members do not. Also, while there might be fierce competition among different works of art for long-term recognition, there is still space for lesser-known art to coexist meaningfully with better-known art. To some extent this is true of software – some users might prefer one e-calendar over another because of differing functions, though one program or one version of a program is simply better. Yet a superior software program can have its dominant position reinforced by the fact that software is particularly prone to network effects.[51] The more individuals who adopt a program, the harder it is for a new program to displace it because of the transaction costs for individuals to switch programs. Such network effects are much less prevalent with other forms of cultural creation because artwork is not generally created to accomplish practical tasks – e.g., switching one's movie preference simply entails renting different movies, unlike changing one's penchant for word processing programs, which forces one to laboriously transfer files from one format to another.

---

[47] Yochai Benkler, *Coase's Penguin, or, Linux and the Nature of the Firm*, 112 YALE L.J. 369, 378 (2002).
[48] *Id.* at 379. [49] *Id.* [50] *Id.* at 381.
[51] DAVID SINGH GREWAL, NETWORK POWER: THE SOCIAL DYNAMICS OF GLOBALIZATION 198 (2008).

Benkler formulates this second requirement of successful peer production in a similar vein. He suggests that fruitful peer production "must have low-cost integration, which includes both quality control over the modules and a mechanism for integrating the contributions into the finished product."[52] He argues that "[i]f a project cannot defend itself from incompetent or malicious contributions and integrate the competent modules into a finished product at sufficiently low cost, integration will either fail or the integrator will be forced to appropriate the residual value of the common project – usually leading to a dissipation of the motivations to contribute ex ante."[53]

In summary, collaborative, peer-based production projects are attractive, yet this mode of continuous modular creation works for software but cannot often keep artwork alive and evolving and hence will not be adopted by the vast majority of cultural creators. Thus, a commons exchange is necessary to improve the odds that websites and digital artwork that do not easily fit within the free software model live on and evolve after their initial owners can no longer maintain them.

Possible Problems or Concerns

Copyright trolls attempting to hoard copyrighted works in order to extort settlements from potential infringers are one potential concern. Yet they will probably not be enticed by the selection available on a commons exchange because the works most likely to be put up for adoption are those under Creative Commons licenses or not currently economically successful. Further, it has been argued that a commons exchange should encourage those letting go of their creations to simultaneously attach an open Creative Commons license. Finally, the copyright assignment contract can expressly forbid the use of the adopted work for either any commercial use or copyright troll-like behavior.[54]

Jonathan Zittrain has voiced concerns about free software projects that are informative for how a commons exchange might work. First, since proprietary software generally does make its source code available, it is difficult for free software projects to know if a company is stealing its code for profit without

---

[52] Benkler, *supra* note 47, at 379.   [53] *Id.*

[54] While defining such activity could be challenging, the contract could potentially focus on aspects such as the adopter agreeing to not bring any suits against individuals or nonprofits using the material in certain ways. A similar analysis has been incorporated into fair use determinations where the nature of the use of copyrighted material is considered. 17 U.S.C. § 107(1).

complying with the free software license.[55] An asymmetry exists in that free software "is much more vulnerable to claims of infringement by proprietary code authors, since the source code to free software is, by definition, available for examination by would-be plaintiffs."[56] Second, the "collaborative nature of free software development makes it harder to determine where various con- tributions are coming from, and whether they belong to those who purport to donate them."[57] Given such concerns, the possibility of baseless or legitimate lawsuits against open collaborative projects is worth protecting against. To counter such risk, "[t]he open source community sought to address these concerns by offering Open Source Risk Management ('OSRM')."[58] A commons exchange could consider providing a similar arrangement.

Another potential issue is that some individuals might have difficulty under- standing why anyone would want to adopt an existing cultural creation as opposed to creating one on their own. First, there will always be individuals who prefer to create from scratch, which should not be discouraged. Yet even those who do must realize that their creation is built on the backs of previous artists with similar thoughts, theories, and styles of expression. Thus, building off existing art is similar to taking over someone else's website. Adopting artwork is a more explicit recognition of this grand collaborative project spanning all artists over centuries.

Second, there is no need to re-create the wheel. For example, if someone has carefully listed many of the festivals in Italy, why not build from this existing resource instead of attempting to re-create it? Alternatively, it will often be less wasteful to adopt a repository of bird photos than to start building one de novo. Just imagine if everyone discarded all the buildings in a city in order to build anew. Such duplication would be incredibly expensive and waste countless time and effort. Instead, what usually happens is that people acquire an existing building and make it their own – painting the walls a different color, hanging artwork and curtains, or replacing old wiring, pipes, and appliances. This is the essence of what could be done with existing websites – those who newly adopt a site can alter its aesthetics, update some links and data, and potentially even rewrite some code, not take a bulldozer to the entire website.

Third, some people will find it less daunting to adopt an existing cultural creation and gradually modify it than to start from scratch. Adoption helps ease the way into the creative process.

---

[55] Jonathan Zittrain, *Normative Principles for Evaluating Free and Proprietary Software*, 71 U. Chi. L. Rev. 265, 286 (2004).
[56] *Id.*   [57] *Id.*
[58] Niva Elkin-Koren, *What Contracts Cannot Do: The Limits of Private Ordering in Facilitating a Creative Commons*, 74 Fordham L. Rev. 375, 419 (2005).

Fourth, art enthusiasts collect paintings or books for various reasons.[59] Some build an extensive library as a tool to improve their thinking and writing. Others collect paintings to ensure the survival of the art or to enshrine it as a source of inspiration in their lives. Adopting cultural creations can serve the same ends.

A further concern is that failed adoptions will occur. Approximately 1 to 10 percent of completed adoptions dissolve, while 10 to 25 percent of adoption proceedings end in disruption – "an adoption process that ends after the child is placed in an adoptive home and before the adoption is legally finalized, resulting in the child's return to (or entry into) foster care or placement with new adoptive parents."[60] Yet we would never think of preventing people from adopting children in need, nor should we in the case of cultural creation. Further, the default alternative – losing vast amounts of cultural creation – would be the practical equivalent of all adoptions failing. A commons exchange should continually monitor failed adoptions in order to improve success rates. Part of such an examination should be asking both parties to an adoption whether it was successful and, if not, why it failed.

While a commons exchange would provide information on specific websites and digital artwork that creators are attempting to hand over – the creator's name and contact details; the site's title, URL, and subject matter; and a mission or content summary – those putting material up for adoption should have the option to select how much and what type of information to ask for from applicants wanting to adopt their work. For example, a commons exchange could allow those placing a website up for adoption to solicit biographies, CVs, references, examples of past work, and even essays from prospective adopters and to conduct interviews over Skype.

Also, impostors could claim that they own a website. This fraudulent activity would effectively be dealt with by requiring any site owner who initiates an adoption request to upload a commons exchange "adopt me" logo to her site before the commons exchange would recognize her adoption request. The idea is that only the legitimate owner of the site could post the commons exchange logo.

Verifying the proper owners of digital artwork would be more difficult, yet there are numerous ways to minimize concerns. One way is to require both parties to take steps to verify their identities to the commons exchange and to each other. One widely used verification method is requiring anyone

---

[59] *See generally* INTERPRETING OBJECTS AND COLLECTIONS (Susan M. Pearce ed., 1994).

[60] CHILD WELFARE INFO. GATEWAY, ADOPTION DISRUPTION AND DISSOLUTION 1–6 (June 2012), www.childwelfare.gov/pubs/s_disrup.cfm.

registering with a commons exchange to complete her application by clicking on a link emailed to her. Parties should also be encouraged to do their due diligence online as to the artwork in question and each other. As mentioned earlier, creators putting work up for adoption on a commons exchange should be able to ask applicants for numerous types of information, even references. Further, as online communities develop, users often establish ways to monitor each other such as trustworthiness ratings.[61] If in one night Airbnb helps 140,000 people trust complete strangers enough to rent a place to stay from them – sometimes on couches or air mattresses – then developing methods to build confidence between commons exchange users seems eminently achievable.[62]

A last concern is that a commons exchange would help preserve ethically suspect cultural creations by facilitating connections among individuals with similar extreme views. Such a service could even be more critical to the preservation of extremist websites because an owner of such a site, relative to owners of less extreme sites, is less likely to have a large enough social network of individuals with similar beliefs to find someone to take over her site.

In the long run, scholars from Socrates to Thomas Jefferson have believed that truth and justice should prevail in the marketplace of ideas. Justice Oliver Wendell Holmes Jr. stated in a dissenting opinion: "Persecution for the expression of opinions seems to me perfectly logical. If you have no doubt of your premises or your power and want a certain result with all your heart you naturally express your wishes in law and sweep away all opposition ... But when men have realized that time has upset many fighting faiths, they may come to believe even more than they believe the very foundations of their own conduct that the ultimate good desired is better reached by free trade in ideas, that the best test of truth is the power of the thought to get itself accepted in the competition of the market, and that truth is the only ground upon which their wishes safely can be carried out."[63] Getting to this future period of harmony might take a while, but the alternative – censorship – is not worth the short-term apparent accord.

That said, certain sites would not be welcome, such as those advocating child pornography or abuse of women. This may seem like a contradiction. While a response could fill books, the general view is that content should be

---

[61] *See, e.g.,* Feedback Scores, Stars, and Your Reputation, eBay, http://pages.ebay.com/help/fe edback/scores-reputation.html (last visited June 9, 2013).

[62] Thomas L. Friedman, *Welcome to the "Sharing Economy,"* N.Y. Times, July 21, 2013, at SR1.

[63] Abrams v. U.S., 250 U.S. 616, 630 (1919).

prohibited if the underlying beliefs are so obviously a violation of John Stuart Mill's harm principle and universal human rights that accommodating them would only lead to immediate harm to the vulnerable groups affected by such despicable practices.[64] A commons exchange would not be alone in having to confront this problem. All major websites that serve as social or communicative springboards, from YouTube to Twitter, face the issue with some success.[65]

Not all great art gets recognized as such during its owner's lifetime, and not all website owners are skilled networkers. A commons exchange will give ideas and creations time to find their audience by preserving the accumulated labor and creativity of the Internet for future generations. This breathing space will encourage more individuals to begin creating by drawing them into a dialogue with others' works, by providing more noncorporate material for them to build on, by allowing them to test their creative waters through the nurturance of others' works, and by providing creators with greater assurance that their works will continue to exist after they pass. A commons exchange will check the power of Hollywood by helping to decentralize the creation and distribution of artwork. It will also keep knowledge perpetually expanding and changing with the times by helping cultural creation live on and evolve under new artistic direction. And someday a commons exchange might even facilitate its own adoption.

COPYRIGHT COLLECTIVE FUNDS

For centuries, people have collected artwork either as individuals or as members of art clubs or confraternity institutions such as the Venetian *Scuole Grandi*. The National Arts Club in New York City even grants lifetime membership to artists who have been asked to donate one piece of art to the club's permanent collection, which includes many well-known American artists of the late nineteenth and mid-twentieth centuries.[66] Art investing opened a new chapter in 1974, when the British Rail Pension Fund established the first art investment fund. This fund invested in more than 2,500 pieces of art over six years with an average 11.3 percent annual return from 1974 to

---

[64] See Wojciech Sadurski, *Joseph Raz on Liberal Neutrality and the Harm Principle*, 10 OXFORD J. LEGAL STUD. 122 (1990) and JAMES GRIFFIN, ON HUMAN RIGHTS (2008).

[65] For example, Twitter prohibits "content promoting child sexual exploitation." *Child Sexual Exploitation Policy*, TWITTER, https://support.twitter.com/articles/37370 (last visited Aug. 25, 2017).

[66] CAROL LOWREY, A LEGACY OF ART: PAINTINGS AND SCULPTURES BY ARTIST LIFE MEMBERS OF THE NATIONAL ARTS CLUB (2007).

1999.[67] Since then the transition from collecting art for the pleasure of it to doing so for profits has only gathered speed.

A second novel investment trend that is gaining in popularity is purchasing a fraction of another individual's future earnings. Pave, one such venture, allows prospects to create a personal profile, and then it uses an income prediction model to set funding rates for the individual for multiyear contracts.[68] Backers are solicited to invest directly in an individual rather than, for example, in an individual's startup company. While ventures like Pave are promising, Pave's accredited investors, generally speaking, concentrate their funds in individuals with relatively stable career prospects such as graduate students in STEM fields (science, technology, engineering, and math), not in young artists.

More legal and institutional experimentation is needed in regard to not only who invests in artwork and human capital but also how. I propose the creation of copyright collective funds, which would be a hybrid of the two previously mentioned recent investment models.[69] Copyright collective funds would make selecting a career as an artist less risky by enabling hundreds of up-and-

---

[67] *What Are Art Funds: Basics of Art Funds and their Managers*, ART FUND ASS'N LLC, www .artfundassociation.com/_what_are_art_funds/basic_af.html (last visited Aug. 25, 2017).

[68] *About Us*, PAVE, www.pave.com/about (last visited Feb. 26, 2017).

[69] A related yet different model is that of the Artist Pension Trust (APT). First, the name itself emphasizes that APT is creating a pension for individual artists, not a collective support organization or insurance for spreading the risk of not becoming commercially successful. This approach has been characterized as a way to plan for an individual artist's future primarily through the sale of that artist's work: After APT's 28 percent cut of the net proceeds of the sale of one of the artist's works, the artist gets 40 percent of the net proceeds from his own piece selling, while only 32 percent of the net proceeds go to a collective pool of funds to be divided among all artists in the trust. A further sign of this distinction is that with APT the artist "remains the owner of his or her works, which are held in the trust's possession until they are sold." Julia Kollewe, *Portrait of the Artist as an Older Man – This Time with a Pension*, GUARDIAN (Sept. 18, 2009, 7:05 PM), www.theguardian.com/money/2009/sep/19/artists-pensions. A final strong indication of APT being primarily about creating pensions instead of spreading risk is that APT artists can withdraw from the fund and in so doing are not obligated to continue providing more pieces of art to APT (though APT will sell the works it already has). *Id.* Second, APT's premise rests on catering to the art world elite – APT's "art professionals" identify "artists with the highest potential of success." Thus, whereas copyright collective funds aim to assist all artists in a world covered by a Rawlsian veil of ignorance, APT pulls back the veil to cherry-pick the future all-stars while neglecting everyone else. APT picks the prom winners only, while copyright collective funds pick everyone at the prom. Third, this elite selection process is tied to a different model of reimbursing artists. APT takes a 28 percent cut of all net proceeds (after deducting a sales commission, VAT, transportation fees, installation costs, production costs, others taxes, etc.). This financial arrangement could have been very different – APT could have decided to have its 28 percent from each sale cover the sales commission, taxes, and other costs. To put this in context, the standard for-profit commission that art galleries take is 50 percent of the sale of the work, not 50 percent of

coming artists to jointly invest in a fund where the buy-in is simply a contractual pledge to give the fund ten pieces of original artwork if notified to do so during the thirty-year life of the fund. Ultimately, only the most commercially successful artists, perhaps only five to ten individuals, would be called upon to contribute artwork, which would be auctioned with the proceeds being equally distributed to all the artist-investors.[70]

Copyright collective funds provide a novel arrangement for artists, who are not strangers to collective action. Artists have historically banded together in numerous different types of groups from traditional art collectives (an informal group sharing space or buying supplies in bulk) to art cooperatives (formally incorporated to advance artists' goals) to art communes and colonies (artists living together).[71]

A 0.1 percent share of a copyright collective fund might not sound too enticing, but it would only take one Damien Hirst (a billionaire) or Jeff Koons (half a billionaire) in the group to make each individual's return substantial.[72] Copyright collective funds would encourage more existing artists to stay with the profession either on a full-time or part-time basis. The funds could also encourage some individuals to decide to become artists in the first

net proceeds – i.e., the galleries pay the costs as part of their 50 percent take. To this end, APT distributes part of its proceeds to "its 120 financial backers (who have provided $10 million in funding so far)." *Id.* A further display of how APT differs financially from proposed copyright collective funds is that APT is "owned by MutualArt, a holding company." *Id. See also About Us & FAQ,* Artist Pension Trust, www.aptglobal.org/en/About & www.aptglobal.org/en/About/FAQ (last visited May 31, 2017).

[70] Copyright collective funds have advantages over third-party, for-profit investment ventures in human capital such as Pave. First, copyright funds do not siphon off profits to distribute to outside investors; all art sale proceeds are evenly divided among all artists in the fund. This nonprofit model of investing is important not only practically but also philosophically and in terms of public perceptions. Second, copyright funds do not automatically require repayment, which could create real hardship for individuals later in life under the for-profit schemes. Yes, such for-profit ventures provide funding up front rather than years later, but it must be repaid in the human-capital direct investment schemes. It is a loan, not an insurance-like investment vehicle. Finally, entrepreneurs usually need infusions of cash for their businesses. The same is true for someone wanting to sell a stake of their future earnings – e.g., she needs funds to pay for tuition. Yet depending on the field of art, most artists do not need significant amounts of cash to create in the here and now. Essentially, artists are much more likely to pursue their interests, even if only on a part-time basis, without third-party, for-profit investment. Hence copyright collective funds are a better match for artists, helping to smooth out the vagaries of art market success through providing funding in the future.

[71] For example, the Health Alliance for Austin Musicians provides "access to affordable health care for Austin's low-income, uninsured working musicians." Health Alliance for Austin Musicians, *Our Story,* MyHAAM.org (last visited Aug. 25, 2017).

[72] Husnain, *Top 10 Richest Painters Net Worth,* Articles Teller (Mar. 20, 2016), https://articlesteller.com/top-10-richest-painters-2016/.

place. Both outcomes would occur for two reasons. First, copyright collective funds would modestly improve the financial outlook of such a career choice. Second, they would diminish the sense that the vagaries of the art market unjustly reward only a handful of artists who are not necessarily the most gifted or profound.[73]

Copyright collective funds could take numerous forms from informal associations that discard the "fund" in their name to formal hedge-fund-like entities. The latter approach could be accomplished through various legal regimes or legal exemptions. Such funds could be enabled by the US Securities and Exchange Commission rules on crowdfunding mandated by the Jumpstart Our Business Startups (JOBS) Act of 2012, which provides an exemption from the registration of securities for "certain crowdfunding transactions."[74] If copyright collective funds attempt to rely on the JOBS Act crowdfunding exemption, they would have to follow numerous requirements, including caps on the amount of money raised and limits on how much money individual investors could invest – i.e., the present value of artist-investors' commitment to donate art in the future if called upon to do so.[75]

Previously, crowdsourcing has enabled a few artists to pursue their work but only through collecting small donations given altruistically or in exchange for a perk – e.g., a numbered copy of a print – not in exchange for a portion of any financial returns or profits from the artists' activities, which would go beyond crowdsourcing to become crowdfunding. While investing through crowd-funding was technically legal before the JOBS Act, it was limited to a small group of wealthy investors, not open to the general public. Further, while crowdfunding was enacted to help entrepreneurs, copyright collective funds, as a possible variation of crowdfunding, have the chance to help emerging artists.

Alternatively, copyright collective funds could conceivably be realized through the Securities Act, given that it does not apply to securities issued by "a person organized and operated exclusively for ... benevolent, fraternal, charitable ... purposes, and not for pecuniary profit."[76] To make such an arrangement work, a copyright collective fund would have to argue that it is

---

[73] Just as sensing injustice within the workplace can affect buy-in from employees, sensing injustice regarding who is recognized as an accomplished artist within the art world could dampen people's desire to pursue a career in the field. Larry W. Howard & Cynthia L. Cordes, *Flight from Unfairness: Effects of Perceived Injustice on Emotional Exhaustion and Employee Withdrawal*, 25 J. Bus. & Psychol. 409, 422 (2010).

[74] U.S. Sec. & Exch. Comm'n, Regulation Crowdfunding: A Small Entity Compliance Guide for Issuers (2016), www.sec.gov/info/smallbus/secg/rccompliance guide-051316.htm.

[75] *Id.*   [76] 15 U.S.C. § 77c(a)(4).

not operated for profit but rather exists for benevolent purposes. A second requirement of this exemption to the Securities Act is that "no part of the net earnings of [the fund] inures to the benefit of any person, private stockholder, or individual."[77] An argument could be made that the point of the fund is to support the arts through supporting the fund's artist-investors. If this argument is unsuccessful in meeting this second requirement, the structure of copyright collective funds could be altered so that emerging artists could legally commit to donating artwork in the future to a nonprofit that could then sell it to raise funds to further its mission instead of distributing shares to individual artists. The idea would be to get hundreds of emerging artists to pre-commit to helping others if they become successful in the future.[78]

There are numerous organizational aspects of copyright collective funds that would be interesting to consider. For example, establishing a nonprofit that helps promote copyright collectives would greatly facilitate their adoption and operation. It could assist in signing up artists, providing standardized copyright fund contracts, deciding when and which artists would have to hand over artwork, coordinating the sale of such work, distributing the earnings to all artist-investors, and allowing fellow artist-investors to get to know each other and track the success of their fund online. There would be numerous ways to select artists to join a particular fund – by geography, age, artistic medium, or educational affiliation. While such criteria would make starting a new fund easier, they might do so at the expense of diversification to a certain extent. Also, a group of artists could decide to set up its own copyright collective fund. Furthermore, the idea behind copyright collective funds could even be expanded beyond art – e.g., to include high-tech entrepreneur cooperatives.

Finally, copyright collective funds could allow members to sell their stake in order to raise funds quickly rather than waiting for possible payouts in the future. If funds allow this, future payments would flow to the new stakeholder, but the original artist-investor would continue to be responsible for producing ten pieces of art if called upon to do so by the fund. The fund could allow such transfers only after a certain period following the establishment of the fund or permit only members facing demonstrable life crises to sell their share. Regardless, the JOBS Act crowdfunding rules would generally allow transfer

---

[77] *Id.*
[78] Further legal forms or limitations that might be appropriate for copyright collective funds, include examining the Securities Act Section 3(a)(11) exemption on intrastate offerings, direct participation plans, or attempting to convince the SEC that copyright collective funds are not investment contracts under the Securities Act and thus should not qualify as securities.

of an equity stake only after a one-year holding period, though exceptions to this rule exist.[79]

One potential concern with copyright collective funds is that they might be too expensive to operate. Aside from the remote possibility that artist-investors would be required to submit artwork to the fund at some future point decades away, members would not incur any additional costs outside of periodically updating their contact information with the copyright collective fund – a standard transaction cost for many investments. As for the coordinating nonprofit, it would likely initially need philanthropic support or have to consider partnering with an established art nonprofit or art school. Yet an attractive aspect of copyright funds is that in the medium to long term the central nonprofit could become self-sufficient by charging the funds a small fee to cover its provision of administrative support.

Another possible concern is that a famous artist who is a member of a copyright collective might refuse to give artwork to the fund if called upon to do so. Such recalcitrance would do little for the artist's image in the eyes of her peers or the public. The negative press in combination with a legally binding contractual obligation would make such obduracy unlikely.

Some naysayers might argue that the time commitment to produce ten works of art would be too demanding a contractual requirement. This is not so if the fund allows the artist to submit recent work as well as current work created over a reasonable span of time. Moreover, numerous artists do pro-duce rapidly. Picasso made at least 70,000 works of art.[80] Further, the most famous artists often have a cadre of assistants facilitating production – Koons has more than 120 assistants.[81]

Another objection could be that some artists would sign up for numerous collectives. In moderation, that would be a good thing. If an artist joins five different funds and then becomes a star, the other 4,995 members of the five funds would be elated by the added revenue. The likelihood that the artist would become a star is not diminished by her five memberships, and the danger that she would not be able to provide fifty works in this scenario is inconsequential. Besides, such funds could require applicants and members to disclose how many funds they belong to or are in the process of applying to. Further, given that copyright funds would be largely organized around

[79] U.S. Sec. & Exch. Comm'n, *supra* note 74.

[80] Jonathan Jones, *Nightmare at the Picasso Museum*, Guardian (Oct. 16, 2014, 1:00 PM), www .theguardian.com/artanddesign/2014/oct/16/-sp-nightmare-picasso-museum-paris.

[81] Dion, *Jeff Koons Has More Than 120 Assistants*, Art News Blog (Aug. 7, 2009), www .artnewsblog.com/jeff-koons-has-more-than-120-assistants/.

a limited number of affiliations such as university alumni groups, it is unrealistic to anticipate that an artist might sign up for dozens of such funds.

Another concern is that artists would deliver art of poor quality. To prevent an artist from submitting ten subpar works to the fund, a contractual clause could stipulate that the works must sell above a certain price – e.g., 75 percent of the average sale price of all the artist's works sold over the preceding two years. If the works fail to meet such a floor, the artist would have to submit additional art in order to make up the shortfall.

Finally, some skeptics might worry that copyright collective funds could interfere with an artist's contract with a music label, publisher, or art gallery. Given that most artists would join a collective fund before being signed, the point could be moot. Further, outside of contemporary music contracts, which might cause challenges, the structure of publishing contracts and art gallery representation would easily allow for writers and visual artists to join copyright collective funds.

Committing one's life to art should be less risky. Copyright cooperatives will not turn everyone or even most people into artists. However, the establishment of copyright collective funds would encourage a few more individuals to take the risk of devoting at least part of their lives to creating art.

ENTERTAINMENT CONSUMPTION TRACKER, CREATION ALARM CLOCK, AND SELF-TAXATION

We have numerous contraptions to wear on our wrists or put in our shoes to check our heart rate, tally the number of steps we take, or determine how much we have slept. The point of these gadgets is not only to monitor our vitals but to get a poignant reminder of how active we have been, which is meant to nudge us toward biking across continents, swimming across oceans, or at least taking the stairs.[82]

We should create such a tracker to calculate how much entertainment we consume. Given that we devour entertainment in numerous ways – cell phones, tablets, computers, the TV in our living room, the TV in our bedroom, the TV in our kitchen, the movie theater down the street, even artwork not on screens – it would be a challenge to easily yet precisely record all of our consumption. Yet we do the vast majority of our consumption on digital

---

[82] Alternatively, I do not know of a similar device that reminds us of our sedentary nature, though it's possible to have a watch or fitness band zap you if you have been inert for too long – a gentle or not-so-gentle reminder that we damage our health from all the sitting we do.

devices connected to the Internet, a development that Tim Berners-Lee has celebrated as the "Internet of Things."[83] Thus, the more the Internet of Things takes hold and the more coordination between different devices takes place – e.g., between our car radio and cell phone – the easier it will be to obtain a precise gauge of our consumption. To further increase the accuracy of the tally, the app, by asking the user a few questions, could get a decent sense of how much offline consumption one does – e.g., how many magazines one reads each week or how often one goes to an art gallery or museum. Finally, if or when wearable or insertable electronics become widespread, appraising one's media consumption will be more exact. For example, the failed, yet-to-be-relaunched Google Glass could theoretically run such a media consumption tracker app.[84]

In addition to the previously mentioned apps that encourage us to exercise more, there are apps that track different forms of consumption with an eye to ensuring we don't go overboard. For example, there is an app that measures how much caffeine you consume, at least nine apps that count your alcoholic drinks, and a few that touch on media indirectly, such as apps that monitor the number of times you check your phone or that help you remember which TV shows or anime you've already watched.[85] Despite the superfluity of tracking apps, we still need a way to track all our consumption across all platforms to figure out if we consume more or less than the American average of ten hours a day.

The entertainment consumption tracker could do more than tell you the total number of hours you spend consuming entertainment each day; it could also itemize all the content. The app could mimic American Express's online pie charts demonstrating how much you spend each month, with each merchant, and how much on different categories such as travel versus food. Thus, the tracker would show you variances in how much media you consume

---

[83] Adam Conner-Simons, *Web Inventor Teaches Web Course – Learn about "Internet of Things" through edX*, MIT COMPUTER SCI. & ARTIFICIAL INTELLIGENCE LABORATORY (Jan. 26, 2016), www.csail.mit.edu/iot_professional_education_course_2016.

[84] Steven Levy, *Google Glass 2.0 Is a Startling Second Act*, WIRED (July 18, 2017, 7:00 AM), www.wired.com/story/google-glass-2-is-here/.

[85] Kristin Ambrosino, *9 Top Drink-Counting Apps*, MEN'S FITNESS, www.mensfitness.com/life/gearandtech/9-top-drink-counting-apps (last visited Mar. 10, 2017); *Caffeine Tracker: Kofe+*, GOOGLE PLAY, https://play.google.com/store/apps/details?id=sleeping_vityaz.trackmycaffeine&hl=en (last visited Mar. 10, 2017); Katy Hall, *These Apps Help You Realize How Much Time You Waste on Your Phone*, HUFFINGTON POST (Nov. 5, 2014, 7:43 AM), www.huffingtonpost.com/2014/11/05/apps-smartphone-use-_n_6096748.html; *Entertainment Tracker Pro*, GOOGLE PLAY, https://play.google.com/store/apps/details?id=com.sazzad.etpro&hl=en (last visited Mar. 10, 2017).

over an average day, week, or month; how much time each day or month you spend watching a particular TV show or browsing a particular website; and how you divide your time consuming different art forms.

Why stop there? The app could also put entertainment consumption in perspective as one aspect of life by helping you measure and then compare the time you spend on other activities. Conceivably, it could help you track everything you do in your entire day, such as how much you sleep, work, exercise, and talk to friends. Most important, it could demonstrate how much of your life you spend creating – using rich graphics to compare creation rates with consumption rates in various ways.

The basic idea is simple – create a tool that could help individuals determine if they are overconsuming entertainment and, if so, provide clues as to where to cut back by showing individuals what they are consuming. The hard data might surprise many, but it would be challenging to refute.

We also need a wakeup call to create, so let's literally create an alarm clock app to remind us. Especially in combination with an entertainment consumption tracker, a creation alarm clock could help us prioritize creativity. The app would allow you to set your own schedule or allow friends to select times to create together so that you get a "go create" wakeup ring or text alert. Research in India has shown that weekly text message reminders stressing the importance of oral hygiene significantly improve "oral hygiene compliance."[86] If digital reminders work for an activity as mundane as brushing your teeth, they should work miracles for playing an instrument, planting a flowerbed, or drawing a picture.

The information collected by an entertainment consumption tracker on its own could be psychologically cathartic or alarming. It might not be enough to motivate individuals to change their habits, even if coupled with a creation alarm clock. Still, the data could go beyond mere enlightenment and friendly reminders and underpin additional tools to incentivize people to reduce passive consumption.

Some weight-loss programs motivate individuals by having them commit to donating money to a charity if they do not meet their goals. A more general version of this idea is the "Commitment Contract" offered by StickK, a company that supports behavior change "by helping people eliminate" the

---

[86] Harshal R. Jejurikar et al., *Does Text Messaging Reminder Help in the Orthodontic Compliance of Patients to Maintain Their Oral Hygiene*, J. ORAL HYGIENE & HEALTH (July 31, 2014), www.esciencecentral.org/journals/does-text-messaging-reminder-help-in-the-orthodontic-compliance-of-patients-to-maintain-their-oral-hygiene-2332-0702.1000152.php?aid=32307.

gap between dreaming about a goal and actually achieving it.[87] "A Commitment Contract is a binding agreement you sign with yourself to ensure that you follow through with your intentions – and it does this by utilizing the psychological power of loss aversion and accountability to drive behavior change."[88] In short, individuals "hate losing things and often give into immediate gratification (e.g. eating a donut) at the expense of our long term goals (e.g. losing weight)."[89] StickK fights back against these two traits through "two factors that effectively help people achieve the behavior change they desire: incentives and accountability."[90] For example, not only can you commit to giving away money if you are unsuccessful; you can also enable a referee to encourage and monitor your compliance. According to StickK, "[f]inancial stakes increase your chances of success by up to 3x," while a "[r]eferee increases your chances of success by up to 2x."[91]

An entertainment consumption tracker could be merged with a behavior-changing program like StickK. Individuals could set a ceiling for how much entertainment they could view a day, commit to part with cash if they go over the limit, and enlist family and friends to help hold them accountable. Of course, the precise incentives could vary. For instance, if an individual exceeds her daily allowed media consumption, she could be required to give cash to a favorite charity, hand it out to random strangers on the street, or even donate it to a political party that she disagrees with in order to make parting with it more painful. Likewise, how individuals are held accountable to their family or friends could vary. An individual could ask her friends for encouragement and carrots or for strict monitoring and sticks. For instance, she could request that friends dole out chores like cleaning a friend's garage or cutting a neighbor's grass.

The data gathered by an entertainment consumption tracker, like the data collected by a fitness band, could allow you to compete with friends, family, and even strangers as well as against your personal best. For example, you could create friendly contests with your work colleagues as to who could consume the least entertainment or create the most art. Given the digital nature of the data, you could run daily comparisons to see how much you might need to up your game. Conceivably, you could enter more than one such competition with different friends and even wager on the result – e.g., the loser would have to write a sonnet on the virtues of the winner's Chihuahua or the superiority of the winner's alma mater.

---

[87] *How It Works*, STICKK, www.stickk.com/tour (last visited Aug. 26, 2017).   [88] *Id.*
[89] *FAQ – About StickK*, STICKK, www.stickk.com/faq (last visited Aug. 26, 2017).   [90] *Id.*
[91] *How It Works, supra* note 87.

There are other existing ways to attempt to limit one's consumption. While several of these methods are effective to a certain degree, they are not as successful as self-taxing to reduce overconsumption. For example, more than 450,000 people use the Freedom app that helps you concentrate by disabling all online activity for a prescribed period of time or by blocking certain apps or websites that you find particularly distracting.[92] The simple idea is that if your browser is enabled, you will be distracted by all the websites you have forgotten to check in the past five minutes. As with similar attempts to reduce online distractions, the goal is less to limit our options than to remind us of our propensity to go down Internet rabbit holes more frequently than we would ideally like. Such methods could also be combined with the idea of self-taxation to limit consumption of entertainment.

In summary, there are lots of apps for tracking addictive consumer behavior, from drinking beer to checking one's phone, but we need a more comprehensive method for monitoring and moderating our consumption of entertainment. We should also consider trying creation alarm clocks, taxing ourselves if we overconsume, and getting into friendly competitions with family and friends to help us reach our goal of consuming less and creating more.

FREE GRANT ART

Art is speech. When the French artist Abraham Poincheval literally lived inside a bear carcass for weeks while allowing visitors at the Musée de la Chasse et de la Nature to observe him "hibernating," I believe he thought he was conveying something. The performance piece *Fuck for the heir Puppy Bear!* by a collective of Russian artists called Voina (War), which entailed public sex but thankfully left actual bears out of it, probably meant to communicate a lot.[93] Moving beyond bear-themed art to works involving mutilation, American artist Chris Burden wanted to speak to us when he had a friend shoot him in an art gallery from 15 feet away with a .22 rifle. At the Tate Modern, Franco B, an Italian artist, once strolled down a catwalk bleeding from his wrists. Apparently importantly, his entire body was painted white. Afterward he was quoted as saying, "'Art is about creating language and

---

[92] FREEDOM, https://freedom.to (last visited Aug. 26, 2017). For an older formulation of a strategy, see Home Entertainment Equipment Control Apparatus, www.google.com/patents/US5051837 (last visited Mar. 12, 2017).

[93] Sadly, Voina forgot to leave animals alone when they threw cats at workers at a McDonald's. Katherine Brooks, *20 of the Most Confusing Performance Art Pieces of All Time*, HUFFINGTON POST (June 30, 2014, 9:01 AM), www.huffingtonpost.com/2014/06/24/worst-performance-art_ n_5512731.html (last updated June 30, 2014).

memories. Language is like a virus that can invade you, and I love that.'"[94] Australian artist Casey Jenkins addressed us in a 2013 piece she summarized as "'spending 28 days knitting from wool that I've inserted in my vagina.'" Likewise, Swiss artist Milo Moiré had a point when she "push[ed] paint eggs out of her vagina onto an empty canvas" in her performance piece called *Plop Egg Painting*.[95] I'll spare you examples of poop-themed artwork and instead conclude this arc with two less dramatic works. In 2010, Marina Abramovic, a Serbian artist, stared at Museum of Modern Art visitors for 736 hours, which induced British actress Tilda Swinton to take a nap in a glass box at the same New York City institution three years later.[96]

Whether the preceding examples exude a profound message or tell a banal story, art is, at least partially, about communicating with others – getting an aesthetic, philosophical, social, cultural, economic, political, emotional, or personal message across to the audience. Even art we dislike was probably effective in communicating with us.

Since artists speak through their work, there is debate about the appropriateness of governments financially supporting artists. This free speech debate has at least two components. First, a government should not favor one message over another, which, some argue, is what occurs when the government awards grants for new artwork. While the state funding another abstract expressionist spinoff movement might not sound free speech alarms, a possible end of the spectrum is Nazi propaganda. Even if we are not talking about explicitly politically sponsored art with a nefarious purpose, government funds can affect who is heard above the crowd.

Second, art funded by governments is art that can be more easily censored. Again, the extreme is Soviet apparatchiks debating whether a Dmitri Shostakovich symphony, without any words in it, was sufficiently patriotic and hence could be released or instead whether the composer himself should be "released" to a gulag. At about the same time Shostakovich "voluntarily" withdrew his Fourth Symphony before its premier, he began "sleeping in the hallway of his apartment complex in expectation of arrest, not wishing to wake his wife when the moment occurred."[97] Such censorship occurs to this day in democracies. For example, the National Portrait Gallery withdrew "a four-minute video called 'A Fire in My Belly' after complaints from the Catholic League and politicians ... who objected to images of ants crawling over

---

[94]　*Id.*　[95]　*Id.*
[96]　All the examples in this paragraph come from the same piece by Brooks. *Id.*
[97]　Philip K. Decker, *Surviving Stalin's Terror and Censorship*, Real Clear Hist. (July 11, 2014), www.realclearhistory.com/articles/2014/07/11/surviving_stalins_terror_and_censorship.html.

a crucifix."[98] While the Germans may be less apt to have caved in this particular instance, they have laws that restrict free speech protections of artists to such an extent that artists can face "several years in jail if convicted," mysteriously under the justification that without such censorship laws there would be a greater danger of more government censorship – e.g., a rise of another Nazi movement.[99] For example, in 2016 – yes, 2016 – Chancellor Angela Merkel "cleared the way for the prosecution of German comedian Jan Böhmermann," who wrote a poem mocking Turkey's president, allegedly in violation of a "German law against insulting heads of state."[100]

While in general Germany is less prone than the United States to find government funding of artwork controversial, there is another related yet neglected question that is more on point with our focus on copyright and the public domain.[101] If the government has chosen to sponsor some speech in the name of art, then why should it also charge the public (who are effectively the patrons of the art) in order to consume it? All artwork created through the generosity of a government grant should immediately go into the public domain rather than spend decades if not a century or more under copyright restrictions. Furthermore, honors such as being named a poet laureate should be bestowed on artists with the understanding that all the artwork they create during their tenure would flow directly into the public domain. In the United States at least, given the relatively modest funding available to artists through government entities such as the National Endowment for the Arts (NEA) and the Library of Congress, this proposal would not transform the public domain overnight. For example, the poet laureate distinction is given to only one individual a year and comes with a $35,000 stipend plus $5,000 for travel.[102] The idea behind having such awardees voluntarily relinquish their copyright in government-sponsored

[98] Ed Morrissey, *3 Reasons Why Tax Dollars Shouldn't Fund Art*, Hot Air (June 8, 2011, 10:05 AM), http://hotair.com/archives/2011/06/08/3-reasons-why-tax-dollars-shouldnt-fund-art/.

[99] Rick Noack, *Merkel Allows Prosecution of German Comedian Who Mocked Turkish President*, Wash. Post (Apr. 15, 2016), www.washingtonpost.com/news/worldviews/wp/2016/04/15/merkel-allows-prosecution-of-german-comedian-who-mocked-turkish-president/.

[100] *Id.*

[101] There are other aspects to the debate over whether governments should fund artists beyond the quality of the art and free speech issues. For example, some argue that such funding is unnecessary given that "Americans give around $13 billion a year in private donations to the arts." Morrissey, *supra* note 98.

[102] While the Library of Congress administers the "Poet Laureate Consultant in Poetry" award, which was established in 1937, the stipend "is funded by a private gift from Archer M. Huntington." *United States Poets Laureate: A Guide to Online Resources*, Library of Congress, www.loc.gov/rr/program/bib/poetslaureate/faq.html (last visited Aug. 26, 2017).

works is simply another measured step toward building greater recognition for the public domain in the hope that the more robust it is, the more likely it is to play a part in getting the general public to create on their own. Let the government-funded speech speak to people. And let the people borrow from that speech in their own creations.

This proposition is less controversial when one considers that works of authorship created by the US federal government never receive copyright protection.[103] This is because the government wants to disseminate such works as broadly as possible – just imagine the due process concerns raised if citizens had to pay copyright royalties to reproduce or publicly read statutes and judicial opinions.[104] This prohibition against copyright in any work "prepared by an officer or employee of the U.S. government as part of that person's official duties" does not automatically extend to works of authorship created for the federal government by independent contractors.[105] Federal government entities have the option to oblige independent contractors to waive their copyright to such works if doing so is in the country's interest. To go from having the option to require federal contractors to put their works in the public domain to expecting the same of artists given grants from taxpayers' wallets is not a monumental leap.[106]

Currently, for example, the NEA allows grant recipients to retain their copyright on "any materials [they] develop from the work undertaken during the period of support without prior approval from us."[107] The NEA further states: "Unless otherwise specified in the award, we are not entitled to receive royalties from work supported or made possible by a grant or cooperative agreement; however, we retain a royalty-free right to use such work for

---

[103]   Copyright Act § 105.
[104]   The Copyright Act of 1976 does not prevent state governments and local municipalities from receiving copyright in works they have created, excluding laws, regulations, and judicial opinions. Copyright Act § 101.
[105]   *Id.*
[106]   The leap is minimal given the United States' conception of copyright as providing an economic incentive to generate more expression as opposed to the EU's vision of copyright as protecting art because it is an extension of the artist's personality.
[107]   Nat'l Endowment for Arts, General Terms & Conditions for Grants and Cooperative Agreements to Organizations 17 (Dec. 2012), www.arts.gov/sites/defa ult/files/GTC-2014-new-address.pdf. The NEA mischaracterizes how copyright works in its use of the phrase "You may arrange to copyright" (immediately preceding the text quoted here). Copyright protection automatically subsists "in original works of authorship fixed in any tangible medium of expression." 17 U.S. Code § 102. No arranging is necessary, though an author can register her work with the US Copyright Office. In fact, there is no need for an artist to affirmatively act unless she wants to get rid of her copyright and donate the work to the public domain.

Federal government purposes (e.g., the use of final report final products to document the results of our award programs), including placement on our Web site."[108] So, the NEA grants itself the privilege to use the artwork royalty-free but does not provide the same opportunity to the rest of us.[109]

Given that federal government entities have the ability to require independent contractors to give up their copyright in material they create under a government contract, federal entities such as the Library of Congress, the NEA, and the National Endowment for the Humanities could presumably implement such a change on their own without any legislation. Artists and scholars would then be free to accept the condition or decline the funding that is on offer.

Such progress has already been made for certain educational materials generated by government grants. For example, the Department of Labor stipulates that all grant recipients place a Creative Commons Attribution license on all material created with grant funds.[110] The Department of Education puts grant applicants "on notice that a term and condition of grant awards that contemplate creation or modification of curricular or educational materials will require grantees to grant an open license to the public that enables free use and reuse of all materials with attribution."[111]

Furthermore, numerous federal government institutions now have policies on sharing source code not only with other government agencies but also with the public – policies they implemented well before the White House's Office of Management and Budget (OMB) "finalized its source code policy for federal agencies, which will make code open for sharing and re-use across all federal agencies."[112] The OMB's 2016 "policy will come with a pilot program where agencies will release at least 20 percent of their newly-developed custom code," written by third parties, as open source.[113] A similar trend is to

[108] *Id.*
[109] This is the case even though the NEA's own website states: "The National Endowment for the Arts does not retain copyright on any Endowment-created material within the Web site, such as guidelines and grant listings." *Copyright Status Notice*, NAT'L ENDOWMENT FOR ARTS, www.arts.gov/site-policies/copyright (last visited Dec. 2, 2016).
[110] *Licensing Policies, Principles, and Resources*, PROJECT OPEN DATA, https://project-open-data .cio.gov/licensing-resources/ (last visited Mar. 12, 2017).
[111] *Id.*
[112] Greg Otto, *OMB Finalizes Policy on Open Source Code from Agencies*, FEDSCOOP (Aug. 8, 2016), www.fedscoop.com/omb-code-gov-open-source-tony-scott-august-2016/. For existing examples before the OMB announcement, see *Licensing Policies, Principles, and Resources, supra* note 110 (including examples from NASA to the Department of Defense).
[113] *Id.*

freely share data collected by the federal government with the public.[114] Also, it has been argued that the public should have free access to the research articles describing government-funded science along with peer-reviewed educational resources that stem from government grants.[115]

One potential concern is that artists opposed to copyright-free grant art would boycott the NEA and related government grant-making bodies. While some might create a fuss and a few might actually withdraw their applications, the threat seems hollow. Celebrity artists don't need the NEA's money – some have hundreds of millions more than the NEA distributes in a year. Meanwhile, many emerging artists would happily accept the honor and funding because the copyright amounts to less than peanuts – only widely known artists generate any substantial revenue from copyright. Even in the remote event of a boycott, the loss of potential applicants would simply open up grant opportunities to others.

This leads to a related concern – that freeing grant art from copyright is picking on the little artist. But since the copyrights of little-known artists are financially worthless, the emerging artist will not be sacrificing anything.[116] One could argue that in thirty years the artist might be a superstar and hence the copyright could turn to gold; however, the copyright royalties of famous artists are dwarfed by their ability to sell one painting for millions. So, once more, little is financially stripped from the artist. Yes, the artist would lose the ability to limit who uses a creation she might have poured her heart into, but this loss of control is exactly the point: It is the freedom to borrow from others and experiment for others. Further, such a policy is a bargain, a condition of accepting the grant. The artist can simply say no.

114   *The Third U.S. Open Government National Action Plan*, DATA.GOV (Oct. 28, 2015), www.data
       .gov/meta/open-government-national-action-plan/. OPEN GOV'T PARTNERSHIP, THIRD
       OPEN GOVERNMENT NATIONAL ACTION PLAN FOR THE UNITED STATES OF AMERICA
       (Oct. 27, 2015), https://fas.org/sgp/obama/nap3.pdf.
115   Billy Meinke, *Public Access to Publicly Funded Materials: What Could Be*, CREATIVE
       COMMONS (Sept. 25, 2013), https://creativecommons.org/2013/09/25/public-access-to-
       publicly-funded-materials-what-could-be/. Also, the proposed Public Access to Science Act,
       which was ultimately unsuccessful, would have amended "Federal copyright law to declare
       copyright protection unavailable to any work produced pursuant to scientific research
       substantially funded by the Federal Government to the extent provided in the funding
       agreement entered into by the relevant Federal agency pursuant to this Act." H.R. 2613,
       108th Cong., 1st Sess. (2003), www.congress.gov/bill/108th-congress/house-bill/2613?q=H.R.
       +2613+%28108%29.
116   A final issue is that this policy of requiring grant recipients to donate their work to the public
       domain should be limited to grants to artists and not spill over, for example, to the art of kids in
       grade school if any grant money goes to supply them with paint and brushes. This makes sense
       and could easily be accounted for.

PUBLIC DOMAIN AWARDS, A CITY CHAMPIONING THE PUBLIC DOMAIN,
AND PUBLIC DOMAIN PASSPORTS FOR KIDS

We have the Pritzker Prize, the Pulitzers, the Grammys, the Emmys, and the Tonys. If you take any individual art form, such as film, beyond the most famous awards, such as the Oscars and Golden Globes, there are more than three dozen less well-known film awards in the United States alone, with hundreds of similar awards abroad. The public domain needs its own awards and possibly, in due course, an awards ceremony to honor recipients. Given the amorphous nature of the commons – encapsulating the universe of artwork that is free for anyone to view, copy, modify, or reimagine – it is obviously less fit for its own awards than a particular art form such as literature or architecture is.[117] Yet the public domain has few individuals or institutions fighting for it, let alone serving as its public relations firm. The point of having public domain awards would be to motivate individuals to greatness, to honor their greatness, and to publicize and promote the commons and creativity in general.

A nonprofit could raise awareness of the commons by recognizing artists who have done the most for the public domain – awarding lifetime achievement as well as the best creations put into the commons each year. The awards could be given in different categories to acknowledge each art form – e.g., the best new film in the public domain – and/or in subcategories to acknowledge each genre – the best new documentary, the best new action film, and so on.

The public domain awards would raise awareness most efficiently if the categories are subdivided into separate awards for famous, emerging, and amateur artists. In addition to highlighting the egalitarianism of the commons, these distinctions might encourage other artists at the top of their fields to embrace the commons as the digital embodiment of our creative capacity and culture. For example, Gerhard Richter donating paintings into the public domain might motivate Vik Muniz or Jenny Saville to do the same. Cindy Sherman setting her photos free could nudge Andreas Gursky to follow suit. The same could be said for famous sculptors, playwrights, poets, recording artists, and directors. Not only could one famous honoree's donations lead her to become more of an advocate for the public domain; the public celebration of her donations and advocacy could spur other artists to contribute to and support the commons. Further, to raise funds for the nonprofit that would

---

[117] For an excellence conceptualization of the commons, *see generally* Michael J. Madison, Brett M. Frischmann, & Katherine J. Strandburg, *The Complexity of Commons*, 95 CORNELL L. REV. 839 (2010).

coordinate the awards, all it would take is the willingness of a few famous artists to auction off one work each.

While the public domain awards may not surpass the prestige or renown of the Oscars or Pulitzers anytime soon, the point would simply be to get the public, over the long term, to understand what the public domain is and what it does to sustain our culture. Plus, low-cost marketing strategies to publicize the awards could prove surprisingly effective in generating buzz. First, to advertise the event's egalitarian spirit, the organizing committee could open up the voting to everyone online. Just as donating artwork to the public domain can give an artist a sense of affinity to the cause, so can casting a vote. Second, the committee could persuade a few celebrities to make public service ads letting people know how they can participate by voting online. Third, over time the organizers could create critics' choice awards to complement the general awards determined by online voters. The panel of critics could include famous artists across numerous art forms. The opportunity to get recognition from heroes and stars could help motivate emerging and amateur artists to excel. Fourth, since all works under consideration would be absolutely free to view and modify, the awards website would provide a great online gathering place for individuals to check out and discuss the winners. If other nations establish their own public domain awards, all the national awards sites could interlink to create a global network of free work.[118] Finally, as the ceremony's éclat increases, we could see Lady Gaga on the red carpet wearing others' copyrighted material as a political protest instead of raw meat.

Not only does the film industry use awards ceremonies to publicize its wares; it has deliberately branded a city in its wake – Los Angeles. The Internet has Silicon Valley. The hub of finance is New York, while government has Washington, DC. The public domain needs its own city. The reason for this is at least twofold. First, given how Hollywood is not only a moniker for the film industry but a physical location makes us think about film more often than we otherwise would. Whenever we picture LA, it is difficult not to think of the film industry. The mind roams from smog to celebrities, plastic surgeons, and beaches, in no particular order. Second, the association between the place and the industry gives the city economic incentives to promote film. Doing so increases tourism and creates a critical mass of expertise in the industry, which has positive spillover effects – more

---

[118] Since there is no global public domain, a certain amount of work would have to go into ensuring that all the nominated and award-winning pieces from each nation could be freely shared globally.

creative individuals are drawn to the same location, and their interaction sparks new ideas.[119]

Since the point of the public domain awards is to publicize the importance that this free artistic space – the commons – has for our culture, we should raise the profile of the public domain, which currently lives in the ether, by giving it an unofficial physical capital.[120] Associating the public domain with a city would allow advocates of the commons to borrow the publicity efforts LA has long used to promote the film industry beyond simply hosting award ceremonies. Whichever city agrees to become the symbolic center of the public domain, be it Portland, Seattle, or Austin, it could emulate serious and quixotic ideas from other cultural hubs. On the lighter side, the city could create public domain stars on the city sidewalk to engrave with the names of artists who have significantly contributed to the commons. Such plaques or displays could even include samplings of the artists' work, given the art would be in the public domain. If numerous branches of sports and music have their own halls of fame, as do intellectual property lawyers, so could the public domain.[121] The city could build an equivalent of Hollywood's forty-five-foot-tall, 350-foot-long hillside sign that was originally built in 1923 – e.g., imagine a sign along the slope of Grouse Mountain just north of Vancouver or floating on Elliott Bay west of Seattle. The city could heavily promote the existing Public Domain Day.[122] The metropolis could create a public domain amphitheater to rival the Hollywood Bowl – possibly even carved into a hillside, as the Greeks were apt to do. It could brand a part of the city with the moniker "Public Domain Town" or "Commons Corner" (or, hopefully, something catchier). Seattle could even fund a public domain arts festival. If New York City can have a museum devoted to the media (the Paley Center for Media) that hosts exhibits, screenings, and a library of historic broadcasts, Portland could conceivably build a public domain museum with a sculpture park. Austin could create its own Times Square or Piccadilly Circus – a public square or busy intersection surrounded by enormous digital billboards displaying public domain art on an ever-continuous rotating basis.

---

[119] *See generally* RICHARD FLORIDA, THE RISE OF THE CREATIVE CLASS (2011).

[120] Barcelona is promoting collaborative projects or collective communities such as co-ops to provide access to the Internet and renewable energy sources – i.e., they are promoting different commons but not adopting the public domain to explicitly advocate for it. David Bollier, *Barcelona's Brave Struggle to Advance the Commons*, DAVID BOLLIER: NEWS & PERSP. ON COMMONS (Nov. 22, 2016, 1:16 PM), www.bollier.org/blog/barcelonas-brave-struggle-advance-commons.

[121] IP HALL OF FAME, www.iphalloffame.com (last visited Aug. 26, 2017).

[122] *Public Domain Day 2017*, CTR. FOR STUDY PUB. DOMAIN, https://law.duke.edu/cspd/pub licdomainday/ (last visited Feb. 9, 2017).

Ideally, the metropolis that decides to embrace the public domain would come up with a beguiling name to link its city to the commons. One path I would discourage is any attempt to make a play on "Hollywood." We already have the portmanteaus of Bollywood in India and Nollywood in Nigeria, which has even spun off its own Kannywood in Northern Nigeria for Hausa-language cinema. Attempting to go down this path would symbolically suggest that what the public domain city aspires to is to pay homage to Hollywood and the legal regime that validates it – excessive copyright law. We need a new nomenclature that breaks away from this assumption and instead counters it with an entirely new paradigm.

While publicity efforts such as building a giant "Public Domain Town" sign, hosting an annual awards ceremony, and placing stars on sidewalks would not transform the commons, especially since much of it exists online, symbolism is important and the public domain would benefit from such high-profile advertising. Furthermore, if a city volunteers to adopt the public domain, it would likely do more than provide free public relations. It would consider ways to build a public domain ecosystem to attain a critical mass of artists, scholars, and organizations interested in cultivating the public domain through hosting festivals; organizing conferences; endowing a few professorships at local universities to study the public domain from legal, social, and economic perspectives; and potentially helping the local government lobby Congress. For example, the city could subsidize rents to attract nonprofits advocating for a more robust public domain. It could do the same for startups interested in using the public domain to help society but also to make a dollar – e.g., using public domain creations for art and music therapy to reduce medical care costs.

Why would any city decide to adopt the public domain? For the very reason mentioned earlier – economic growth through increased jobs and tourism. This is a realistic proposition that at least one city would likely gamble on given how many cities have seriously explored Richard Florida's argument about the benefits to a city of cultivating a creative class through pursuing more robust art scenes. For example, if a United Nations Public Domain Programme is established, where better to locate the new institution than in the city synonymous with the public domain? Yet beyond self-interested motivations, a city might decide to do so because a large portion of its residents believe in the animating ideas underpinning the public domain and the importance of cultivating it.

To encourage more adults to care about such considerations, we need to start young. Through public relations campaigns aimed at youths, Big Copyright deliberately perpetuates misleading justifications of the theory underlying copyright law and what the law actually says. Even the Boy

Scouts in Los Angeles offer a "Respect Copyright" merit badge, for which the Motion Picture Association of America penned the curriculum.[123] These campaigns "teach a series of simplifications, even falsehoods, when it comes to the ownership of art and ideas"; for example, one lesson falsely states that "intellectual property is no different than physical property."[124]

The public domain needs better public relations across the board, yet it desperately needs a counterweight campaign to resist Big Copyright's inculcation of children. Just as the public domain awards could increase the profile of the commons, public domain passports could introduce kids to the joys of exploring and adding their own creations to the public domain. For every work they release into the commons, they would get a stamp that allows it to travel anywhere in the world unimpeded by copyright. Or, conversely, a digital passport could be issued to the child's creation so she can track each port of call along its journey by the stamp it receives every time another player opens the file. A variation of this idea would be to create an augmented reality app like Pokémon Go that lets a child release her creation into the public domain so her friends can try to "capture" it on their own devices in museums, in outdoor sculpture parks, and in front of architecturally significant buildings. Each of these passport ideas would encourage children to not just create but share their art with friends and talk about each other's work.[125]

Passports are symbols of both freedom and restraint. They enable us to experience the boundless world but only through limitations, bureaucracy, and a loss of privacy. The idea of public domain passports for kids would turn the restrictive aspects of passports on their head or, alternatively, emphasize the endless possibilities that passports can represent. They would do this by underscoring how art is about communicating freely and sharing ideas across all forms of boundaries for the betterment of us all.

Each public domain passport could include a very brief explanation of the public domain, what open licenses are, how the passport works, and how borrowing from others is vital to creation. The best open license for the passports is the Creative Commons Zero Public Domain Dedication tool, which is a legal document that one can attach to one's artwork to dedicate it to the public domain.[126] It is a "tool for freeing your own work of copyright

---

[123] Lewis Hyde, Common as Air: Revolution, Art, and Ownership 7 (2010).

[124] *Id.* at 8.

[125] I'd like to thank Malcolm McDermond for this Pokémon variation of public domain passports.

[126] CC0, Creative Commons, https://creativecommons.org/choose/zero/ (last visited Aug. 26, 2017). The CC0 tool is distinct from the Public Domain Mark, also created by Creative Commons. The Public Domain Mark is meant to be attached to works already in the public

restrictions around the world."[127] Further, CC0 also allows you to waive "related or neighboring rights that you may have in all jurisdictions worldwide, such as your moral rights (to the extent waivable), your publicity or privacy rights, rights you have protecting against unfair competition, and database rights and rights protecting the extraction, dissemination and reuse of data."[128]

While the public domain passports would be easy enough to create, ideally a nonprofit organization would be established to publicize and distribute the passports. Alternatively, an existing nonprofit could agree to take on such a project by adding a youth outreach branch to its mission. The nonprofit would attempt to get free copies of the public domain passports in schools to accompany art, music, and English classes and would distribute them to kids at airports or hotels. The nonprofit could consider partnering with existing kids' organizations such as the Boys & Girls Clubs of America and with airlines. For example, a national air carrier, such as United, could agree to hand out the public domain passports to kids on flights and offer works in the public domain to view. International versions of the passports could be created in Spanish, French, Arabic, Mandarin, and Russian, among other languages. The nonprofit organization could not only publicize the value of the public domain but also aim to correct Big Copyright's inaccurate teaching about copyright laws. It could talk about the exemptions to copyright for educational and other purposes and how one can use fair use to borrow from other artists. Of course, the passports themselves would be free for anyone to use, unimpeded by copyright restrictions.

RESULTS-BASED COPYRIGHT REFORM PRIZES

From the Bill & Melinda Gates Foundation to XPRIZE, numerous organizations are offering large financial prizes to the first individual or entity to accomplish a specified task – e.g., develop a cure or vaccine for a disease.[129] This strategy dates back centuries, at least to 1714, when the British government offered a £20,000 prize to the first individual to find a solution to the problem

---

[127] domain worldwide, while the CC0 enables you to strip the copyright protection surrounding a work not already in the public domain. *Id.*

[127] *Id.* [128] *Id.*

[129] Owen Barder, Michael Kremer, & Heidi Williams, *Advance Market Commitments: How to Stimulate Investment in Vaccines for Neglected Diseases,* in THE ECONOMISTS' VOICE: TOP ECONOMISTS TAKE ON TODAY'S PROBLEMS 52, 56 (Joseph E. Stiglitz, Aaron S. Edlin, & J. Bradford DeLong eds., 2008) and William W. Fisher & Talha Syed, *A Prize System as a Partial Solution to the Health Crisis in the Developing World,* in INCENTIVES FOR GLOBAL HEALTH: PATENT LAW & ACCESS TO ESSENTIAL MEDICINES 181 (Thomas Pogge et al. eds., 2009).

of determining longitude at sea to within half a degree.[130] Even Napoleon in 1795 tendered a 12,000-franc prize for a better method of preserving food that was easily transportable and capable of supplying an army.[131] Countries seeking solutions to strengthen their military dominance on sea and land initiated these challenges. Yet private results-based prizes were also offered. For example, a hotelier named Raymond Orteig offered a $25,000 prize in 1919 to the first pilot to fly directly from Paris to New York or vice versa, with the aim of boosting his profits through increased tourism.[132] After numerous aviators lost their lives to the pursuit, Charles Lindbergh captured the prize in 1927.

The idea of provoking change through offering substantial results-based prizes might sound ambitious or unreachable, yet XPRIZE prides itself in setting far-flung goals. Its first prize was a $10 million competition for the creation of a "reliable, reusable, privately-financed, manned spaceship."[133] XPRIZE not only leveraged talent, it "leveraged investment in an industry that started from nothing."[134] Discoveries from the competition helped generate a "private space industry worth over $2 billion today."[135] Relevant to the concern of alleviating harm caused by excessive copyright protection, XPRIZEs do not only fund scientific inventions – e.g., one current $7 million XPRIZE is to increase adult literacy, while a potential future prize deals with happiness.[136]

XPRIZE believes certain criteria are critical for success. Without listing its near dozen standards, the most instructive for a copyright prize are as follows. First, a bold and audacious yet achievable goal that targets a market failure needs to be set. Second, this goal should be measurable and winnable by a small team. Third, the problem should be presented in a "solution-agnostic"

[130] JONATHAN BETTS, TIME RESTORED: THE HARRISON TIMEKEEPERS AND R. T. GOULD, THE MAN WHO KNEW (ALMOST) EVERYTHING 84 (2006). "Up until the middle of the eighteenth century, navigators had been unable to determine their position at sea with accuracy and they faced the huge attendant risks of shipwreck or running out of supplies before reaching their destination." *Id.* at 83. "The Government prize of £20,000 was the highest of three sums on offer for varying degrees of accuracy, the full prize only payable for a method that could find the longitude at sea within half a degree." *Id.* at 84. John Harrison, a self-taught carpenter, ultimately claimed the prize.
[131] JOHN W. KLOOSTER, ICONS OF INVENTION: THE MAKERS OF THE MODERN WORLD FROM GUTENBERG TO GATES 101 (2009).
[132] RICHARD BAK, THE BIG JUMP: LINDBERGH AND THE GREAT ATLANTIC AIR RACE 28–29 (2011). The preceding examples can also be found at *Our Story*, HEROX, https://herox.com /our-story (last visited Aug. 27, 2017).
[133] *Mojave Aerospace Ventures Wins the Competition That Started It All*, XPRIZE: ANSARI XPRIZE, http://ansari.xprize.org/teams (last visited Aug. 26, 2017).
[134] *Id.* [135] *Id.*
[136] *A $7 Million Global Competition to Transform the Lives of Low-Literate Adults*, XPRIZE: BARBARA BUSH FOUNDATION ADULT LITERACY XPRIZE, http://adultliteracy.xprize.org/ (last visited Aug. 27, 2017).

manner, while the objective and rules should be clearly defined. Fourth, the challenge should be "designed to affect the foreseeable future" within a reasonable time frame of two to seven years.[137]

While a company or foundation often sponsors prizes to the tune of millions of dollars, the exact prize amount varies and does not inevitably have to be so large. This is especially the case for assuaging the harms of excessive copyright protection because a copyright challenge might not require as much financial investment as building a reusable spaceship. Furthermore, the prize bounty does not necessarily have to come from one entity. We can save time by not bothering to ask Big Copyright for funding and instead approach a few technology companies that potentially view a more moderate copyright regime as beneficial to their self-interest. This is not inconceivable given certain companies issue open source software while generating revenue through providing services, and others, even Google perhaps, view information in all its forms as its comparative advantage and might feel encumbered at times by the current copyright laws.

Since a corporate benefactor is probably a long shot, we should approach foundations and wealthy individuals with the aim of convincing them of the gravity of our cultural condition. Anu and Naveen Jain wanted to tackle the problem that "one in three women globally have faced physical or sexual violence in their lifetime," with the rates dramatically higher in certain regions of the world. For example, in New Delhi, more than 90 percent of women have experienced "some form of sexual violence in public spaces in their lifetime."[138] To empower communities to respond quickly to threats against women, the Jains established their own $1 million XPRIZE that urges teams to develop technological "safety nets."[139] Conceivably, a similar prize could challenge software developers, scholars, policy wonks, and artists to find innovative ways to resist Big Copyright, reform copyright law, support the public domain, and help individuals make room in their lives for creativity. We just need to make our case to potential benefactors.

Alternatively, the funds for the results-based prize could be crowdsourced along the lines of HeroX, "a platform where you can support a cause you believe in, help fund a prize, or post challenges to inspire others."[140] HeroX

[137]   *What Is an XPRIZE?*, XPRIZE, www.xprize.org/about/what-is-an-xprize (last visited Aug. 27, 2017).

[138]   *Technology for Safer Communities*, XPRIZE: Anu & Naveen Jain Women's Safety XPRIZE, http://safety.xprize.org/ (last visited Aug. 27, 2017).

[139]   *Id.*

[140]   *Sponsors & Partners*, XPRIZE, www.xprize.org/about/foundation-partners-sponsors (last visited Aug. 27, 2017). *See also* HeroX, *supra* note 132.

currently has more than $25 million in prizes committed to different challenges.[141] Created as "a means to democratize the innovation model of XPRIZE,"[142] HeroX not only provides the digital platform to collect funds from others but helps with marketing and community management of crowd-sourced results-based prizes.

While the idea of using incentive prizes to reform copyright has not yet been explored, the idea that we could eliminate our entire copyright system and replace it with a government-sponsored system of prizes for creative works of authorship has been discussed within the copyright literature.[143] If reformers decide against the "repeal and replace" idea, they could ask the public for help with determining what goal to set for an incentive prize aimed at reforming copyright law. The HeroX website allows contest organizers to create a modest challenge that awards a prize to the individual who has the most convincing idea for defining a prize competition or setting rules for it. In other words, the prize system itself can be crowdsourced – copyright reformers can challenge the public to help define and structure it. Plus, contest organizers can even ask the public to "crowd vote" for the optimal refinement of their vision.[144] For example, the public can help decide how to set the prize parameters for alleviating the harm caused by copyright orphans or increasing artists' pay within a particular art form. Voting could also be used to refine how to measure phenomena such as the total number of copyright orphans or how to assign decreases in copyright orphans to the efforts of different, competing teams.

This renaissance in results-based prizes can be used in the copyright context to create one or more challenges that lead to legislative reform, help reduce negative externalities caused by the current excessive copyright regime, or encourage the public to start creating more and consuming less.

WORLD EASE OF ARTISTIC CREATION INDEX

Society at times appears to be obsessed with rankings. While we have traditionally followed them in sports, they have exploded into many aspects of life. We rank products – from cars and washing machines to socks, wines, TV episodes, dog toys, and dogs themselves – while marketers measure and rank our online activities. We rank professionals – doctors, plumbers, lawyers,

---

[141] *Id.* [142] *About HeroX*, HEROX, https://herox.com/about (last visited Aug. 27, 2017).

[143] At least one treatise scholar avers: "Congress has withheld comprehensive subsidies to the arts on the ground that the marketplace rather than government patronage is the best guarantor of diverse expression." PAUL GOLDSTEIN, GOLDSTEIN ON COPYRIGHT 46 (3d ed. 2016).

[144] *FAQ*, HEROX, https://herox.com/faq (last visited Aug. 27, 2017).

electricians, dentists, etc. We rank institutions – law firms, hospitals, restaurants, and universities. Plus, we don't just have one ranking of universities; we have many – not just of different intellectual disciplines but regional rankings, national rankings, world rankings. We might even have a ranking of different university rankings or at least composite rankings that aggregate the scores of different university rankings into a combined mark. We rank cities; we rank nations. Select a matter relevant to countries, and there is a good chance that a ranking exists for it from cost of living to crime. We rank at least seven different ways developed countries assist developing countries – foreign aid, migration, technology transfer, finance, trade, security, and environmental policies.[145]

Rankings can be dangerous. Whether a ranking does more good than harm hinges on what subject matter is ranked, how it is measured, how accurately it is measured, and what is excluded. There are concerns about rankers comparing oranges and apples, consumers fixating on rankings, rankings reinforcing inequality, and individuals and institutions attempting to game rankings. Any particular ranking could be subject to legitimate criticism on potentially all the previously mentioned grounds.[146] Yet we realize that ignoring rankings, however arbitrary or wrong, can negatively affect us if others rely on them. Thus, to minimize the harm, we need to convince existing rankers to alter their criteria or close shop, or else we need to create a better ranking system and compete against them.

Existing rankings either attempt to equate creativity with more, not less, intellectual property protection or simply scold countries for weak IP protection. For example, as previously mentioned, the USTR issues the "Special 301" Report, which reviews the global status of IP protection and enforcement.[147] From the perspective of the USTR, the report aims to publicize which countries are not doing enough to enforce existing excessive IP protections, which in the view of the USTR will reduce investment and

---

[145] Developed countries have varied widely in how much and in what ways they have attempted to assist different developing countries. The Center for Global Development's Commitment to Development Index measures the previously mentioned seven ways developed countries attempt to help others. See Petra Krylová & Owen Barder, *Commitment to Development Index 2015*, CTR. GLOBAL DEV. (Dec. 4, 2015), www.cgdev.org/publication/ft/commitment-development-index-2015.

[146] For an example of gaming legal rankings, see *Villanova Law Censured for Grade Inflation*, NBC PHILADELPHIA (Aug. 16, 2011, 11:23 AM), www.nbcphiladelphia.com/news/local/Villanova-Law-Censured-for-Grade-Inflation-127837313.html (last updated Aug. 16, 2011, 8:07 PM).

[147] *Special 301*, OFFICE U.S. TRADE REPRESENTATIVE, https://ustr.gov/issue-areas/intellectual-property/Special-301.

innovation. The report only pays lip service to establishing ever-more-restrictive IP laws because the laws on the books in most countries are already so extreme. Thus, the Special 301 Report grumbles about "troubling 'indigenous innovation' policies that may unfairly disadvantage U.S. rights holders in foreign markets" in addition to complaining about instances of international unauthorized copying and counterfeit trademarked products.[148] The USTR avers: "The United States uses the review and resulting Report to focus our engagement on these issues, and looks forward to constructive cooperation with the trading partners identified in the Report to improve the environment for authors, brand owners, and inventors around the world."[149]

Another example is the Global Creativity Index, which ranks nations on their talent, technology, and tolerance – metrics that aim to indicate creativity and prosperity.[150] While the ranking is mostly well meaning – for example, measuring racial and ethnic tolerance, tertiary education levels, the size of the creative class, and research and development spending – it makes two mistakes. First, it assumes more patents directly lead to more creativity and prosperity. More important for our purposes, it doesn't measure or address barriers to creativity for artists and creators. The sixty-eight-page report published in 2015 doesn't even mention copyright once; it doesn't broach whether countries' excessive copyright policies deter individuals from creating in many instances, let alone contemplate how to reduce such negatives.[151]

The Consumers International IP Watch List was a worthwhile endeavor that had the correct vision of how copyright, if excessive, can inhibit creation; however, it relied on surveys that were on average more than five years old, and its rankings missed the essence of where the most harm occurs from excessive copyright.[152] First, the rankings were generated from survey questions that one could only respond to with "Yes," "No," or "In part," which severely limited room for refinement. Further, it did not clearly define ideal policies, so it was unhelpful in forcefully communicating how bad the situation is in all countries. Instead of emphasizing how far away from a healthy copyright regime countries are, it further exaggerated differences through comparing countries against each other on an arbitrary A to F gradient. Finally, instead of concentrating on how excessive copyright encourages vast overconsumption, creates

[148] *Id.* [149] *Id.*
[150] Richard Florida, Charlotta Mellander, & Karen King, *The Global Creativity Index 2015*, MARTIN PROSPERITY INST., http://martinprosperity.org/media/Global-Creativity-Index-2015.pdf.
[151] *Id.*
[152] *Consumers International IP Watch List 2009*, OPEN SOC'Y FOUND., www.opensocietyfoundations.org/reports/ip-watch-list-2009.

an army of copyright orphans, and does little to financially assist more than a handful of elite artists, it focused on access to and use of copyright material – a worthy concern but only one failure in a basket of problems with the copyright regime. Asking questions such as "May quotations be used for any purpose?" as an indicator of journalists' freedom to access and use copyrighted material is valuable but doesn't strike at the heart of copyright's ills.

Those interested in copyright reform should consider creating a new ranking as a way to counter the misconceptions of copyright perpetuated by Hollywood.[153] One method to do so is to create a new world ease of artistic creation index – a ranking that encourages more artistic creation, not the discovery of new inventions; a ranking that counters the USTR's "Special 301" view that ever-more copyright protection is optimal.

The methodology for the new creativity ranking could take one of two forms. First, it could measure how far away from a reasonable copyright regime countries are presently, concentrating on how too much copyright leads us to overconsume, in addition to gauging policies to reduce copyright orphans, increase non-celebrity artists' incomes, and increase the ability of individuals to legally borrow from others. It is impossible, at least at present, to precisely define each facet of an ideal copyright regime – e.g., whether six months or two years of copyright protection is ideal. Yet we know that where the current length of copyright stands – at the entire life of the author plus seventy years after her death – is overkill. While there would be debate about the specific Platonic form, such debate would highlight most countries' misguided policies of maximizing copyright protection beyond sanity. Further, the importance of generating an imperfect baseline of reasonable copyright protection stems from the fact that almost every country in the world has incredibly excessive levels of protection; hence there are few meaningful distinctions between countries.[154] Some variation exists – e.g., in database protection, moral rights, and para-copyright measures – yet it is simply too little. Hollywood has imposed amazing copyright uniformity across the globe through international treaties. The emphasis needs to be on how all countries are far away from moderation, not on how one country's excessive copyright length compares to another country's excessive copyright length.

Another approach could be to have copyright law as only one of numerous variables measured by the index. Whereas the first form of the creativity

---

[153]   For an excellent exposition of the need for an access to knowledge index, see Lea Shaver, *Defining and Measuring A2K: A Blueprint for an Index of Access to Knowledge*, 4 I/S: J. L. & Pol'y Info. Soc'y (2008).

[154]   This approach would be contrasted to how some rankings grant the top country a score of 100 and normalize all other countries' scores in relation to the top country's position.

ranking would focus on how excessive copyright law reduces creation by making us overconsume, by limiting our ability to borrow from others' work, and by putting most of the cash in the pockets of a few elite artists, the second form of the ranking would include measures of excessive copyright but also track the amount of funds dedicated to community art programs, the proportion of students receiving art or music instruction at school, the cost of art museum tickets, and the average amount of entertainment individuals in different countries consume. Thus, this second form would look more directly at how much citizens in countries are actually creating and less at how excessive copyright law reduces the amount they create.

Big Copyright exploits the use of rankings to propagate its preferred vision of copyright maximalism. We need to counter such exploitation with our own ranking providing an alternative narrative.

COPYRIGHT-FREE FESTIVALS

The world rushes to reimagine the physical world on the Internet – e.g., virtual books, bookstores, and libraries as well as digital communication and entertainment. Working in reverse, we need to take some of the innovation online and introduce it within our brick-and-mortar existence. The idea of an online creative commons needs to be re-created in physical space. Groups across the country could establish copyright-free festivals where individuals freely share their work for a weekend or longer by getting together to create and experiment with other attendees' works.

Everyone at the festival would grant everyone else in attendance a nonexclusive license to use the work he or she brings to the event for at least the length of the festival, if not longer. The license would allow all attendees to freely use each other's works in any manner they deem fit. If so desired, Creative Commons licenses could be modified to limit borrowing simply for the duration and on the grounds of the festival. Alternatively, a more generous system would enable attendees to take their creations, and the material borrowed from others contained within their art, with them when they return home and freely use or dispose of both as they see fit. A third option, the most open of all, would allow festival attendees to use other attendees' work for the length of their lives. This third option would in essence be a Creative Commons license that is only handed out to festivalgoers, allowing them to use any art from other festivalgoers to encourage attendance.

Just as with Creative Commons licenses, such open source festivals would only put a dent in copyright restraints, but such festivals should be a welcome addition to a rising movement to redress how legally perilous borrowing has become at the behest of Hollywood's lobbyists. Further, open source festivals, as with Creative Commons, would play a modest role in reducing the problem of overconsumption caused by our copyright regime because the essence of such festivals would be creating on one's own.

Given the digital nature of Creative Commons, such licenses are more efficient in disseminating free works relative to a copyright-free festival, yet there are positive benefits of copyright-free or open source festivals that cannot be had in cyberspace. Foremost are the numerous positive benefits of face-to-face human contact, such as improved mental health and higher-quality and hence more satisfying communication.[155] In addition to such psychological benefits, copyright-free festivals could attempt to be the artistic equivalent of deliberative democracy theory within the artistic realm.[156] The festivals could encourage artists with different artistic, economic, and political visions to mix in hopes of inspiring existing artists or teaching new ones. Regardless, the festivals do not have to be better than Creative Commons licenses, simply different – engaging artists already using Creative Commons licenses in a new way and attracting artists altogether unfamiliar with such open licenses. Given the diversity of people's preferences, there will be some who will get benefits out of festivals that they could not receive online, just as there will be some for whom the reverse will be true.[157]

Copyright-free festivals are similar to yet distinct from copyright-free zones. The difference is that festivalgoers can only use each other's art, while artists in a copyright free zone can import and borrow from any works in existence.

A possible concern is that artists might not be interested in creating at the festival if attendees are not allowed to distribute their work afterward. First, depending on how the open licenses are written, artists could distribute their work created at the festival after the fact. Second, as mentioned with copyright-free zones, even if artists couldn't distribute their works after the festival, the process of creation and the close proximity of many artists could prove to be good practice and insightful nonetheless.

---

[155] See generally Alan R. Teo et al., *Does Mode of Contact with Different Types of Social Relationships Predict Depression in Older Adults? Evidence from a Nationally Representative Survey*, 63 J. AM. GERIATRICS SOC'Y 2014 (2015) and Ned Kock, *The Psychobiological Model: Towards a New Theory of Computer-Mediated Communication Based on Darwinian Evolution*, 15 ORG. SCI. 327 (2004).

[156] See generally AMY GUTMANN & DENNIS THOMPSON, WHY DELIBERATIVE DEMOCRACY? (2004).

[157] Getting a few well-known artists to agree to attend copyright-free festivals could do wonders to promote such gatherings. Also, we would need to think of ways to easily display each artist's artwork to everyone else at the festival to facilitate borrowing.

NONCORPORATE ART ALERT AND COPYRIGHT ANTI-MATCH

Our world has been socialized – not in the sense of surpassing capitalism but in the sense that almost anything we do online can have a social media component. Even without Facebook, Snapchat, Instagram, Twitter, LinkedIn, and countless other social platforms, we still can't browse for eateries without being presented with the option to see whether our friends have been to the restaurant and, if so, what they think of it.

This is particularly true with media and art. Entertainment sites that were born without social networking functions, such as Hulu, Netflix, and *The Washington Post*, now have them in spades. While not all of such social connectivity regarding artwork leads us to consume more corporate artwork, a ton of it does.

It is not inevitable that we should use social networking to further cement Big Copyright's already seemingly indestructible hegemony. To resist it, let's create an app that encourages friends to share the noncorporate artwork they interact with. Of course, the app would not enable – and could even block – the sharing of corporate artwork. Big Copyright doesn't need any more free advertising, so let's stop being its foot soldiers. An app that tells you what noncorporate art your friends are viewing would attempt to level the playing field for artists. Equally importantly, it would expose users to more diverse works with potentially more revealing truths. The app could be integrated with Facebook and other social platforms so enthusiasts can spread the word. In addition to possibly increasing the income of non-celebrity artists, such a noncorporate art alert app would reduce passive consumption since it is unlikely that the forms, messages, and production values of noncorporate works are conspiring to immobilize us on the couch.

The recommendations we get from friends might vary little in style or content from what we are comfortable with. This is not necessarily bad. Getting recommendations from friends can be quite helpful and satisfying, though we have been made aware of the dangers of having our views unquestioned in the political realm for some time. If all the news one reads is presented through the lens of a political ideology one already believes in, then one reduces the chances that one will question one's beliefs.[158] This same risk exists within culture, not just politics. Further, culture and politics are inextricably linked. A painting of struggling farmers depicted nobly by Jean-François Millet can affect us in numerous subtle and implicit ways. Beyond the range of thoughts and emotions that art can evoke, works sometimes intend

---

[158] *See generally* DELIBERATIVE POLITICS: ESSAYS ON DEMOCRACY AND DISAGREEMENT (Stephen Macedo ed., 1999).

to convey explicitly political messages. This concern that we frequently test our beliefs through exposure to alternative views is a cornerstone of the theory of deliberative democracy and should apply to art as well as politics.[159]

While a noncorporate art alert would aim to broaden one's exposure to noncorporate works through sharing with friends, an alternative is to create an app where users could enter the names of corporate works they like and be given recommendations of noncorporate art to sample instead. Some of the noncorporate recommendations would clearly share similarities with the corporate work (e.g., in subject matter, genre, or style), while other recommendations would be significantly different to egg on the individual to try something new.[160] Thus, some of the recommendations would push one's boundaries (and buttons), especially in regard to political, economic, and cultural viewpoints.[161] As a result, the copyright anti-matching machine would get users not only to contemplate noncorporate work but also to experience art outside their established preferences in style or content.

Both a noncorporate art alert and a copyright anti-match app would aim to decrease our overall consumption of entertainment by shifting our focus toward noncorporate works and away from corporate works crafted in addictive mediums by an army of creators whose job is to hook us instead of inspire us.

---

[159]   Beyond a diverse cross section of art helping us reflect on our political commitments, it can potentially improve our own innovation. Howard Tullman, CEO of Tribeca Flashpoint Media Arts Academy, suggests that having varied artwork in your office can help spur innovative thoughts. Elysabeth Alfano, *Does Business Need the Arts to Be Innovative? Five Executives Weigh In*, HUFFINGTON POST (Jan. 23, 2013, 4:29 PM), www.huffingtonpost.com /elysabeth-alfano/business-art-innovation_b_2450438.html (last updated Mar. 25, 2013).

[160]   Artsy runs an interesting endeavor called The Art Genome Project, which "maps the characteristics (we call them 'genes') that connect artists, artworks, architecture, and design objects across history. There are currently over 1,000 characteristics in The Art Genome Project, including art historical movements, subject matter, and formal qualities." While sharing similarities to the copyright anti-match machine, it doesn't rely on the distinction between corporate and noncorporate art – it concentrates on fine art – nor is it used to prove dissimilar works as results. *About*, ARTSY, www.artsy.net/about (last visited June 7, 2017).

[161]   I am not attempting to presume a one-way street in terms of political positions. For example, Ken Johnson, a liberal art critic at *The New York Times*, has stated that "the orders of the art world are pretty tightly policed ideologically ... There's a lot of kinds of expressions or sensibilities that aren't allowed in these. You could say that it's a 'liberal festival' ... No, the only thing that would be shocking in the art world is if a great Teabagger painter came along ... Oh ... I shouldn't say that. I should say ... if some ultra right-winger, conservative." *The Art World: A Boring Festival of Liberals?*, EDWARD WINKLEMAN (May 5, 2011), www .edwardwinkleman.com/2011/05/art-world-boring-festival-of-liberals.html (providing a partial transcript of a *Leonard Lopate Show* that Ken Johnson appeared on).

INSTRUCTION COMMONS

Not knowing how to vary brushstrokes or how to write a stanza rarely stops toddlers from creating with abandon, yet older children and adults are not so bold. Part of why some individuals are reluctant to create could be because they do not know how. This makes a good deal of sense when it comes to numerous things in life – e.g., it would probably be a bad idea to try to fly a plane without instruction.

To help alleviate this hesitancy, an instruction commons site could be established, where one could type in the name of a famous painting or song and the site would explain the artistic techniques involved in making the artwork. For example, users could learn how Vincent van Gogh applied brushstrokes, how Ansel Adams captured light, how Gustav Holst arranged harmonic progressions, or how Constantin Brancusi carved stone. Additionally, beginners could take a comprehensive step-by-step course in a particular art form where each new lesson allows them to select a famous work to serve as the basis for learning the new technique. Furthermore, experienced artists looking to improve on a particular aspect of their artwork could be presented a range of masterpiece-centered lessons relevant to the focus area they want to explore.

Many artists learn from existing works they admire either consciously or unconsciously. For centuries, the visual arts were taught through explicit imitation – e.g., students attempted to perfectly duplicate existing master-pieces. This was not only a sign of respect and admiration for the artists who came before but an effective way to learn. It is not until aspiring artists have "thoroughly assimilated" others' works that they can begin to develop their own voice out of the totality of culture and history – as T. S. Eliot explained, an artist is compelled "to write not merely with his own generation in his bones, but with a feeling that the whole of literature . . . has a simultaneous existence and composes a simultaneous order."[162] The instruction commons would make this foundational aspect of creating – that we cannot help but borrow and learn from existing artwork – explicit, organized, and comprehensive.

While there are a flood of sites that provide general instruction on how to tattoo, write poetry, garden, and generate digital graphics, fewer show you how to learn from replicating existing creations. There are some artistic forms for which instruction in re-creating specific items or tasks is available, yet it tends to be because of the nature of particular artistic forms – cooking and knitting versus

---

[162] William Patry, How to Fix Copyright 91 & 97 (2011) (citing T. S. Eliot's essay "Tradition and the Individual Talent," www.bartleby.com/200/sw4.html).

film or music.[163] While one still needs to learn certain general cooking techniques such as whipping and kneading, given the nature of cooking, much of the instruction entails following detailed recipes for specific meals. One such website for knitters, crocheters, spinners, weavers, and dyers, Ravelry, which receives millions of hits each month,[164] enables members to share educational materials, such as patterns, on how to make a plethora of individual designs.[165]

Tailored instruction on how to re-create existing works is not necessarily a better way to master an art form than general guidance – e.g., how to hold your hands above piano keys properly, how to cut fabric when making dresses. Yet such general instruction can also be learned from studying a masterpiece. Training centered on the re-creation of masterpieces makes learning more exciting because it adds relevance and concreteness – your aim isn't the abstract challenge of learning to paint but a specific goal, for example, reproducing a Joan Miró canvas. Further, such precise instruction is not too much to ask of beginners (e.g., replicating a small Georges Seurat painting) yet also provides challenges to experts (e.g., mirroring a Bartolomé Murillo). Finally, it gives artists time to find their own voice or create their own style. Knowing how to use different brushstrokes and how to mix paint does not make deciding what to paint any easier, but replicating famous works can help a budding artist get more comfortable with an art form and view creativity as a great source of excitement instead of a daunting task.

An instruction commons could provide both general and specific education in a variety of art forms broadly defined. It could be a one-stop portal for individuals with a range of expertise, from neophytes to amateurs to full-time artists.[166] Such an instruction commons could enable visitors to provide helpful services to each other. For example, Ravelry brings the knitting community closer through ancillary services such as connecting knitters looking for a rare wool yarn with knitters who have it. Members not only answer such calls but do so generously – at times sending the yarn free of charge. Something similar

---

[163] Not only will YouTube most likely provide you with a free video on how to change a shower faucet; it will probably offer a video on how to change your specific faucet – i.e., a video on the quirks of installing your particular brand and make of faucet.

[164] *Ravelry.com Website Traffic and Information*, Traffic Estimate, www.trafficestimate .com/ravelry.com (last visited Feb. 9, 2017).

[165] *About Us*, Ravelry, www.ravelry.com/about (last visited Feb. 9, 2017).

[166] Different individual components of an instruction commons exist to varying degrees, though I have found no comparable sites. For example, both Artyfactory and Artists Network provide only a handful of examples of how to use existing paintings to learn a technique, provide instruction in only some art mediums, and charge fees and/or are not open collaborative projects. *See generally* Artyfactory, www.artyfactory.com/ (last visited June 7, 2017) and Artists Network, www.artistsnetwork.com/ (last visited June 7, 2017).

could be done for finding resources such as studio space, in-person instruction, or extras for an amateur film.

It's possible that a commons offering free instruction and resources would become a household name. If Wikipedia's growing popularity can lead doubters to become users and contributors, then broad recognition of an instruction commons can spur more individuals to become learners, creators, and instructors. Plus, there is something alluring and reassuring to a beginner about a site that has all the instruction you need, a site where knowledge building is collaborative and insights are tested – a site that lets you know where to begin, no matter what creative activity you want to start.

Currently, we have plenty of 800-pound gorillas in other online domains – Facebook in social media, Google in search, Amazon in online retail, eBay in auctions, etc. – yet no similarly sized gorilla exists for learning how to create in any art form. We have large sites for specific art forms, such as Ravelry for knitting and crocheting, but the dominant site in each art form is not usually known outside of its membership or others interested in that specific art. We generally think of centralization as potentially troubling from an economic competitive standpoint or from the perspective that multiple sources of information guard against bias, yet if we had a Google of artistic instruction, its brand power could focus minds to create. Further, we could guard against competition concerns by making it a nonprofit and defend it from informational bias concerns by encouraging as many people as possible to collaborate in building up the content.

As with promoting the public domain, innovative as well as time-tested strategies could be deployed to get the word out about the instruction portal, including enlisting famous artists as spokespeople. Taking a cue from social media marketing, we could ask portal enthusiasts to mention their experiences to others. For example, we could create a logo that artists could attach to their works in the same vein that Creative Commons licenses attached to existing works advertise the value of such licenses. An instruction commons logo would not have to be attached to a license – it could simply be an option for users who are grateful to the portal and willing to spread news of its existence.[167]

---

[167] Theoretically, the use of the instruction commons logo could go beyond a voluntary arrangement to more of a license model. In essence, users of the creative portal would agree to affix the logo to future works they create if the portal was helpful in teaching them more about a particular craft. The instruction commons logo could be attached to a simple license that states that you should attribute your instruction to the portal. Thus, it would be similar to Creative Commons' approach to attribution rights, yet instead of mentioning whose artwork you incorporated into your own creation, it would be declaring where, in part, you learned to create. To keep the idea distinct, we could call it a recognition right that new creators would be acknowledging when they attach the logo to their creations.

6

Cooperating with Big Copyright

Love your enemy. It will ruin his reputation.
                    —Archbishop Desmond Tutu

Providing Big Copyright with incentives to cooperate – to not block copyright reform or to address problems created by copyright non-legislatively – can have significant positive benefits in general. Yet the approach is difficult to employ as a tool to decrease the production of corporate artwork and hence reduce overconsumption, since the raison d'être of Hollywood is profits. Given the numerous problems with the current copyright regime beyond encouraging overconsumption, such as poor pay for the majority of artists and untold copyright orphans, it is imperative to also consider practical proposals that incentivize Big Copyright to address these other concerns, even if the effects on overconsumption may be unclear, marginal, or nonexistent.[1]

Dangle a large enough carrot in front of corporations, and they will not resist. Yet the same does not necessarily work for activists, given the nature of their motivations. Activists do not have to love the idea of working with Hollywood, nor should they give up their efforts to build, over the long term, society-wide support for their positions; in the short term, however, they must compromise to stay true to their stated goals. Some communist intellectuals undermined socialism because they felt that temporary measures slowed progress and sullied their purity of purpose. Oscar Wilde wrote of

---

[1] Any augmentation in creation by citizens or artists encouraged by the reform proposals will not further increase consumption because citizens do not overconsume work by average citizens or even famous individual artists; they overconsume corporate work created by Big Copyright. Furthermore, on average, citizens overconsume certain art forms such as TV and movies that are highly dependent on copyright and whose current practice creates tendencies in the brain that lead to overconsumption.

denying the poor charity so that society would more quickly open its eyes to the horrors of capitalism and hence more readily embrace communism.[2] His twisted logic infantilized the poor – as if they did not already know how hard their lives were or forgot such hardship when it was temporarily relieved by a private charity and as if they could not understand the effects of capitalism or charity's relationship to different economic systems. Copyright minimalists have the moral high ground. They should not be co-opted by copyright abolitionists or by their own ideal vision of copyright into maintaining the current excessive copyright regime; they should not replicate Wilde's mistaken calculation, especially given that partial freedom now will strengthen the movement for the arduous long-term fight ahead.

In the words of Alexander Bickel, "No society, certainly not a large and heterogeneous one, can fail in time to explode if it is deprived of the arts of compromise, if it knows no ways of muddling through. No good society can be unprincipled; and no viable society can be principle-ridden."[3] Edmund Burke previously expressed a similar sentiment, stating, "All government, indeed every human benefit and enjoyment, every virtue and every prudent act, is founded on compromise and barter. We balance inconveniences; we give and take; we remit some rights, that we may enjoy others; and we choose rather to be happy citizens than subtle disputants."[4] At a minimum, compromise is a necessary evil.

I cannot improve on Archbishop Tutu's advice on loving one's enemy. So I will jump right into examples of potential collaboration, for partnership is a close second to love.

TIERED REVENUE-BASED COPYRIGHT REGIME

I propose a tiered revenue-based copyright regime.[5] It would give the "one-in-a-million" copyright holder the ability to cash out her lottery ticket without having to derail our culture. It would do this by presenting

---

[2] See generally OSCAR WILDE, THE SOUL OF MAN UNDER SOCIALISM AND SELECTED CRITICAL PROSE (Linda Dowling ed., Penguin Classics 2001) (1885–1891). Marx advocated a similar argument in his critique of petty-bourgeois socialism. KARL MARX, THE COMMUNIST MANIFESTO 81–82 (Frederic L. Bender ed., Samuel Moore trans., Norton 1988) (1848).

[3] ALEXANDER M. BICKEL, THE LEAST DANGEROUS BRANCH: THE SUPREME COURT AT THE BAR OF POLITICS 64 (Yale University Press, 2d ed. 1986).

[4] Edmund Burke, On Moving His Resolutions for Conciliation with the Colonies (Mar. 22, 1775), in 1 SELECT WORKS OF EDMUND BURKE 221, 278 (E. J. Payne ed., Liberty Fund 1999).

[5] There is a different and unrelated proposal for using tiers within copyright law based on the originality of copyrighted material. See generally Gideon Parchomovsky & Alex Stein, Originality, 95 VA. L. REV. 1505 (2009).

all artists with two different copyright terms, which they would have to choose between. The first tier would provide a fixed, nonrenewable copyright term of ten to fourteen years, while the second tier would offer a one-year copyright term that could be indefinitely renewed as long as the work is successful enough to meet or exceed a revenue threshold.[6]

The effect of a tiered revenue-based copyright regime on overconsumption is unclear. One could draft scenarios where consumption increases, decreases, or largely stays the same. For example, such a copyright system might increase Hollywood's profits and at the same time reduce overconsumption through having Hollywood continue to charge for its perennial winners yet having the public consume fewer corporate works of marginal interest. A two-tiered revenue-based copyright regime will break the gridlock between Big Copyright lobbying for longer copyright terms and public domain advocates insisting that terms are already remarkably excessive. It will solve the problem of exceedingly long copyright terms for most artwork in exchange for giving Big Copyright the opportunity to have much longer copyright protection on its most successful commercial works. It will immediately free millions of orphaned works, and its structure will institutionally preclude orphans from reemerging. It will require all artists seeking copyright protection to register each work and thus will keep most noncommercial art in the public domain. It will increase the speed at which the overwhelming majority of commercial art moves into the public domain because artists selecting the first tier would have only ten to fourteen years of copyright protection – a much shorter term than current law provides. Moreover, it will free much of the commercial art in the second tier within one or a few years of copyright registration, for the revenue-based annual renewal system will be a final filter to ensure that only the most profitable works continue to be excluded from the commons.[7]

---

[6] *See generally* Martin Skladany, *Unchaining Richelieu's Monster: A Tiered Revenue-Based Copyright Regime*, 16 STAN. TECH. L. REV. 131 (2012).

[7] This proposal addresses only copyright length, not other ills plaguing copyright like its excessive breadth and depth. Further, the proposed copyright regime is limited to artwork – e.g., I do not consider copyright on software. Also, it is assumed that if a tiered revenue-based copyright regime is implemented, the United States would have to withdraw from at least the Berne Convention, which compels all signatories to subscribe to a minimum copyright term of the life of the artist plus fifty years and requires that no formalities be placed on artists. I do not see withdrawal from Berne as an insurmountable impediment. Nor do Landes and Posner, who explicitly state that withdrawal from Berne is not only possible but necessary to their proposed indefinitely renewable copyright scheme: "This would require the United States to withdraw from the Berne Convention." WILLIAM M. LANDES & RICHARD A. POSNER, THE ECONOMIC STRUCTURE OF INTELLECTUAL PROPERTY LAW 215 n.15 (2003). But see Christopher Sprigman, *Reform(alizing) Copyright*, 57 STAN. L. REV. 485, 552 (2004).

Proposal Details

In the tiered revenue-based copyright regime,[8] copyright holders would have to select one of two tiers or tracks of copyright protection for their artwork.[9] Both tiers would require registration of artwork, preferably online given the lower transaction costs and ease with which the public can check on the copyright status of registered works. Online registration might also encourage the public to track the revenue claims of copyright holders.[10]

Tier One would grant a work automatic copyright protection for a set period of time – e.g., ten or fourteen years – without any option to renew the copyright. Protection for ten years is reasonable because, as already stated by James Boyle, this is the upper range of protection from which almost all copyrighted artwork will bring in revenue.[11] The suggested alternative of fourteen years is simply a historical nod to the length of the initial term in US copyright law, minus the possibility of a fourteen-year extension. While such relatively short terms might seem radical to some, *The Economist* has proposed going back to this original term from 1790.[12] A third possible term length would be twenty years to align copyright terms with patent terms. The point of Tier One is to introduce copyrighted works into the public domain as soon as possible.

Tier Two would grant only one year of automatic copyright protection but would allow the protection to be renewed indefinitely for a fee as long as the copyrighted work meets or exceeds a revenue threshold. Every year the copyright holder would have to submit verification that the work meets or exceeds the revenue benchmark in order to obtain another year of copyright protection. Different revenue benchmarks could exist depending on the type of work copyrighted.

The structure of Tier Two would include five additional key features. First, the revenue threshold would be set high – i.e., the revenue that a copyrighted

---

[8] Hala Essalmawi tangentially mentions using revenue as a determinant of copyright length. Hala Essalmawi, *Options and Alternatives to Current Copyright Regimes and Practices*, in ACCESS TO KNOWLEDGE IN THE AGE OF INTELLECTUAL PROPERTY 627, 630 (Gaëlle Krikorian & Amy Kapczynski eds., 2010).

[9] This regime would also mandate altering when copyright protection generally starts to some formulation of publication or registration, again harking back to previous copyright requirements.

[10] This last possible function is similar to Beth Simone Noveck's idea of peer-to-patent, allowing the public to comment on the appropriateness of patent applications. BETH SIMONE NOVECK, WIKI GOVERNMENT: HOW TECHNOLOGY CAN MAKE GOVERNMENT BETTER, DEMOCRACY STRONGER, AND CITIZENS MORE POWERFUL 3–15 (2009).

[11] JAMES BOYLE, THE PUBLIC DOMAIN: ENCLOSING THE COMMONS OF THE MIND 11 (2008).

[12] *Copyrights: A Radical Rethink*, ECONOMIST (Jan. 23, 2003), www.economist.com/node/1547223.

work would have to produce each year would be substantial. Second, the revenue threshold for each copyright would increase from year to year at a rate higher than the inflation rate. For example, the adjusting revenue threshold could be set to increase at the rate of inflation plus 2 percent each year.[13] Third, copyright holders would have to pay a substantial fee to renew their copyright if it meets the vigorous revenue requirements. Fourth, the renewal fee would be ever increasing at a rate higher than inflation, e.g., it could be benchmarked to the rate of inflation plus 2 percent per year. Fifth, a limit would be placed on the percentage of works copyrighted through Tier Two that could be renewed each year. For example, a maximum of one-tenth of 1 percent or 1 percent of all copyrighted material could be renewed each year. If more than one-tenth of 1 percent or 1 percent of copyrights meet the revenue threshold for renewal in a given year, the threshold would automatically increase. If this occurs, only the highest revenue-generating copyrighted works would continue to receive copyright protection. The number of works in Tier Two that are allowed to retain their copyright each year could be either a percentage of all current copyrighted works or a percentage of only the works in Tier Two. The latter restriction would make it more difficult for a work to be renewed.

Tier Two would cater to large business enterprises that are confident that they have just created the next Mickey Mouse. Tier One would most likely cater to the vast majority of creators who are risk-averse, doubtful that they could satisfy the revenue benchmark of Tier Two, or not willing to pay the substantial annual renewal fees.

The value of having two tiers in a copyright regime is similar to the value of the legal formalities that artists formerly fulfilled in order to obtain copyright protection. Both ideas attempt to filter art into different categories in order to get more works into the public domain more quickly. Since the proposed tiered revenue-based copyright system includes a registration requirement for all works, most noncommercial works would immediately flow into the commons, and copyright orphans would be kept to a minimum. Plus, a tiered regime would not only distinguish between commercial and noncommercial art but also divide commercial art into two tiers to accelerate the speed at which most of it enters the public domain. The two tiers would allow commercial artists to judge how risk averse they are in their calculations of the likely revenue from their

---

[13]   This proposal is similar to the idea "that the older a copyrighted work is, the greater the scope of fair use should be." Joseph P. Liu, *Copyright and Time: A Proposal*, 101 MICH. L. REV. 409, 410 (2002).

artwork. For example, if an artist has doubts about the earning potential of a piece, she would likely opt for the nonrenewable protection provided through Tier One. This calculus would partly determine how quickly commercial art enters the public domain, depending on which tier the artist chooses.

The revenue-based structure of Tier Two is attractive not only because it would move more commercial artwork more quickly into the public domain but also because it would make the consuming public the final arbiter of copyright protection.[14] The public's implicit consent to renewal would come in the form of a good number of people having enough interest in a copyrighted work to pay for access to it. For this reason, a revenue-based renewal system is more likely to be deemed constitutional than a copyright system that allows for unlimited renewals based simply on the actions of the copyright holder, as with Landes and Posner's proposal for the automatic unlimited renewal for a fee, which will be discussed later.

A tiered revenue-based copyright regime could be modified in numerous ways. First, the number of years of automatic copyright protection under Tier One could be reduced or extended to ensure that copyright reform is significant yet feasible within the current climate.

Second, there could be more than two tiers. For example, a Tier Three could grant five to seven years of automatic copyright protection plus annual renewal into perpetuity as long as the copyrighted work meets a revenue benchmark. Of course, Tier Three's revenue benchmarks would be significantly higher than those of Tier Two. Tier Three would provide more upfront security to copyright holders but at the cost of greater difficulty in renewing because of higher revenue requirements.

Third, the revenue requirements under Tier Two could be timed differently. Instead of having annual revenue benchmarks, Tier Two could have two- or three-year benchmarks.[15] Or the length of time of each successive benchmark could steadily increase or decrease over time. For example, the first benchmark period could be one year, the second benchmark period two years, and so on.

[14] A copyright holder could advertise heavily to boost revenue targets, but she could not buy her way out of the revenue requirements by selling use rights to herself so that she would meet the revenue requirements. This ban would have to include careful restrictions on internal transfer pricing between subsidiaries of conglomerates or possibly not counting such sales.

[15] Under such a revision – e.g., a three-year renewal period – the revenue threshold could be formulated in several ways: (1) an average revenue threshold for all three years, (2) a peak threshold whereby the copyright would be renewed if in one of the three years revenue exceeds the threshold, or (3) an annual revenue threshold for each of the three years.

Fourth, the annual revenue benchmarks could be set to increase by only the inflation rate instead of a rate higher than inflation or by a rate that would actually decrease over time – i.e., make benchmarks easier to meet.

Fifth, the registration requirement could be limited to Tier Two, with Tier One being the default option that would automatically apply if an author does not take the affirmative steps to select Tier Two.

Sixth, the renewal fee under Tier Two could be increased to deter strategic copyrighting. Landes and Posner suggest a "stiff renewal fee" because their proposal for "indefinite renewals" is potentially vulnerable to "[a] more serious concern" that "copyright holders might renew their copyrights for strategic purposes, hoping one day to 'hold up' an author who wanted to copy their work. This practice would resemble strategic patenting."[16] Regardless of whether a large renewal fee ameliorates the problem, a tiered revenue-based copyright system is not likely to be susceptible to such risk because the holder's decision is not the final factor determining renewal.

Seventh, the renewal fee for artwork in Tier Two could be lowered to offset the difficulty of meeting revenue benchmarks. The fee could be nominally constant, without taking inflation into account, over the life of a copyright. Alternatively, the real value of the fee could be held constant – i.e., adjusted for inflation regularly. Or this substantial renewal fee could nominally decrease over time. It could even go in the opposite direction of the trend established for the amount at which the revenue threshold is set.

This proposal to reform copyright is feasible because corporate America can be persuaded to accept a system that offers indefinite copyright protection on its blockbuster creations for as long as such an arrangement increases its overall profits. The motivation behind a tiered revenue-based copyright regime is to give Big Copyright what we know it wants – the promise of possibly infinitely extendable copyrights – in exchange for increasing the scope and vitality of the public domain. Should the open commons movement care whether Mickey Mouse is perpetually copyrighted as long as the copyright term is significantly shortened for most works, the problem of orphan works is solved, the fair use doctrine is broadly construed, and substantial similarity provisions are narrowly tailored? Even if we should, the current regime is suboptimal because it ensures that Big Copyright will always demand longer copyright terms, paralyzing society under a one-size-fits-all copyright regime. A tiered revenue-based copyright system would dissolve corporate America's insistence on a monolithic copyright system.

---

[16]   Landes & Posner, *supra* note 7, at 221.

Advantages over Other Proposed Revisions to the Copyright Term

The benefit of a tiered revenue-based copyright system is that it dramatically expands the public domain without trampling on the toes of Big Copyright. Numerous other schemes attempt to do the same: the Shawn Bentley Orphan Works Act of 2008 and the Orphan Works Act of 2008, Christopher Sprigman's reformalization of copyright proposal, and the indefinitely renewable copyright regime suggested by William Landes and Richard Posner.[17]

The Shawn Bentley Orphan Works Act of 2008 proposed, among other things, to significantly reduce remedies, under certain circumstances, for infringement of orphan works. While it passed the Senate, a similar House bill, the Orphan Works Act of 2008, died.[18]

The Shawn Bentley Orphan Works Act of 2008 tried to limit "the remedies in a civil action brought for infringement of copyright in an orphan work, notwithstanding specified provisions and subject to exceptions, if the infringer meets certain requirements."[19] These conditions included "perform[ing] and document[ing] a reasonably diligent search in good faith to locate and identify the copyright owner before using the work" and, if the copyright holder was known, providing attribution to her.[20] Compensation would be restricted to reasonable compensation for the copyrighted artwork. No compensation would be necessary if the use was by a nonprofit institution and was "performed without any purpose of commercial advantage and is primarily educational, religious, or charitable in nature."[21]

Both orphan works acts had real promise in attempting to increase access to copyright orphans yet not as much as a tiered revenue-based copyright system. Neither orphan works act aspired to reduce the length of copyright; each simply aimed to reduce the potential cost of using orphan works if one follows the procedures within the proposed acts. A tiered revenue-based copyright regime is superior to both orphan acts on three grounds (1) It gets the vast majority of noncommercial artwork into the public domain much more quickly, (2) it also moves more commercial artwork into the commons more rapidly, and (3) it has a greater chance of enticing, not antagonizing, Big

---

[17] This list is not meant to be exhaustive.
[18] S. 2913, 110th Cong. (as passed by Senate, Sept. 27, 2008) and H.R. 5889, 110th Cong. (2008).
[19] Cong. Research Service, S. 2913 (110th): Shawn Bentley Orphan Works Act of 2008 Official Summary, www.govtrack.us/congress/bill.xpd?bill=s110-2913&tab=summary (last visited Oct. 31, 2012).
[20] *Id.* [21] *Id.*

Copyright because it offers Hollywood a substantial incentive in the form of much longer copyright terms on the most successful works.

Sprigman has argued that the reformalization of copyright by creating new-style formalities would allow for substantial reform to "take place without damaging the interests of copyright owners who would otherwise have strong incentives to oppose the creation of a less restrictive copyright regime."[22] He writes:

> The simplest solution would be to preserve formally voluntary registration, notice, and recordation of transfers (and reestablish a formally voluntary renewal formality) for all works, including works of foreign authors, but then incent compliance by exposing the works of noncompliant rightsholders to a "default" license that allows use for a predetermined fee. The royalty payable under the default license would be low. Ideally, the royalty to license a work that a rightsholder has failed to register. . . should be set to approximate the cost of complying with these formalities (i.e., the total cost of informing oneself about the details of compliance and then satisfying them).[23]

Sprigman argues that such a reform would "ease[] access to commercially valueless works for which protection (or the continuation of protection) serves no purpose and [would] focus[] the system on those works for which protection is needed to ensure that the rightsholder is able to appropriate the commercial value of the expression."[24]

Sprigman's new-style formalities reform is a reasoned policy option that should be seriously considered. It has at least one benefit over a tiered revenue-based copyright regime: Sprigman's view that the Berne Convention would permit such new formalities, though he admits "there are arguments both ways."[25] While his reform would improve access to commercially unsuccessful work, it would not immediately place it into the public domain like a tiered revenue-based copyright system would. My proposal opens the door to bringing much more commercial artwork into the public domain much more quickly for two reasons. First, the nonrenewable term of Tier One would free the vast majority of registered artwork within ten to fourteen years. Second, artwork registered under the annual renewal system of Tier Two would also quickly enter the commons if it fails to meet the revenue thresholds necessary to maintain copyright protection. This would especially be the case if there is a yearly percentage cutoff as to how much commercial artwork could continue to be protected.

---

[22] Christopher Sprigman, *Reform(alizing) Copyright*, 57 STAN. L. REV. 485, 568.
[23] *Id.* at 555.   [24] *Id.*   [25] *Id.* at 556.

Testifying in 1906 before Congress against the need for copyright term limits, Samuel Clemens, aka Mark Twain, said, "There is only about one book in a thousand that can outlive forty-two years of copyright. Therefore why put a limit at all? You might just as well limit a family to 22. It will take care of itself."[26] Following in the footsteps of Twain, Landes and Posner propose a copyright regime of indefinitely renewable copyrights in which copyright holders could pay a fee to have their copyrights renewed after short fixed terms.[27] Under their proposal, all new and existing copyrighted artwork would need to be registered, and copyright holders could extend their copyrights as many times as they desire.

Landes and Posner's proposal has numerous attractive characteristics, yet a tiered revenue-based copyright regime has more advantages. First, my proposal is more effective in moving commercial artwork into the commons. Whether we consider it a good thing or a tragedy, a substantial portion of our culture comprises commercially successful artwork (films, music, TV, etc.). Landes and Posner's scheme would lead (unless stiff renewal fees are contemplated) to most commercially successful artwork being absent from the public domain for an extremely long time. My proposal is more capable of moderating the amount of successful commercial art that stays locked up; it pushes all but the most profitable copyrighted works into the public domain and does so within a reasonable time frame.

Second, both proposals create some transparency by requiring registration, but my proposal is more transparent and less susceptible to abuse because it prevents copyright holders from having full control over the terms of their copyright protection. Under Landes and Posner's proposal, the decision to renew lies solely with the copyright holders, who can continue to pay for copyright protection indefinitely. They can refuse to ever allow anything into the commons, either to prevent their opponents from potentially benefiting from their creations or out of a pack rat mentality. Under my proposal, copyright holders may choose to pursue renewal, but whether a renewal is granted depends on whether the work in question meets the revenue threshold. Ultimately, it would fall to the public to decide, through their pocketbooks, whether a copyright should be extended.

This benefit of the public's implicit consent as the determining factor for renewal ties into the third advantage: A tiered revenue-based copyright regime

---

[26] Clemens's testimony was reprinted in Samuel L. Clemens, *Copyright in Perpetuity*, 6 GREEN BAG 2d 109, 111 (2002).

[27] William M. Landes & Richard A. Posner, *Indefinitely Renewable Copyright*, 70 U. CHI. L. REV. 471 (2003).

would have a better chance of meeting constitutional objections than the system proposed by Landes and Posner. This is because a tiered revenue-based copyright regime would not guarantee copyright holders direct control or indefinite protection. Landes and Posner simply state that their "concern is with the economics rather than the constitutionality of indefinite renewal."[28] In a footnote they go on to say, without explanation, that "[i]n light of" *Eldred v. Ashcroft,* "it is unlikely that a system of indefinite renewals, which has more to commend it than the Sonny Bono Act, would be held unconstitutional."[29]

Fourth, a tiered revenue-based copyright system can be modified. For example, while my proposal requires registration of all artwork, it could easily be altered to eliminate that requirement for the fixed-term tier. Such flexibility is not possible with Landes and Posner's proposal.

Potential Problems

A tiered revenue-based copyright system is not a perfect solution, but it is better than the current copyright system and the proposals described previously. Following are responses to some of the most common criticisms of this proposition that have not already been discussed.

Very few, if any, variables can be perfectly and costlessly measured. While measuring copyright revenue will not be immune from some abuse and some complications in calculation, the proposed regime's features will not be easy to abuse or impossible to assess. Also, Landes and Posner's suggestion that transaction costs would drop under their proposal of indefinite copyright renewals is applicable to a tiered revenue-based copyright system:

> The aggregate transaction costs [of the proposal] ... would depend on the number and possibly the value of licenses (holding tracing costs constant), the transaction costs per license, and the administrative cost of operating the renewal system. Since the number of licenses would depend in part on the total number of works renewed, aggregate transaction costs could actually fall compared either to a system of automatic renewals or to a single term of life plus seventy years.[30]

Past and present-day examples of copyright payment and/or registration systems that are arguably more complex than the measurements required by my proposal also suggest that a tiered revenue-based copyright regime is practically feasible. Historically, obtaining copyright was more costly and time-consuming than it is under current law. Copyright was intelligently structured

---

[28]   LANDES & POSNER, *supra* note 7, at 211.   [29]   *Id.*   [30]   *Id.* at 217.

as a quasi-test of an artist's intent to seek copyright protection. These historical requirements, which began to be eroded from 1909 onward, entailed registration of the artwork, the deposit of copies of the artwork with the Copyright Office, and placing a notice of copyright protection on every published copy of the work.

One contemporary real-world example of a complex copyright arrangement is the 1992 Audio Home Recording Act (AHRA), which enables manufacturers of digital audio equipment to sell digital tapes and recorders if they pay royalties on all such sales.[31] The royalties are divided among background musicians, vocalists, featured recording artists, record companies, composers, and music publishers.[32] While the percentage each of the groups receives is fixed by statute, the law does not mandate how individuals within these groups must be compensated. This example demonstrates that law can be functional even if many variables cannot be perfectly measured or observed.

A second example is the American Society of Composers, Authors, and Publishers (ASCAP). It is a performing rights organization of more than 450,000 composers, lyricists, songwriters, and publishers[33] that licenses billions of nondramatic public performances of their copyrighted artwork each year and then distributes the royalties to its members.[34] ASCAP is

> guided by a "follow the dollar" principle in the design of [its] payment system. In other words, the money collected from television stations is paid out to members for performances of their works on television, the money collected from radio stations is paid out for radio performances, and so on . . . The value of each performance is determined by several factors, including the amount of license fees collected in a medium (television, cable, radio, etc.), how much we receive in fees from the licensee that hosted the performance, and the type of performance (feature performance, background music, theme song, etc.).[35]

In fact, royalty calculations for an individual musical work are more complicated than the preceding summary suggests. ASCAP multiplies five variables (use weight, licensee weight, "follow the dollar" factor, time of day weight, and general licensing allocation) together and then adds radio feature premium

---

[31]   Audio Home Recording Act of 1992, Pub. L. No. 102–563, 106 Stat. 4237 (1992) (codified as 17 U.S.C. §§ 1001–1010).

[32]   17 U.S.C. §§ 1004–1008.

[33]   *What Is ASCAP?*, ASCAP, www.ascap.com/about/ (last visited Dec. 20, 2012).

[34]   *ASCAP Payment System: How You Get Paid at ASCAP*, ASCAP, www.ascap.com/members/payment/ (last visited Dec. 20, 2012).

[35]   *Id.*

credits and TV premium credits to arrive at a final tally.[36] The general licensing allocation drives home the point that intricate systems for approximating values that cannot practically be precisely measured can successfully work. The general licensing allocation is calculated by the following method: "Fees collected from non-broadcast, non-surveyed licensees (bars, hotels, restaurants and the like) are applied to broadcast feature performances on radio and all performances on television, which serve as a proxy for distribution purposes."[37]

While these examples are not perfect precedent for proving that revenues can be measured accurately enough without bankrupting artists and regulators, they serve as positive indicative guides. Measuring the revenue of copyrighted artwork will not be flawless or even elegant, but it is practicable on a large scale.

A second potential concern is that this proposal would make access to the most successful commercial artwork more expensive and hence more restricted.[38] In this regard, it could be viewed as harmfully revising the definition of a free society. Any such restriction, however, would be a minor impediment relative to the benefits the proposed reform will bring. Yet we need to be brutally honest about how much cultural freedom we can realistically expect to win in the short term. We should be willing to give Disney more of what it wants so that it stops deforming and shackling most of our culture. Such a calculation is by necessity utilitarian. My assertion is simply to redo the calculus – lock up a much smaller amount of content for a longer time in order to allow a vast amount of content to become free much sooner.

Many copyright scholars, including myself, desire to significantly shorten copyright's length. If we do nothing now because we do not have the necessary mobilization for radical reform, then the most successful commercial artwork will be locked up for a long time regardless.

Some might claim that a tiered revenue-based copyright regime with one tier having an annual revenue requirement would annihilate the commercial

---

[36]　*ASCAP Payment System: Royalty Calculation*, ASCAP, www.ascap.com/members/payment/royalties.aspx (last visited Dec. 20, 2012).

[37]　*Id.*

[38]　A related potential concern is the possibility expressed by Felix Cohen many years back: "The vicious circle inherent in this reasoning is plain. It purports to base legal protection upon economic value, when, as a matter of actual fact, the economic value of a sales device depends upon the extent to which it will be legally protected." Felix Cohen, *Transcendental Nonsense and the Functional Approach*, 35 COLUM. L. REV. 809, 815 (1935). While Cohen's observation can be piercing in other contexts, it does not fit the facts or the nature of this proposal. As is clearly evidenced by the existence of millions of copyright orphans, legal protection does not always automatically create economic value.

art market because the public would simply wait a year before paying to see or listen to any artwork with a renewable copyright. Such an argument overlooks current marketing practices and consumer behavior.

As previously discussed, the current Hollywood practice is to roll out a film gradually in different forms. Many movies are first available only in theaters. When released on DVD or online, some movies can initially only be bought, with the option of renting coming a month or two later. Most of these steps occur within a year, and a marketing push often precedes each step to create and maintain a movie's "must-see" status.

Even if a large enough group of individuals is willing to wait for a copyrighted work to fail to meet a revenue benchmark so that it would be released into the public domain, there would be no certainty ex ante that the work would not meet the revenue cutoff. Hence, such a group could wait for decades or longer to see a Mickey Mouse movie for free. Such uncertainty could even create a situation similar to the prisoner dilemma: While it would be in the group's best interest to wait a year and deny the copyright holder enough revenue to meet the benchmark, individual members might prefer to purchase the product the day of its release instead of having to deal with the uncertainty of trusting others not to buy it immediately. This is not to claim that some individuals might happily resist all the marketing, live with the uncertainty, and wait for a work to go off copyright, but this group is likely to be small and hence would not significantly chip away at the commercial art market.

Another concern is that Big Copyright might agree to this proposal but then, over the long term, fight to change the provisions of the bargain. While such a possibility is unfortunate, whenever reaching across the aisle, one has to consider such behavior. *Si vis pacem, para bellum*; if you wish for peace, prepare for war.[39] In fact, Big Copyright should plan for the same contingency – public domain advocates continuing to push for shorter copyright terms – though neither side should necessarily expect any success if it ventures away from a compromise built on a tiered revenue-based system.

Two main concerns exist.[40] First, Big Copyright might attempt to compromise the stringency of revenue thresholds or increase the length of renewal periods. Yet Big Copyright has little incentive to prolong copyright

---

[39] FLAVIUS VEGETIUS RENATUS, VEGETIUS: EPITOME OF MILITARY SCIENCE 63 (N. P. Milner trans., 2d rev. ed., Liverpool University Press 1996) (ca. 430–435).

[40] Another concern is that Big Copyright could always reissue a lapsed copyright in a form different enough to get a new copyright. This already occurs and is difficult to eliminate outside of abandoning copyright entirely. The saving grace is that the related works are not identical.

on all artwork if it does not own most of it and if much of what it owns is essentially worthless after a decade. Second, Big Copyright might also strategize to bring back copyright orphans in one form or another to reduce the size of the public domain so that there is less competition for its holdings. Such potential competition from works in the public domain is uncertain, given that orphan works are often orphaned because they were unsuccessful commercially. Also, Big Copyright could benefit from a clearing of copyright orphans into the public domain because all artists – commercial as well as noncommercial – would gain an enormous amount of newly available free material to borrow from. Furthermore, Big Copyright would have to seriously consider whether any added revenue that might result from breaking the compromise is worth (a) the potential financial cost of lobbying to make an extra buck on lackluster holdings and (b) the risk of breaking faith with society, given the danger of being painted evil like Big Pharma. Finally, it must be remembered that one of the biggest strengths of a tiered revenue-based copyright regime is that relative to the current copyright system it would reduce rent seeking on copyright's term length.

If Big Copyright accepts a tiered revenue-based copyright regime, incentives could be built into the new legislation to discourage powerful commercial interests from later lobbying to loosen the requirements. First, Big Copyright could be required to contribute money to a nonprofit that would lobby to ensure that the new copyright system's term provisions are not altered in the future to favor Big Copyright. Second, a poison pill, distinct from the version previously noted, could be attached to the tiered revenue-based copyright regime bill – i.e., if the regime is altered for the benefit of Big Copyright, the poison pill dilutes its copyright ownership but not everyone else's. Alternatively, the bill could require a transition period during which all copyright holders (or just those who pushed for the bill that alters the tiered copyright regime) have their copyright diluted (i.e., scope of protection weakened).

Activists dedicated to reducing the length of copyright protection should consider negotiating a deal that will entice Big Copyright to set orphans free and to accept dramatically reduced copyright terms for the vast majority of artwork in exchange for gaining longer protection for its most successful commercial works.

BESPOKE RECORDINGS

Sir Tim Berners-Lee, founder of the World Wide Web, states: "'Record labels have a very strong voice when it comes to arguing for their particular business model, which is in fact out of date.'"[41] As a result, "laws have been created which make out as if the only problem on the internet is teenagers" sharing music.[42]

Of course, the rise of the Internet may well have cut into the recording industry's revenues. Alejandro Zentner estimates that "peer-to-peer usage reduces the probability of buying music by 30 percent."[43] On this basis, he calculates "sales in 2002 would have been around 7.8 percent higher."[44] While the possible sources of declining music sales will be examined later, it is worth noting that some scholars claim that the music industry's difficulties "have very little to do with illegal file-sharing," because other industries, such as the "personal computer software market (with 57 percent average piracy, yearly)" have not experienced the same significant revenue decline.[45] As Berners-Lee implies, the recording industry is hurting financially because it has been slow to consider altering its business model in the face of rapid transformation around it. It is understandable that an industry that has relied on a tool – copyright law – for decades would reflexively react to a changing world by demanding that the tool's powers be expanded, but as Berners-Lee points out, "[w]e mustn't allow record companies' fear that their business model isn't working to upset the openness of the internet."[46]

Recording labels are not alone in needing to rely less on copyright by finding alternative revenue sources. Copyright has largely been ineffective at supporting unknown musicians and non-elite music nonprofits – e.g., music outreach programs for kids as opposed to the Berlin Philharmonic.

Big Copyright does not have to abandon copyright; it simply needs to stop being reactionary and experiment with numerous new revenue-generating strategies beyond suing customers and attempting to impair freedom, creativity, and innovation on the Internet. Musicians have been more willing than recording companies to experiment with alternative revenue sources, such as relying more on touring, promoting the concept of tipping musicians, or asking fans to voluntarily pay what they think

---

[41] Olivia Solon, *Berners-Lee: Don't Let Record Labels Upset Web Openness*, ARS TECHNICA (Apr. 18, 2012, 7:21 PM), https://arstechnica.com/tech-policy/2012/04/berners-lee-dont-let-record-labels-upset-web-openness/ (quoting Sir Tim Berners-Lee). For more information on bespoke recordings, see Martin Skladany, *Bespoke Recordings: The Limits of Intellectual Property and the Revival of the Music Industry*, J. L. TECH. & POL'Y (2014).

[42] *Id.*   [43] Alejandro Zentner, *On Music Purchases*, 49 J. L. & ECON. 63 (2006).   [44] *Id.*

[45] DAVID KUSEK & GERD LEONHARD, THE FUTURE OF MUSIC: MANIFESTO FOR THE DIGITAL MUSIC REVOLUTION 83 (2005).

[46] Solon, *supra* note 41.

a recording is worth.[47] Belatedly, record companies have only recently begun to seriously consider alternative business models such as subscription-based Rhapsody and satellite-based Pandora, yet more experimentation is required.[48]

On May 30, 2013, David Lang premiered *The Whisper Opera*, a piece he specifically composed to be "so quiet and so intimate and so personal to the performers that you needed to be right next to them or you would hear almost nothing."[49] His vision: "A piece like this would have to be experienced live."[50] In this vein, "the score to the whisper opera states clearly that it can never be recorded, or filmed, or amplified."[51]

Unlike paintings, which cannot be perfectly reproduced and hence are each one-of-a-kind cultural creations, music's fixed tangible form is frequently encapsulated in recordings using vinyl, magnetic tape, or electronic bits. Given that music's physical medium makes it susceptible to being not only recorded but also effortlessly copied, Lang desired to compose music that was impossible to record in order to remind us of the beauty of music performed live. But the prevalence of recordings has also prevented musicians from benefiting from the scarcity dynamics associated with unique paintings.

Yet such scarcity could be engineered by establishing legal, technical, and institutional mechanisms to support the creation of bespoke recordings (e.g., a one-of-a-kind recording by pianist Martha Argerich) and bespoke compositions (e.g., a unique composition by Jennifer Higdon) that would not be copied or released publicly but instead would be privately auctioned.[52] Each bespoke musical recording would be as unique as an Artemisia Gentileschi painting or a Camille Claudel sculpture and would be sold to music lovers or investment funds. In a sense, bespoke recordings would be a new unique form of distribution – of almost nondistribution.

Walter Pater once observed, "All art constantly aspires towards the condition of music," in the sense that of all fields of art, music perfectly unifies

---

[47] Cate Czarnecki, *A Tip Jar for the Digital Age*, OFF BEAT (Jan. 30, 2013), www.offbeat.com /2013/01/30/a-tip-jar-digital-age/, and Tobias Regner, *Why Consumers Pay Voluntarily: Evidence from Online Music*, JENA ECONOMIC RESEARCH PAPERS, No. 081 (2010), http://hdl .handle.net/10419/56912.

[48] *See generally* John Eric Seay, *Legislative Strategies for Enabling the Success of Online Music Purveyors*, 17 UCLA ENT. L. REV. 163 (2010).

[49] David Lang, The Whisper Opera (2013), http://davidlangmusic.com/music/the-whisper-opera.

[50] *Id.*   [51] *Id.*

[52] Martha Argerich could be asked to either record a performance of a piece she has never publicly played or to create a new, unique recording of a piece she has previously performed.

content and form given its nonrepresentational nature.[53] This magnifies the transcendent nature of art, for "wherever it is we believe great art takes us, music takes us there in a more unambiguous, direct and unhindered way than any other art form."[54] While this aspiration is certainly lyrical and thoughtful, and possibly even true, bespoke recordings would be an attempt to reverse it in terms of form. The motivation to do so would be to allow music to benefit financially from the uniqueness inherent in other artistic forms.

To conceptualize more fully the value of bespoke recordings, it might be helpful to contrast them to the first or master version of a publicly released recording. Such a master recording can be analogized to the first print of a series, while bespoke recordings can be equated with unique paintings. Yet even such a comparison to a limited print series is far from perfect because unlike a print series that is capped at, for example, 200 authorized prints, a master recording can have an unlimited number of subsequent copies. Not surprisingly, limited edition prints sell for a small fraction of a unique painting by the same artist. Hence, a bespoke recording would be much more valued by collectors and investors than the master copy of a publicly released recording.

Along with advocating for the creation of bespoke recordings, I propose establishing a nonprofit that would encourage emerging and established musicians to annually either compose a bespoke piece or produce a unique recording for auction, with the proceeds going to music nonprofits of their choosing. Since many of the musical outreach programs would likely center on classical music, it would make sense to initially ask contemporary classical performers to record bespoke pieces, yet the nonprofit should also encourage musicians from other fields to donate unique recordings.

Just as a round of golf with Tiger Woods has been auctioned off for $30,000, so have there been a few ad hoc music charity auctions where philanthropists have bid for a private evening with a composer or soloist.[55] For example,

---

53   WALTER PATER, STUDIES IN THE HISTORY OF THE RENAISSANCE 124 (Oxford University Press 2010) (1873, though the quote only appears in the third edition of the book from 1888, when "The School of Giorgione" essay was added).

54   Comment by Denis, Feb. 1, 2010, on *All Art Constantly Aspires towards the Condition of Music – You Don't Say!*, WUTHERING EXPECTATIONS (May 7, 2008), http://wutheringexpectations.blogspot.com/2008/05/all-art-constantly-aspires-towards.html.

55   Alexandra Peers, *At Charity Auctions, Doing Good while Doing Well*, N.Y. TIMES (Feb. 12, 2006), www.nytimes.com/2006/02/12/business/yourmoney/at-charity-auctions-doing-good-while-doing-well.html?mcubz=3. Also see the work of the Foundation for Contemporary Arts, which is "based on the belief that visual artists – painters and sculptors – were sufficiently concerned about the state of the performance arts – dance, theatre and music – enough so to donate artwork to benefit performing artists." The foundation uses the proceeds from the sale of donated visual art to run a grant program for those in the performance arts. *About,*

a private forty-minute performance in one's home by Philip Glass was estimated to fetch $10,000 at a charity auction.[56] The hammer prices have been
modest because such an evening, though magical, is not also a valuable
financial asset that can be enjoyed and then resold at a later date. The intent
behind bespoke recordings would be to create the same demand that allows for
an individual sculpture by Alberto Giacometti to sell at auction for
$104.3 million or for Paul Cézanne's painting *The Card Players* to reportedly
change hands for $250 million in a private sale in 2011 – i.e., to generate
significant proceeds that can make a real difference in steadying the financial
future of nonprofit music programs and recording labels.[57]

Initially, bespoke recordings could be auctioned at less than 1/1000th of the
price of a Warhol or 1/100th of the price of a contemporary work, such as a Jeff
Koons. However, as the market for unique recordings and compositions grows
over the decades, such charitable music auctions could raise millions a year
for worthy music nonprofits. In 2005, in the United States alone, live art
auction sales were more than $12 billion.[58] If over time bespoke recordings
only capture the equivalent of 10 percent of the live art auction sales in a year,
it would equate to $1.21 billion. Even if only a portion of this amount is
donated, it would be a revolution in funding for music nonprofits.
Worldwide art gallery sales are estimated to be more than 20 billion euros
(roughly $26 billion).[59] While bespoke recording galleries may or may not
evolve, the fact that art gallery sales are estimated to be more than twice the
size of the live art auction market is an encouraging sign for the possible future
depth of the bespoke recording market.

The investment returns of artwork have been robust. Jianping Mei and
Michael Moses created the Mei-Moses art index, which "shows average
annual art returns were 7.7 percent between 1875 and 2000, compared with
6.6 percent from equities."[60] Further, the art auction market is so established

FOUNDATION FOR CONTEMPORARY ARTS, www.foundationforcontemporaryarts.org/about
(last visited June 7, 2017).

56　*Enjoy a Private Concert in Your Home with Music Icon Philip Glass*, CHARITY BUZZ, www
.charitybuzz.com/categories/31/catalog_items/262314 (last visited Feb. 10, 2013).

57　*Daily Chart: The $cream*, ECONOMIST: GRAPHIC DETAIL (May 3, 2012), www.economist
.com/blogs/graphicdetail/2012/05/daily-chart-2.

58　*$250,000 in 60 Minutes?*, AUCTION RESULTS, www.auction-results.org/news1.html (last vis-
ited Feb. 10, 2013).

59　Graham Bowley, *For Art Dealers, a New Life on the Fair Circuit*, N.Y. TIMES (Aug. 21, 2013),
www.nytimes.com/2013/08/22/arts/for-art-dealers-a-new-life-on-the-fair-circuit.html?
mcubz=3.

60　Nazanin Lankarani, *Art Funds Feel a Revival as Economy Thaws Out*, N.Y. TIMES (Sept. 5,
2009), www.nytimes.com/2009/09/05/business/global/05rinartfund.html?mcubz=3.

and deep that art exchanges, similar to stock exchanges, have begun to spring up. In 2009, the government of China established the Shenzhen Cultural Assets and Equity Exchange (SZCAEE).[61] In France, Pierre Naquin launched a similar art exchange "offering in January 2011 his first thousandth parts in the works of Sol LeWitt and Francesco Vezzoli."[62] If in the long term bespoke recordings develop into a successful new revenue source for the music industry and music nonprofits, a similar bespoke recording exchange could be considered.

Other high-value fields auction off material at astounding prices even though a sizable portion of bidders ultimately consume the product. For example, the worldwide wine auction market was $389 million in 2012.[63] Wine investment funds are gaining ground, at least one wine fund index tracks prices over time, and numerous high-net-worth individuals hold tens of thousands of bottles. Wine can only be consumed once and will ultimately go bad at some point if not drunk, as opposed to being listened to over and over again throughout the centuries, yet both individuals and institutions treat it as a serious investment class.

Almost any artwork can be imperfectly copied if one is given access to the work, yet pieces retain their financial value if they can be distinguished from illicit or unacknowledged copies or, more important for bespoke recordings, if unauthorized duplicates can be effectively prevented from being produced. In the digital age, it has commonly been assumed that the reproduction of art is inevitable, but the market for unique musical recordings can be structured to ensure that bespoke pieces can be authenticated and copies can be prevented. Yet copyright law does not solve this concern; intellectual property laws are practically incapable of providing assurance to collectors and investors that reproductions of a bespoke recording do not exist. To do so, numerous legal, technological, and institutional safeguards must be implemented.

First, a registration or title system would be created. It would contain a universal list of existing bespoke music pieces, both compositions and recordings. It would also designate who owns a recording in a similar way to how land registries work.[64]

The existence of a bespoke recording registry would make it more difficult to claim falsely that an undiscovered masterpiece was found in

---

[61] Artprice, Art Market Trends 2010 at 6, http://imgpublic.artprice.com/pdf/tren ds2010_en.pdf.

[62] *Id.*

[63] Peter D. Meltzer, *Worldwide Wine Auction Revenues Fall in 2012*, Wine Spectator (Jan. 15, 2013), www.winespectator.com/webfeature/show/id/47905.

[64] Kevin Gray & Susan Francis Gray, Land Law 59 (2007).

one's attic – i.e., for fake bespoke recordings, as opposed to illicit copies of a genuine bespoke recording, to be successfully passed off as authentic.[65] The music registry would also provide assurance to potential subsequent buyers that the current holder of a recording is in fact the legitimate, legal owner of a piece. Finally, the registry would reduce the motivation to steal unique pieces. A stolen bespoke recording could not be sold in the open market without legal risk, given that clear documentation of who the legitimate owner is would exist. Thus only individuals willing to buy a known stolen recording and keep it a secret, as opposed to treating it as an investment, would provide any type of a market for thieves.[66] While bespoke recording registries would minimize the risk of theft, the unusual nature of bespoke recordings would already create a strong disincentive to attempt to steal such works. Essentially, bespoke recordings would only retain their financial value if potential buyers are confident that the piece has never been copied.

Second, buyers and sellers would enter into contractual agreements containing numerous provisions that would provide legal assurance to the buyer, including, for example, representations from the owner about whether the piece was ever copied. Another such clause could be that any owner of a bespoke recording, into perpetuity, could never make more than a set number of copies for sale. The purpose of such a clause would be to prevent a bespoke recording owner from publicly releasing the bespoke recording for profit, causing potential consumer confusion – and, in the eyes of recording labels at least, creating undesired competition, since the bespoke recording owner might begin to look like a recording label that represents the artist. Such a provision against public release should not apply to the bespoke recording being given away for free to the public.

Third, the physical device on which the bespoke recording exists could be outfitted with numerous technological anti-counterfeiting protections, including having artists sign the score or the physical device containing the musical piece they composed or recorded; software encryption; varying anti-counterfeiting measures from one unique piece to another to make it more difficult for a potential thief or counterfeiter to know whether she properly disabled all safeguards; and transmitting the recording only through bone

---

[65] Plus, the overwhelming majority of such bespoke recordings will be by living composers and performers, who, if need be, can verify a piece's authenticity.

[66] This is not to claim that such an illicit market in artwork is small or relatively unexceptional. JANET ULPH & IAN SMITH, THE ILLICIT TRADE IN ART AND ANTIQUITIES: INTERNATIONAL RECOVERY AND CRIMINAL AND CIVIL LIABILITY 3 (2012).

conduction, "sending vibrations to the inner ear through the skull," instead of using traditional speakers.[67]

Fourth, secure storage facilities could be established to allow owners of bespoke recordings the option of storing their works there. Some of these facilities could simply be housed within freeports around the globe. The work would never leave the premises, and even owners would be thoroughly searched for recording devices before being allowed access. Other safeguards could include metal detectors being calibrated to a sensitive setting,[68] requiring that individuals not bring anything into the listening studio, sweeping for recording devices using magnetic field detection devices, and using infrared photography to detect heat signatures of any recording devices.[69] The facility could implement measures to prevent employees from illicitly copying any bespoke recordings. For example, each bespoke recording could be stored on a device that is locked in a vault that can be opened only with a key held by the owner. Alternatively, the digital equivalent of this could be implemented, where the bespoke recording owner would have a digital password that is unknown to anyone at the storage facility.[70]

Some owners of bespoke recordings might prefer to have their pieces at home so they can listen to them at any time. This would not necessarily be the most common preference for several reasons. First, many owners of recordings might not be individuals but investment funds or other corporate entities that acquire recordings solely for investment purposes. Second, even owners who are individuals might favor storing the recordings outside their home for safekeeping as evidenced by the common use of safety deposit boxes at banks and freeports. Third, both individual and corporate owners would likely be concerned not only with securing the physical safety of their recordings but also with maximizing the works' financial value. Finally, given that individuals happily travel to concert halls to hear performances, it might not be so

---

[67] *Poll: Would You Get Earphones Implanted into Your Head?*, GUARDIAN: MUSIC BLOG (Aug. 7, 2013), www.theguardian.com/music/musicblog/poll/2013/aug/07/poll-earphones-implanted-head.

[68] There are other measures to take including not having any windows in the listening studio so that exterior laser-bounce listening devices cannot be deployed. Such devices can pick up very sensitive displacements. *See generally* Chen-Chia Wang et al., A New Kind of Laser Microphone Using High Sensitivity Pulsed Laser Vibrometer, Paper Presented at Conf. on Lasers & Electro-Optics and Conf. on Quantum Electronics & Laser Sci. (May 4–9, 2008), https://ntrs.nasa.gov/archive/nasa/casi.ntrs.nasa.gov/20080018709.pdf (on file with NASA).

[69] Recording devices, including digital ones, create miniscule signals, which can be detected. *How to Detect Hidden Listening Devices*, BUZZLE, www.buzzle.com/articles/how-to-detect-hidden-listening-devices.html (last visited July 4, 2017).

[70] Other possible measures include constant video surveillance and guards working in tandem.

unreasonable that some people would travel to a secure facility to listen to an utterly unique recording.

The secure facility could also buy insurance against an employee illegally copying a bespoke recording to compensate the owner in such an event. Past and present insurance practices strongly suggest that a respected insurer would issue such a policy. For example, insurers have issued policies for Heidi Klum's legs, America Ferrera's smile, and Bruce Springsteen's vocal chords.[71] More on point, it is standard practice for a movie being made to get errors and omissions insurance against, among other things, copyright infringement claims.[72]

Fifth, as already mentioned, a bespoke recording nonprofit would be set up to encourage artists to donate unique recordings, auction the works with the proceeds going to musical nonprofits, and implement the first four measures: maintaining the bespoke recording registry, tailoring contractual agreements, implementing the anti-counterfeit protections, and coordinating with or supervising the secure bespoke recording storage facility.

Part of the process of convincing well-established and up-and-coming composers and performers to donate a bespoke composition or recording each year would be persuading record labels to understand the creative, professional, and social benefits – not to mention the indirect benefits to corporate bottom lines – of encouraging their signed artists to submit pieces to be auctioned for charity. Even if record labels do not appreciate such benefits, depending on how artists' recording contracts are written, musicians would not need the blessing of their labels to make donations of bespoke pieces to charity.[73]

As for guiding the growth of such donations, an effective strategy could be to first promote bespoke recordings in one musical field. Contemporary classical music is a good possible place to start given that it is the closest cousin to artistic fields that demand the highest premium at art auctions, many music outreach programs specialize in teaching individuals how to play orchestral instruments, and it is a small musical subfield in terms of record sales. This last consideration is important because experimenting with bespoke recordings in

[71] *Celebrity Body Insurance: Stars Who Insured Their Body Parts*, HUFFINGTON POST (Feb. 21, 2013), www.huffingtonpost.com/2013/02/21/celebrity-body-insurance-parts_n_2721783.html.
[72] Melvin Simensky & Eric C. Osterberg, *The Insurance and Management of Intellectual Property Risks*, 17 CARDOZO ARTS & ENT. L.J. 321, 325–27 (1999).
[73] While it is likely that such contracts prohibit for-profit unauthorized recordings being distributed by anyone but the label, not-for-profit recordings may or may not be covered. See Richard E. Caves, *Contracts between Art and Commerce*, 17 J. ECON. PERSPECTIVES 73, 78–79 (2003).

a subfield that is not a high priority for the for-profit music industry would lower the odds that major labels would attempt to squash the idea initially. If bespoke recordings prove to be successful in classical music, major labels will want to expand such recordings into other musical fields.

During the systematic push to develop classical bespoke recordings, famous popular musicians could be approached for help establishing the idea of such a market. Success would take time, likely more than a decade. Such a timeline would be ambitious and should not be considered a mark against the idea. The time to develop a mature market for bespoke recordings should be compared to the much longer time it took for the art auction world to mature.

Ideally, the bespoke recording nonprofit would be funded with foundation support until the market for bespoke recordings is large enough that a small fraction of auction sales could cover administrative costs and the vast majority of proceeds could be donated to worthy music endeavors. The nonprofit's ability to ultimately become completely self-funding is another attractive feature of this proposal – a rarity in the nonprofit world.

Finally, if bespoke recordings are successful, the bespoke recording non-profit could expand the idea to include different music genres or other art forms such as dance, poetry, fiction, performance art, or video in the hope of raising added funds for nonprofits specializing in these fields.[74]

Benefits

There are at least four benefits of bespoke musical recordings, which would assist numerous actors including music nonprofits and local communities, the public at large, professional and emerging musicians, and the recording industry.

First, bespoke recordings could benefit music nonprofits and the local communities they serve. In the long run, bespoke recordings would generate significant new funds for different music nonprofits such as those teaching underprivileged children how to play musical instruments or those offering music therapy. Expanding the reach of music nonprofits so that they could encourage more kids and adults to play, compose, and listen to music would

---

[74] One copy of one particular video game exists. *Chain World*, Wikipedia, http://en.wikipedia .org/wiki/Chain_World. I thank Michael Margitich for bringing this to my attention. Also, as I was writing up the idea of bespoke recordings as a law review article, the music group Wu-Tang Clan was working on such a unique album: *Once Upon a Time in Shaolin*, which they released in 2015. Emily Saul, *"Pharma Bro" Plays $2M Wu-Tang Clan Album to Celebrate Verdict*, N.Y. Post (Aug. 4, 2017, 6:40 PM), http://nypost.com/2017/08/04/pharma-bro-plays -2m-wu-tang-clan-album-to-celebrate-verdict/

bring enjoyment[75] as well as cognitive and health benefits.[76] Increased funding to music outreach and therapy programs would also improve the lives of participants in that composing or playing an instrument allows us to go beyond consumption – to search for beauty and meaning, to struggle to master a skill, and to communicate. Thus, bespoke recordings directly attempt to address a major concern of overconsumption – getting individuals to create more and consume less.

Second, while encouraging more individuals to get involved with music is a good in and of itself, a beneficial consequence of letting a million flowers bloom is that some may be breathtaking. This brings us to the second desirable aspect of bespoke recordings – they would make it more likely that new musical geniuses would be found. This is primarily because of the expanded musical outreach programs that would be funded by bespoke recordings. These musical outreach programs would get more children and adults involved with music, increasing the odds that someone with exceptional potential is introduced to composition or performance. While cultivating genius is a mysterious endeavor, expanding music access to segments of the population that would likely not, for example, ever be exposed to classical music or jazz will increase the probability of uncovering more exceptional talent. This is not only because more people would be introduced to music but also because people with diverse backgrounds bring, by definition, different experiences to bear on artistic activities, potentially allowing them to express themselves in inventive and captivating ways and to reinterpret fields.

Third, cultivating a market for unique recordings would increase the salaries of composers and performers. The more mature and liquid the bespoke recording market becomes, the higher the income musicians could demand. Famous musicians would not be the only ones to benefit from the development of a bespoke recording market. While young or up-and-coming artists could not command hammer prices remotely comparable to those of established musicians, making bespoke recordings and selling them at auction either for profit or for charity would give them valuable exposure to serious music connoisseurs and potential patrons and investors. Not only are music lovers on the lookout for new talent to enrich their musical understanding; art patrons search for hidden talent to foster and investors seek emerging artists to enrich their own pocketbooks. Furthermore, fans or investors with smaller

---

[75] Listening to "peak emotional moments" in music releases dopamine. Robert J. Zatorre & Valorie N. Salimpoor, *Why Music Makes Our Brain Sing*, N.Y. TIMES (June 7, 2013), www .nytimes.com/2013/06/09/opinion/sunday/why-music-makes-our-brain-sing.html?mcubz=3.

[76] *See generally* KEVIN F. MCCARTHY ET AL., GIFTS OF THE MUSE: REFRAMING THE DEBATE ABOUT THE BENEFITS OF THE ARTS (2004).

pockets would be drawn toward more affordable bespoke recordings by emerging musicians. Both the art and wine auction markets sell a significant number of artworks and bottles of wine that are imminently affordable, which suggests that young musicians could use bespoke recordings as a method to enhance their visibility. For example, the average price per lot – usually either one bottle or a case of 12 bottles – of wine in 2012 was $2,792.[77]

Bespoke recordings would also help artists more easily give back to their communities. Nationally televised Live Aid-like concerts aside, arguably the most impact that a musician can make in one night is performing a charity concert where either the ticket sales are donated to charity or the tickets are subsidized or free and distributed to individuals who usually do not get a chance to attend concerts. Yet organizing a charity concert is no small feat, and musicians are not necessarily also businesspeople. Further, there are risks that the concert might not be a success and reflect poorly on the musician. With bespoke recordings, there is little chance of failure – the artist can always record a second take, and there is no pressure to fill a house. The unique recording could fetch less than expected, but this could be more easily explained away than a half-empty concert hall. There is less demand put on others' time – i.e., there is no need to plan a marketing campaign, sell tickets, hire ushers, etc. Also, in the long run, the financial impact of auctioning a bespoke recording for charity can be much greater than the impact of hosting a concert. For example, assuming you could fill all 2,804 seats in the Isaac Stern Auditorium of Carnegie Hall at $100 each – a tall order – the total evening's take would be $280,400 before subtracting the spectacular fees associated with putting together a concert in the middle of Manhattan.[78] It might take two decades, but exceeding such a take by auctioning off bespoke recordings by famous musicians will become relatively commonplace over time – just think of how little such a sum buys at art auctions.

Fourth, by promoting the market for bespoke recordings, the recording industry would gain a financial lifeline from for-profit unique recordings as well as positive press and increased demand for the distributed work of signed artists who donate bespoke recordings to charity. These benefits could make the industry less inclined to lobby Congress for greater intellectual property protection and overreaching powers to monitor the Internet. This may appear to be the weakest of potential benefits because there is no definitive way to

---

[77] Meltzer, *supra* note 63.
[78] *Information: Isaac Stern Auditorium / Ronald O. Perelman Stage*, CARNEGIE HALL, www .carnegiehall.org/Information/Stern-Auditorium-Perelman-Stage/ (last visited July 4, 2017).

ensure that a financial resurgence would lead the recording industry to be more reasonable. Yet there is a significant countervailing force: society. Big Copyright needs to understand the value of gaining the approbation of society, not its opprobrium. Either the music industry is overconfident that fans hooked on its products are not paying attention, or it has not seriously considered the fact that public perception of its actions can substantially affect its profits. Its history of massive lawsuits against individuals – more than 30,000 suits in total[79] – and recent attempts to lobby Congress for even greater control are out of touch. What other industry sues its own customers and then attempts to gain the power to shut down their Internet access without proper judicial process? Such harsh tactics are not only out of step with society but conservative methods of profit maximization. The resulting negative perceptions of the industry do it no favors. For example, savvy consumers still desiring to support artists will do so through going to see them in concert because they know an artist earns more from live performances than from royalties on record sales. Moreover, fans fed up with labels may feel justified in downloading copyrighted songs without paying for them.

Consumers may become even more upset with the music industry if it adopts bespoke recordings as a revenue source but continues its misguided attempts to monopolize culture. Nonetheless, bespoke recordings are a perfect way for the music industry to experiment with alternative funding sources because they are in no danger of eroding sales elsewhere, unlike other potential sources of income for the industry.

Bespoke recordings are a promising tool but not a comprehensive solution to the revenue struggles of the music industry. This does not make bespoke recordings a deficient idea; in fact, they have no significant drawbacks. Bespoke recordings could be separately pursued along with other new revenue-generating ideas, for example, the broadcasting of live concerts in movie theaters across the country, as has been pioneered by the Metropolitan Opera. These high-definition opera broadcasts "from the Met stage" are also available at some public schools.[80] In addition, live concerts can be broadcast over the Internet for a small fee.

One potential concern is that if a bespoke recording market is established, only a fraction of unique pieces would be donated to the public over time. This would create greater inequality of access to certain recordings, but to put

[79]   *RIAA v. The People: Five Years Later*, ELECTRONIC FRONTIER F. (Sept. 30, 2008), www.eff
       .org/wp/riaa-v-people-five-years-later.
[80]   *The Metropolitan Opera HD Live in Schools*, METROPOLITAN OPERA, www.metoperafamily
       .org/metopera/about/education/index.aspx (last visited Feb. 10, 2013).

this into perspective, it is quite similar to the private sale of a Mary Cassatt painting or a Zaha Hadid building.

Ralph Waldo Emerson observed, "In the Greek cities, it was reckoned profane, that any person should pretend a property in a work of art, which belonged to all who could behold it."[81] Yet there is much art that is inherently private and personal, and society accepts that a substantial amount of such artwork – e.g., paintings and sculpture – will remain in private hands. The numerous reasons for such tolerance are applicable to bespoke recordings.

First, to block the development of bespoke recordings would be philosophically illiberal because their creation and sale would not harm anyone.

Second, the nature of capitalism, and the basis for much of our wealth as a nation, depends on the private production and consumption of countless goods, including artistic masterpieces. Creating new methods for musicians to be able to financially support themselves should be celebrated. During the Renaissance and early modern period in Europe, when recordings did not exist, composers and performers had to find other ways to sustain themselves. Some made their living through music but had to devote a significant amount of time to activities not directly related to their composing – e.g., Johann Sebastian Bach was a church organist,[82] and Antonio Vivaldi was a music director of an orphanage[83] – and many, like Joseph Haydn, accepted the awkward power dynamics of patronage.[84] To this day, it is not uncommon for musicians to work jobs outside of music – e.g., Morton Feldman worked in his family's textile business, while Philip Glass drove a taxi.

The third reason for accepting the private ownership of some artwork is the abundance of artwork – it is estimated that the "active universe of songs" is 8 million, while the "available music catalog worldwide" comprises roughly 50 million recordings.[85] Most new musical compositions will continue to be released to the public, even if bespoke recordings are spectacularly successful. This is because musicians want to be heard by a large audience – they want to touch others' lives with their work.[86] As Glenn Gould suggested, the purpose of art is the "lifelong construction of a state of wonder and serenity."[87] Also, for

[81] RALPH WALDO EMERSON, THE CONDUCT OF LIFE 53 (CreateSpace 2013) (1860).
[82] THE WORLDS OF JOHANN SEBASTIAN BACH 145 (Raymond Erickson ed., 2009).
[83] KARL HELLER, ANTONIO VIVALDI: THE RED PRIEST OF VENICE 42–43 (1997).
[84] OXFORD COMPOSER COMPANIONS: HAYDN 325 (David Wyn Jones ed., 2002).
[85] KUSEK & LEONHARD, *supra* note 45, at 90. Cf. supra page 99 n 78.
[86] Ian Rogers, *"You've Got to Go to Gigs to Get Gigs": Indie Musicians, Eclecticism and the Brisbane Scene*, 22 J. MEDIA & CULTURAL STUD. 639, 642 (2008).
[87] KEVIN BAZZANA, WONDROUS STRANGE: THE LIFE AND ART OF GLENN GOULD 337 (2005).

a musician's bespoke recording to be highly sought after, she must be widely known – a result that would be hard, though not impossible, to achieve without releasing public recordings for wider distribution and frequently touring.

The reason bespoke recordings are ultimately good for society is that the positive benefits described earlier – improving the finances of musicians and the recording industry, increasing funding to music nonprofits, encouraging the discovery of new musical talent, and reducing the impetus for Big Copyright to shackle the Internet – outweigh the fact that most bespoke recordings will remain private.

Big Copyright cannot be allowed to impede creativity, innovation, and free speech simply because technology has evolved to the point where copyright can no longer further contort itself to accommodate the interests of Big Copyright. That technology can make certain intellectual property laws less relevant is not a new phenomenon, yet Big Copyright has been unwilling to accept copyright's diminishing importance and limited revenue-generating capacity, at least in regard to certain fields of art. Bespoke music recordings will alleviate the music industry's overreliance on copyright.

Bespoke recordings can breathe life back into the music industry by increasing income for both musicians and record labels. Further, donated bespoke recordings can be auctioned off to fund music outreach and therapy programs, which would bring scores of individuals in greater contact with music, encourage creation, and foster the next generation of music appreciators, composers, and performers. By facilitating an extreme form of ownership for isolated recordings, we might prevent the overall expansion of the copyright regime and avoid draining the vitality of the Internet.

FAN FICTION AND FANTASY SPORTS CHARITY LEAGUES

Fan fiction (fanfic or fic) is a "literary format with its own subgenres" where fans take existing material from TV shows, movies, video games, novels, and comics such as characters or plots as a starting-off point to generate new stories.[88] It "has been around for centuries but only recently gained a name and a culture."[89] While the community's range of creations is very broad, "the vast majority of stories tend to be things that would make sense even to people

---

[88]   Gavia Baker-Whitelaw & Aja Romano, *A Guide to Fanfiction for People Who Can't Stop Getting It Wrong*, DAILY DOT (June 17, 2014), www.dailydot.com/parsec/complete-guide-to-fanfiction (last updated Mar. 8, 2017, 3:24 PM).

[89]   *Id.*

who have never read fanfic in their lives: romances where old friends are reunited and enemies recognize a mutual attraction, continuations of long-cancelled TV shows, and explorations of details that never got enough screen-time in canon."[90]

The fandom environment is not only highly creative, it is highly collaborative: "[T]he way fanfiction is produced and consumed is nothing like the process of producing or consuming a novel, which is typically a very lonely venture on both ends of the reader/writer relationship."[91] For example, fanfic writers and readers get together to write collaboratively but also to edit others' work (as beta readers) and to establish fandom publishing houses. The Archive of Our Own (AO3) is one of the more popular hosting sites for fanworks, with more than a million registered users and "fanworks in over 22,000 fandoms" in 2016.[92] To give more perspective on the scope of fan fiction, more than 35,000 amateur artists along with more than 500,000 fans twice a year "converge on a man-made island in Tokyo Bay for a three-day convention."[93] While fan fiction is distinct from fan art, fan videos, and podfic, my suggestion that follows applies to all forms of fanworks.

We should consider the idea of institutionalizing the encouragement of friendly competition among different fandoms in the name of charity. Fan fiction group leagues could be set up in a similar vein to sports leagues. Such charity leagues could arrange fan fiction teams in groups of ten or twenty, mixing, say, a *Buffy the Vampire Slayer* team with a *Star Trek* team. Each week, every team in the league would compete against another in the league, with the team in each matchup that raises the most money for charity winning. At the end of the season, the top fan fiction team would be crowned league champions and could possibly enter a regional tournament, which might even lead to a national championship contest. Each league could possibly set its own rules on how it wants to compete – collecting funds for charity or number of hours volunteered by each team or a combination of the two – along with a myriad of other details, e.g., whether the winning team receives a physical or digital trophy or whether there should be caps on how much money each team member could personally donate to prevent the skewing of results by wealthy fans.

Currently, to the best of my knowledge, there are fan fiction institutions – such as the Organization for Transformative Works, which engages in

[90] *Id.*   [91] *Id.*

[92] *Archive of Our Own*, ORG. FOR TRANSFORMATIVE WORKS, www.transformativeworks.org/archive_of_our_own/ (last visited Feb. 12, 2017).

[93] Nathaniel T. Noda, *Copyrights Retold: How Interpretive Rights Foster Creativity and Justify Fan-Based Activities*, 20 SETON HALL J. SPORTS & ENT. 131, 132 (2010).

outreach and social activism on behalf of fan fiction creators – yet there is nothing equivalent to a fanfic charity league. Another group doing good is the Vlogbrothers' Nerdfighteria, which has "local meetup groups worldwide," encourages fans to start social projects,[94] and runs an annual fundraising drive, the Project for Awesome, which raised more than $2 million in 2016.[95] Community members are encouraged to make short videos about a charity they like and upload it to the Project for Awesome website, where members vote for their favorite videos, which "helps determine the charities that receive funding."[96]

Similar charity leagues could be set up for sports fans. Currently, sports aficionados who love statistics can get together and create their own fantasy teams of real professional athletes in a particular sport. Drafts are held so that players in the league alternate in selecting sports stars for their teams. Once each fan has a complete team, each week two different fans compete against each other to see which fantasy team wins, based on how well the actual athletes did that week in their real National Football League (NFL) or Major League Baseball (MLB) games. We could set up fantasy sports charity leagues to bring these existing fantasy sports leagues together to do good.

For baseball, we could establish an MLB Charity League, an umbrella nonprofit organization that would assist in creating fan-based charity teams for each real franchise. Charity teams would compete with each other to donate the most money or volunteer hours to nonprofits. So, for example, Red Sox fans could have a rivalry with Yankees fans to see which fan base gives more in donations each year. To help inaugurate the charity league, one or more MLB players per team could be recruited as spokesmen. Furthermore, MLB players could donate alongside fans to charity teams. If one professional sports league has the vision to pursue a charity sports league, other professional sporting leagues would surely follow.[97]

The charity team that donates the most money in a particular year would be crowned that year's MLB Charity League World Series winner. The victor

---

94 Aja Romano, *DFTBA: Behind the Vlogbrothers' Nerdfighters Movement*, DAILY DOT (Aug. 20, 2012), www.dailydot.com/society/hank-john-green-vlogborthers-nerdfighters/ (last updated Dec. 11, 2015, 8:56 AM).

95 *Project for Awesome 2016: Online Creators Decreasing World Suck*, PROJECT FOR AWESOME, www.projectforawesome.com/about (last visited July 4, 2017).

96 *Id. See also* Alex Kruse, *Fanfiction Fanfilms for Charity*: WIRED, CROWDRISE, www .crowdrise.com/fanfictionfanfilmsfo (last visited July 4, 2017).

97 Currently, there is a related Beard-A-Thon fundraiser for National Hockey League fans who "pledge to grow a playoff beard for the duration of their team's playoff run," with donations, raised from their family and friends, given to charities. *About Beard-A-Thon*, BEARD-A-THON, www.beardathon.com/noteam/what-is-beardathon.aspx (last visited July 4, 2017).

could be determined either by (a) simply seeing which Charity Team donates the most money in a year or (b) mirroring MLB's playoff structure. In this latter scenario, the ten charity teams to donate the most money during the regular season would enter the MLB Charity League Playoffs. Then, over a one- or two-week period, charity teams would go head-to-head to determine which teams would advance to the next round. This would be repeated until two charity teams remain to compete in the MLB Charity League World Series. The MLB Charity League would keep track of yearly champions just like MLB does on the field, providing charity teams further incentive to donate to worthy causes – aspiring to create charity baseball dynasties. Conceivably, charity baseball could even keep track of top individual donors to compose charity all-star teams, charity baseball hall of fame inductions, etc. Also, other metrics besides total donations could be used to rank teams – e.g., hours of donated service at MLB Charity League events or donations per fan.[98] Furthermore, such fantasy charity leagues could be created for university sports to help raise scholarship funds. For example, during a Penn State versus Ohio State football game, the scoreboard could display a real-time running tally of charity team donations. When the football game ends, so would your team's chance to donate more to your alma mater.

What do these charity leagues have to do with copyright? My major concern is that copyright leads to overconsumption that crowds out important aspects of life, such as creating, volunteering, and spending time with friends. If time spent on these valuable activities can be increased in ways other than decreasing copyright, we should consider those paths. Improving lives – not decreasing copyright – is the primary goal. The creation of fan charity leagues would bring benefits to people currently overconsuming entertainment. Added fan activity would probably not increase or decrease the consumption of the underlying artwork or televised sports but would likely increase the creative and collaborative activities of members of fan groups.[99] Creating fan teams would encourage some members to meet in person, which would help build friendships around shared interests. Such developing solidarity could lead to added creative social endeavors such as attending a Comic-Con together, actually playing baseball, or making a film or novel collectively.

Another benefit of building fan charity leagues is that group members would be not only creating and interacting more but also ramping up their volunteering and fundraising efforts for worthy causes. It is a good trade to

---

[98] This last metric could be determined possibly by the team's city population, taking into account that some cities have more than one franchise.

[99] Also, it could decrease members' consumption of artwork unrelated to the fan group.

substitute two hours of consumption for two hours of socializing more, creating more, and helping more.

Fan charity leagues would potentially interest Big Copyright and corporate sports franchises because they offer another angle for raising brand awareness and extracting additional profit. The more involved the fanfic charity leagues are, the more Big Copyright wins, assuming many creative works with their own large fan associations will, if not initially, certainly ultimately, be held by corporations. Further, the more options for participation within the fanfic charity leagues, the greater the chances that membership will grow, which would also benefit the copyright holder.[100] Big Copyright's gains would likely come from higher attendance at corporate-sponsored events and higher sales of paraphernalia associated with the artwork such as costumes, toys, gear, T-shirts, and games. If so, such a boost to Hollywood would also benefit individuals. Research shows that individuals obtain more happiness when they spend money on an experience – e.g., going to a Dragon Con event to interact with other fans rather than buying a consumer good.[101] Further, if one buys a consumer good, it is more valuable if the good leads to interaction and experiences rather than isolation. Buying a *Star Wars* costume and acting out scenes with other fans is healthier and more satisfying than sitting on one's couch watching the movie series one more time. The same can be said of Hollywood's sister – the corporate sports world. Fantasy football, basketball, baseball, soccer, and hockey charity leagues would unite fans to go to more games, rather than watching from home, because competing in leagues would reinforce identification with the team and other fans as well as spur members to volunteer and donate to charity. Universities would love another funding source to help students with financial need.

A potential concern is that creating fan charity leagues would bring about a dangerous level of symbiosis with big brands in sports and entertainment. Conceivably, perilously strong bonds might be fostered, yet it is difficult to understand exactly how this might occur any more than it already does. More likely, active participation in a creative community will lessen overconsumption. Again, I think it is worth the trade-off that fans spend more on

---

[100]   Tushnet suggests: "Copyright owners should be able to defend their creations against pure copying and against harm to market share. These two uses form a boundary that is easily policed and that fulfills the legitimate goals of copyright law. When no lucrative market share is sought and productive use is made of copyrighted characters, fan fiction should be recognized as expressing a protected and valuable form of human creativity – if only in the margins." Rebecca Tushnet, *Legal Fictions: Copyright, Fan Fiction, and a New Common Law*, 17 Loy. L.A. Ent. L. Rev. 651, 686 (1997).

[101]   Elizabeth W. Dunn, Daniel T. Gilbert, & Timothy D. Wilson, *If Money Doesn't Make You Happy, Then You Probably Aren't Spending It Right*, 21 J. Consumer Psychol. 115 (2011).

merchandise and corporate-sponsored creative events if it enables them to form stronger friendships, create more socially, and volunteer more.

COPYRIGHT PAYBACK MACHINE

In response to the conflicting challenges of attempting to seek retribution against those who committed injustices and attempting to bring a torn country together in reconciliation, South Africa established an innovative truth commission. While the compromise was imperfect, as all compromises must be, the solution was a creative remedy that worked. In situations where traditional recourses are ill advised or impractical, new remedies must be sought.

Not all unauthorized downloads are equal. In fact, some unauthorized downloads are ethically virtuous. Others are clearly against the spirit of copyright law – e.g., when an individual goes onto a peer-to-peer network and helps herself to 6,000 copyright-protected songs without Creative Commons licenses. Hollywood realizes that suing potentially millions of individuals might be impractical, so we are in need of an unorthodox solution.

Undoubtedly, many of us have at some point in our lives done something we regret. Sometimes we can erase the guilt through apologizing or attempt to make up for it with actions. Yet at other times the chance forever disappears – e.g., when you are not openly disrespectful to a stranger but too curt or unwelcoming. We can attempt to partially compensate for it by keeping the misdeed forefront in our minds to help us remember to be kinder in the future, yet it would be wonderful if there was a way to get back in touch with the person and reengage. Such a tool would be helpful to some individuals who have illicitly downloaded art, which they consumed but did not use in their own process of creation.

Tracking down an artist whom you have taken from without permission or payment would not be a strict impossibility. Yet practically speaking it could take a good deal of time to find a way to do it. Local artists might not post contact information because of a lack of focus on marketing, while celebrity artists might purposefully not provide contact information because they do not want to be inundated with mail. Plus contacting them would involve a substantial amount of legal uncertainty in regard to advertising your potential copyright infringement.

As everyone is aware, a digital song is not the same beast as a candy bar. Thus, it would not sit right to simply buy another candy bar twenty years later from the same merchant to make up for the one you stole when you were eight years old. Going on iTunes and paying for a second digital copy of a song you already have saved on your computer does not harm the artist in the way that a merchant would be harmed by doling out two candy bars but only getting paid for one. Thus, to attempt to correct your unauthorized download, you could simply buy another copy of a song you previously downloaded illicitly. Yet this would not always be practically possible – e.g., a book could be out of print. Further, on some level, doing so seems less satisfying in terms of righting a wrong.

The issue is a mix of Aristotelian commutative justice – a conception of the just exchange of goods – along with the informed ethical principle – the idea that there is ethical value to open, as opposed to ignorant or disguised, ethical action, especially action meant to elicit forgiveness.[102] When looking at both downloads collectively, no violation of corrective justice is necessarily triggered – i.e., the artist was not a victim who suffered palpable harm at the hands of an aggressor. Within a commutative justice perspective, the concern is that while the artist ultimately did not lose anything because the consumer later bought a second copy, the first exchange, when the consumer downloaded a pirated copy, was chimerical. The illicit download does not recognize the artist as a party to a transaction that should ideally maintain equality between the parties within a commutative justice framework.

Attempting to make up for the initial illicit download through simply buying an authorized, second download also does not sit well ethically within the context of informed, purposeful individual action and interaction with others. When buying the second download, the consumer masks his intention for both the current and the previous acts; he is not confronting the artist honestly. This matters not only to the consumer who wants to erase his guilt but also to the artist who would experience a different range of emotion if informed that a consumer is righting a wrong years later, not simply buying her song online. It is also important to the consumer to honestly confront the artist to learn from the experience, which will inform his future actions much more than simply buying a second copy of the song.[103]

---

[102]   ARISTOTLE, THE NICOMACHEAN ETHICS 1129–34 (D. Ross trans., Oxford University Press 1925) and Martin Skladany, *The Executive as Executioner and the Informed Governance Principle*, 3 CRIM. L. & PHIL. 289 (2009). I am introducing the idea of an "informed ethical principle" here – i.e., to my knowledge, it is a newly coined concept within ethical thought. I am basing it off the informed governance principle, which I also introduced as a new term within political theory, in the previously cited article, to argue that if our president and state governors are not against the death penalty, they have an ethical obligation to personally execute a death row inmate in order to learn more about the institution of the death penalty.
[103]   This reasoning would suggest that ideally the former illicit downloader would make himself known personally to the artist. Yet, given the potentially crippling nature of copyright infringement remedies, the illicit downloader who now wants to make up for his past act has to do so anonymously.

Here is where copyright minimalists and maximalists could come together and spill sweat instead of blood.[104] Collectively, they could establish a nonprofit that runs an app and website that would allow consumers to pay back artists whom they took from in the past – a copyright payback machine.[105] Reparations would be anonymous, but consumers would be offered the option to digitally save a receipt of the payment. Anonymity is important because the payback machine could not provide absolute absolution, since it could not speak on behalf of the artist; yet this could be a second area of collaboration – getting Congress to alter the law to release the consumer from potential liability. Offering a receipt would open the door to amnesty in the event the consumer is sued before the laws are changed. The receipt could be used to show remorse and possibly affect damage awards, though statistically speaking the risk of suit would in almost all instances be vanishingly remote. Conceivably, individual artists could contact the payback machine to reach an agreement to absolve from potential copyright infringement liability anyone who illicitly downloaded one of their works but subsequently pays for it through the payback machine.

To help fund administration of the payback machine, the nonprofit running it would charge a small upfront fee on top of the cost of the pirated work. Also, the app could even collect payback funds for orphaned works.[106] Additionally, the payback machine could feasibly allow the consumer to leave a personal yet anonymous note apologizing for his or her past actions.[107]

Hopefully, consumers would take advantage of an easy option to right a wrong, not just for the sake of the artists but also for themselves. A copyright payback machine could give artists a modest financial boost while giving consumers a second chance.[108] Further, a payback machine would also prove helpful in terms of easing fluctuations in consumer purchasing power. An innovative publisher, Semaphore Press, allows law students to

---

[104] This phrase may come from David Hume.

[105] The name is an homage to the Internet Archive's wonderful Wayback Machine, which allows users to see what a particular website looked like in the past. *Wayback Machine*, INTERNET ARCHIVE, https://archive.org/web/.

[106] What to do with the funds would be a challenging and interesting issue. For a fascinating account of the history of the cy-près doctrine, see CAROLINE R. SHERMAN, THE USES OF THE DEAD: THE EARLY MODERN DEVELOPMENT OF CY-PRÈS DOCTRINE (2018).

[107] Gary Chapman and Jennifer Thomas identify five different forms apologies can take or "languages of apology," including expressing regret, accepting responsibility, making restitution, genuinely repenting, and requesting forgiveness. *See generally* GARY CHAPMAN & JENNIFER THOMAS, WHEN I'M SORRY ISN'T ENOUGH (2013).

[108] For a complex and potentially ambiguous take on attempting to right wrongs, see Gayatri Chakravorty Spivak, *Righting Wrongs*, 103 S. ATLANTIC Q., 523 (2004).

pay what they'd like for downloading an entire casebook. The company suggests students pay $30, though they can download the materials for free. While such an arrangement has many interesting aspects to it, one of them is helping law students smooth their consumption over years. For example, if a student has no money now but really needs the book, she can download it for free today; a few years later, when she's working and able to pay, she can donate back to the authors by downloading a new copy. While this is not ideal, as described previously, Semaphore's decision to structure the payment system in this way easily enables customers to smooth consumption without actually illicitly downloading a casebook.

Big Copyright might agree to come together with copyright minimalists to create a payback machine because of the additional revenue and the possibility of a more effective way to instill the norm that unauthorized copying simply to consume is sometimes uncouth. Hollywood has largely found that scare tactics either do not work or are socially unacceptable – the days of suing thousands of individual consumers are largely over for certain entertainment industries. The payback machine would be a more gentle, more receptive way to get people to realize that certain types of uses of others' work are beyond the pale.[109] While copyright minimalists and maximalists will continue to disagree about whether many different types of uses of another's artwork are or should be permitted under copyright, downloading a song from a file-sharing site instead of paying a dollar for it does not generate a ton of disagreement, though some think the act warrants jail time while others think of it as resistance that is necessary to bring down all of copyright.

One potential concern is the risk that the payback machine could be hacked and the list of payers publicly released. This is a general concern with all online transactions, and it is no more likely to occur here than elsewhere. However, consumers' credit card information could be handled independently from all the other information involved in the transaction, so even if the payback machine were hacked, it would only reveal who donated a payment, not to which artist or for which work. Further, free software for anonymous payments is being developed, such as GNU Taler, to mitigate this concern.

---

[109] While I have found online threads discussing how to try to pay an artist back for having illicitly downloaded her work in the past, I have not found anyone proposing a copyright payback machine. Suggestions revolve around whether to simply buy the artist's work, attend her concert, or buy merchandise from her. For example, see *I've Illegally Downloaded a Record and Now Want to Pay for It. What Is the Channel That Will Reward the Artist with the Most Money?*, QUORA, www.quora.com/I-ve-illegally-downloaded-a-record-and-now-want-to-pay-for-it.-What-is-the-channel-that-will-reward-the-artist-with-the-most-money (last visited Feb. 26, 2017).

A second possible concern is that the payback machine could be a stealth scheme to avoid liability. While such a claim could be made, it is difficult to see how it would hold true. For example, unless an artist who holds copyright in her own work explicitly agrees to release individuals from liability if they use the payback machine or unless the law is changed, consumers who visit the app would still be technically on the hook if a copyright infringement case were brought against them. Further, numerous uses of the payback machine would likely occur after individuals are legally off the hook – after the three-year statute of limitations for copyright infringement.[110]

TAX IDEAS & CHARITABLE PARTNERSHIPS

There is modest scope for progress in alleviating the numerous harms of excessive copyright protection through the tax code and through charity. Following are a few inchoate ideas.

Tax Breaks for Donating Copyrighted Art to the Public Domain

It all started to go downhill with Richard Nixon – specifically, the IRS's policy on art donations. In 1969, Nixon donated his vice presidential papers to the National Archives and took a tax write-off that many thought was inflated – above the fair market value for the papers.[111] In response, Congress took it out on artists by eliminating their ability to write off the fair market value of art they donated to 501(c)(3) nonprofits. Going forward, artists would only be able to deduct the costs of the materials – paper and ink – that were used to create the art. Oddly, this change in the tax code applied to artists, not collectors, so a collector of another's artwork could donate it to a nonprofit and receive a tax deduction worth the market value of the art.[112] This change brought an immediate halt in donations. The year before the shift, the Library of Congress received more than 100,000 donated literary manuscripts. The year after – zero.[113] Works are still donated to museums but in fewer numbers and mainly by wealthy donors who purchase an artist's work and then

---

[110] "No civil action shall be maintained under the [Act] unless it is commenced within three years after the claim accrued." 17 U.S.C. § 507(b).

[111] Michael Rips, *Painters Deserve Their Deduction*, N.Y. TIMES (Apr. 21, 2017), www.nytimes .com/2017/04/21/opinion/painters-deserve-their-deduction.html?emc=eta1. Rips offers a highly original solution to bring back the full market value deduction to artists that relies on the 2010 Supreme Court ruling in *Citizens United v. Federal Election Commission*.

[112] *Id.*   [113] *Id.*

turn around and donate it to a museum, relying on the IRS's disparate treatment of donations from artists and collectors.

There is a recent bill, the Artist-Museum Partnership Act, to bring parity back between artists and collectors, by allowing artists to deduct the fair market value of their physical work if they donate it to a museum.[114] While I support such an effort, it does not fully take into account our digital world, nor does it recognize the public domain. It makes sense that we cannot realistically expect an artist to donate a painting to the public domain – the painting needs a physical roof. There is less of an immediate need to donate digital photographs or videos to an institution as opposed to the public domain. Plus, famous works, including digital pieces, will always be welcomed by museums, less so the work of millions of artists working in obscurity.

While artists can already freely donate their art to the public domain using a Creative Commons CC0 license (no rights reserved), why should they not at least get to deduct the costs of creating the work, as do famous artists if they donate to a museum and who arguably need such a tax deduction less?[115] There may be a nonlegal, simple fix to this situation: establish a nonprofit, provisionally and poorly titled the Public Domain Tax Vehicle, that would accept anyone's donation of digital artwork, unlike archives and museums, which are selective in what they are willing to accept. After receipt of the work, the nonprofit would commit to putting a Creative Commons CC0 license on it in order to release it into the public domain. Such a fix would unlikely bring riches to artists. The point would be to create more parity between famous and non-famous artists in the law and encourage the development of the public domain.

Of course, we could do better. If Congress passes the Artist-Museum Partnership Act, it would allow all artists to get the fair market value of the physical work that they donated to the Public Domain Tax Vehicle, not just the cost of the materials. Hollywood might be responsive to such an expanded deduction because it would give it the option to offload a bunch of content.

Better yet, we could encourage Congress to go beyond the proposed bill and allow all artists to write off the fair market value of their copyright if they dedicate their art directly to the public domain – without the need to use the

---

[114] NAT'L OPERA AM. CTR., TAX FAIRNESS FOR ARTISTS AND WRITERS (2016), www .operaamerica.org/Files/OADocs/AdvocacyPDFs/2016/06_TaxFairness.pdf.

[115] In my opinion, while ideally all non-famous works should be adopted by others and simultaneously also be put under a Creative Commons license, so that the works can evolve or simply be preserved under another's stewardship yet be accessible freely to others as inspiration, I recognize that donating non-famous works to the public domain without adoption is also a worthy option.

Public Domain Tax Vehicle. Would this lead some to claim their childhood scribbles to be billion-dollar masterpieces? Possibly, but we have the IRS, whose job is to discourage overvaluation. What about work from an artist who has never sold anything in her life? Establish another nonprofit, called Be the First to Buy a Piece of Art from an Up-and-Coming Artist, to help facilitate fair market values.

Alternatively, we could push for a tax credit. The government could even theoretically give ex ante grants to average citizens to create art. Finally, the government could pay any citizen who voluntarily presents proof that he or she has created a work of art.[116] Do we really want to live in a society that pays people to create? Numerous European countries have no compunction about distributing cash grants and/or subsidies to couples to induce them to have more children.[117] Given variations in culture, many Americans might reflexively cringe at such an idea, but what is at stake, if people take advantage of the art deductions, credits, or grants, is so great that knee-jerk reactions should not eliminate the option before serious consideration of the proposal.

Freeing Art from Freeports

There is an extraordinary amount of exquisite artwork – primarily paintings, drawings, and sculpture – in glorified storage sheds. The facilities combine Fort Knox security with a touch of industrial aesthetic – i.e., literally countless vaults or storage units in warehouses. These secure facilities are called freeports. The security freeports provide is largely incidental to their real value as tax havens.

The tax savings can be substantial. At the Geneva Freeport, no import or transaction taxes have to be paid as long as the artwork stays at the facility.[118] For example, even if a piece of art is sold while it is at the freeport, as long as it

---

[116] To maximize the effectiveness of this strategy, it would be wise to provide ex ante or ex post financial payments to citizens instead of tax deductions. Tax deductions would not help individuals who do not have deductions that exceed the standard deduction available to all filers. Furthermore, many people do not file federal income taxes – 47 percent of American households did not pay any federal income tax in 2009. David Leonhardt, *Yes, 47% of Households Owe No Taxes. Look Closer.*, N.Y. TIMES (Apr. 14, 2010), www.nytimes.com/2010/04/14/business/economy/14leonhardt.html.

[117] See the Child Benefits section in Gerda Neyer, *Family Policies and Low Fertility in Western Europe* (Max Planck Institute for Demographic Research, Working Paper No. 21, 2003), www.elfac.org/Publications/politicaseuropa.pdf.

[118] David Segal, *Swiss Freeports Are Home for a Growing Treasury of Art*, N.Y. TIMES (July 21, 2012), www.nytimes.com/2012/07/22/business/swiss-freeports-are-home-for-a-growing-treasury-of-art.html?mcubz=0.

remains in the freeport, no taxes are due.[119] Only once the artwork leaves the freeport – "either because it's been sold or because the original owner has moved it – are taxes owed in the country where it winds up."[120] This is because when the idea of a freeport sprung up, it was meant more as a distribution facility for agricultural goods, a place to store food before it was dispersed throughout the country.[121] It was not conceived of as a place to store priceless art, cars, wine, and gold bars for decades, yet given its "'temporary exemption of taxes and duties for an unlimited period,'" it was only a matter of time until it turned into a tax minimization tool.[122]

While little is known of exactly what lies within these vaults, one art dealer recalled a job he held more than twenty-five years ago in which he was doing inventory on more than a thousand works by Picasso in just one freeport facility.[123] Only customs officials know, and will not disclose, how much art is stored in the 565,000-square-foot Geneva Freeport, which is roughly the size of ten football fields, let alone the numerous other freeports throughout Switzerland.[124] This is in addition to freeports scattered around the world in places such as China, Singapore, and Luxembourg. David Segal cites an underwriting director of AXA Art Insurance as saying, "'I doubt you've got a piece of paper wide enough to write down all the zeros,'" in an attempt to estimate the value of all artwork held at the Geneva Freeport.[125]

This is a tragedy. We do not know the bounds of our cultural treasures because of the taxman. Unlike many artists, Galileo Galilei was persecuted for his ideas, yet Galileo's works have freely circulated, while works by Vincent van Gogh and Gustav Klimt continue to be confined in art prisons. To alleviate such wasting away of brushstrokes, we should give those who have tucked away art in freeports a tax incentive to digitize their work and display it on a central nonprofit art site.[126] To ensure anonymity, if desired, art owners would be given the option to not reveal their interest in the work. Alternatively, some owners might not particularly care about the tax break but instead be excited by the creation of such an online repository, which would

---

[119] *Id.*   [120] *Id.*   [121] *Id.*   [122] *Id.*   [123] *Id.*   [124] *Id.*   [125] *Id.*

[126] Le Freeport Luxembourg "is encouraging clients to loan works to local museums to improve the small country's cultural offering." Jessica Tasman-Jones, *Hidden Treasure: A Look into the World of Freeports*, CAMPDEN FB (Jan. 23, 2015, 11:48 AM), www.campdenfb.com/article/h idden-treasure-look-world-freeports. A Swiss lawyer, Christophe Germann, has made a more radical proposal – "arguing that free ports be forced to open their doors to let people see public displays of the private collections, a worthy trade-off for the tax benefits collectors receive," instead of creating a voluntary online repository in exchange for new tax breaks. Graham Bowley & Doreen Carvajal, *One of the World's Greatest Art Collections Hides Behind This Fence*, N.Y. TIMES (May 28, 2016), www.nytimes.com/2016/05/29/arts/design/o ne-of-the-worlds-greatest-art-collections-hides-behind-this-fence.html.

allow them to share their works online. Others might revel in the ability to proudly have their name publicly associated with owning masterpieces, proving Thorstein Veblen's theory of conspicuous consumption correct – so much of the joy of buying luxuries comes from displaying them to others. Further, the same incentive to share a high-quality digital reproduction online can be provided to individuals who store famous works in their homes. This would provide both the owners of the work and the public with numerous advantages over the current *Raiders of the Lost Ark* scenario that incentivizes the storage of art instead of its display.[127]

Individual art collectors and corporate investment firms would be attracted to the idea of the online repository and tax break because it could save them money, increase the value of their work, and/or allow them to act altruistically by sharing the work with the public.[128] For at least some individual or corporate investors, publicly displaying their work might have a beneficial effect on the value of the work. For example, an individual Caspar David Friedrich painting might catch the eye of a collector who views it online and decides she must have it at any cost.

There would be numerous benefits to society from encouraging artwork that is locked up – artwork that may have never been shown to more than a handful of people in centuries – to be viewed online. The increased access to artistic masterpieces would hopefully invigorate the passions of existing fans of fine art and introduce new individuals to the fields. This would be beneficial because the increased audience for fine art could help reduce the overconsumption of corporate works. At a minimum, experiencing fine art does not dampen our brain activity and hence does not foster dangerous levels of overconsumption. Plus, experiencing unearthed masterpieces could directly inspire some to create.

A concern could be backlash from enabling the rich to profit more through this new arrangement. While this is strictly correct – wealthy art owners would be attracted to the idea at least in part because of the money – the criticism neglects to highlight the benefits from such a policy. Furthermore, the public's unwillingness or inability to pressure lawmakers to close the vast gap in

---

[127] It is not lost on me that I advocate for creating bespoke recordings, unique musical compositions or recordings, and locking them up in freeports. The difference is that the visual fine art world is financially incredibly robust relative to the contemporary classical music world. Successful artists like Damian Hirst and Jeff Koons could fund art education programs to the tune of hundreds of millions by themselves. We don't have the equivalent opportunity for classical musicians to do the same. Bespoke recordings would be a necessary compromise to get more funding to musical nonprofits in order to enrich childhoods with classical music.

[128] Of course, this would not apply to any art held illegally, such as artwork looted by the Nazis during World War II.

income inequality and eliminate tax avoidance schemes allows freeports to continue to exist. Combining such political feebleness or apathy with the fact that very few among the general public know about the existence of freeports makes it unlikely that encouraging the placement online of pieces hidden away for centuries in some instances will instantaneously propagate revolt. Allowing for such lending will bring masterpieces to the masses, at least digitally. Currently, the locked-up works are infrequently visited only by "collectors who are ferried in white limos from the tarmac to the warehouse."[129]

Art Elections and Donations to Digitize Works

The ultra-wealthy are not the only ones squirreling away artwork. Museums do it as well – sometimes in the same freeports used by the rich. While for different reasons, a lack of wall space instead of a lack of desire to pay tax, the result is the same – art hidden from the world.

We need to also encourage museums without the Metropolitan Museum of Art's $4 billion endowment, which enables the revered New York City institution to pay millions in compensation to its most senior employees (including $500,000 bonuses), to digitize all their stored items and freely display the reproductions online.[130] While the permutations are numerous, one possible way to fund such an endeavor is to encourage individuals to donate the cost of digitizing one piece within the museum's collection. Wealthy patrons could also make donations on behalf of others, such as public elementary school art programs.

Then museums could hold monthly or semiannual elections for which newly digitized pieces should be publicly displayed in the museum. Everyone who donated to digitize a work or was given a vote through another's contribution could vote for his or her favorite. The contest would be meant to highlight the newly digitized works but also use a novel method to engage patrons with the museums. The contest could take numerous forms from a simple most-votes-wins format to a more intricate structure resembling an NCAA basketball tournament, with single elimination contests in multiple rounds. If the contest gains popularity, firms could sponsor it as they do sports stadiums, sports leagues, sports tournaments, etc.[131] Not only could this give

---

[129]　Segal, *supra* note 118.

[130]　Isabel Vincent & Melissa Klein, *Money-Losing Met Hands Execs Hefty Raises*, N.Y. Post (Mar. 13, 2017), http://nypost.com/2017/03/13/money-losing-met-hands-execs-hefty-raises/.

[131]　*Europe's Most Successful Football Stadium: Emirates Stadium*, Populous, https://populous .com/project/emirates-stadium/ (last visited July 2, 2017).

companies online publicity; their contribution could be recognized next to the displayed winning piece at the museum.

Corporations Endowing Art

Museums court corporate donors through, for example, sponsoring exhibits. Such institutions should consider a novel approach – asking corporations to endow a piece of art within a museum, which would allow the firm to display the work in its offices for a specified period of time every few years. Firms could be attracted to the idea because it would not only allow them to build goodwill through such financial donations but also provide an added perk of being able to display the work at their headquarters – providing enjoyment, impressing visitors, and further publicizing their generosity, subject to tax code alterations. The advantages for art museums would be equally beneficial – e.g., adding long-term financial support while enabling them to rotate their displayed works more regularly, especially if one firm endows numerous pieces and/or if many firms participate in the program.[132]

These collective ideas do not directly address overconsumption but rather aim to get more nonaddictive art out in the open through expanding the public domain, unearthing purposefully hidden gems, or increasing funding options for art museums.

NETFLIX OFFERING POEMS

We could encourage entertainment companies to offer public domain works to consumers through their expertise in gatekeeping.[133] Do we want companies economically exploiting works that are in the public domain – i.e., making a profit off works that are freely available to anyone who simply seeks them out? It might sound crazy, but the idea would be to steer individuals away from corporate and quasi-addictive art forms (TV, film) toward other mediums in hopes of lowering the overall levels of consumption.

---

[132] Once the entire collection is digitized, the museum could even consider allowing patrons, upon a donation, to request a work come out of storage for a particular event – e.g., a wedding anniversary.

[133] Barnes & Noble sells hard copies of works by famous authors that are in the public domain for five dollars each. *B&N Classics: Your Choice $5 Each*, BARNES & NOBLE, www .barnesandnoble.com/b/bn-classics-your-choice-5-each/_/N-2mie (last visited July 2, 2017). *See also* Bill Goldstein, *MEDIA; Publishers Give Classics a Makeover*, N.Y. TIMES (Feb. 10, 2003), www.nytimes.com/2003/02/10/business/media-publishers-give-classics-a-mak eover.html.

Companies with business models that do not rely on sales of individual works online might consider it. For example, Netflix and Hulu, which make their money from subscriptions that provide unlimited access to a large, fixed group of artwork, might be open to the idea because such additions would be costless while expanding the offerings to their customers. The likes of Redbox might not appreciate the idea because any money they make from selling a poem for five cents might not be enough to compensate for any possible reductions in consumption of the entertainment they rent out – TV and movies.

Amazon is a mixed hybrid, offering some artwork for free such – as digital copies of novels in the public domain by Charles Dickens and Mary Shelley – even though it operates a business selling individual copies of other works and runs an unlimited, buffet-style revenue model, Amazon Prime Video. Tellingly, Amazon does not cross-market free Dickens novels to customers browsing for movies on Amazon Prime Video. It might want to maintain such content silos because it thinks doing otherwise would distract or annoy customers, yet others such as Netflix could experiment with such cross-marketing and with offering public domain content that its competitors do not. Furthermore, just as non-entertainment companies currently sponsor shortened commercial breaks for viewers of certain TV shows, such companies could conceivably sponsor the inclusion of individual poems, short stories, etc. on Hulu for a certain period of time.

REJECTION TRACKER

Social media is too often about spinning a narrative. It is turning oneself into a character in one's own novel – a novel that is devoid of the richness of genuineness because it elevates a simplistically positive, flat conception of the self. We live in a world where for many "editing one's life to make it appear perfect is more appealing than naturally existing."[34]

When Proust said, "Happiness is beneficial for the body, but it is grief that develops the powers of the mind," he was talking about our individual solitary paths, not a collective experience. In fact, portraying only one's happiness through social media may harm others because our self-portraits are often wildly exaggerated. By stressing the positive and censoring the negative in our lives, we make those who read our feeds and tweets feel inadequate and

---

[34]   Josh Noble, *Study: Social Media Making People Anti-Social, Jealous*, STUDY FINDS (Feb. 1, 2017), www.studyfinds.org/study-finds-social-media-jealousy-facebook/.

envious.[135] If only we too saved a puppy on top of Mount Everest and were constantly found smiling with a gaggle of friends including George Clooney, the Queen, and, of course, the puppy we saved, then we too would be living happy lives. If only we communicated the setbacks, tragedy, and sorrow, we might make connections instead of simply further alienating others in lonely sorrow.

Science faces the same problem. Usually only successful scientific research is published, not the millions of failed experiments, which contain valuable information – i.e., clues to what does not work.[136] This asymmetry leads to countless research hours and funds being unknowingly duplicated. Amazingly, this bias against publishing failed experiments was found to be the result of researchers simply not bothering to "write up and submit null findings," though the reason for each failure needs to be further explored.[137]

Unlike this needless waste in science, personal failure should be looked at more positively. For example, whereas in France business failure can be equated with personal deficiencies, in other countries failure is elevated as a badge of honor. There have been a few artistic efforts to highlight failure, for example, the web series *Failure Club* by Morgan Spurlock, a reality show that encourages seven New Yorkers to not bow to the fear of failure. Still, even in cultures that celebrate mistakes, failure is less publicized than it could be; failure should be seen so it can serve as inspiration to others.[138]

Jane Park, the CEO and founder of Julep Beauty, writes about how, on the advice of Starbucks founder Howard Schultz, she kept a spreadsheet to track the number of rejections she received in the process of raising the first million dollars for her startup. The tally came to fifty-eight rejections, compared to Schultz's 217 rejections.[139] More important, by thinking of the nos along the path to success as simply part of the process, she was able to persevere and find the motivation to continue. It is this view of failure as part of life instead of

---

[135] Hanna Krasnova et al., *Envy on Facebook: A Hidden Threat to Users' Life Satisfaction?*, 11th International Conference on Wirtschaftsinformatik (2013), www.ara.cat/2013/01/28/855594433 .pdf?hash=b775840d43f9f93b7a9031449f809c388f342291.

[136] There are a few journals that specialize in null results, including the *International Journal of Negative & Null Results* and the *Journal of Negative Results in BioMedicine*.

[137] Annie Franco, Neil Malhotra, & Gabor Simonovits, *Publication Bias in the Social Sciences: Unlocking the File Drawer*, 345 Sci. 1502, 1502 (2014).

[138] Lanford Beard, *Yahoo!: Morgan Spurlock Launches "Failure Club,"* Ent. Wkly. (Nov. 23, 2011, 3:00 PM), http://ew.com/article/2011/11/23/morgan-spurlock-failure-club-new-series-yahoo-screen-exclusive/.

[139] Jane Park, *I Created an Excel Doc to Keep Track of My Rejections*, Elle (June 10, 2016), www .elle.com/culture/career-politics/advice/a37004/i-kept-an-excel-doc-of-my-failures/.

a moral judgment of one's worth that needs to be better understood, tracked, and shared with others.

We need to create a website that allows people to easily track all the rejection in their artistic lives and chart it over time – e.g., all the publishers that reject a manuscript, all the bad auditions and dismissive casting directors, all the record labels that won't even listen to a demo, all the art galleries that overlook an ambitious portfolio. While the default setting for the rejection tracker would be a private list viewable only by the user as a screen saver or securely online, you could decide to allow a select group of friends or the world to see your failed endeavors.[140]

For those already creating, the rejection tracker would help monitor failures as a motivational tool. The point is: If you're not registering a certain number of rejections each year, you're not truly giving it your all. The rejection tracker would also serve to help alter your perspective by reminding you that, just as unsuccessful startup endeavors are badges of honor, your artistic failures should be celebrated.

Any user who stumbles across rejection tracker profiles that have been made public or views profiles shared by friends or family will be inspired by the artists' persistence. Non-artists might wonder what it is about creativity that drives artists to continue struggling amid an ocean of rejection. The artists' determination might inspire non-artists to look more closely at art and find beauty or a gripping message or simply be spurred to think that they too could create. Seeing failed attempts as a noble endeavor could motivate more people to try their hand at art. Further, the rejection tracker could enlist celebrity artists to share their failures, before and after their breakthrough into the public eye. For example, Walt Disney got canned from a newspaper because "his editor told him he lacked imagination"; Oprah Winfrey was "pulled off the air as an evening news reporter and was told that she was 'unfit for TV'"; and Michael Jordan was "cut from his high school basketball team."[141] We are inspired by heroes' successes when in fact we should probably be more inspired by their failures.

---

[140]   There is a related app called Failure Games, which every day releases a new challenge such as "telling a joke or . . . asking a complete stranger to have lunch with you. Some will be harder than others, but every challenge will be designed to get you more at ease with taking chances and with the possibility of failure." Eric Fernandez, *Overcome Fear with Our New App: Failure Games*, APPSUMO (Nov. 1, 2013), www.appsumo.com/failure-games-app/.

[141]   Susie Moore, *Why Rejection Can Actually Be a Really Good Thing*, HUFFINGTON POST (Oct. 12, 2016), www.huffingtonpost.com/susie-moore/why-rejection-can-actually-be-a-really-good-thing_b_8270928.html.

In a certain light, crafting an unrealistically perfect narrative of our lives is artistic creation. It is fiction that must be imagined by someone. Given my desire to get more individuals creating, you might expect me to celebrate such a development. Yet think of how many relentlessly positive novels you've read as an adult compared to the picture book collection of your youth. While beauty, generosity, and sacrifice are to be revered, what is happening on social media resembles marketing more than art. Beer commercials leave out beer guts, with images of models permanently smiling and laughing on the beach. Further, while a positive attitude in life is priceless, ignoring the cracks and faults in life is reckless. Philosophers have struggled for centuries with the idea that without evil there cannot be genuine good. We need to appreciate both the good and bad to be autonomous instead of automatons. We need to acknowledge setbacks because they illuminate the good. We need to appreciate that doubt, melancholy, and anger have value, no matter how painful they may be to experience. Our failures often contain praiseworthy lessons. Our imperfections are beautiful.[142] They help us relate to each other, appreciate our friends, and sympathize with the downtrodden, and they remind us to treat everyone with respect, not caricature interactions with adults as if they were children or means instead of ends.

The rejection tracker could be used for numerous other purposes – tracking job applications, sports defeats, mountains unscaled, school rejections, business ventures gone wrong, etc.[143] A similar tracker could surely be created to note one's successes, though doing so might not be as interesting or educational. Further, there is a greater tendency for individuals to do so already on their own – e.g., awards on their desk, diplomas on their walls, pictures of family and friends sprinkled around their house, and, of course, social media.

Whether the rejection tracker is called Botched It or Flop Watch or Badge of Honor, the site could employ reflective provocations to get individuals curious. For example, the advertising campaign could ask: "Famous artist X failed Z times before you got up for breakfast, so why not have a go?" Or the tagline could read: "Try, probably fail, don't just consume." Such promotion would benefit wonderfully from the willingness of a few famous artists to help not just publicize the app but also share their failures. This last point touches on why Hollywood might want to collaborate on such a project. If entire

---

[142] I do not mean this in the sense of glorifying self-pity – the "exhibitionism of self-harm, suicide, depression, or self-loathing under the pretext that it is beautiful, romantic, or deep." Anne-Sophie Bine, *Social Media Is Redefining "Depression,"* ATLANTIC (Oct. 28, 2013), www .theatlantic.com/health/archive/2013/10/social-media-is-redefining-depression/280818/.

[143] *See generally* Shelley J. Correll, *Constraints into Preferences: Gender, Status, and Emerging Career Aspirations,* 69 AM. SOC. REV. 93 (2004).

industries exist around reporting the breeds of dogs celebrities have, what they don't eat for breakfast, and what they look like without makeup, the idea of getting celebrities to share their failures could generate more buzz and cash than the movies the stars act in.[144] Exaggerations aside, there is promise in getting celebrities to connect with and relate to fans in unique, genuine ways.

---

[144] Another reason Hollywood might want to cooperate with a rejection tracker is that studios could potentially license good storylines from some of the public profiles.

Conclusion

Art enables us to find ourselves and lose ourselves at the same time.

— Thomas Merton

I am not sure that Merton was right that we find ourselves in art. It seems that art is compelling because we find much more than just ourselves there. But he was right that we do lose ourselves in art, and if we consume without measure, we risk losing ourselves entirely. Only creation brings us back to ourselves again.

Art is supposed to inspire us intellectually and emotionally – to help us cope with the hardships of life, the monotony of monotony, the frustrations of the bureaucratic state, and the indignities of modern industrial production where workers are treated like tools before being replaced by them. Instead, excessive copyright protection has turned the last refuge of humanity – art – into a slick corporate weapon that is wielded by Hollywood to effectively imprison vast swaths of society. "We the people" are "doing time" in front of a screen.

Dramatically reducing copyright would dampen the overconsumption of commercial art and encourage people to resist the ossification of their personalities by creating art on their own. More critically, we would be building a democracy of people who make rather than people who sample. A society that creates, not clicks. In so doing, we would encourage citizens to stop defining themselves solely as critics – identifying themselves by the products (such as a television show, wine region, or style of music) that they like – and start defining themselves also as creators.

Currently our law provides substantial financial incentives to Big Copyright to flood the market with polished entertainment that the average individual binges on for ten hours a day, which prevents him or her from spending more time with family, volunteering, relaxing, and – yes – creating. All I suggest is that if we are going to have a copyright regime, it should not be blind to this reality – no one desires that a friend or child spend more than half her waking hours consuming; no one thinks the government should support a law that has this practical consequence. No other law or social phenomenon causes Hollywood to release a deluge of works. Further, while no one can forecast the exact drop in production of artistic works by Big Copyright if the length and scope of copyright are reduced dramatically, it is reasonable to believe that Big Copyright would produce less, since this is the central premise of copyright and what Hollywood believes to be the bedrock of creativity.

It is widely assumed that the Internet can enable anyone to become a creator, and in fact millions have been so empowered. Nevertheless, the majority of Americans do not create and in fact use the Internet to consume more and more entertainment that is more hyped, more polished, and more addictive than ever before. I am not saying we all need to create every minute or even every day, nor am I saying creating is more valuable than sleeping or even consuming. I am simply saying that if the average American frees up a substantial portion of her day, every day, it is conceivable that at least a small percentage of individuals will spend a portion of this extra time learning to play the guitar, writing poetry, or knitting. Even this small percentage would translate into millions of individuals, which would be a worthy accomplishment.

Moreover, those of us who are not consuming ten hours of entertainment a day can be tempted to deny the willing subjugation or the harm that follows from such overconsumption because it is so foreign, so difficult to believe unless witnessed in person. Yet if we do not acknowledge the extent of the problem and do not try to beat back the norm of overconsumption, which was created by extreme copyright laws, at what point do we personally start to become responsible for the perpetuation of the existing copyright regime? Big Copyright has been enormously successful at co-opting and capturing us all. Even those of us who fight for copyright reform still live in a media world governed by Big Copyright and are liable to accept its premises as inevitable. I hope this book, which is itself under copyright, will nonetheless provide some succor to the resistance.

Epilogue

The nation is bound together by its creative artists and not by parallel lines of rusting steel.

— Pierre Berton

Countries are not defined by railroads or bridges but by individuals and communities and the art they create, which shapes their culture and informs their governance. If all citizens were artists, broadly defined, our politics would be more equal and just, since we would all contribute collectively to our culture and political system. We would have the cultural equivalent of direct democracy.

Just as we let politicians represent us in government, we allow Hollywood to create our culture in our place, and we "vote" on our culture through consumption. While representative democracy may be the best we can hope for politically, we must do better than a representative culture. Our Hollywood-mediated culture has led to less political freedom and justice because Hollywood speaks for us, decides what values are important to us, and coins the terms we use to communicate. It does this not with our liberty or equality in mind but with a single-minded focus on its own profits. As a result, our representative culture has closed off a vast majority of citizens from creativity, from active participation in civil society, from life.

Without a direct culture, many find a saving grace in employment, since numerous jobs allow us to create at work. Even jobs that do not enable creativity during working hours still offer valuable benefits, such as a sense of contributing to society, an opportunity to provide for one's family, and a community of peers.

Over time, as robots take over the building of railroads and much else, it will become increasingly important that we become a nation of artists. The policy to dramatically reduce copyright in order to inspire more citizens to create will only gain in importance if our workforce is displaced by robotics, as experts are predicting. The existing discussion, as characterized by Bill Gates, Steve Wozniak, Elon Musk, Bill Joy, Stephen Hawking, and others, touches only on how to deal with such a transition from an economic welfare standpoint – e.g., by providing greater financial subsidies to displaced workers.

Reforming copyright law could lessen the negative consequences of future upheaval in employment. Encouraging individuals to create on their own becomes even more important when fewer people are working. At present, hundreds of millions of Americans are allowing Hollywood to structure the majority of their free time. If their jobs become obsolete, if they are deprived of opportunities to create at work, they will need a culture with fewer Hollywood creations and a robust, diverse, expansive public domain to fuel their creativity, assist their transition to new activities, and empower them to speak up and contribute to the greater good. Since the consumer revolution, the link between labor and consumption has been strong. It will be our collective task to encourage displaced workers to find new, meaningful ways to contribute to a world that may no longer need their labor.

Index